D1603600

THE LIFE AND WORK OF
S.M. Dubnov

The Modern Jewish Experience

Paula Hyman and Deborah Dash Moore, *editors*

THE LIFE AND WORK OF
S.M. Dubnov

DIASPORA NATIONALISM AND JEWISH HISTORY

BY *Sophie Dubnov-Erlich*

TRANSLATED BY *Judith Vowles*
EDITED BY *Jeffrey Shandler*

INTRODUCTORY ESSAY BY *Jonathan Frankel*
AFTERWORD BY *Victor Erlich*

*Published in association with the YIVO Institute
for Jewish Research*

Indiana University Press
BLOOMINGTON AND INDIANAPOLIS

Originally published as Sofiia Dubnova-Erlikh, *Zhizn' i tvorchestvo S. M. Dubnova* (New York, 1950), © 1950 by Sofiia Dubnova-Erlikh. Photographs courtesy Archives of the YIVO Institute for Jewish Research

The paper used in this publication meets the minimum requirements of American National Standard for Information Sciences—Permanence of Paper for Printed Library Materials, ANSI Z39.48-1984.
⊗™

Manufactured in the United States of America

Library of Congress Cataloging-in-Publication Data

Dubnova-Erlikh, Sofiia.
[Zhizn' i tvorchestvo S.M. Dubnova. English]
The life and work of S.M. Dubnov : diaspora nationalism and Jewish history / by Sophie Dubnov-Erlich ; translated by Judith Vowles ; edited by Jeffrey Shandler ; introductory essay by Jonathan Frankel ; afterword by Victor Erlich.
p.   cm. — (The Modern Jewish experience)
Translation of: Zhizn' i tvorchestvo S.M. Dubnova.
"Published in association with the YIVO Institute for Jewish Research."
Includes bibliographical references and index.
ISBN 0-253-31836-X (alk. paper)
1. Dubnow, Simon, 1860–1941. 2. Historians, Jewish—Biography.
I. Shandler, Jeffrey. II. Title. III. Series: Modern Jewish experience (Bloomington, Ind.)
DS115.9.D8D82 1990
909'.04924'007202—dc20
[B]   89-46342
                                                                           CIP

1   2   3   4   5   95   94   93   92   91

CONTENTS

CHRONOLOGY / ix

S.M. Dubnov: Historian and Ideologist by Jonathan Frankel	1
Introduction	37
1. *Sources*	39
2. *On the School Bench*	43
3. *Rebellion*	46
4. *Wandering*	52
5. *In the Northern Capital*	59
6. *The Preacher of Free Thought*	70
7. *At the Crossroads*	76
8. *History Was Revealed to Me*	83
9. *The Odessa Literary Circle*	90
10. *The Spirit of the Past*	97
11. *Works and Days*	101
12. *Between Journalism and Poetry*	107
13. *Thoughts on Old and New Jewry*	112
14. *Farewell to the South*	119
15. *In the "Jerusalem of Lithuania"*	125
16. *Year of Revolution*	129
17. *The Moral of Terrible Days*	134
18. *Back in St. Petersburg*	140
19. *Unity in Variety*	145
20. *At Work on the* Magnum Opus	152
21. *On the Eve of War*	158
22. *The Thunder of Guns*	163

23. *The Great Upheaval*   169

24. *Into the Whirlpool*   174

25. *An Island amid the Elements*   179

26. *Meeting the West*   187

27. *Fulfilling the Vow*   192

28. *The Golden Autumn*   199

29. *Seventieth Birthday*   205

30. *In a New Nest*   210

31. *Victory over Loneliness*   218

32. *Work Continues*   224

33. *The Twilight of Europe*   230

    Epilogue   245

    From the Author   248

    Life with Grandfather by Victor Erlich   249

                    GLOSSARY / 257

                EDITOR'S NOTES / 259

                BIBLIOGRAPHY / 274

                    INDEX / 277

                Illustrations on pp. iv, 35, and 64–69.

CHRONOLOGY

1860	Simon Dubnov born 18 September, in Mstislavl, Belorussia.
1880	Dubnov moves to St. Petersburg.
1881	Dubnov's first historical writing published in *Russkii Evrei*.
1883	Dubnov marries Ida Freidlin.
1885	Sophie Dubnov born.
1890	The Dubnovs move to Odessa.
1891	Dubnov issues a call to gather documents and to help organize Jewish historiography of Eastern Europe.
1892	At Dubnov's initiative the Jewish Historical-Ethnographic Association is established by the Association for the Dissemination of Enlightenment.
1894	Dubnov's first work on Hasidism is published in *Kaveret*.
1897	The first of Dubnov's *Pis'ma o starom i novom evreistve* (Letters on Old and New Jewry) is published in *Voskhod*.
1898	Dubnov's first textbook of Jewish history, *Uchebnik evreiskoi istorii*, appears.
1901	The first part of *Vseobshchaia istoriia evreev* (World History of the Jews) is published in Odessa.
1905	The Dubnovs move to Vilna. Dubnov articulates the principles of national-cultural autonomy at two Jewish conferences.
1906	The Dubnovs move to St. Petersburg. Dubnov organizes the Folkspartey.
1909	Dubnov's annotated edition of *Oblastnoi Pinkes* (Community Record Book of the Jews of Lite) is published in St. Petersburg.
1914	*Noveishaia istoriia evreiskago naroda*, Dubnov's history of modern Jewry, is published in St. Petersburg.
1918	The fortieth anniversary of Dubnov's career is celebrated in St. Petersburg.
1922	The Dubnovs leave the USSR and move to Kovno, Lithuania, where the plan for Dubnov to hold a chair in Jewish history is not fulfilled. The Dubnovs then move to Berlin.
1925	The first complete edition of *Vsemirnaia istoriia evreiskogo naroda* (World History of the Jewish People) is published in Berlin.
1927	Dubnov participates in the Zurich conference for the defense of Jewish minority rights.

1930   Celebration of Dubnov's seventieth birthday, at which the
            Festschrift zu S. Dubnows siebzigstem Geburtstag appears. The
            Dubnov Fund for the publication of a general encyclopedia
            in Yiddish is established.

1930–1931   *Toldot Ha-Hasidut* (History of Hasidism) is published in Tel Aviv.

1932   *Yidishe geshikhte dertseylt far kinder*, a Jewish history text for chil-
            dren, is issued in Berlin.

1933   The Dubnovs move to Riga.

1934   The first volume of *Kniga zhizni*, Dubnov's autobiography, is
            published in Riga.

1935   Celebrations of Dubnov's seventy-fifth birthday. The second
            volume of YIVO's *Historishe shriftn* is published in his honor.

1940   The third volume of Dubnov's memoirs is published in Riga.

1941   Dubnov is murdered on 8 December in the Riga ghetto.

THE LIFE AND WORK OF

S.M. Dubnov

S. M. Dubnov

Historian and Ideologist

by Jonathan Frankel

This essay is dedicated to the memory of Alexander Erlich.

In the early years of this century, Simon Dubnov, then a man in his forties, was already a well-known figure in the Russian-Jewish intelligentsia. But among what was then a rapidly growing social stratum of writers, journalists, artists, men of the professions, politicians, ideologists, and revolutionaries he was not unusually prominent, certainly not famous.

Today, though, some fifty years after he was killed by the Nazis in Riga, he continues to command attention within the Jewish intellectual world,[1] while the vast majority of his contemporaries are all but forgotten. Time has demonstrated that Dubnov enjoys two abiding claims to fame.

First, in his *Letters on Old and New Jewry*, which he began to publish in article form in 1897, he put forward in well-elaborated terms the theory of what is variously known as Diaspora nationalism or Jewish national autonomism. Essentially, this theory states that even with the destruction of their state in 70 C.E. and their dispersal across the world, the Jews have remained a nation (albeit "nonterritorial" in character); that until the French Revolution and emancipation, the Jews had always been granted a large measure of internal self-government in the host states; that in the modern era, they should therefore lay claim in the various countries of the Diaspora not only to civil but also to national (that is, national minority) rights; and that national autonomy would enable them not only to run their own internal (above all, educational) affairs but also to defend their political interests more effectively both at home and abroad. Although Dubnov may not have been the first person to advocate Jewish autonomism —Chaim Zhitlowsky, for example, like Dubnov himself, had been preparing the ground for the theory since the early 1890s—his powerful presentation of it as an all-embracing ideology ensured that it came to be associated to a large extent with his own name.

However, it is not Dubnov the ideologist but Dubnov the historian who is surely the better known today. His history of the Jews throughout the ages, first published in the 1920s in a ten-volume German edition (translated from the Russian manuscript), rapidly became, and still remains, a standard work.[2] Together with the histories by Heinrich Graetz and Salo Wittmayer Baron[3] it belongs to an extremely rare, and by now probably extinct, genre: the attempt to encompass single-handedly the whole of Jewish history within one massive and conceptually unified work of high scholarship.

The publication of Dubnov's *Weltgeschichte* marked the culmination of a lifetime devoted to research on and the writing of Jewish history. His characteristic interests, methodology, and historiographical theories had already made a profound impact on his students in Russia before the First World War, and they in turn had begun to disseminate his ideas in Germany. But it was only with the appearance of the ten-volume history that readers in the West, or at least in Central Europe, could begin to familiarize themselves with the full scope of his work.

Almost by chance, though, a number of Dubnov's works had by then been available for some time in English translation. The credit for this somewhat surprising situation was almost entirely due to the enthusiasm of Israel Friedlaender, a Polish Jew who had studied in Berlin and who became a member of the faculty of the Jewish Theological Seminary in New York in 1904.[4] His German version of Dubnov's historiographical essay of 1893[5] formed the basis for the English edition, *Jewish History: An Essay in the Philosophy of History*, translated by Henrietta Szold and published in Philadelphia in 1903. Friedlaender himself translated and initiated the publication of Dubnov's three-volume *History of the Jews in Russia and Poland*, which came out, again in the United States, during the period 1916–20.

Friedlaender was killed in the Ukraine while on a relief mission in 1920, and the translation of Dubnov's writings was not taken up again until after the Second World War. In 1958, The Jewish Publication Society of America brought out a selection of his essays under the title *Nationalism and History*. It included, *inter alia*, the bulk of *Letters on Old and New Jewry* (translated from the authorized but very truncated Hebrew edition of 1937[6]) as well as a highly perceptive and informed introduction by the editor, Koppel S. Pinson.[7] Some ten years later, the English edition of Dubnov's world history began to appear, in five bulky volumes.[8]

What has hitherto not been available in English (with the exception of an unpublished dissertation[9]) is a biography of Dubnov. This missing link has now been fitted into place with the publication of the present volume, Sophie Dubnov-Erlich's biography of her father, which was first published in Russian in 1950. To a considerable extent, her work is based on the autobiography that Dubnov began publishing in Riga in 1934.[10] It shares much of the characteristic reticence of those memoirs, and one may well ask whether preference should not have been given to translating the autobiography first. (Certainly, it is to be hoped that Dubnov's *Kniga Zhizni* [The Book of My Life] will appear in English at some time. The second volume, in particular, is an extraordinary document, consisting largely of diaries kept in Petrograd during the 1917 revolution and the Civil War.)

But the autobiography is a sprawling work of some nine hundred pages and does not go beyond 1933. Moreover, Sophie Dubnov-Erlich had to reconstruct not only the last nine, but actually the last twenty, years of her father's life from her own memories and from scattered written sources, published and unpublished. In 1950, she was still under the impression that all the copies of the third volume of the autobiography had been destroyed by the Germans shortly after its publication in Riga. It was only some years later that a single surviving book (mailed out by Dubnov as a personal gift on the eve of the Nazi invasion) was found in Australia, in the private library of Isaac Steinberg.[11]

The present work not only covers Dubnov's entire life story in compact form but also brings out, more strongly perhaps than does the autobiography, various personal aspects of that story. Most notably, it portrays the heavy burden borne by Ida Dubnov, as the wife of a penurious and highly dedicated scholar; and it conveys the depth of Dubnov's love of nature —for the shores of the Black and the Baltic seas, for the White Russian and Finnish forests. For the first time English readers can glimpse the man behind the hitherto disembodied ideologist and scholar.

The central theme which provides Dubnov's memoirs with a strong sense of purpose and unity, and which finds clear reflection in his daughter's biography, is the idea of a life divided into three highly distinct phases.[12] In his childhood and until his early teens, Simon Dubnov grew up cocooned, as it were, within the safe confines of Mstislavl, an exceptionally beautiful but otherwise not unusual Belorussian *shtetl*. As the descendant of a long line of distinguished rabbis and the grandson of the local rabbi, an outstanding talmudist, the young Dubnov was automatically put through all the stages of the traditional educational system, rapidly advancing from biblical to talmudic studies, and from the *kheyder* to his grandfather's lessons in textual explication (*shiurim*). In a different period, Dubnov would in all probability have ended up as a rabbi himself.

But in 1874, he started attending a state school, where he acquired for the first time a real knowledge of the Russian language (to use in addition to his mother tongue, Yiddish, and his excellent Hebrew). And for the next ten years he advanced very far along the path of alienation from the traditional micro-world in which he had grown up. An uncritical faith in the divine inspiration of the Jewish law, whether written or oral, gave way first to deism and then to materialism and positivism, as he avidly read his way through Chernyshevsky and Pisarev, and Russian versions of Buckle, Spencer, Mill, and Comte. He rebelled against the "blind patriotism,"[13] the unquestioning loyalty to the Jewish people, of his childhood and found himself increasingly subjected to an inner "storm of cosmopoli-tanism."[14] By the mid-1880s he had become an awesome "legend" among the youth of his native district—the rabbi's grandson who, when visiting Mstislavl, stayed at home working on Yom Kippur, when all the other Jews were at the synagogue.[15]

Eventually, though, a clear reaction set in, and Dubnov found his belief in positivism giving way to skepticism and doubt. In the late Tolstoy (par-ticularly in *A Confession*) and in Ernst Renan, he heard echoes of his own need to make good a growing "loss of faith."[16] From the late 1880s he began his way back, seeking a bridge between the old and the new, the particular and the universal.[17] By 1897, he had reached the point where he could present publicly his own complete world view—a secular Jewish nationalism. This ideology envisaged the gradual transformation of tradi-tional culture within a pluralistic modern nation and of traditional self-government within the structures of national autonomy and the twentieth-century democratic state.

There is no doubt—and it would be absurd to argue otherwise—that Dubnov's triadic concept reflected certain key changes in his ideological development. That is demonstrated by the political positions he took in 1881 and 1905, during the two great crises which then swept over the Jewish people in the Russian empire.

The massive wave of pogroms which originated in Elizavetgrad in April 1881 found Dubnov, then a mere twenty-one years old, living impecuni-ously in St. Petersburg, without a long-term residence permit and therefore in constant danger of police harassment. But despite his extreme youth, he was already a budding journalist, having published a few articles, and so was able to formulate his response to the crisis in the Russian-language Jewish journals published in the capital: *Razsvet, Russkii Evrei,* and *Voskhod.*

The task Dubnov took upon himself during the years 1881–84 was to champion the embattled positions of the Russian-Jewish Enlightenment, or *Haskalah,* movement as it had developed over the previous half-century. In the face of the challenge posed by the pogroms, the rise in popular anti-Semitism, and open governmental hostility, it was the duty of the Jewish intelligentsia, as he saw it, to demonstrate loyalty to and even to accentuate its basic beliefs, while avoiding at all costs the stampede to reassess basic values.

What this meant in practice was, above all, a consistent and sharply argued hostility to the claim of the new Palestinophile movement that its program could potentially solve the Jewish question in Russia or even worldwide. Dubnov pointed out that the existing Jewish community in Palestine was so ultra-Orthodox that it would do everything in its power to ensure that new immigrants would abandon agricultural work (exchang-ing "the plough for the prayerbook"[18]); that the country was *de jure* in the hands of Turkey, which was bound to be hostile, and *de facto* in those of the Great Powers, which were afraid to tamper with the *status quo.*

He maintained that it was the height of irresponsibility to encourage extraordinary excitement and manifestly exaggerated expectations, as Peretz Smolenskin and other ideologists of the new movement were doing.

There could be no single or simple panacea for a problem of such magnitude, Dubnov argued. In order to meet the crisis one had to pursue a number of different and parallel policies simultaneously. Thus he was among the very first to advocate a planned campaign to organize the large-scale emigration of Jews from Russia and their resettlement in new agricultural colonies in North America. In his article of August 1881 in *Razsvet*, he envisaged the campaign as a joint effort of the Jews in Russia, Western Europe, and America. Only the United States could provide the Jews with "firm ground not poisoned by the destructive miasmas of national enmity and religious intolerance."[19] At the same time, a significant reduction of the Jewish population in the countries of origin could defuse the anti-Semitic threat in "Russia and Germany—that is, in two-thirds of Europe."[20]

However, for the majority of the Jewish population, which had no choice but to stay in the tsarist empire, the long-term goal had to remain what it had been for many decades: the attainment of full civil rights, equality before the law. Obviously, nothing of the kind was to be expected in the Judeophobic atmosphere of 1881, but in anticipation of yet another reversal in tsarist policy, the Russian Jews should meanwhile rebuild their own way of life, thus strengthening their claim to emancipation and preparing themselves to make full use of it when it finally came. Thus, redoubled efforts had to be made to develop modern education within the Russian Jewish world, and Dubnov emphasized particularly the training in technical skills planned by the organization ORT, which was founded in St. Petersburg in 1880.[21]

Still more important, though, as he argued with vehemence in the years 1882–84, was the urgent need to reform the theology and ritual of the Jewish religion as it had developed in Eastern Europe. This issue lay at the very center of his entire conception of Jewish history in this period. He shared fully the idea considered almost axiomatic by most modern Jewish thinkers in the West: Since the destruction of the Judean state in 70 C.E. the Jews had transformed themselves from a nation into a religion, or as Dubnov put it in 1881, "The history of the Jewish people is primarily the history of Judaism pure and simple."[22]

It followed logically that any basic changes in Jewish life had to begin with reform of the religion. Dubnov eagerly pursued the basic concept of Reform as developed in Germany in the 1840s: that of an essential Judaism, primarily Mosaic and Prophetic, with the Oral Law seen as a necessary evil, a shell developed to protect the kernel during the centuries of medieval persecution. The time had now come to cleanse the kernel of all its outmoded accretions. Referring to the leading ideologist of German Reform Judaism (himself a famous historian), Dubnov wrote that "the Russian Jews are still awaiting their Geigers."[23] And, as he put it in 1883, in his well-known essay "What Kind of Self-Emancipation Do the Jews Need?":

> I know of no word in Jewish history so terrible as *rabbinism*; for the Jews it has been a hundred times worse and more destructive than the Inquisition; the latter destroyed people physically, the former spiritually. The Inquisition was active at a specific time; rabbinism remains at work without cease.[24]

Between such ideological positions as these and Dubnov's political role in the next major upheaval, the 1905 revolution, there certainly was a yawning gulf. Throughout the revolutionary period, 1905–1907, Dubnov was an unflagging spokesman for the view that the Jewish people in Russia had to claim not only civil but also national rights. He was living in Vilna for most of that time, and so when the Union for the Attainment of Full Rights for the Jewish People in Russia held its founding conference in that city in March 1905, Dubnov was on hand to see that this demand was included in its program. Later the same year, he pioneered the idea, which was adopted by the Union but never implemented, that it was time to call together a democratically elected National Assembly to represent the Jewish people in Russia.

During the revolutionary years, Dubnov had the satisfaction of seeing the concept of national autonomy, although in many variant forms, adopted by nearly every Jewish party in the Russian empire. But his hopes that all the movements—whether Zionist, Bundist, territorialist or liberal, "bourgeois" or "proletarian"—would unite to lay the immediate foundations for that autonomy were sadly disappointed. By 1907 he found himself with no choice but to work within the narrow confines of yet another party—albeit one named the Folkspartey (People's Party)—which advocated not only national autonomy but also organized assistance for Jewish emigration overseas, particularly to America.[25]

Even before the revolution, Dubnov had for many years been rethinking his concept of the essence of Jewish history. The position he finally adopted turned out to be the exact reverse of his viewpoint in the early 1880s. As he put it succinctly in the introduction to his *World History*, written in St. Petersburg in 1910, "Judaism has been formed in the image of the nation, of the society, and not vice versa."[26]

There was, then, a strong factual basis for the triadic concept of his life, which Dubnov emphasized in his autobiography. At the same time, though, it should be noted, he had his own logic for stressing this particular theme in his life story. As he explained many times, he was convinced that his personal experience reflected nothing less than the major trend in modern Jewish history. The negation of tradition, which had led to the triumph of "assimilationism," had, in turn, produced its own negation and the growing ascendancy of Jewish nationalism. Dubnov saw in this process a guarantee that the ideology he shared was being carried forward on an upward curve, that it had the force of history on its side and would inevitably triumph throughout the Jewish world.

But beyond that, he also argued that this type of triadic process—thesis, antithesis, synthesis—represented a basic law of historic development. As he saw it, this law was rooted not in metaphysics, as Hegel would have it, or in economics, as Marx believed, but in the workings of sociopsychology.[27] Sooner or later, traditional societies are bound to end in rebellion; radical change in turn produces reaction, and the interaction between these two forces culminates in some new and higher stage of social organization. Ultimately, it was this dialectical logic which alone ensured human progress.

In short, the tripartite framework was meant to emphasize the typical —Dubnov's life as a paradigm reflecting the inevitable ideological metamorphosis of the Russian-Jewish intelligentsia, a "pilgrim's progress." This theme was taken up eagerly, of course, in the biographical essays of such nationalist historians of the next generations as Benzion Dinur and Yehuda Slutsky.[28]

However, the Jewish world in which Dubnov lived has long since been destroyed, be it physically by the Nazis or culturally by the Soviet dictatorship. And today's vantage point, of necessity, opens up entirely different perspectives on his life. The deep and prolonged ideological conflict between the Jewish nationalists and the so-called assimilationists—between "the freedom in slavery" of East European Jews and "the slavery in freedom" of the Jews of Western Europe (to use Ahad Ha-Am's terminology) —which dictated the structure of Dubnov's autobiography, no longer commands the attention of the Jewish people.

What perhaps stands out most clearly today is how very much, beyond the typical, Dubnov remained, throughout, an exceptional and in important ways a unique figure within the Russian-Jewish intelligentsia, both as ideologist and, still more, as historian. In part, this was due to his individualistic temperament. Even though Dubnov was open to persuasion (and Ahad Ha-Am, for example, clearly exerted a major influence on his thinking during his Odessa years[29]), he could never be stampeded into the mainstream. As a result, he often took up oddly anachronistic positions. For example, in the years 1883–84 he could do battle for the hopelessly outmoded idea of Reform Judaism in Russia as if he were still in the 1870s; and in 1890 it was his old-fashioned article in praise of Western Jewish "mission" theology[30] which provoked Ahad Ha-Am's famous counterattack.[31]

In these cases Dubnov would eventually change his mind and fall into line with prevailing opinion in the Jewish nationalist camp. However, of more fundamental importance was the extent to which he remained doggedly loyal throughout the sixty years of his intellectually active adult life to a number of key concepts and articles of faith. Continuity rather than discontinuity was the particular hallmark of his life and thought.[32]

Dubnov always made it clear—starting with his earliest articles of 1881 —that throughout its thousands of years of history the Jewish people has, as he saw it, been engaged in a harsh but necessary struggle for survival. The threats to its existence came from without (physical dangers) and from within (the loss of morale). Even in the early and mid-1880s, which Dubnov would later term his "cosmopolitan" phase, he sought not the disappearance of the Jewish people, but its modernization, its transformation into a "civilized nation" which could contribute its part to "the enlightened future of mankind."[33]

Time and again, Dubnov explained the key turning points in Jewish history (such as Yohanan Ben-Zakai's move to Yavne) by the fact that "the *instinct of national self-preservation* was unusually developed among all members of the nation."[34] Or as he put it in April 1881, "The most characteristic mark of Jewish history is the struggle of the people for its spiritual existence."[35] From beginning to end the key actor in, and the subject of, Jewish history was the "people." And Dubnov can be characterized as a life-long Jewish "populist," so long as it is borne in mind that populism in Russia often implied an idealized view of the people not as it actually was, but only as it might become.

Secondly, Dubnov's view of Jewish history as the struggle of a people for its "national self-preservation" was organically linked to his lifelong evolutionism. He always believed that the basic social unit in which men came to organize their lives was the nation, and that change resulted from the interaction, the rivalry, and the mutual influence among the peoples of the world. The law of "the survival of the fittest" applied to nations no less than to species.

Violence, of course, played a crucial role in history; but another immutable axiom of Dubnov's credo was that the evolution of mankind gradually reduced the relative importance of brute force in human affairs, while increasing the power of moral, spiritual, and intellectual factors. That was why the Jewish people, despite—or rather precisely because of—the fact that it had lost its state and country some two thousand years before, could nonetheless expect to exert a positive and important influence on the future development of mankind. For Dubnov, evolution did not mean endless conflict, bloody in tooth and claw, but on the contrary—beyond the inevitable ups and downs—the ultimate advance of man. He always remained a humanist, and even when he became a nationalist he retained his faith in universalism, in progress as the basic law of history.

In his scheme of things, the modern era ushered in by the French Revolution represented a new and higher stage of historical development, and Dubnov always retained his enthusiasm for the principle of the rights of man proclaimed so dramatically in 1789. The declaration of liberty and equality—meaning equality before the law, not social revolution—never lost its hallowed status in his eyes. In the 1880s he interpreted liberty primarily in terms of individual freedom and civil rights. From the 1890s he broadened the concept to include the right of all nations to equality and free development. He thus saw his nationalism as an extension, not a negation, of his deeply rooted and unwavering liberalism.

For him, the modern Jewish nationalism developed in Eastern Europe did not imply any disillusionment either with Western society or with Western values. He became highly critical, of course, of the "assimilationism" of Western Jews—meaning the claim that Jewry constituted a religious persuasion alone and not a nation—but he was never anything but a "Westerner."

Throughout his life Dubnov argued that the message that the Jewish people had brought, and could still bring, to the world combined the joint perspectives of the particular and the universal. The spiritual peaks of Jewish history had been reached when the barriers isolating the Jews from the outside world had broken down and when the Jews had come to see the fate of their nation as inextricably linked to that of mankind as a whole. Such moments he always identified with biblical Prophecy, with Maimonides and—in marked contrast to the prevailing opinion in his own nationalist camp—with Moses Mendelssohn.[36] Thus, what he came to term "Prophetism"—the imperative demands of social justice and the vision of universal peace as overshadowing the demands of religious ritual—constituted yet another fixed principle in his world view.

Given this particular system of beliefs, then, it is hardly surprising that Dubnov found himself increasingly out of tune with the ideologies becoming dominant after 1881 in the Russian-Jewish world. He was an evolutionist, but Zionism, territorialism, and Marxism all spoke of social change in revolutionary terms. He was a liberal in an age when liberalism was under attack by Zionists (and proto-Zionists) for being impotent in the face of racial incitement, and by socialists for being at best a transitional stage on the way to a totally new order. And he was a populist, who thought in terms of the Jewish people everywhere and as a whole; in opposition to the Zionists or the territorialists, who focused primarily on the nation of the future, renewed in its own land; and as against the Bundists (and other Jewish Marxists), who stressed class divisions and class war.[37]

However paradoxical it may seem—for he was only a child at the time —in many ways Dubnov would always remain a man of the 1860s. This may be explained in large part by the nature of his education. Because of his very late start in Russian elementary school, he found himself too old to enter the seminary for Jewish teachers in Vilna, and, despite enormous expenditures of time and effort, he could never gain entry to a university. As a result, he was basically self-taught, when it came to secular studies, and most of his early reading had to be clandestine, hidden from the eyes of both governmental and (even more so) Jewish communal authorities.[38]

The works he devoured in his teens were largely of the kind which had held sway among the Russian intelligentsia in the previous decade. Obtained and read conspiratorially, they made a profound and ineradicable impression. Thus, Dubnov's belief that evolutionary theory guaranteed human progress can be dated back to his reading of Comte, Buckle, and Spencer. His passionately held liberalism owed most to John Stuart Mill's *On Liberty*, which came upon the young Dubnov like a revelation from on high;[39] and his "Westernism" was reinforced by his early encounter with Dobroliubov, Pisarev, and Chernyshevsky. As for his Jewish populism, it too originated partly in Russian radical thought, but also in yet another discovery of his youth, Heinrich Graetz's *History of the Jewish People*. (Here, however, we are not dealing with a work popular in the 1860s, for Graetz's remarkable impact on the Russian-Jewish intelligentsia was only beginning to gain momentum in the late 1870s.)

Although Dubnov the political ideologist was thus in many ways out of step with his contemporaries—and even more so with the next generation—he was not entirely alone. Ahad Ha-Am, in particular, shared many of the same articles of faith—anti-utopian evolutionism, an organic, quasi-biological concept of national history—and they eventually became close friends. Dubnov the historian, however, was beyond question a unique figure in the Russian-Jewish world.

As he himself would frequently point out, the Jewish intelligentsia in Russia in the latter half of the nineteenth century was far too involved in current problems and in strategies for the future to concern itself with the past for its own sake. In an era of highly engagé politics, historical studies were bound to be seen as a superfluous luxury, unless they could be called in to reinforce party ideologies. "Hardly any educated people," wrote Dubnov in April 1881, "knows its own history as little . . . as the Jewish people."[40]

But from the very first, Dubnov made it clear that he regarded the study of history not only as a means to understand the present and plan for the future but also as an end in itself.[41] His interest in history had developed in early childhood, nurtured by his antipathy for the Talmud, by his love for biblical narrative, and by the discovery of a copy of *Yosipon* (a medieval Hebrew version of Josephus) in his grandfather's library.[42]

Starting in 1881, an astonishing flow of Dubnov's articles on a broad range of topics in Jewish history appeared week after week in *Razsvet* and *Russkii Evrei*. Even though Dubnov would later dismiss these youthful efforts as "an immature youthful debut,"[43] they clearly revealed his passionate interest in the past, his urge to catch the imagination of the general public, his boundless energy, and his vaulting ambition to understand Jewish history as a single whole, which would become his hallmark as a historian. It was already apparent then that the author was not only an ideologue, an *intelligent*, but also a scholar-in-the-making, an intellectual.

What could not have been predicted, however, was that this provincial young man—poverty-stricken, with only an elementary school education, unable to enter (let alone teach in) a university, and hounded by the police —would actually create a new profession for himself as a free-lance but full-time historian of the Jewish people.

A number of outside factors combined with Dubnov's own personal inclination to make this career possible. Thus, for example, during the mid-1880s Dubnov had hoped to become a general European historian, and at one time, he had been tempted to write a full-length study of Condorcet,[44] but there was no way for him to finance the time and travel involved in such a project.

By contrast, by keeping up a steady output of articles on Jewish history, as well as political commentary and book reviews, for the Russian-Jewish journals, Dubnov could eke out a very modest living. True, from 1883 he was totally dependent on the one such periodical then extant, the monthly *Voskhod*, and its tight-fisted publisher, Adolph Landau. However, despite its chronic problems with the censor (it was closed for six months in 1891), *Voskhod* proved to have great staying power, and for over twenty years it formed the basis for Dubnov's life as a professional historian.[45]

The exclusive concern with Jewish (as distinct from general) history which had been forced on Dubnov by circumstances now gradually became his all-consuming interest. Working on his study of Hasidism in 1889 he noted in his diary: "I have stopped tormenting myself with [the] accursed questions. All my religion, philosophy, poetry are concentrated in this work."[46] In 1892, in a diary entry referring to his attempts to arouse public interest in the Russian-Jewish past, he stated: "I have, as it were, become a missionary for history."[47]

Only after many years did Dubnov gradually begin to build up new sources of income. Starting in the mid-1890s, his textbook for use in Jewish schools in Russia, which was frequently reprinted, and a series of ever-expanding histories of the Jewish people brought in a small but steady trickle of royalties. After 1905 he started to lecture on Jewish history in unofficial institutions of higher learning in St. Petersburg, first at the Free University and then at Baron David Günzburg's Courses in Oriental Studies. And it was because of a similar post at the new Jewish People's University, obtained for him by Bolshevik well-wishers, that he was just able to keep body and soul together during the Civil War years of 1918–21. Finally, by the 1920s, the royalties on his books, then being published in several languages, and occasional articles in the New York Yiddish press (*Forverts, Tog*) provided the minimal financial independence he needed to live in Berlin and, later, in Riga.[48]

Dubnov was always aware of what an unprecedented path he had carved out for himself. When Ahad Ha-Am was forced to take up employment with the Wissotsky Tea Company in 1902, Dubnov commented in his diary, "What a regime this is, in which an editor and outstanding writer has to become a businessman. Now I remain alone as a professional writer."[49] In his own way, then, he had created for himself a "home university,"[50] an ideal he had first discovered in 1881 in reading about Buckle's way of life as an independent man of letters.

Always presiding, as it were, over this home university was the dominating presence of Heinrich Graetz. Although the two men never met and do not appear to have corresponded, it would be hard to imagine a tutor having a more powerful or more fruitful influence on a student than Graetz exerted on Dubnov. All but overwhelmed, the pupil measured himself almost from the first against his master, seeking ways to go beyond him and somehow to emancipate himself. Before the eyes of the homeless *ekstern* in St. Petersburg, Graetz loomed as a figure of gigantic proportions, the professional historian who combined meticulous scholarship with an all-encompassing vision, encyclopedic knowledge with the ability to popularize, limitless industry with imagination and inspiration.[51]

In a book-length essay, written in 1892 on the occasion of Graetz's death, Dubnov gave free rein to this sense of awe, noting that the great Breslau historian had been connected "inseparably to the heart of the people."[52] He termed Graetz a "nationalist in the best sense . . . [which] in no way excludes universalist ideals."[53] Dubnov further observed that Graetz had been forced to mix his own clay and bake his own bricks before he could design and construct his "grandiose historical monument,"[54] a task "which only a man of genius possessed of the most diverse gifts could undertake."[55] Through his lifelong tie to Graetz, Dubnov became a bridge between German-Jewish academic scholarship—the Wissenschaft des Judentums—and the new school of Russian-Jewish historians, who grew up largely under his influence.[56]

Given Dubnov's deep commitment to the ideal of objective scholarship, the relationship between his dual roles as historian and as political ideologist, as intellectual and as *intelligent* was bound to be both multifaceted and complex. In many ways, the interaction between his two personae proved fruitful, but it also involved inner conflicts and contradictions. While writing his history of the Jewish people, Dubnov would not infrequently find inspiration in the more dramatic events of his own day. For example, in 1905, he hurried to reach the chapter he had to write on 1789 in order to describe the French Revolution at the moment that he himself was living through the experience of a great insurrection.[57]

The mounting wave of revolutionary activity in Russia also influenced Dubnov's attitude toward the Jewish revolt against the Romans in 66–73 c.e. His description of the revolt written in the 1890s and entitled simply "The War with the Romans" tended to follow Josephus' interpretation,[58] but the volume he published in 1904 carried an account far more sympathetic to the Zealots and was called "The Great National War." It was replete with the highly charged terminology of contemporary Russia: the "revolutionary movement" (*revoliutsionnoe dvizhenie*), the "provisional government" (*vremennoe pravitel'stvo*), the "people's assembly" (*narodnoe sobran-*

ie), and the "liberation movement" (osvoboditel'noe dvizhenie).[59] It was not that Dubnov wrote history as a form of propaganda, but that the excitement of the day made it much easier to aim for his goal of "comprehending the past as if it were as alive as today."[60]

However, it was also part of what he called his "historist" creed to comprehend the present in historical terms.[61] And his determination to measure contemporary issues against the yardstick of history was one more factor making it impossible for Dubnov to identify himself fully with— or, for that matter, to disassociate himself fully from—any of the major Jewish political parties which began to crystallize after 1881. Thus, for example, he could never bring himself to join the Zionist (or proto-Zionist) movement, if only because of his abiding antipathy to its doctrine of "negating the Diaspora" (shlilat ha-galut) and to its claim to possess a comprehensive solution to the Jewish question. However, because of his commitment to historical continuities, he soon came to see the aspiration to establish modern Jewish life in the ancient homeland, thus creating a synthesis of the old and the new, as an entirely natural enterprise which, however limited in scale, still deserved sympathy. As early as 1883 we find him hoping that the Hibbat Zion movement would "achieve something by its determined efforts" in Palestine, thus helping "to thin out the Pale of Settlement."[62]

Conversely, although from the 1890s Dubnov was a declared supporter of Diaspora autonomy, he could never bring himself to share the view of the majority of autonomists that Yiddish should be declared the sole national language of the Jewish people. He agreed that it should develop into a modern language to be used in Jewish education and in everyday life, but he could not countenance the idea of an official dethronement of Hebrew, the age-old language of the Jewish nation worldwide. In a debate with Moyshe Rafes and other Bundists in 1916, he condemned their eagerness to break with "the 'old,' with the historic culture, with everything except speaking Yiddish. . . . A nation is not only a totality of individuals but also a totality of generations living out the entire evolution of its historical life."[63]

Logically enough, then, Dubnov repeatedly placed his hopes on projects for some unified organization which, standing above party, would take the broad and long view of the national interest—be it the Jewish National Assembly (of 1905), the Folkspartey (in 1907), the Russian Jewish Congress (of 1917), or the World Jewish Congress (of 1936).

If, however, Dubnov's two roles reinforced each other in many ways, adding passion to his writing of history and a sense of historical continuity to his politics, this duality also brought with it major tensions. At one level, nothing more was involved than the mundane but nonetheless perpetual and nerve-wracking problem of how to divide his time. Given the vast scope of his plans as a historian and the high levels of scholarship to which Dubnov aspired, he needed every possible moment to devote to his major academic projects. But he could not simply deny the pull of politics and public affairs. He believed that he had an important message to deliver and so had no right to isolate himself. As a result, there were times when his work as a historian slowed to a standstill, as in the summer of 1905.[64] More often, though, there were long periods when he took an oath to devote himself entirely to historical scholarship, or, as he put it in his diary in 1907, "to live out the rest of one's days in uninterrupted work."[65] This inner conflict could never be resolved as long as Dubnov lived in Russia. But his decision as an exile in 1922 to settle in Berlin rather than in independent Lithuania meant that he had finally decided to retreat into his "home university."

A far more profound contradiction, though, threatened the attempt to combine the roles of historian and ideologist. From his very earliest writings, Dubnov devoted great attention to the tragic aspects of Jewish history, to the frequent expulsions from one country or another, to the coerced conversions, constant humiliations, and massacres. In doing so he was in part simply following Graetz, who had treated martyrdom as a central theme in his magnum opus. Beyond this, Dubnov was responding directly both to the pogroms which swept over southern Russia (particularly the Ukraine) in 1881–82, 1903–1906, and 1918–20, and to the great Jewish exodus from Russia to the New World during the period 1881–1914.

Furthermore, when he developed his own historiographical conception in opposition to Graetz, stressing sociology rather than theology, Dubnov did not lessen this emphasis, but, on the contrary, assigned pivotal weight to the mass migrations which had punctuated the history of the Diaspora. One after the other, the great "hegemonic" centers of Jewish life had been undermined or totally eliminated by their host societies and states, and time after time new communities had been built up elsewhere only by extraordinary effort.[66]

This story, however heroic it appeared in Dubnov's telling, was hardly of the kind to inspire optimism. Graetz had seen the work of Providence within the seemingly random flux of tragic events, but Dubnov always wrote secular history. Deprived of metaphysics, he had to rely on the laws of progress and of evolution in order to sustain the belief that this oft-repeated pattern of construction, destruction, and reconstruction had an inner logic, purpose, and message. It was this axiom, in turn, that buttressed his faith in the viability of Jewish autonomism.

In a real sense, then, Dubnov's system of thought was always threatened by tension between his latently cyclical vision of Jewish history and his linear, albeit dialectical, concept of human advance. To what extent, though, he himself was fully aware of this potential contradiction is unclear; certainly, for very long periods he saw catastrophe not as a threat to his faith in progress but as a challenge to be met and overcome.

In 1882 his acute sense of historical analogy inspired him to publish articles about the massacres perpetrated by Khmelnitskii's armies in 1648–

52,[67] the "Hep! Hep!" riots of 1819, and the great German-Jewish migration
to the United States, which began in the 1820s.[68] Similarly, he was soon
prompted—no doubt by the extraordinary upsurge of popular enthusiasm
for a Jewish Exodus from Russia in the years 1881–82—to bring out essays
on the Sabbatean and Frankist movements.[69] (In these writings he antici-
pated a major preoccupation with Jewish mysticism, not only in his own
subsequent work, but also in twentieth-century Jewish historiography as
a whole.)

As Dubnov implied in the early 1880s, the lesson to be learned from
these past events was that the Jewish people in Russia—like the German
Jews faced by the Teutonomania of 1819 and after—had to respond to disaster with caution, with reason, with measured steps and not with messianic
fantasies. By flocking blindly after Sabbatai Zevi (in the very period that
they had hounded Spinoza out of the community), the Jews had opted
for the path of mysticism and obscurantism which would culminate in the
disastrous rise of Hasidism as a mass movement in the eighteenth century.
Instead of seeking to benefit from and to participate in the Enlightenment,
they had deliberately elected to remain alone in their own Middle Ages.[70]

From the late 1880s, Dubnov, of course, changed direction. The task
of the historian, he now concluded, was not to seek out and learn from
errors in the past conduct of the people but to discover and analyze the
causes of mass behavior. In his full-scale study of Hasidism, published
in *Voskhod* in the years 1888–91,[71] Dubnov argued that the triumph of mysticism in Jewish life had to be understood as the natural reaction of the
Jewish people, of their collective consciousness, to the destruction of
Ukrainian Jewry by Khmelnitskii.

By applying the methods of social psychology, the observer could penetrate the inner workings of the nation's life. Religious enthusiasm, being
the product of emotion and faith, of the deepest yearnings of the masses,
could reveal more to the historian than could the study of rational thought:
"It is in the mystic tendencies of a given epoch that the general situation
of the people, as it then was, finds its clearest expression."[72]

Dubnov's history of Hasidism, which was first published in book form
in 1930 and constitutes a central landmark in modern Jewish historiography, opened a new phase in Dubnov's life.[73] The decade and a half from
1888 to 1903 constituted the *anni mirabiles* of his intellectual creativity. Dubnov had come to maturity and was pioneering new paths only sporadically
explored by Graetz.[74] Given his new determination to describe the past
not as the eternal conflict between philosophical truth and error but in
terms of mass psychology, he could now openly criticize the way in which
the great Breslau historian had dismissed Jewish mysticism as a deviation
from the essence of Judaism. As Dubnov wrote in 1892,

If Graetz gives credit to the study of the Talmud in that it preserved the Jewish
mind from stagnation . . . then how much more should he have recognized

that the Kabala saved Jewish religious *feeling* from fossilization. . . . The Kabala, it is true, intoxicated, but it also inspired strength.[75]

These words encapsulate the central theme developed by Dubnov in the 1890s. In times of extreme adversity, the Jewish people had in the past found new ways to maintain its sense of purpose, its hold on life, its faith. It was for the historian to understand and explain, not to condemn, these collective reactions to mass suffering, however repellent they might appear to the modern mind. But Dubnov argued that what had been true of the past applied equally to the present. Faced by the savage enmity of the tsarist regime, the Jewish people had once again to withdraw into itself, fall back on its own psychological and spiritual resources, produce a positive inner response to the external challenge. For the rapidly growing Russian-Jewish intelligentsia, profoundly estranged from the traditional faith, religion could no longer serve as a primary source of inspiration. Only a real understanding of the Jewish past, a sense of its continuity and rhythm, could endow the modern Jew with a sense of allegiance, direction, and hope. "The Jewish national idea," Dubnov wrote in 1891, "is based primarily on *historical consciousness.*"[76] Or again: "The main support of national unity is *historical consciousness.*"[77]

Here, too, Dubnov clearly felt that he was advancing into areas largely unexplored by Graetz. To open up the history of the Jews in Russia and Poland from the earliest times until the present (a relatively marginal theme in Graetz's book) now became his primary ambition. The Russian Empire of his day, after all, contained most of the Jews in the world, and yet the history of that community, stretching back to the Middle Ages, had not been systematically studied. It was often held in contempt as a story of obscurantism and superstition, and was all but unknown even to the vast majority of educated Jews. In a long article of 1891 (also published as a booklet), he drew up the blueprint for what he now envisaged as his life's work.[78]

The immediate task, he wrote, was to hunt down and organize systematically the primary materials scattered in a variety of collections—governmental and ecclesiastical, Russian and Polish, communal and private, *misnagdish* and Hasidic, elitist and popular, published and unpublished. Dubnov's enthusiasm was such that he was able to bring about the establishment of the Historical-Ethnographical Commission in 1892. Among its founding members were Maxim Vinaver, Leon Bramson, and Julius Brutzkus.[79]

This undertaking was only the first of a long line of such organizations and initiatives inspired by Dubnov in order to advance the study of Russian-Jewish history. Perhaps the most notable among them was the important journal *Evreiskaia Starina*, which he founded in 1909. YIVO, established in 1925, was in large part the creation of his ex-students and disciples.[80] And, as a senior academic associate, he followed its growth closely from its foundation until his last days. In letters written in 1940 he told of his plans to move to Vilna in order to work and teach at the Institute, which had suffered greatly from the German conquest of Poland.[81]

From his belief that only knowledge of the past, of the "collective historical fate,"[82] could save the present-day Jew from "corrosive pessimism,"[83] it was only a short step to his theory of Diaspora autonomy. Salo W. Baron has argued that Dubnov's historical writings paid "special attention to Jewish self-government . . . due to his own political 'autonomism.'"[84] But in all probability, it was the constant interaction between Dubnov as historian and as ideologist which led to his heightened interest in Jewish autonomy both as a historical phenomenon and as a political program.

Thus in his essay of 1891 he could specifically criticize Graetz and the entire school of German-Jewish historians for their failure to use municipal archives in order to examine the "internal way of life and the self-government" of the Jewish communities.[85] By 1894 Dubnov was beginning to publish rare documents relating to the history of communal self-rule in Eastern Europe, which, he argued, had *"civilized* the Jewish masses, disciplined them, maintained the idea among them of strict legality and law."[86]

What Dubnov did in his *Letters on Old and New Jewry* (which began to appear three years later) was to argue powerfully that national self-government for the Jews in the Diaspora was a phenomenon even more suited to the modern than to the medieval world. The Jews had every right to declare themselves *"not a state within a state but a nation within a nation,"*[87] *"an equal member among the European nations."*[88] Given the increasingly vociferous demands for greater freedom by the oppressed nationalities within the multinational states, it could only be a question of time until a new constitutional system, granting equality to all national groups, was attained. "This is not a dream," he declared in 1899, "but a historical necessity,"[89] and the Jews, too, could fit into the new order of things if they only chose to do so. Although the fact is often overlooked, Dubnov regarded his concept as suited not only to Eastern Europe, but in many ways even more to the liberal West, and particularly to the United States.[90]

It was the great error of the Zionist movement, he declared, that it denied these realities, ignoring the opportunity contained therein for the "political rebirth of the ten million Jews in the Diaspora,"[91] and that it "despaired of historical progress, of the moral improvement of mankind."[92]

In the 1890s, then, Dubnov envisaged history, be it universal or Jewish, as moving neither in circles nor along a straight line, but as making a complex ascent by sharp zigzags. There was no such thing as unbroken progress, but mankind (and the Jewish nation within it) had proved its ability to surmount the greatest catastrophes and to continue to advance. For this reason, he could look forward with great confidence. He even argued that the Jewish nation, lacking a territory of its own, represented the highest form in the evolution of nationalities, dependent as it was entirely on "cultural-historical" and "spiritual" factors,[93] with "no possibility of striving for political victories, territorial annexations or the subjugation of other peoples."[94] The idea of a Jewish "mission" to mankind, which he had once so admired in the thought of modern Judaism in the West, thus implicitly reemerged here, with the role of the Jewish people now being to demonstrate that a nation could exist in total separation from statehood and so serve as a force for peace rather than war.[95]

As the year 1900 arrived, Dubnov noted in his diary that if the eighteenth century had witnessed an intellectual revolution and the nineteenth had been an age of revolutionary change in politics, science, and technology, then the twentieth century in all probability would become an era of "moral" and "ethical revolution."[96] A mere three years later, in April 1903, Kishinev became the scene of a pogrom in which dozens of Jews were brutally murdered and hundreds were wounded. This event proved to be only the first in a series of such attacks, which culminated in late October 1905 with pogroms in hundreds of places, leaving thousands dead.

Dubnov, who had been living in nearby Odessa since 1890, felt the impact of the Kishinev pogrom to the full. A committee in that city, consisting of Ahad Ha-Am, Bialik, Dizengoff, Ben-Ammi, Rawnitzki, and Dubnov, issued a manifesto to the Jews of Russia, calling on them to prepare armed resistance against future pogroms. The committee sent Bialik to Kishinev to report on what exactly had happened during the slaughter.[97] Dubnov responded very quickly, both in 1903 and in 1905, publishing his analysis of the events in two influential articles: "A Historic Moment," which appeared within weeks of the Kishinev pogrom; and "Lessons from the Terrible Days," printed after the October massacres.

Now, for the first time, the latent tension between the historian and the ideologist in Dubnov became painfully manifest. He found himself trapped between a tragic view of the recent events and a political philosophy based on the axiom of human progress.[98] As his own life became increasingly entangled in the cataclysms of twentieth-century Europe, this paradox became ever more painful. However, given his beliefs and his character, it was one from which there could be no escape.

In some respects Dubnov reacted to the pogroms of 1903–1906 in ways very reminiscent of his stance in the years 1881–84. Now, as then, he saw emigration to the United States as the only response which could lead to an immediate improvement in the lot of the Russian Jews. He again called for a concerted effort to organize the migration. He also still argued, as he had in the 1880s, that although colonization in Palestine deserved support, it could in no way solve the problems of the vast majority of the world's Jews. Finally, he once more insisted that the struggle for emancipation, for equal rights in Russia, had to be pursued with redoubled energy, for many millions of Jews would inevitably remain in that country.

What was most striking, though, was the radical change of tone in the

Dubnov of 1903–1906. Some twenty years before, he had used his gift for historical analogy in order to argue against panic. But now he himself wrote in a white heat, and the parallels from the past which poured onto the page clearly suggested that the Jews in Russia were eternally fated to suffer periodic massacre. He rejected out of hand the thesis that the pogroms were simply inspired by the tsarist regime, a move in its counterrevolutionary strategy. He insisted that they were to a large extent the manifestations of popular hatred deeply rooted in history and in the collective psyche.

If in the 1880s he had been alarmed by the messianism of such proto-Zionists as Peretz Smolenskin, he now turned with real fury on the Marxist camp, which, as he saw it, was being carried away by the revolutionary triumphs of 1905 and, in large part, had come to expect the imminent triumph of socialism in Russia. Addressing the Bund, he asked,

> How has this mystical *Russian* nationalism taken such a hold on you Jewish Social Democrats, our brothers and sisters, who have only this minute felt one of the historic "missions" of the Russian people on your broken skulls, making 1905 a parallel to 1648 (note 1648 not 1848)?[99]

> The thousands and tens of thousands of workers, peasants, *meshchane*, and *raznochintsy*, across the entire expanse of Russia from Odessa to Tomsk, who broke Jewish heads, tore out the eyes of children, raped women and tore them to pieces, burnt, looted . . . did they do all this as counterrevolution? No, they did what their fathers and their brothers have done in years past [and] will do again in the future under favorable conditions. . . .[100]

Writing immediately after Kishinev, Dubnov even appeared to cast doubt on his belief in evolutionary progress:

> We are again living through events which show that history moves more along a circular route than along a straight line. Today the martyrology of the Jews in southern Russia has come full circle—from the massacre in Uman of 1768 to 1903. . . . We have reached a fateful frontier. . . . In our history . . . the signposts dividing one epoch from another have been stained with the blood [of our martyrs, the heroes of passive resistance]. The Crusades, the Inquisition, the expulsions, Khmelnitskii, the Haidamaks, . . . the repressive legislation, [the persecution by the Russian regime]—such are the dominant marks of division in our history.[101]

The Jewish masses, he wrote in December 1905, understand the truth better than do the socialist intelligentsia:

> Take into account this direct sense of the people, this psyche of the sufferers, these emotions and moods, which, more than abstract ideas, are the driving force of history! And this popular consciousness, which grasps recent events more correctly, tells us: "Do not trust Amalek, be it as the government, or as the people, because the old Russia can reappear in the new!"[102]

It can be argued that given this bitter indignation, this sense of betrayal and fateful foreboding, Dubnov should, according to all logic, have now radically reviewed his political program. To have any chance of lasting success, the plan for Jewish national autonomy required the establishment of a stable, sophisticated, and tolerant parliamentary regime. How could the Russian people—which Dubnov feared as politically primitive, predisposed to mass violence, and heir to age-old national hatreds—possibly establish, let alone maintain, so complex and fragile a constitutional system? His own analysis appeared to require a sharp change of direction. To argue, as he did with force, that another era had begun in Jewish history, that once again the Jews had to move on, settle in new lands of refuge, and reestablish their communal life, surely suggested that mass emigration had to become the top political priority.

The two most important new centers of the future, Dubnov now predicted with great confidence, would be the Jewish communities in the United States, where many millions would settle, and in Palestine, where a far smaller society would revive the Hebrew language and create an unadulterated national life.[103] He himself insisted that an organized effort was essential to ensure that the emigration went as smoothly as possible, that it be directed not to Western Europe—where it would only inflame anti-Semitism—but overseas.[104] He argued that the emigrants should not settle in over-crowded centers like New York but in selected places in the American West, where their presence would not encourage anti-alienism.[105] In December 1906 he even said outright that "regulating the emigration movement . . . could become our main national task if it were to turn out in the near future that the temporary triumph of black political reaction made the large-scale transformation of Russia impossible."[106]

In reality, though, Dubnov kept his basic political ideology intact not only in the period preceding the First World War but also in the interwar years 1919–39. The Folkspartey, which he helped to found in 1906, devoted only two words in its lengthy program to "directing emigration";[107] and, for his part, Dubnov would always maintain that Diaspora autonomism was of crucial importance for the future of the Jewish people in Eastern Europe and elsewhere.

As first Russia and, after 1914, Europe as a whole stumbled from one catastrophe to another, Dubnov developed more sympathy for Zionism, and after 1917 he often talked of eventually settling in Palestine himself.[108] But he was still repelled by the claims that Zionism offered an overall answer to the Jewish question—be it politically, as understood by Herzl, or culturally, as Ahad Ha-Am would have it.[109] The most that he granted was the strictly hypothetical concession that "if we possessed some cosmic lever which could transfer the Diaspora to a 'Jewish state' we would be delighted to use it."[110] As for territorialism, he regarded the idea of selecting and colonizing some newly chosen piece of land as antihistorical and as nothing more than an exercise in idle utopianism.[111]

Dubnov sought to close the gap between his pessimistic appraisal of the Jewish situation in Russia and his essentially optimistic constitutionalist strategies by emphasizing the role of time. It was wildly unrealistic, he now argued, to expect a basic transformation of Russian society to take place over any but a very prolonged period. Even if the tsarist regime was forced to grant equal rights, it would take many decades for a population of former serfs to become a population of responsible citizens, of free men. The examples of Germany, Austria, and France demonstrated that formal emancipation did not guarantee the Jews full equality, and in Russia the process would be more difficult: "How much time is needed for this metamorphosis, for the reeducation of these savage masses in the spirit of a constitutional *Rechtsstaat*, for the end to the rule of the fist, which has penetrated so deeply into Russian life?"[112]

To this question he could give no definite answer, but there could be no let up in the fight for equal rights, for full emancipation, for national self-government. There was no other choice for the millions of Jews who would always live in Eastern Europe, and eventually those who battled under the banner of "self-help" and "self-defense"[113] could expect to win their reward: "We shall fight for these rights as a nation which respects itself. . . . And however long this struggle for the right may take, we nevertheless will not lose our faith in the future triumph of our cause— the cause of truth and justice."[114]

The shock effect that the pogroms and the aborted revolution produced on Dubnov not only challenged his most basic ideological assumptions but also contributed to a change in his way of life and, it would seem, in his development as a historian. A few months after the Kishinev pogrom, he decided to move with his family from Odessa to Vilna, and three years later they returned once again to St. Petersburg. Dubnov had hoped to find a quiet refuge in Lithuania, away from the turmoil of Jewish life in the Odessa of 1903,[115] but as a result of these moves he found himself entangled in a web of organizational and political obligations in the capital, where he was to remain until 1922.

Time would prove that his thirteen years in Odessa had been the most creative period in his life. The mild climate, the calm domesticity, the active Jewish community, and the circle of friends (above all, Ahad Ha-Am and Mendele Mokher Sforim) with whom he could discuss and exchange ideas all served to inspire his most original work as both ideologist and historian.[116] Away from Odessa, Dubnov tended more to defend than to rethink his preconceived ideas.

In the years following the revolution he also abandoned what he had for so long seen as his life's mission as a historian. He now merged his work on Russian-Jewish history with that on the world history of the Jews, which he had hitherto seen primarily as an exercise in popularization. Thus, the writing of his *Modern History of the Jews*, which covered the period from the French Revolution to the most recent times (and would eventually serve as the last three volumes of the *World History*), occupied much of his energies in the years 1910–13 and was completed only in 1920.[117]

This work, as Raphael Mahler has rightly pointed out,[118] can be seen as Dubnov's attempt to demonstrate—to himself, perhaps, most of all—how the bitter realities of Jewish life in tsarist Russia could be reconciled with his own faith in progress. By his division of the book into broad periods of liberalism and emancipation, broken up by intervals of counterrevolution and reaction, he drove home the view that, however tragic, even major setbacks could do no more than delay the onward march of mankind. Seen from this perspective the Russian experience was a determined, prolonged, but ultimately futile stand by the tsarist regime and its supporters against the constitutionalism advancing from the West.

Dubnov was fated, of course, to live through the subsequent crises of Russian and European Jewry: first in St. Petersburg, then in Berlin, and finally in Riga. During the years 1914–21 he experienced firsthand the World War, the Revolution, and the Civil War; and then in the period 1929–41, the rise and expanding influence of Nazism. In essence, he reacted very much as he had done when faced by the pogroms and aborted revolution of 1903–1907.

He again remained unwaveringly loyal to the basic articles of his faith, to the liberal creed, to his humanistic form of Jewish nationalism, to his belief in the ultimate salvation of mankind. And now, too, he searched the horizon constantly for a break in the storm clouds. In the summer of 1917, to take one example, he elaborated in detail the principles of national autonomy in his brochure *What Do the Jews Want?*, declaring: "On 27 February the eyes of Russian people were opened. . . . The new revolution liberated all the peoples of Russia. . . . The Jewish people became a member with equal rights in the family of nations in Russia."[119]

When in the winter of 1918–19 all seemed lost at home, Dubnov still looked with hope to the West, to the postwar order being constructed by Woodrow Wilson and the other Allied leaders. "Somewhere far off in Paris," he noted in his diary on 31 January 1919, "the foundations of a new historical epoch are being laid; a peace conference is deciding the world's problems."[120]

Similarly, in the early 1920s he found satisfaction in the fact that his ideas on Jewish self-government were being partially implemented in the newly independent Baltic and Polish states. (An entry in his diary on 20 May 1920 noted that his "ideal of autonomy for the twentieth century" was actually being realized.[121]) Even in July 1933, when he was about to flee Nazi Germany, he could write that at least the terrible wave of anti-Semitism had forced many German Jews to reconsider their assimilationist strategy, noting that his own *Weltgeschichte* was now "being read in enforced leisure time by those intellectuals—unemployed lawyers, doctors, etc.—who previously would not give a thought to our national problem," and that it was providing them some "spiritual support."[122]

However, as during the 1905 revolution, Dubnov's sensitivity, developed to a high level by a lifetime of historical study, would not permit him to find refuge in the tenets of his own optimistic ideology. The same fury which he had earlier unleashed against the utopian maximalism of the Marxist socialists kept him in a state of unabating outrage as he observed the rise of the Bolsheviks in 1917 and their subsequent consolidation of power. As early as 14 May 1917 he noted privately that

> The degeneration of the Russian revolution into Pugachevshchina is evident in everything. The European revolution in Russian translation means a pogrom on the left together with a reactionary pogrom from the right. What will happen to Russia in a month or two? Civil war and terror, brought by the soldiers fleeing the front; state bankruptcy; real famine.[123]

With the establishment of the Bolshevik dictatorship in October, and during the next four years, his diary entries expressed profound bitterness at the overthrow of the short experiment in liberty. Even though he knew that he was putting his own personal freedom and even his life in danger from the Cheka, Dubnov lashed out at the new regime variously as "oprichniki",[124] "the old Moscow with Ivan the Terrible at its head,"[125] "the most infamous of all despotisms,"[126] "a handful of usurpers,"[127] "a mass of Autocrats,"[128] "the work of latter-day Razins and Pugachevs,"[129] an "Egypt"[130] in which everybody had become a "serf,"[131] "Asiatic socialism,"[132] "*kulak* socialisim,"[133] and (referring to the Red Army outside Warsaw) a "Hannibal at the Gates."[134]

For a long time Dubnov hoped passionately for the defeat of the Red Army, but when he belatedly absorbed the news of the unprecedented pogroms perpetrated against the Jews by the anti-Bolshevik forces in the South, he had to admit that the Whites were "really Black pogromists and not heroes."[135] By contrast, he demonstrated remarkable perspicacity in grasping at once that the draconian terms of the Versailles Treaty could only lead to the perpetuation of conflict in Europe. "It is something terrible . . .," he wrote on 14 May 1919, "worse than Bismarck's treaty of 1871. . . . And this is done by the World League, the League of Nations. . . . I am burying one more dream, the dream of triumphant pacifism, of a holy alliance of the nations for eternal peace."[136]

Steeled by his personal experience in the years 1914–21, Dubnov watched the political development of Europe and the world in the interwar years with the deepest anxiety. He believed Bolshevism to be unredeemable and could see no hope for the future of the Jewish community in Russia. He saw "tsarist injustice and pogroms being reborn in Poland"[137] and acknowledged in 1922 that by moving to Berlin he had placed himself on a "volcano."[138] Germany, he wrote a year later, "for all its culture, can sink either into a Black or into a Red sea,"[139] and in the same year he noted that the "hope for European peace is flickering out."[140] Even America, he had to admit, had shockingly disappointed expectations. If 1881 had seen the beginning of the great Jewish migration from Eastern Europe, then 1925 (following the passage of the new Immigration Act) marked its end.[141] And in the 1930s, he was quick to adopt the concept of totalitarianism (or "totalism,"[142] as he termed it) to describe the forces of darkness closing over Europe from the Stalinist Left as well as from the Nazi and Fascist Right.

Given the relentless unfolding of tragedy which overtook East European Jewry from 1914 and the Jews of Central Europe from 1933, it is hardly surprising that Dubnov often found himself wracked by doubt. Was it possible in such times to maintain belief in the triumph of humanity, universalist nationalism, the rule of law? His diaries reveal at least some of this agony of the soul. "It will be terrible to die," he wrote of the World War in August 1917, "if there is no certainty that this deluge will not repeat itself, if there is no certainty that peace will reign between states, nations, classes."[143]

Dubnov asked himself, in December 1919, whether his old friend and colleague Michael I. Kulisher had maintained his belief in progress right up to his recent death. "If so, then it was easier for the one who has gone than for those remaining behind."[144] An entry dated Shavuos 1920 described Dubnov looking up at the great sky of late spring in Petrograd in wonder and doubt: "Is this the attraction of the part to the whole or is it all a mirage? Perhaps the soul of man is full but the world is empty, soulless?"[145] A year later, at a gathering called to mark the fortieth anniversary of Dubnov's first publications, the assembled guests found themselves, as the author noted, compelled to "try to soften my pessimism."[146]

In 1900 he had looked forward to the new century for the completion of tasks neglected by the last, but now he found himself reluctantly drawn to the idea that this was to be a century of destruction. "The streams of lava," he wrote in 1919, "are flowing over the old culture, clearing a way for the new—will it be better or worse? I am inclined to think worse."[147] He returned to this thought when he published the first volume of his memoirs some fifteen years later.

> An entire epoch, our epoch on the edge of two centuries, is at an end, and many signs give grounds for fearing that the twentieth century will not be the continuation but the negation of the nineteenth. The ways of thought associated with that century—a century into which my life and that of my contemporaries is interwoven—have for the time being been forcefully severed by a historical cataclysm.[148]

Nonetheless, in the post-Kishinev period, Dubnov refused to abandon, or even modify, his basic political credo and program. Once more, he relied on time as the only escape from the trap set for him by the historical catastrophe overtaking Europe and European Jewry in particular. The metaphor of the Flood occurs in his diary—a period of total destruction, but one that was followed by a new and higher stage in man's development. "In all probability," he noted in June 1919, "we will again have to go through the stage of a culture low in its ethics before reaching the higher level."[149] He ended his public eulogy on Kulisher with the call "to keep our faith [in progress]; otherwise reason will be eclipsed, and God in the souls of men will die."[150]

In the final volume of his autobiography, published after the outbreak of the Second World War, Dubnov spoke with assurance of the future era which would in its turn negate the present epoch: "A pessimist, not expecting anything good from life, often acquiesces in all its horrors. . . . A true idealist, not losing faith in the final triumph of good, never acquiesces in the temporary triumph of evil and preserves his 'divine discontent.' "[151]

Of the Jewish people, in its time of greatest trial, he declared: "Our great sorrow is that we have been persecuted in every generation. Our greatness lies in the fact that we outlived the persecutions and the persecutors, all the Hamans of our history."[152] He predicted that the time would come when

> this generation of deformed youth, all this mass of pogromists called Iron Guards, Storm Troopers . . ., this generation of the moral desert, will either be corrected or will die out [and] a new society based on the love for man, on brotherhood and social justice, will be born in Europe.[153]

But for all his determination to remain undaunted even as his world collapsed about him, Dubnov could not sustain the extraordinary originality and productivity which had marked his life in the period before 1914 and particularly during the Odessa years. More and more, he devoted his time between the two world wars to overseeing the revision and publication of his major, but largely pre-existing, works—his history of Hasidism, the *Letters on Old and Modern Jewry*, his *World History of the Jewish People*, the *Pinkes* of the Jews of Lithuania[154]—in a variety of languages and editions. As he explained when he published the first volume of his autobiography in 1934, it was of vital importance in an age of regression, in a period of the Flood, to preserve for posterity the achievements of the generation about to be swept away: "We, its last representatives, have an obligation to set up a memorial to this disappearing epoch."[155]

In sum, then, it is no exaggeration to say that Dubnov's life and work were from the very first inextricably intertwined with the mounting tragedy of Russian and then of European Jewry. Dubnov wrote his first articles on history and politics in 1881, was one of the founders of the defense committee in Odessa following the Kishinev pogrom, and lived through and was politically active in the revolutions of 1905 and 1917. He survived the Civil War in St. Petersburg only by the skin of his teeth, witnessed the Nazi rise to power as an exile resident in Berlin, and was killed in Latvia by the German invaders at the end of 1941.[156]

Dubnov could have found refuge in America during the interwar period. Overtures were made to him by, among others, the Jewish Theological Seminary.[157] On the face of it, nothing would have been more natural than his joining the great stream of Jews moving West, a movement he himself had predicted and encouraged as early as 1881. But strong family ties worked against such a step; besides, as both historian and ideologist, he felt that his place was in Europe—where the present was organically integrated with the past, the new with the old—rather than in America, which belonged so clearly to the future. As the Nazis extended their hold over Europe, Dubnov made no attempt to escape. "One cannot desert the flock which still remains in Europe . . .," he wrote to Rawnitzki in 1940. "Providence, it seems, has decreed that I should remain with my brothers in the vale of tears and suffer together with them in the hour of danger."[158]

The constant succession of crises not only disrupted his life but also exposed his hard-won and highly integrated world view to ever greater stress and strain. On the one hand, as a historian he was ideally placed to sense, and to warn against, impending disaster. Describing Jewish history over the millennia, he had isolated what he saw as perhaps its central theme—the almost rhythmic pattern of communal construction, of persecution and destruction, of exile and migration, of reconstruction in the lands of refuge, one center always replacing another, albeit at enormous cost.

On the other hand, as an ideologist, he was committed to the cause of political liberation and Jewish emancipation in Russia and indeed in all of Europe. It was of key importance to his entire way of thought that history had taken a radically new turn with the Enlightenment and the French Revolution, that the medieval era, with its endemic violence and intolerance, had been forced to retreat.

But what if no ethical watershed divided the medieval from the modern? What if history forever follows not a linear but a cyclical path? More and more, Dubnov asked himself these questions, and they burst forth in his awesome articles following the pogroms of 1903 and 1905. But here was an intellectual problem which he could never resolve to his own satisfaction.

He discovered reluctantly, painfully, but inexorably that he would have to live out his life as an exile from 1922 on, as a nineteenth-century man in the ever more hostile world of the twentieth century. His belief in measured change, in constitutional liberalism, in humanistic nationalism, in a united Jewish politics, was rendered more anachronistic with every passing year. Of course, he could have escaped political isolation by modifying his ideology. He would have been welcomed by the Zionist, Territorialist, or Bundist movements if he had only been ready to deemphasize one aspect or another of his overarching theory of Jewish nationalism. But for him that would have been a betrayal of the truth.

The only course open to him, he concluded, was to retreat into semi-isolation and do his best to ensure that his historical works, his political message, and his life story be made as accessible as possible. They would be rediscovered by later generations in a different and better time.

Fifty years after his death, from today's perspective—which, of course, is itself only transient—it is impossible not to admire Dubnov's unyielding integrity, however lonely and costly it proved to be. What is more, his faith that time would eventually salvage something from what had every appearance of a lost cause has been justified.

It is clear today that it was Dubnov who, in many important ways, set the agenda for Jewish historiography in the twentieth century. He did so as the disciple of, but also in opposition to, Graetz. Dubnov not only pioneered the systematic study of the Jewish past in Eastern Europe but also, in contrast to Graetz, wrote history which used anthropological rather than theological terms of explanation. Dubnov's historiography emphasized the impact of external sociopolitical factors on the internal life of the Jews; the key importance of sociodemographic change, particularly migration and resettlement; the centrality of the mystic movements in the national experience; and the unbroken political role of Jewish self-government throughout the ages. Thus, for all the criticism to which his work is subject, Dubnov's reputation as a historian will, in all probability, only grow with the passage of time.

As for his political ideology, which condemned Dubnov to marginality for decades, it, too, has weathered better than could have been expected. His conviction that the triumph of totalitarianism would eventually prove transient looks far less naive half a century later than it did in 1940. His analysis of the Jewish future has similarly proved remarkably prescient. Although he underestimated the destructive power of anti-Semitism and the full potential of Zionism, he rightly predicted as early as the turn of the century that Palestine and America were both destined to be the new centers of the Jewish world. And that world, as he insisted it would be, is now multicentered. Within it, his concept of cultural autonomy in the Diaspora, well adapted to modern concepts of ethnicity and ethnic rights, is again surprisingly applicable.

Perhaps the last word should come from Dubnov himself. A note in his diary from 1926 reads: "When I think of my life I am convinced that what is most characteristic is that ever since early youth I have gone *my own way*, deviating neither to right nor left."[159] And in 1892, when disassociating himself from Graetz's judgment on such Jewish "heretics" as Elisha ben Abuya, he wrote,

> But does history glorify only those people who, thanks to fortunate conditions, achieved practical success and condemn those who "thought and suffered"

but did not achieve it? That can only end up in the theory of "vae victis" [woe to the conquered].[160]

NOTES

1. Although there is as yet no full-scale scholarly biography of Dubnov, there are numerous biographical and analytical articles about him. In addition to the works cited in the notes below, see, e.g.: Israel Friedlaender, *Dubnow's Theory of Jewish Nationalism* (New York, 1905); Josef Fraenkel, *Dubnow, Herzl and Ahad Ha-Am* (London, 1963); and Lionel Kochan, "The Apotheosis of History: Dubnow," in *The Jew and His History* (London, 1979), pp. 88–98. An entire edition of *He-avar* was assigned to essays on Dubnov: *He-avar: hoveret Shimon Dubnov: le-mleat mea shana le-holadeto*, vol. 8 (1961). (Alfred A. Greenbaum's forthcoming book in Hebrew on Russian-Jewish historiography will include a chapter on Dubnov, which the author has kindly permitted me to consult.)

2. *Weltgeschichte des jüdischen Volkes: Von seinen Uranfangen bis zur Gegenwart*, translated by Aaron Steinberg, 10 vols. (Berlin, 1925–29).

3. Heinrich Graetz, *Geschichte der Juden von den ältesten Zeiten bis auf die Gegenwart*, 2d ed., 11 vols. (Leipzig, 1863–1902); published in English as *History of the Jews*, 6 vols. (Philadelphia, 1956). Salo W. Baron, *A Social and Religious History of the Jews*, 18 vols. (New York, 1952–83).

4. For a recent biography, see Baila R. Shargel, *Practical Dreamer: Israel Friedlaender and the Shaping of American Judaism* (New York, 1985).

5. "Chto takoe evreiskaia istoriia? Opyt kratkoi filosofskoi kharakteristiki," *Voskhod*, October–November 1893, pp. 111–42; December 1893, pp. 78–112.

6. *Mikhtavim al ha-yahadut ha-yeshana ve-he-hadasha* (Tel-Aviv, 1937). The Yiddish edition, by contrast, is unabridged, being a translation from the Russian book of 1907: *Briv vegn altn un nayem yidntum*, introduction by Chaim Szlama Kazdan (Mexico City, 1959). For a new, scholarly, and full edition, see *Lettres sur le Judaisme ancien et nouveau*, edited and with an introduction by Renée Poznanski (Paris, 1989).

7. *Nationalism and History: Essays on Old and New Judaism*, edited and with an introduction by Koppel S. Pinson (Philadelphia, 1958).

8. *History of the Jews*, translated by Moshe Spiegel, 5 vols. (New York, 1967–73).

9. Robert M. Seltzer, "Simon Dubnow: A Critical Biography of His Early Years," Ph.D. diss., Columbia University, 1970.

10. *Kniga zhizni: Vospominaniia i razmyshleniia*, 3 vols. (Riga, 1934–35; New York, 1957).

11. Sophie Dubnov-Erlich, "Predislovie," ibid., III, p.vii.

12. See below, e.g., pp. 84, 224.

13. *Kniga zhizni*, I, 90. Dubnov apparently quoted this phrase from a letter he had written in 1878.

14. Ibid., I, 34.

15. Ibid., I, 175–76; II, 234–35.

16. Ibid., I, 221.

17. For an excellent analysis of this period of reassessment, see Robert M. Seltzer, "Coming Home: The Personal Basis of Simon Dubnow's Ideology," *AJS Review* 1 (1976):283–301.

18. "Vopros dnia," *Razsvet* 35 (28 August 1881):1386.

19. Ibid., p.1387.

20. Ibid.

21. *Razsvet* 34 (21 August 1881):1349.

22. "Neskol'ko momentov v istorii razvitiia evreiskoi mysli," *Russkii Evrei* 16 (15 April 1881):628.

23. Ibid., p.631.

24. "Kakaia samoemantsipatsiia nuzhna evreiam?" *Voskhod*, May–June 1883, p.240.

25. On Dubnov and the founding of the Folkspartey, see Robert M. Seltzer, "Jewish Liberalism in Late Tsarist Russia," *Contemporary Jewry* 9/1 (1987–88):47–66; and Oscar I. Janowsky, *The Jews and Minority Rights (1898–1919)* (New York, 1933), pp.114–18.

26. *Vsemirnaia istoriia evreiskogo naroda* (Berlin, 1924; dated St. Petersburg, 1910/Berlin, 1924), I, xv.

27. *Kniga Zhizni*, III, 134–38.

28. Benzion Dinaburg [Dinur], "Shimon Dubnov (le-yovalo ha-70)," *Tsiyon [Zion]*, 1/2 (1936):95–128; Y. Slutsky, "Kritikus," *He-avar*, 8 (1961):43–59.

29. Robert Seltzer, "Ahad Haam and Dubnow: Friends and Adversaries," in Jacques Kornberg, ed., *At the Crossroads: Essays on Ahad Haam* (Albany, 1983), pp. 60–73.

30. Kritikus [Dubnov], "Literaturnaia letopis': Vechnye i efemernye idealy evreistva," *Voskhod*, December 1890, section 2, pp.15–24.

31. Ahad Ha-am, "Avdut be-tokh herut," *Kol kitvei Ahad Ha-am* (Tel-Aviv, 1947), pp.54–59. (First published in *Ha-Meliz*, 1891.)

32. Koppel Pinson made this same point: "Dubnov, however, never became a revolutionary. . . . Capable though he was of deep emotion and sentiment, yet throughout his life sober and practical realism always triumphed over romantic enthusiasm. Dubnow always remained a moderate humanitarian reformer." ("Simon Dubnow: Historian and Political Philosopher," in Dubnow, *Nationalism and History*, p.7.)

33. "Kakaia samoemantsipatsiia nuzhna evreiam?" *Voskhod*, May–June 1883, p.221.

34. "Neskol'ko momentov v istorii razvitiia evreiskoi mysli," *Russkii Evrei* 18 (1 May 1881):710.

35. Ibid., 16 (15 April 1881):628.

36. Compare Dubnov's assessments of Moses Mendelssohn over a span of almost sixty years: "Mendelson russkikh evreev," *Razsvet* 30 (24 July 1881):1192; and *Vsemirnaia istoriia evreiskogo naroda* VII (1937):284–94.

37. Sophie Dubnov's marriage to Henryk Erlich, an active Bundist and later a leader of the Bund in Poland, introduced this ideological conflict into the inner family circle, but close personal ties were maintained nonetheless. On the public debate between Dubnov and Erlich in the late 1930s, see below, p.229. Cf. p.216.

38. *Kniga zhizni*, I, 50–56.

39. Ibid., pp.100–102.

40. "Neskol'ko momentov v istorii razvitiia evreiskoi mysli," *Russkii Evrei* 16 (15 April 1881):629.

41. See, e.g., the viewpoint stated by Dubnov in his article on Isaac Baer Levinsohn: "To truly evaluate the achievement of great thinkers, it is essential to observe them in the context of their own epoch." And: "*Historico*-critical evaluation and substantive criticism are not the same. Historical criticism is *relative*, conditional; but logical or rational criticism is absolute and to apply it to historical figures would be false and unjust." ("Mendelson russkikh evreev," *Razsvet* 30 [24 July 1881]:1192; 36 [4 September 1881]:1429.)

42. *Kniga zhizni*, I, 30–31.

43. *Vsemirnaia istoriia evreiskogo naroda*, vol. 1 (Berlin, 1924), p.xix.

44. *Kniga zhizni*, I, 187.

45. On the Russian-language Jewish press and for an extensive examination of *Voskhod* and Landau's role, see Yehuda Slutsky, *Ha-itonut ha-yehudit-rusit ba-mea ha-tsha-esre* (Jerusalem, 1970); and Slutsky, *Ha-itonut ha-yehudit-rusit be-reshit ha-mea ha-esrim* (Tel-Aviv, 1978).

46. *Kniga zhizni*, I, 231.

47. Ibid., p.268.

48. Dubnov noted in his diary on 31 January 1923: "For the first time in my life I have succumbed to an honorarium: 25 dollars for an article which at the present rate is one million marks." (Ibid., III, 21.)

49. Ibid., I, 405.

50. Ibid., I, 120.

51. On Dubnov's relationship to Graetz, see Lionel Kochan, "Graetz and Dubnov: Two Jewish Historians in an Alien World," in C. Abramsky, ed., *Essays in Honour of E. H. Carr* (London, 1974), pp.352–66; and Robert Seltzer, "From Graetz to Dubnov: The Impact of the East European Milieu on the Writing of Jewish History," in David Berger, ed., *The Legacy of Jewish Migration* (New York, 1983), pp.49–60.

52. "Istoriograf evreeistva: Genrikh Grets, ego zhizn i trudy," *Voskhod*, February 1892, p.51.

53. Ibid., July 1892, p.111.

54. Ibid., p.104.

55. Ibid., March 1892, p.66.

56. Some of the Russian-Jewish historians who had been students of Dubnov or were influenced by him were Zalman Shazar [Rubashev], Julius Hessen, Elias Tcherikower, and Benzion Dinaburg [Dinur]. Among the students at Baron David Günzburg's Courses in Oriental Studies, where Dubnov taught, were Shazar, Joshua Gutmann, Yezekiel Kaufmann, and Solomon Zeitlin. *He-avar* 6 (1958) contains many essays on Baron David Günzburg and the Courses in Oriental Studies.

57. *Kniga zhizni*, II, 31.

58. Samuel Bek [Bäck] and Marcus Brann, *Evreiskaia istoriia ot konsta bibleiskogo perioda do nastoiashchego vremeni*, revised and supplemented by S. M. Dubnov (Odessa, 1896), I, 173.

59. *Vseobschaia istoriia evreev* (St. Petersburg, 1904), I, 336–38.

60. *Kniga zhizni*, II, 194.

61. Ibid. On Dubnov's "historism," see below, p. 91; and Robert M. Seltzer, "Coming Home . . .," *AJS Review* 1 (1976):294–97.

62. "Literaturnaia letopis': Palestinofil'stvo i ego glavnyi propovednik," *Voskhod*, July–August 1883, section 2, p.34.

63. *Kniga zhizni*, II, 198.

64. Ibid., p.28.

65. Ibid., p.74.

66. Dubnov's emphasis on Jewish history as marked by the rise and fall of "hegemonic centers"—transformations caused by socioeconomic and political change in the host societies—was set forth most systematically in the introduction to his *World History*, but it also shaped his earlier work, published in St. Petersburg in the years 1904–1906. (It should be noted that those sections of the *World History* which cover the period between the post-biblical era and the French Revolution in large part involved re-editing rather than a total rewriting of the earlier three-volume work, *Vseobshchaia istoriia*.)

67. "Bedstviia evreev na Ukraine v 1648–1652 gg," *Razsvet* 24 (13 June 1882):

915–19; 25 (20 June 1882):956–61; 37 (12 September 1882):1434–36; 39 (28 September 1882):1498–1500; 40 (3 October 1882):1532–34.

68. "Istoricheskii ocherk poseleniia evreev v Amerike," *Razsvet* 20 (16 May 1882):759–62; 21 (23 May 1882):795–99.

69. "Shabbatai Tsevi i psevdomessianizm v XVII veke," *Voskhod*, July–August 1882, pp.136–63; September–October 1882, pp.13–44; "Iakov Frank i ego sekta khristianstvuiushchikh," January–February 1883, pp.17–49; March 1883, pp.71– 93; April 1883, pp.90–116; September 1883, pp.44–67; October 1883, pp.1–19.

70. "Shabbatai Tsevi . . .," *Voskhod*, July–August 1882, p.137.

71. "Vvedenie v istoriiu khasidizma," *Voskhod*, January–February 1888, pp.83– 100; March 1888, pp.3–18; "Vozniknovenie khasidizma," May–June 1888, pp.113– 41; July 1888, pp.81–100; August 1888, pp.3–21; September 1888, pp.3–16; October 1888, pp.27–44; "Vozniknovenie tsadikizma," September 1889, pp.3–21; October 1889, pp.3–18; January 1890, pp.23–42; March 1890, pp.83–100; "Istoriia khasids-kogo raskola," April–May 1890, pp.74–92; Iune 1890, pp.37–45; July 1890, pp.67– 84; August 1890, pp.3–20; September 1890, pp.33-41; October 1890, pp.3–24; November 1890, pp.43–71; December 1890, pp.125–45; January 1891, pp.58–74; February 1891, pp.95–115; October 1891, pp.6–36; November 1891, pp.121–44; December 1891, pp.92–112.

72. "Vvedenie . . .," *Voskhod*, January–February 1888, p.86.

73. *Toldot ha-hasidut be-tkufat tsmihata ve-gidula*, 3 vols. (Tel-Aviv, 1930–31).

74. But see Graetz's study of Frankism: *Frank und die Frankisten: eine Sekten-Geschichte aus der letzten Hälfte des vorigen Jahrhunderts*, Jahresbericht des jüdisch-theologischen Seminars (Breslau, 1868).

75. "Istoriograf evreistva," *Voskhod*, May 1892, pp.62–63.

76. *Ob izuchenii istorii russkikh evreev* (St. Petersburg, 1891), p.6.

77. "Chto takoe evreiskaia istoriia?" *Voskhod*, October–November 1893, pp.120–21.

78. *Ob izuchenii istorii russkikh evreev*, 1891.

79. The Istoriko-etnograficheskaia komissiia was established originally as a sub-section of OPE, The Society for the Dissemination of Enlightenment among the Jews in Russia. In 1908 it became the Evreiskoe istoriko-etnograficheskoe ob-shchestvo.

80. On Dubnov's relationship to YIVO, see below, pp.215, 216–17, 219, 221, 225, 228, 238, 239, 244.

81. Letter dated 20 May 1940 to Yehoshua H. Rawnitzki, in Simon Rawidowicz, ed., *Sefer Shimon Dubnov* (Jerusalem, 1954), p.331.

82. *Ob izuchenii istorii russkikh evreev*, p.6.

83. Ibid., p.4.

84. Salo W. Baron, *History and Jewish Historians* (Philadelphia, 1964), p.78.

85. *Ob izuchenii istorii russkikh evreev*, p.15.

86. "Istoricheskie soobshcheniia: podgotovlenye raboty dlia istorii russkikh evreev," *Voskhod*, February 1894, p.104.

87. "Pis'ma o starom i novom evreistve," *Voskhod*, January 1898, p.31.

88. Ibid., p.28.

89. *Voskhod*, June 1899, p.60.

90. *Voskhod*, December 1901, pp.12–16. Dubnov here predicted correctly that the Jews in the Austrian Empire, particularly in Galicia, would soon establish their own "national political party" to compete for seats in the Reichsrat; and he argued that the Jews in the United States "can and should" elect representatives to the Congress with "strictly national instructions" (p. 16).

91. *Voskhod*, March 1898, p.136.

92. *Voskhod*, June 1899, p.59.
93. *Voskhod*, November 1897, p.14.
94. *Voskhod*, January 1898, p.19.
95. *Voskhod*, November 1897, pp.13–21.
96. *Kniga zhizni*, I, 371.
97. On Dubnov's response to the Kishinev pogrom, see below, pp.122–23.
98. Aaron Steinberg (who, *inter alia*, translated Dubnov's World History from Russian into German) noted this tension, writing that Dubnov saw "world history as a whole as progressing but not as progress. . . . The author, who set out specifically not to write a history of spirit and suffering [eine Geistes- und Leidensgeschichte], found himself compelled to do just that by an inner truth and by his sensitivity to his subject matter. Thus his work finds expression in words of messianic longing." (Aaron Steinberg, "Die weltanschaulichen Voraussetzungen der jüdischen Geschichtsschreibung," in Ismar Elbogen et al., eds., *Festschrift zu Simon Dubnows siebzigstem Geburtstag* [Berlin, 1930], pp.39–40.)
99. "Uroki strashnykh dnei," *Voskhod [Nedel'naia khronika]* 47–48 (1 December 1905):9.
100. Ibid., p.3.
101. "Istoricheskii moment," *Voskhod [Nedel'naia khronika]* 21 (22 May 1903):1. The phrases in square brackets appear in the 1907 version and were presumably omitted in the original because of censorship. (*Pis'ma o starom i novom evreistve*, p.281 and note.) Cf. below p.121.
102. *Voskhod [Nedel'naia khronika]* 47–48 (1 December 1905):6.
103. *Pis'ma o starom i novom evreistve* (St. Petersburg, 1907), pp.358–61.
104. "Istoricheskii moment," *Voskhod [Nedel'naia khronika]* 21 (22 May 1903):5.
105. *Voskhod [Nedel'naia khronika]* 22 (29 May 1903):4.
106. *Volkspartei: Evreiskaia narodnaia partiia* [December 1906] (St. Petersburg, 1907), p.15.
107. Ibid., p.28.
108. See, e.g., his diary entry for 16 July 1919, *Kniga zhizni*, II, 295. Here Dubnov states the hope that he might be "among the saved," those settling in "Erets-Yisrael," but asks whether he has the right to leave behind the mass of Jews in the Diaspora, "to cast off the doomed." Cf. p.339.
109. " 'Utverzhdenie golosa' (Po povodu 'Otritsaniia golosa' Akhad Gaama)," *Evreiskii mir* 5 (1909):48–58.
110. Ibid., p.52.
111. On the distinction made by Dubnov between "real" and "utopian" emigration, see, e.g., *Pis'ma o starom i novom evreistve*, p.360.
112. "Uroki strashnykh dnei," *Voskhod [Nedel'naia khronika]* 47–48 (1 December 1905):4.
113. "Istoricheskii moment," *Voskhod [Nedel'naia khronika]* 21 (22 May 1903):2. The term "self-defense" appeared in the 1907 version, but not in the original (*Pis'ma o starom i novom evreistve*, p.282).
114. Ibid., p.290. This passage did not appear in the 1903 version.
115. *Kniga zhizni*, I, 414.
116. Ibid., I, 246–56. See below, pp.90–96, 124.
117. *Noveishaia istoriia evreiskogo naroda: ot frantsuzkoi revoliutsii do nashikh dnei*, 3 vols. (Riga, 1937–38). This work was first published in full in Berlin in 1923 in Russian, German, and Hebrew editions. A volume covering the period 1789–1881 had appeared in St. Petersburg in 1914.
118. Raphael Mahler, "Shitat Dubnov u-mifalo be-historiografiya ha-yehudit," in Aaron Steinberg, ed., *Simon Dubnow: The Man and His Work* (Paris, 1963), pp.57–72, particularly p.71.

119. *Chego khotiat evrei* (St. Petersburg, 1917), pp.9–10.
120. *Kniga zhizni*, II, 283.
121. Ibid., p.317.
122. Ibid., III, 120.
123. Ibid., II, 226.
124. Ibid., p.262.
125. Ibid., p.250.
126. Ibid., p.351.
127. Ibid., p.333.
128. Ibid., p.245.
129. Ibid., p.340.
130. Ibid., p.245. Dubnov noted here that the hopes for Palestine following the English conquest of Jerusalem was "a point of light in the Egyptian darkness." Cf. p.329.
131. Ibid., p.347.
132. Ibid., p.283.
133. Ibid., p.263.
134. Ibid., p.320.
135. Ibid., p.313 (diary entry 2 February 1920).
136. Ibid., p.289.
137. Ibid., III, 12.
138. Ibid., p.15.
139. Ibid., p.30.
140. Ibid., p.20.
141. Ibid., p.56.
142. Ibid., p.144.
143. Ibid., II, 233.
144. Ibid., p.304.
145. Ibid., p.317.
146. Ibid., p.338.
147. Ibid., p.292.
148. Ibid., I, vii.
149. Ibid., II, 292.
150. Ibid., p.304.
151. Ibid., III, 154.
152. Ibid., p.150.
153. Ibid., p.153.
154. S. Dubnov, ed., *Pinkas ha-medina: o pinkas vaad ha-kehilot ha-rashiyot bi-m[e]dinat lita* (Berlin, 1925).
155. *Kniga zhizni*, I, vii.
156. On Dubnov's last days, see below, pp.245–47.
157. *Kniga zhizni*, III, 14–15. Dubnov noted in his diary on 26 August 1922, "Of course, I shall refuse because it's not pleasant to be living now in the quiet and wealthy land of the dollar, far from the European volcano."
158. In a letter to Y. H. Rawnitzki, dated 20 May 1940 (in S. Rawidowicz, ed., *Sefer Shimeon Dubnov* [Jerusalem, 1954], p.331), he wrote that friends in America had obtained an entry visa to the United States for him. See below, pp.237, 239. On Dubnov in Riga, see Y. Maor, "Dubnov be-tkufat Riga," *He-avar* 8 (1961):26–29; and D. Levin, "Me-riga ha-sovyetit li-[ye]rushalayim–be-daaga (Mikhtavo ha-aharon shel Shimon Dubnov li-[ye]didav be-erets-yisrael," *Shvut* 8 (1981):111–12.
159. *Kniga zhizni*, III, 70.
160. "Istoriograf evreistva," *Voskhod*, February 1892, p.62.

THE LIFE AND WORK OF
S. M. Dubnov

by Sophie Dubnov-Erlich

Introduction

The biography of a human being is not merely a list of facts. Even the most confused, complicated, and inconsistent life has an intrinsic unity. The biographer's task is to reveal that unity methodically in the cumulative effects of the years as they change the aspect of the man. Indissolubly linked to decades of Russian-Jewish history, the life of the historian Dubnov presents no difficulties to the researcher. From the humble *kheyder* where the inquisitive mind of the child sought nourishment in the legends of the Bible and the casuistry of the Talmud, the road leads, straight as an arrow, to the snow-covered square where a shot by a human beast put an end to decades of cerebration.

My father made his biographer's task easier in another, practical way. By the end of his life he had published three volumes of memoirs, encompassing almost eighty years; the final volume was in press when war broke out. True to his historian's instinct, he gave the book, entitled *The Book of My Life*, the subtitle "Materials for a History of My Time." The biography of the *man* merged with the biography of a bygone *era* as it receded into the past. The memoirs were based on the diary my father kept for many years, the testimony of his wish to take stock in times of vicissitude and crisis.

My father's need for summation—for what he called the "integration of the soul"—became particularly urgent in the period of physical old age (he never felt he was an old man spiritually). Originally he had not intended that his memoirs be published during his lifetime; he altered that decision when he concluded that the declining years of his life coincided with the decline of a great era. "We are living now in an era of historic endings," he wrote in 1934, in his isolated little house in the middle of Baltic woods, "when the heritage of the nineteenth century is being eliminated from all areas of public and private life. A whole era, our era on the border of two centuries, is ended. . . . The continuity of the ideological currents of the century, with which my life and the lives of many of my contemporaries were interwoven, has been temporarily sundered by the force of historical cataclysm. And we, the last representatives of a bygone era, are duty bound to erect a monument to it."

To understand a man's life one must begin at the source: family roots and childhood environment. Here, too, as a historian, accustomed to tracing the evolution of phenomena, my father comes to the biographer's aid. He reveals that a distinctive succession of generations can be observed in the Dubnov family: men of a spiritual, ascetic bent were followed by more or less successful, practical men of affairs. More than once in his

memoirs he emphasizes his spiritual kinship with his grandfather, a talmudic scholar, rather than his father, a man burdened by the cares of
scraping out a living. Grandfather and grandson followed different paths,
but they were alike in their passionate and intense work of the mind,
their lives of spartan simplicity and their rationalism, grounded for one
in traditional rabbinical studies, and, for the other, in the philosophy of
positivism. But beneath the sober rationalism of the grandson flowed an
undercurrent of a visionary romanticism springing, perhaps, from a more
remote family tradition. Thus the nineteenth-century positivist was connected through a line of talmudists and *misnagdim* to his distant ancestor,
the seventeenth-century cabalist Yosef Dubno.

The world of my father's childhood, in a small, remote, provincial town
in Belorussia, was in keeping with family tradition. Little Simon, a pupil
of the *kheyder*, was expected to become a talmudic scholar when he graduated from the yeshiva directed by his grandfather. But for the first time
in the Dubnov family, mutiny broke out: the young yeshiva student had
become a *maskil*, an autodidact, and opposed the religio-national thesis
with an individualistic and cosmopolitan antithesis. The years passed,
and the period of "Storm and Stress" was followed by the search for a
synthesis. History, uniting the past with the present, as well as the national
with the human, helped him to find that synthesis.

The curiosity of his early awakened mind and the ardor of his yearning
heart found an outlet in immersion in the little-researched realms of the
many centuries of his people's life. This work, imbued with religious fervor, and rising above deprivation and daily adversity, became the *suprema
lex* of my father's life. But only in his last years did he succeed in attaining
harmony between the outer shell and the inner content of life: the green
parks on the outskirts of Berlin and the pine forests in the vicinity of
Riga created an ideal frame for his indefatigable work, which did not let
up even in his old age. The hermit lived not by the past alone in his forest
retreat: on his table rose a pile of newspapers; the daily mail brought echoes
from all corners of the world; dozens of men knocked at the door of his
modest dwelling; as always everything human stirred him. The volcanic
eruptions of a twenty-year period which foreshadowed catastrophe roused
apprehension; but this eternal optimist did not dread the triumph of Nazi
barbarity.

When catastrophe loomed, my father did not take a single step to save
himself. The life of his people was his life; the death of the great masses
of Jewry became his death. He, the chronicler of the many terrible days
of his people, wrote the final, most terrible page of all in his own blood.

N.B.: The author's notes are marked by asterisks and appear at the foot
of the page. Those compiled by the editor are numbered sequentially
throughout the translation and appear at the end of the book.

1

Sources

The little town in Belorussia stood remote and forlorn among the fields and the pine and birch groves. The town was first built in the days of the appanage princes and still bore the ancient Slavic name Mstislavl. It kept changing hands in the wars between Muscovy and Poland and retained traces of Polish culture long after. In the second half of the nineteenth century, in the age of the emancipation of the serfs, it was a sleepy little town, typical of the western border region, with unpaved streets, duckboard sidewalks, tiny houses rooted in the earth, and endless fences, behind which many dogs barked long and mournfully in the dead of night. The green square in the center of town was surrounded by the houses of the local "aristocracy"—civil servants and well-to-do merchants—with porches, colored shutters, and front yards. Beyond the square lay the Jewish quarter, known as the *shulhoyf*, with a large *kahal* synagogue in the center. It was noisy and dirty, with puddles that never dried up, in which ragged, barefoot children swarmed like sparrows. Petty shopkeepers, artisans, and coachmen crowded the squat little houses. Narrow, crooked streets led to the outskirts of town, where poverty-stricken Russians lived; there vegetable plots straggled, the smell of wood smoke hung in the air, cows mooed. The narrow ribbon of a murky stream, the Vekhra, meandered along. Wild street urchins from the outskirts played rowdy games on its muddy banks overgrown with reeds; and here, too, flocked the little inhabitants of the Jewish quarter, the prisoners of the stifling *kheyder*, in their rare hours of liberty. One swarthy, black-eyed boy often lingered on the bank after the others had gone; not even fear of punishment could force him back to the dusty tomes on time. Crouching in the tall, wet grass, he gazed along a horizon which seemed like the rim of the world, and listened intently to the fragrant, green silence broken only by the moist chomping of grazing cows and the drawn-out cries of the raftsmen floating logs down river. In those solitary hours, the melancholy Belorussian plain, framed by scrubby forest, smelling sharply of wormwood and wild peppermint, and embroidered by the dark blue threads of the river winding through the emerald fields, sank into his soul forever. Years would pass and in all his wanderings the boy, grown to manhood, would carry within him the landscape of his native land, the only landscape in the world to become the landscape of his soul.

He had to leave the green banks and return to the noise, dust, and stuffiness of the *shulhoyf* and the cramped lodgings where his large family lived. The Dubnovs were respected throughout the town for their spiritual lineage (*yikhes*). Since the end of the eighteenth century, when the descendants of the renowned cabalist Yosef Dubno moved from Volynia to Belorussia, the line of scholars in the family had never been broken. On the other hand, they could not boast of their achievements in worldly affairs: if any men with business acumen appeared in the family and succeeded in making a fortune, their sons preferred the volumes of *Halachah* to accounting ledgers and squandered their fathers' fortunes.

When the boy Simon was born, in September 1860, on the second day of Rosh Hashanah, the talmudist Rabbi Bentsion was considered the head of the family. In his youth Bentsion Dubnov had, at his father's insistence, tried to learn a trade, but decided to devote himself to learning. For forty-five years he had taught an advanced course in the Talmud in the Mstislavl synagogue. In the town, legends were told of his strength of character and fanatical dedication. There was a story that when a fire broke out in the Jewish quarter, destroying almost half the houses, Rabbi Bentsion caught sight of the huge glow through the synagogue window, persuaded his terrified students to remain in their places, and went on with his lecture. Later, when the people who had been burned out were sorting through the possessions they had managed to save, he asked a *shamash* from the synagogue to search out a treatise in the Talmud, which he needed to prepare the next day's studies. He accepted the financial disaster with fortitude; the fire had burned down the stone house, left to him by his father, which was his sole source of income. He had become a poor man, but he refused the profitable duties of a rabbinate offered to him by the community and remained a teacher of the Torah.

Bentsion Dubnov was a confirmed *misnagid*, critical of Hasidic mysticism, and he avoided any ecstatic bodily movements in his prayers. This is how he remained in his grandson's memory forever: "He stood erect, his tall figure turned to the eastern wall. He uttered each word of the prayer slowly and distinctly, and only occasionally did he calmly lower and raise his head. But chastely concealed inner exaltation could be felt in his entire being." More than once little Simon was present on Yom Kippur when his grandfather performed the holy rites in the synagogue, overflowing with the congregation: "There he stands before the lectern, a tall, elegant man with a long silvery beard, his tallis thrown over his white robe [*kitl*], and, like a lawyer in a toga before the court, he delivers his speech for the defense to God." Not everything in this discourse was understood by his grandson, but the transitions from angry challenge to deep sorrow and then reconciliation made his child's heart throb in agitation.

Simon's parents were people of a different spiritual cast. They were typical Jewish toilers, weighted down by the cares of supporting a huge family. Meyer-Yakov Dubnov (1833–1887) worked as a steward for his rich father-in-law, who bought up timber from Belorussian landowners and floated it south. He spent the winter far from his family in a wooden shack in a remote part of Polesia, directing the lumbering and sale of timber. When spring came he accompanied the rafts floating downriver to the ports of the great southern towns. He would return home for a short time only in the autumn for the High Holidays—worn out by nine months of traveling, silent, with an unremitting cough. Dependency on his harsh and miserly father-in-law, worries for his family of ten, perpetual minor indispositions which developed into chronic lung disease—all this aged the shy, gentle man prematurely. Illness brought him to the grave at the age of fifty-four. Father and son were attached to one another, but there was no real intimacy between them. Simon's father passed through his life like a silent shadow, leaving a cloud of sadness and a troubling sense of guilt. The only thing he left his son was the consciousness, which grew stronger over the years, that there is no greater curse than being tied to uncongenial work and swamped by material cares.

Joy was an infrequent visitor to the cramped three-room lodgings in the *shulhoyf*. Sheyne Dubnov withered early beneath the burden of care; her dark, gentle eyes, circled by a web of wrinkles, grew dim. A small, thin woman with an elongated, swarthy face and a high forehead beneath the fringe of her wig, she scurried about from dawn to late at night like a tireless ant, dividing her time between house and shop. As Simon tossed on his hard straw pallet in the gray morning shadows, he heard his mother whispering her prayers beside her bed. Her knotted, calloused hands turned the pages of the large women's prayer book (*Korban Minchah*), and silent tears rolled down her hollow cheeks. Having completed her devotions, she plunged into worldly cares: she fed her horde of children before hurrying off to the crockery shop with a heavy bunch of keys. The first peasant carts were already making for the market square, raising clouds of dust. A lean Belorussian in a sheepskin coat and boots smelling of pitch was already waiting at the door of the shop, thrashing the air with his whip. Furious bargaining began: the small woman rummaged feverishly in boxes, pulling cheap white china cups and bowls out of the shreds of dusty straw while the peasant tapped the china with his finger in a businesslike manner and held it up to the light. Then he entered into a violent argument over a few pennies. The woman did not give in: a few extra five-kopek pieces meant the price of repairing a pair of boots for irrepressible Simon or a ribbon in pretty, black-eyed Risa's braid.

Late in the evening the heavy iron-bound door was slammed shut; Simon's mother trudged home, dragging her feet, hoarse, worn out. Her thin, bluish lips rarely smiled for her children; her love for them was perpetual fear and worry, her prayer soundless weeping. But she did not grumble; everyone around her lived like this. A festive spirit entered her scrawny body only on the evening before the Sabbath. Simon loved those evenings: the warm glimmer of the wax candles in the polished family candlesticks, the yellowish twisted braid of challah, the gleaming white of the darned tablecloth—everything breathed unaccustomed peace and comfort. The gentle drudge covered her eyes with her fingers, through which streamed honey-colored light, and shook off the dust of the everyday in an almost soundless prayer.

The children grew up unattended and surrounded by squalor, living in cramped, stuffy quarters, among perpetually busy and care-worn adults. Affection between the oldest and the youngest children is rare in a large family: little Simon could not really be a friend to his taciturn brother Isaac, a talmudic scholar who married young and moved to another town, nor to his older sister Risa, who helped her mother about the house and sang sad songs, secretly dreaming—contrary to time-honored tradition—of marrying for love.

From early childhood to old age Simon felt genuine closeness to his brother Volf (Vladimir), who was a year and a half older. The brothers were very like one another in appearance: the same dark skin, the typical aquiline semitic nose, the broad forehead under a thick mane of hair. But fiery sparks burned in Simon's black eyes, and his movements were quick and decisive, while Volf was a slow, phlegmatic boy. Not surprisingly, the younger brother wielded authority over the older all their lives.

The environment of childhood shapes a man's soul, both when he bends to it and when he rebels against it. The anxiety, bitterness, and resignation which saturated the atmosphere of the Dubnov family bred rebellion and longing for a different life in Simon, but they spawned passivity and melancholia in Volf. Thus their future paths were defined: Simon was to forge his destiny in accord with his inner imperative; Volf was doomed to walk in the paths of dissatisfaction, beneath the lash of a secret knot of guilt, which in a moment of crisis led him to wreck his personal life. The streams which flowed together in youth would subsequently diverge; but neither years nor distance could weaken the sense of a close, friendly bond between the brothers, a firm bond which only death could sunder.

2

On the School Bench

A dusty room with a low soot-blackened ceiling. Long wooden benches around an ink-stained table made of unplaned boards crudely banged together. Sheyne Dubnov brought little Simon, wearing a freshly washed and darned short coat, to the elementary *kheyder* there. The red-haired, good-natured *melamed*, Rabbi Kule, pinched the shy little boy's cheek with fingers yellow from snuff, and began to show him big letters on an alphabet chart.

Adults accompanied the new boys. At each correct answer the child's father would toss him a piece of gingerbread; the children were assured that it was a gift from the angels. The angel gave nothing to little Simon. Sheyne Dubnov had no time for tomfoolery; she hurriedly thrust a few sweets into the boy's pocket and went off to the shop.

Thus began the drudgery of the *kheyder*, lasting from morning to evening. The only interruption was for dinner, which invariably consisted of a crust of bread and milk soup with groats. The teacher was pleased with Rabbi Bentsion's grandson. The boy quickly learned to read and began to study the Pentateuch.

The monotonous *kheyder* day dragged slowly by. Bent over their tattered books, the children read the Bible under the direction of the *melamed* in a loud, ragged chorus and translated it into their native Yiddish. The imagination of the little boy, who had never heard a fairy tale, was incessantly at work. He saw apples ripening in an immense garden of paradise, like the monastery park on the outskirts of town; the glow of a great fire rising over the houses of Sodom; Jacob herding his flocks in a ravine smelling of wild peppermint, like the footpaths leading to the Vekhra. In the evenings, the little schoolboy lay awake for a long time on his hard straw pallet. The small lamp smoked in the stuffy, tightly shuttered room. His brothers and sisters moaned in their sleep. His mother leaned against the cupboard and counted copper coins. She sighed and scratched her head beneath the wig with a knitting needle. But behind the boy's closed eyelids paraded a procession of extraordinary people who talked to the angels and God Himself.

Simon spent three terms of six months in *melamed* Kule's school; it was the gateway to the next level of *kheyder*, where the teaching of the Talmud began. Simon's memoirs give this account of the *kheyder*:

The new rabbi, Itse Pipler, was the complete opposite of his predecessor. Wizened, short-sighted, with a fleshy nose, he was always morose. . . . He kept us, children of eight or nine years, from nine in the morning until eight at night, with an hour's break for dinner, winter and summer alike, in the small, cramped room of the *kheyder*; and browbeat us with his great wisdom, which we obviously could not appreciate. He began to teach us the Talmud straightaway, using the complete texts of the Mishnah and the Gemara. . . . We read about the dispute between the House of Shammai and the House of Hillel, the two schools of law in the Mishnah. The dispute turned on whether one could eat an egg laid by a chicken on a holiday. The finest hair-splitting discussions on this subject were carried on by the scholars so that the question became even more tangled. My head began to spin from reading loudly in unison a strange text, from all the convolutions of thought and the fine casuistical points which the rabbi drummed into our childish heads with shouts and gesticulations and abuse directed at those who did not understand, and sometimes with a strap laid across our backs or hands.

Years would pass and the adolescent would come to the conclusion that studying this treatise was the origin of his later rebellion against tradition.

The books of the Bible, studied during evening hours, were an oasis after the wilderness of the Talmud. By the dim light of a tallow candle the children read in a monotonous singsong the story of Gideon, the tale of the mighty warrior Samson, and the dramatic chronicles of the kings of ancient Israel. The dry, pedestrian teacher did not know how to enliven the biblical texts with his own explanations, and more than once Simon balked in bewilderment at passages he found incomprehensible. The Book of Ecclesiastes, which the schoolboys read in the interim days of Succos, particularly puzzled him. A late cold autumn set in, and a biting wind whipped through the cracks in the shed, which was knocked together from planks. The pupils shivered from the autumn cold as well as from the strange, terrifying words they chanted: "What profit hath man of all his labor/Wherein he laboreth under the sun?/For all this is vanity and a striving after wind. . . . For that which befalleth the sons of men befalleth beasts; even one thing befalleth them; as the one dieth, so dieth the other." "Many times subsequently," Simon writes in *The Book of My Life*, "when the cosmic cold gripped me and chilled my outlook, I remembered that gloomy autumn and the trembling of an eight-year-old boy before the gaping abyss. . . ."

When Simon was eight he read the first book to awaken his interest in history. He found a Hebrew adaptation of the chronicle of Joseph Flavius, known as the *Yosifon*, in his grandfather Bentsion's library. New images invaded the life of the *kheyder* pupil—Alexander the Great, the Greeks and the Romans, the Hasmoneans, heroes and warriors. He plunged into a stormy, colorful age unknown to his schoolmates and teachers. He could only read the book in the evenings, by the feeble light of a lamp burning linseed oil. Exhausted by hours of wandering through the wilderness of talmudic divorce and trade laws, his brain devoured episodes of historical drama, until his mother called out sleepily from the next room, "Simon, you've burned enough oil, time to sleep!" Losing patience, she would get out of bed, groaning, and blow out the oil lamp, dispelling the images which had enthralled the boy.

When he reached his ninth birthday, he moved to the highest class, under the *melamed* Rabbi Zelig, renowned for his erudition and his God-fearing life. An ascetic and a bitter pauper, Zelig spent entire days in the *kheyder* and synagogue, sustained only by coarse bread made of hemp seed, usually kept for cattle feed. The new *melamed* was no stranger to poetry; he told enthralling stories and related the legends of the *Aggadah* and Midrash to his pupils. Then he would suddenly feel ashamed of his weakness and exclaim, "Well, that's enough fun and games, it's time to get down to work," and once again the children sank into the dry scholasticism of *Halachah* and the fine points of the law. "This intellectual food," says *The Book of My Life*, "gave the ten-year-old students of Jewish law a stone instead of bread, and my unsatisfied spiritual hunger drove me to search for nourishment in other realms."

Further study of the Bible was complemented by lessons in the Talmud. In Rabbi Zelig's *kheyder* the boy read the Prophets for the first time, and he was struck by the power and resonance of the text in Isaiah. Unsatisfied by the traditional methods of study, the nine-year-old schoolboy tried to decipher the text for himself with the help of Mendelssohn's commentaries,[1] which were forbidden in the *kheyder*. Emboldened by this, he assumed the role of teacher. As he sat with his schoolmates at the long table in the synagogue in the summer twilight, between the prayers of *minchah* and *ma'ariv*, he passionately declaimed the tirades of the Prophets against the sinners of Zion or the comforting prophecies about the coming of peace on earth. Ignoring the school curriculum, he went through the whole Bible on his own, and this "Book of Books"—with its ardent lyricism, its exaltion of the national, and its occasional social emphasis—became one of the formative influences on his soul.

The soul of the boy rapidly growing to maturity was wide open to the manifold impressions of life, and he keenly felt his isolation and defenselessness in a strange, incomprehensible, and mysterious world. He soon understood not to expect help from adults, who were burdened by their own cares; he would have to think through and decide everything for himself. All about him the hard, torpid life flowed on. Every evening the heavy doors were drearily bolted, and the dark shutters thudded shut, turning the room into a tomb. Everyone around him lived a life of fear, cringing before God, man, and fate. The boys of the *kheyder* knew that the angel of death, with eyes all over his body, came to the gravely ill and cut their throats with a shining sword; they knew that the dead gathered at night in the women's section of the deserted synagogue, summoning to the Torah the living doomed to die soon; they knew that sinners were roasted in frying pans and flogged with steel switches. More than once Simon's heart contracted in terror: a burning red sunset seemed to be the glow of the great red-hot ovens of hell, and, in the twilight, the tombstones that their neighbor, the carpenter, set by the fence to dry became dead men wrapped in winding sheets. Death hovered over everything: its presence could be felt in the doleful speeches of the wandering preachers calling lost souls to repent, and in the heart-breaking songs of the Jewish recruits marching off to military service as though to an execution.

Beyond the boundaries of the *shulhoyf* lay the green lanes of the main avenue and neat houses with light curtains and colorful flowers on the window sills. The boy gazed with a mixture of terror and curiosity at the white fence beyond which rose the tall bell tower of the cathedral, with its painted onion domes glittering festively in the sun. On Sabbath evenings, when the sadness of the end of the day of rest fell over the Jewish quarter, the deep tolling of the bell floated from that direction. Adults in their best clothes and the same urchins who teased and sometimes played with the pupils of the *kheyder* in the dusty side streets on the edge of town hurried to the cathedral cloister.

Left to his own devices, the boy knocked against the sharp corners of life in bewilderment. What could he do? Resign himself, be like everyone else, squeeze his life into the tight space between synagogue and grave, or try to seek his own way? He chose the latter without hesitation.

3

Rebellion

When Simon's older brother Isaac left his parents' house on the eve of his wedding, he slipped his younger brother a slim book by Kalmen Shulman, a writer from Vilna. The book could only be considered forbidden because it was a work of secular rather than religious literature. It was a naive, sentimental description of a journey through Palestine and neighboring countries, interspersed with pious meditations on the transience of everything earthly. It was not the didactic tendentiousness that captivated the boy but the colorful exoticism of the life Shulman depicted, so unlike the gray routine of provincial existence.

During the hours of study, as Simon gazed absently at a page of the Talmud opened to a discussion of the question of responsibility for direct or indirect harm, he would affectionately stroke the rough cover of the tattered book lying on his knees. He had graduated to the final level of *kheyder*, where the schoolboys were to complete the elementary instruction in the Talmud. Avrom-Yoel, the new teacher, a stern and morose old man, often embarrassed the sinner in public. If a pupil, engrossed in his reading, floundered over an unexpected question, the rabbi's bony hand, with a pinch of snuff between the fingers, smacked his cheek painfully.

Simon felt his independence more and more. His father was traveling, his mother was preoccupied by perpetual duties, and his grandfather Bentsion had moved to another house. More and more Hebrew books of secular content came into Simon's hands. The twelve-year-old boy was overwhelmed by Eugene Sue's *Mystères de Paris* in Hebrew translation, the first real novel with a convoluted plot he had read. For several days he walked around in a daze and set Volf on fire with his emotion. The brothers so longed to own this book that they made a heroic decision: to copy the multivolumed novel by hand. However, even by working feverishly at night, they had time to copy only the first volume before the book had to be returned to its owner. Some time later another book became the object of the youths' passionate desires, *Ayit Zavu'a* (The Hypocrite), a novel by Mapu, then a popular Jewish writer.[2] The author, a second-rate fiction writer, depicted the sanctimoniousness and fanaticism of the *kahal* bosses and the nobility of the enlightened youth struggling with their surroundings. When Simon read the first part of the novel he was consumed by the desire to learn the ultimate fate of its heroes. He decided to ask the bookseller, who stocked religious books, to order the heretical tale from Warsaw. When the five volumes in colored covers appeared on the shelf in the bookshop the young lovers of literature were panic-stricken: their meager savings from skipping breakfast were not enough to buy the books. Fortunately it was just before Passover and trade in the crockery shop was brisk. Every day the boys hid a few coppers in their pockets while they were helping their mother and then raced to the bookshop with pounding hearts. The precious books were hidden in a secret place where the lads' clandestine library was kept. Simon became absorbed in reading the dialogues between the representatives of the old and the new generations, searching for answers to the troubling questions he was beginning to ask. The urge to escape the realm of the rigid traditionalists and enter the realm of the enlightened, the *maskilim*, grew ever stronger.

A militant pamphlet, "A Vision of the Sacred Language," was the fruit of these feelings. Written in a naïvely florid style, abounding in biblical quotations, it scourged the hypocrites and fanatics bent on grinding over the Talmud and hating the *Haskalah*. Simon managed to distribute several copies of the pamphlet. It drew open displeasure from the older generation and secret sympathy from the young people.

At this time the boy's mind was working feverishly and intensely. His vague, childish terror in the face of the mysterious and the incomprehensible gave way to protest against hypocrisy, sanctimoniousness, and injustice. Simon saw the dark sides of life early. The poverty which the adults, in shame, tried to hide from others' eyes was no secret to the schoolboy wise before his time, for he often wrote long letters to his father at his mother's dictation. Standing behind the counter in the semi-darkness of the empty shop, his mother sighed and wiped her eyes with a corner of her knitted shawl while the young scribe painstakingly traced in a fine hand the traditional address: "To my beloved, honored and much respected husband Meyer-Yakov, may his light always shine forth." Then the everyday prose began—a list of expenses for lodgings, for the *melamed's* fee, for mending boots. Sometimes, at his mother's behest, Simon composed eloquent missives, strewn with quotations, to her father, the rich grandfather he had never met. The grandfather praised the style but never sent any money.

All around him was the same penury, the same complaints, the same daily cares. The observant boy spent almost the entire day in the synagogue and could not help but notice that the greater part of the congregation prayed carelessly, garbling the familiar words before hurrying back to their worldly affairs. He began to examine the content of the prayers and felt with some surprise that the words, familiar since childhood, said nothing to his heart. Panic-stricken, he tried to pray in the synagogue in his own words or repeated snatches of his favorite psalms, but more and more he began to think it was possible to pray properly only in solitude.

In September 1873, on the eve of his religious coming of age, Simon began to prepare the traditional sermon on a subject from the Talmud. The *melamed* suggested a treatise devoted to the fine points of ritual. As Simon picked his way through the complicated convoluted text, he got stuck in the disputation about how a left-handed man should put on the *tefillin*. According to the law, it should be fastened with the right hand. The arid, barren casuistry of the text troubled him so deeply that he categorically refused to deliver the sermon.

Simon's bar mitzvah was an important milestone: he moved to the yeshiva, to his grandfather Bentsion's school. The yeshiva students spent whole days in the *kahal* synagogue, sitting at long plank tables and chanting the texts. The chanting, so out of harmony with paragraphs on divorce and the slaughtering of cattle, was suffused by youthful longing and languor. It was hardly surprising that heretical books began to appear beneath the heavy folios of the Talmud. Chance helped Simon to penetrate the mysteries of modern Hebrew literature: a friend from the yeshiva introduced him to a local freethinker who secretly kept a collection of *Haskalah* books and journals in his house. The periodicals coming from Vilna and Odessa were a genuine revelation: the superstition of the Hasidim and the charlatanism of the *tsadikim* were often described in their columns, and sometimes even rabbinicism was subjected to cautious criticism.

Henceforth, the young yeshiva student began to devote the Sabbath, a day free of study, to reading forbidden books, avidly devouring political articles, novels, and poetry. The lyric poet Micah Joseph Lebensohn[3] became his favorite. Simon found echoes of his own religious crisis in the poetry of the dreamer who had gone to an early grave. His passion for books finally drove him to a deed he was to regret long afterward. There had been a heated polemic in the letters published in recent issues of the journal *Ha-Karmel*,[4] a battle between the obscurantists and the progressive young generation. Simon read this correspondence over several times, but when he had to return the book to its owner he could not withstand the temptation to tear out the pages which excited him. He later confessed his sin and returned the stolen pages, but his conscience long tormented him and forced him to beg forgiveness in fervent prayers.

Simon's family did not immediately notice the change that had come over the young yeshiva student. His grandfather was absorbed in his own studies, and his mother could not distinguish secular from religious books. But the congregation of the synagogue sometimes noticed the suspiciously thin books peeping out from beneath the heavy folios and heard rabbi Bentsion's grandson enthusiastically reciting lyric verses in the synagogue. Rumors crept through the town and eventually reached his grandfather's ears: a freethinker fascinated by forbidden books had appeared in the Dubnov family. The rebel took up the challenge and began to answer the reports with diatribes directed at "men of darkness who fear the light of knowledge." Such missives were copied out by admirers of florid language; the yeshiva student gained a reputation as a talented but dangerous pamphleteer in his hometown.

Bentsion Dubnov's informers, who predicted that the young heretic would progress from the literature of the *Haskalah* to even more dangerous books, proved right. Simon felt that Jewish literature alone was insufficient to satisfy his appetite for knowledge. The son of the local synagogue *shamash*, who had graduated from the town school, undertook to teach the Dubnov brothers arithmetic and Russian. In the spring of 1874 Simon passed the entrance examination of the state Jewish school. With difficulty his mother resigned herself to her boy's decision to attend the "half-gentile" school; his aggrieved grandfather demanded that he at least not interrupt his talmudic studies. Simon tried in good faith to combine his school studies with the yeshiva classes, but those around him sensed with pain in their hearts that he was moving farther and farther from the traditions forged by generations of God-fearing men.

Work went quickly and well in the new school. Within three months Simon had completed the three-year curriculum and entered the last class, but he did not receive a diploma because the Jewish elementary schools were suddenly closed by government decree. This was a heavy blow for

Simon. His short autobiography, written in the winter of 1875, and solemnly entitled "The Deeds of My Youth," was full of gloom. The young
author contemplates life and death and complains of being persecuted for
aspiring to unite learning and faith: "They call me a heretic. . . . O God,
You try the hearts of men and You know that I am faithful to Your religion,
that fanatics, enraged because I walk in the ways of the *Haskalah* and not
in the ways of ignorance, have slandered me." He describes the closing
of the school in tragic terms, but in conclusion expresses certainty that
"the foolish will be ashamed and the false prophets will be cast down,
for knowledge will prevail in our town."

Simon had obtained only a limited education at the elementary school
but it helped him to master the Russian language and gave him the key
to Russian literature. Chance revealed a supply of Russian books as it
had earlier revealed a store of Jewish books. He gained access to a little
library organized by a small circle of radical young people and pounced
eagerly on the classics, articles in the major progressive journals, and
translations of Börne[5] and Heine. He had barely mastered Russian but
he diligently applied himself to the study of French. The day was too
short for all these studies, so he had to work at night. Finally, prolonged
lack of sleep and intense, chaotic mental exertion undermined his weakened body, and acute anemia caused headaches and frequent spells of dizziness. The old doctor who came to see Sheyne Dubnov when she was
taken ill shook his head reproachfully at the sight of the pale, sickly adolescent and muttered, "He'd be healthy if he read a little less."

Rabbi Bentsion anxiously watched his grandson's behavior, feeling that
a wall had risen between them. Simon gave up his talmudic studies and
came to the synagogue less and less. Those around him looked askance
at his cropped earlocks and short jacket, and whispered disapprovingly
when they saw him standing motionless as he prayed, eschewing the customary movements of the body. His grandfather constantly had to listen
to the complaints of his God-fearing neighbors; even Simon's mother went
to him in tears, fearing that her son would have to pay dearly for his
freethinking in the next world. Rabbi Bentsion summoned his grandson
and paced about the room, delivering an impassioned tirade against
"empty learning," which led one away from the true path mapped out
by the Torah and the Talmud. Simon's retorts further exasperated the old
man, and he threatened to take away and destroy the "harmful" books.

The attempt to return the sinner to the paths of truth failed. Soon a
new blow fell on his parents: Simon and Volf announced their intention
to enter the local school, which was attended mainly by the children of
Russian and Polish landowners. In the seventies Jewish boys from well-to-
do families were also beginning to appear within the walls of the school,
for graduation from the school meant a shortened military service.

Meyer-Yakov Dubnov reluctantly decided not to hinder his sons; at least
the school was better than the barracks. The two brothers passed the exam-

inations brilliantly and soon rose to the top of the class. Simon was particularly distinguished in Russian language and history, Volf in mathematics. Success was easy; the level of intelligence among the students, as well as among the teachers, was low. School homework left plenty of time for reading the classics. Simon recited Lermontov's poetry with particular enthusiasm; the poet "who seeks the storm" was closer to his restless soul than harmonious Pushkin, the favorite poet of his maturity. Turgenev's novels awakened a strange sensation in the heart of the young yeshiva student. The lonely youth was infatuated with each of the author's enchanting heroines inhabiting the "nests of the gentry." But above all he searched in literature for truth, for the meaning of life, for an answer to the question How to live? Particularly dear to him were the tendentious, didactic tales of the progressive Russian and European writers attacking conservatism and hypocrisy and depicting the spiritual quests of rebellious natures. Börne became the sixteen-year old youth's idol. "I heard the voice of protest against despotism for the first time," he recalled many years later. "For the first time I felt the fascination of the spirit of revolution; I . . . was especially enraptured by Börne's struggle for freedom of thought, so similar to my personal experience at that time." The youth could not withstand the temptation to quote from the radical German journalist in the final school essay; this led to his receiving a lower grade and a reprimand from the headmaster for reading unsuitable books.

While he was attending the school, Simon made his first attempt to break into print. He sent the editors of the Warsaw Hebrew weekly paper *Ha-Zefirah* an unsigned open letter in which he campaigned for the reform of the *khadorim* and for compulsory general education for the *melamdim*. He waited excitedly for the editor's reply but it never came. By the will of fate Simon Dubnov's literary debut did not take place until several years later, in the Russian-Jewish press.

On graduating from the school in June 1877, Simon was faced with the question What next? There was no possibility of continuing his education in the provinces. "I must go away, go away," he repeated feverishly as he strode along the wooden sidewalks, turning different plans over in his mind. After wavering a long time he decided to enter the Jewish Teachers' Institute in Vilna. His father had long ago given up hope that his son would become a talmudist and made no objection. The Institute guaranteed its students a stipend during their years of study and their crust of bread on graduation. The youth's heart beat faster at the thought of moving to the "Jerusalem of Lithuania," the center of the Enlightenment movement.

On a sunny summer day, a Jewish coachman driving a crude, clumsy wagon with a canvas roof stopped at the gates of the house where the Dubnovs lived. Simon's mother silently wiped her eyes with the hem of her apron as she waited at the wicket gate. His older brother, who had given up the role of pioneer to his younger brother, stood with bowed head. As the wagon clattered away over the potholes of the dusty street, the young traveler looked back sadly at the squat little houses and the humble green vegetable plots he was leaving behind. His years of wandering had begun.

4

Wandering

A small skinny youth in a crumpled worn jacket, cut from his father's frock coat, wandered aimlessly through the dusty, badly paved streets of the "Jerusalem of Lithuania." He looked sadly at the ragged children playing in the puddles, at the ancient houses with their dilapidated balconies. The temporary lodgings where the newcomer ended up on the recommendation of one of his countrymen were equally unprepossessing. A low window gave onto a smelly courtyard piled with refuse and dilapidated sheds swarming with poor people. But the youth did not lose heart. He felt he was on the threshold of a new life devoted to learning.

However, Simon was not allowed to cross that threshold. He was denied admittance to the Institute. He wrote rhetorically to his father, "I put out to sea, the sea of life. The inscription HOPE shone from the tall mast of my ship; I have lost my last hope and see in horror my ship going to the bottom." When his father received this dramatic epistle he forwarded money for the return journey.

Once again the gray days in his parents' house dragged by. The sole fruit of his journey to Vilna was the purchase of a small book by Lilienblum, *Hatte'ot Ne'urim* (The Sins of Youth),[6] which Simon read with inner trembling. It was the autobiography of a freethinker who had struggled with the fanatics of his native backwater, then fled from them to the city, aspiring to join the Enlightenment movement. But the young men whom he met had already moved on from the vague ideals of *Haskalah* to a Russian education and the realism and positivism propounded by Pisarev[7] and other progressive thinkers. Simon found echoes of his own experiences in the pages of this book.

His grandfather and relatives were inclined to see the hand of God in the failure which had befallen the young pioneer. But Simon was not one to give up easily. He had a new plan: to enter the modern school (a gymnasium without classical languages) and then to try to enter the university. There was such a school in Dvinsk, the district town, and the Dubnov brothers decided to make their way there. They were inspired by the example of Moses Mendelssohn, who had walked all the way to Berlin, spurred on by his thirst for knowledge.

Life in Dvinsk was even harsher than in Vilna: a small, pokey, unheated room and the relentless pangs of hunger; zealous cramming of textbooks; sleepless nights spent avidly reading books by the dim light of a small oil lamp. Money came from their father at irregular intervals. "It is more than a month and a half," writes Simon in his diary on 9 January 1878, "since I stopped eating meat, and I am sustained only by bread, herring, and tea." The youths bought a week's supply of bread and divided it into seven equal parts lest they exceed the daily ration. Simon eventually became so weak that more than once he was forced to abandon his textbooks and lie for long hours on the sofa in utter exhaustion. As always, books played the dominant role in his life. Depping's *History of the Jews in the Middle Ages* made a strong impression on him. While reading this book he wrote in his diary, "Despite the fact that I . . . can find no sympathy for my attachment to the Jewish nation . . . still, the love for our nationality, tossed aside as a paltry thing by our young generation, grows stronger in me." But this was only a temporary mood, induced by reading; his thinking unswervingly followed the path of cosmopolitanism. This tendency was especially strengthened by Buckle's *History of Civilization*, which seemed a genuine revelation to Simon. For the first time a rigorous ordering of historical phenomena, the interaction of the laws of nature and spirit in the process of the development of civilization, was laid out before him. He was struck by Buckle's notion of the predominance of intellectual over moral factors in the dynamics of history. The cosmopolitan tendency at once frightened and fascinated the former yeshiva student. "This great freethinker has undermined my feeling of love for nationalism," he acknowledges in some confusion in his diary.

Preparations for the examinations went badly in conditions of hunger, cold, and loneliness. Simon lay on the hard sofa and recited sad verses about premature death; Buckle's rationalism had not killed his enthusiasm for poetry. But the Dvinsk period soon ended as abruptly as had the Vilna period: the stalwart pioneers were obliged to surrender in the face of physical weakness. Reduced to total exhaustion by hunger, they decided to return to their native hearth for a while and then continue preparing for the examinations in Mogilev, a town in the neighboring province, where they could count on the help of relatives and friends.

The young people of Mstislavl looked at the voluntary "martyrs of learning" with respect. The new currents were reaching the most remote corners by that time. A small circle for self-education was organized in Mstislavl by the young people of prosperous families. The same small library which had once supplied Simon with his first Russian books was the center of the circle's activities. It was now housed at the home of the merchant Chaim Freidlin and run by his daughters, Ida and Fanny, who had recently graduated from a local private school.

Ida Freidlin's gentle, dark brown eyes gaze thoughtfully and a little shyly from the only surviving photograph of her as a girl. Her fair hair is smoothly brushed, her delicate oval face is tender and stern, her lips curve chastely. A calm, unself-conscious, modest beauty.

The girl who, several years later, was to join her life with the hard lot of a dreamer and a wanderer grew up in a comfortable, prosperous home. Her mother, Mera (Miriam) Freidlin, retained the features of a rare beauty until old age. It was said that when she was a shapely sixteen-year-old girl, with golden braids down to her knees, a Polish landowner from the Mstislavl district fell madly in love with her. The young couple met and corresponded in secret, hiding letters in the hollow of an old oak tree, but they were found out. The anxious parents hurriedly gave their romantic young daughter in marriage to a middle-aged Hasid recommended by a matchmaker. When Mera became a widow, she married a solid merchant of her own choosing; the daughters from her second marriage were her favorites. In her prime she was a powerful, magnificent woman who ruled her household with a firm hand and skillfully helped her husband in his business affairs. Her daughters, round-faced and brown-eyed, with their mother's regular features, resembled one another only in appearance: the younger sister, Fanny, was a gay, flirtatious girl, while Ida was thoughtful, stern, and reticent.

When the Dubnov brothers returned from Dvinsk they expressed a wish to join the library circle. The new fraternity's first meeting took place in the main square on a moonlit winter evening. The voices of the young people rang out in the silence of the sleepy streets, as they talked of books and their plans for the future. It was long after midnight when Simon escorted the Freidlin sisters home; gentle brown eyes looked at him shyly from the steps of the snow-covered porch, and a soft voice murmured, "Let's be friends; come and see us." The heavy door thudded shut. As he walked home through the snowdrifts, Simon felt an unexpected burst of zest: something new and bright had entered his hermit's life.

The enforced vacation in his native town was, as always, filled with reading. Buckle had prepared Simon for grasping the rationalist ideas of the eighteenth century. The assertion that an "Age of Reason" inevitably follows an "Age of Faith" in the life of all peoples became the basis of the world view of this young seeker after truth, who had himself undergone the movement from a child's religiosity to faith in the absolutism of reason. The radical literary criticism linking philosophical and social problems also played a role in the formation of Simon's world view.

In the seventies these questions became increasingly urgent against a background of growing social ferment. The idea of young men and women from the gentry and the intelligentsia "going to the people" had led to a mass movement. In 1876 the revolutionary-populist organization Land and Freedom was founded. The trial of Vera Zasulich, who had shot Trepov, the governor of St. Petersburg, created a stir. Simon devoured the newspapers and the opposition journals but he was not drawn to political involvement. Another "burning passion" possessed him. Whereas for the Russian youth, particularly for the young people of the gentry who had access to all the blessings of culture, breaking with the customary forms of life was a protest against social injustice, the Jewish rebels, who were emerging from the lower classes, rebelled against their surroundings in the name of individual freedom. Their rebellion bore a sharply individualistic stamp. The young Jewish freethinkers, drawn to radical Russian social and political journalism, took from it what was particularly relevant to them: the cult of the "critically thinking" individual proclaimed by Pisarev had a greater influence on the formation of their world view than did the altruism of the *narodniki*, burning with the desire to help the "uneducated peasant." Few active revolutionaries came from the Jewish *maskilim*, the men of the seventies; mass involvement in the revolutionary movement, both Russian and Jewish, was the destiny of the next generation. Simon Dubnov was a typical child of his time—an individualist with a rationalist bent.

Lengthy letters from Mogilev, where Simon had gone to prepare to take the examination, began arriving at the address of his new friends, the Freidlin sisters. The eighteen-year-old youth's epistles to the attractive, lively young girls contained virtually nothing intimate; they contained earnest analysis of books Simon had read and attempts at intellectual self-analysis. He referred patronizingly to his recent ideals and the "blind patriotism" of the days in the "Jerusalem of Lithuania" as manifestations of intellectual immaturity. Now he was diligently studying the natural sciences. In a short tract bearing the imposing title "My Philosophy" he set out the idea that, in order to evolve a complete world view, the "critically thinking" man must pass through three cycles of study: of the world, of the earth, and of man; that is, he must become an encyclopedist. These ideas seemed a true revelation to the provincial girls brought up in the merchant class, and the missionary of encyclopedism appeared to be little short of a prophet. Pensive Ida was particularly attracted by the new ideas; a plan to leave her parent's house and enter the university gradually possessed all her thoughts. The Dubnov brothers were fervently sympathetic to her plan and promised every assistance.

Simon immersed himself in work. After hours of cramming dull school books (the course in mathematics gave him particular trouble), he plunged, as though into an invigorating spring, into reading Schiller's dramas and Turgenev's *Nov'* (Virgin Soil), with its exciting depiction of revolutionary young men and women "going to the people." Life knocked urgently for admittance to Simon's book-strewn cell. It spoke from the broadsheets of the underground press, brought by an occasional student visitor, in the news of bold acts of terrorism. Now and then, the youth attended student gatherings where forbidden songs were sung around the samovar, but this did not undermine his reclusive way of life. He was firm in his resolve to overcome all obstacles to reach the fountainhead of learning—the university.

In May 1879 Simon went to the director of the Mogilev gymnasium for information about the examination requirements. The director, a typical provincial bureaucrat, was perturbed by this autodidact's intention to take the examination without knowing classical languages. A reference to the fact that classical languages were not a prerequisite for admission to the Natural Science Faculty ultimately enraged the director. Squinting maliciously, he scrutinized the pale youth with the stubborn mouth. Before him stood a freethinking Jew boy, his head obviously stuffed with Pisarev's nonsense and other dangerous ideas. His duty as a patriot and a servant of the tsar lay in barring this rebel from the path to learning. Simon realized that he could not count on getting the gymnasium certificate in Mogilev. He decided to begin studying classical languages and to make his way to the nearby town of Smolensk, where he had heard he would be likely to find a temporary job.

Once again the coachman in his dusty, shapeless smock drove the taciturn passenger with a heavy basket packed with books over the bumpy road leading to the railroad station. Once again Simon led the solitary life of a hermit in a strange town, in a pokey little room looking onto an overgrown wasteland. The room cost four rubles a month; its inhabitant earned eight rubles teaching Latin and Russian. From time to time, his father, distressed by his son's breach with his home and family, sent him small sums of money.

In the quiet evenings, Simon, fortified by a wretched supper, enthusiastically scanned the hexameters of the classics. A small oil lamp hanging over the rickety table burned until late at night, shining on his bent head. When his young body rebelled against the crippling strain, his mood swung between ecstasy and depression. *The Book of My Life* describes these moments:

At times, attacks of melancholia made it impossible for me to work. I would walk about the room and think of how I was sacrificing my life for the sake of my life's goal; I read especially deep meaning into a verse by Lermontov, which I often repeated:

I was in the thrall of but one thought alone,
The only, but a consuming, passion,
It lived in me like a worm,
It gnawed at me and burned my soul.[8]

When Simon had been depressed by loneliness in the past, he had prayed with the words of the Psalms. Having lost his childhood faith, he turned in bleak moments to the language of poetry. And he felt that he too could write lines like those in which Koltsov[9] laments his joyless youth and the exhausting battle with "the evil witch of fate."

Preparing for the examination became more difficult each year, as the discrepancy between Simon's wide literary and philosophical interests and the dull school requirements became ever clearer. Two books immediately became the base of his world view and occupied an honored place on his desk: an exposition of the philosophy of positivism associated with Auguste Comte, and John Stuart Mill's treatise *On Liberty*. The first of these books was valued because it set out a complete system of thought intended to take the place of religion and metaphysics. Mill's treatise expounded the principles of rational individualism, which the youth thought were proved by his personal experiences, in succinct, brilliant, and precise formulations. The protest against the tyranny of the milieu, the spirit's highest aspiration according to the English apostle of liberalism, was the basic fabric of the young freethinker's life.

In his letters to the Freidlin sisters, Simon outlined the contents of his favorite books in detail, adding his own commentaries. But sad news came in reply: their parents declared that the girls were not to think of higher education. Matchmakers were already coming to see Chaim Freidlin, vying with one another to present bridegrooms possessing every conceivable virtue: a knowledge of the Torah and some capital. The girls' mother had long ago forgotten the romantic episode of her youth and refused to countenance their dreams. Now only flight from their parents' home could save the sisters from a traditional marriage to a man of their parents' choice and from being swamped by a petty, bourgeois life.

One rainy autumn evening a cautious knock at the wicket gate dragged Simon away from his studies. To his astonishment, before him stood two female figures bundled up almost to the eyebrows. Flushed with excitement the travelers began to tell the story of their flight, both talking at once. It seemed that a gymnasium student, who had been exiled to their provincial town under police supervision for "political unreliability," had undertaken to organize everything; he had made arrangements with a peasant who agreed to take the girls to Smolensk. The runaways had slipped out of the house and ridden to Smolensk in a peasant cart.

In a bleak hotel room the three young people excitedly discussed what to do next. The girls decided to go on to Kiev and prepare for the university there. They had little money and they had been able to take only a few things from home, but they were intoxicated with youth, rainbow hopes, and a sense of freedom. Fearing pursuit, the Freidlin sisters left the next day. Long letters from Kiev began to arrive at Simon's hermit's cell: the girls were working hard but their supply of money was exhausted. Simon sent them a month's wages; then help came from their mother, acting unbeknownst to their stern father. Two months later came the news that their father was gravely ill. Ida and Fanny returned home to find him already dead.

Soon the Smolensk hermit had to return to Mstislavl as well. When the lodgings of the seditious gymnasium student who had organized the Freid-lin sisters' flight were searched, Simon's letters were found. It was an anx-ious time. Simon's parents were afraid he would be jailed in a strange town. On his return to Mstislavl he was immediately summoned for ques-tioning. When the police discovered the purpose of his presence in Smo-lensk they left him in peace, but his study plan had already been disrupted. Simon stayed in Mstislavl for several months, and he was not sorry that he did so.

He moved into an isolated house on the edge of town, surrounded him-self with books, and became immersed in further study of the philosophy of positivism and of Mill's works, writing summaries and commentaries. As before, he shared his thoughts on what he read with the Freidlin sisters, whom he visited every day. In 1880 he writes in his diary,

> March, April, May in my home town. Quiet working days at S———'s lodg-ings: radiant, smiling nature, green and trees all around—all this heals my troubled spirit. Yes, there is a *vis mediatrix* [a healing power] in nature. Bright, sunny, fresh mornings; days of uninterrupted work, marvelously quiet eve-nings . . . calm and undisturbed sleep—this is the picture of my present life. But always close by are those whose heavy cross has brought forth so many sighs. . . . We worked together soberly. But the drowsiness and the lethargy of the environment make themselves felt. I long to be on the banks of the Neva in the center of intellectual development.

At this time Simon was equally friendly with both sisters. They shared the same intellectual interests, the same aspirations to education, and the same dissatisfaction with their surroundings. The phrase "We worked to-gether soberly" emphasizes, perhaps deliberately, the purely comradely na-ture of their relationship. His youthful longing, nourished by reading lyri-cal poetry and by his secret dreams of Turgenev's women, withdrew, for a time, into the shadows. The young positivist put his heart and soul into science; he was a "critically thinking individual," and above all he had to "work soberly." It did not occur to this disciple of Comte and Mill that he was walking, under different circumstances, down the path taken by his forebears, the ascetics who had subordinated all their human needs to the study of the Torah.

5

In the Northern Capital

Simon Dubnov was about twenty years old. He had won complete independence for himself. His elders had finally ceased to interfere in his life. He returned from Smolensk firmly resolved to put an end to the pointless and irksome wanderings from town to town in the Pale. Both Smolensk and Mogilev were provincial centers, but one could find there only faint, belated echoes of the cultural life in the capital. Loneliness weighed heavily on the young autodidact. He was beginning to understand that the company of thoughtful people had as much to offer as reading books. Besides, his brother Vladimir (Volf) had moved to St. Petersburg and invited him to come to that city of writers and scholars, schools of higher education, and rich libraries.

One clear summer day the train from the West rumbled in under the arches of the St. Petersburg station. A shabbily dressed passenger with a wicker basket tightly tied with rope got out of a third-class carriage and looked around in a daze. His older brother was waiting for him on the platform. A ramshackle coach rattling over the cobblestones took the young men along the murky canal and through the outlying working-class district. The brothers settled on the edge of the city, where the police were more lenient toward Jews without the right of residence in the capital (a right granted only to privileged categories). Every day they went to the Public Library in the center of the city in a *konka*, an old-fashioned, two-shafted vehicle pulled by a team of horses. The young men usually climbed up to the upper deck, where the tickets were cheaper. From the top they had a splendid view of the city, with its broad avenues teeming with people and the wide steel ribbon of the river set in granite. The huge city overwhelmed the young provincial: he wandered for hours past palaces holding dark secrets and narrow canals beneath hump-backed bridges; he lingered before the statue of Peter and the bronze horse rearing up, ready to gallop away into space, Russia, the world. He stared intently at the faces of the passersby in the Haymarket, which was jammed with carts, and on the gray Voznesenskii Prospekt, as though he expected to glimpse the figure of Raskolnikov in a shabby coat at the crossroads, or thought that a Gogolian clerk hunched over in an old-fashioned overcoat would surface in the crowd. This fantastic city, erected in the middle of wastes and swamps by stubborn, human will, was saturated with history and literature. It aroused restlessness, summoned one to intense work, stirred up vague hopes. Simon was inspired by the vigor of the thousands of autodidacts who had come here from all corners of the vast country and who were walking along the muddy, slippery pavements with the collars of their shabby jackets turned up against the wind. They were all hurrying to dinner in cheap cafeterias like the one where every day the Dubnov brothers stood in a long line for a bowl of hot soup. And they, too, clumped reverentially in their clumsy, battered boots over the carpet of the wide staircase leading to the main reading room of the Public Library. This library, with its endless bookshelves along the walls, its cozy green lamps above the wide tables, and its atmosphere of intense studiousness, became Simon's precious haven of intellectual work.

Soon after his arrival Dubnov came to realize that in the capital it was easier to satisfy one's spiritual hunger than one's physical hunger. He had not been able to arrange any lessons, and he was not fit for manual labor. Marcus Kagan, an energetic journalist and a fellow countryman from the Mogilev province, repeatedly advised him to look for work on the Russian-Jewish weeklies, but the thought of making the noble study of literature a source of wages seemed little short of sacrilege to the young enthusiast. However, he gradually became accustomed to the idea. In July 1880 he wrote to friends: "He [Kagan] advises me to join the fraternity of scribblers and be paid a fee in the event that I don't set up any private lessons. Although such an attitude shocks my esteem for literature, if the march of events forces me to it, I will not accuse myself of desecration through evil intent. For man there is something more holy: freedom and independence."

Several weeks later he finally despaired of finding any pupils and went to the editorial office of *Russkii Evrei*. The editor wanted to test the novice's literary abililties and proposed that he write a "Letter from Mstislavl." The "Letter," signed with the initials S.D., was soon published. It spoke of the wretchedness of social life in the province, of the abomination of a *kheyder* education and the necessity for Jewish schools offering a general education and practical courses.

Success encouraged the young author, and at the end of August he writes: "Since I love history passionately I have decided to write a whole series of studies on the medieval history of the Jews for *Russkii Evrei*. My knowledge of Hebrew will help me here. . . . I am now reading the sources on which I will base my article." Several volumes of Graetz's *History of the Jews*, which had only just appeared in Russian translation, came into the young man's hands, and he felt a burst of literary zeal. But while the editors were expecting the promised article on a historical subject, Dubnov unexpectedly plunged into writing an autobiographical novel. It bore the title "The Path of Thorns" and the subtitle "From the Diary of a Student Friend." The novel was a hodgepodge of lyrical verse and dialogues on philosophical and social subjects. It was not difficult to recognize Ida

Freidlin in the heroine of the novel, an emancipated Jewish girl who had broken with her family and milieu. In the dialogues the author developed his cherished ideas, which had been clamoring to be set down on paper. In the voice of one of the interlocutors he says:

> Judaism in all its . . . manifestations is a sense of strict religious duty developed . . . into the systematic crushing of individual freedom. This spirit of legalism in the Jewish religious system . . . and the imposition of legal terms of reference on each and every individual action, however trivial, is bound to strike the impartial observer. . . . A Jew who thinks, who dares to have his own opinion, feels the intrusion of religion into his most mundane affairs at every step. . . . That is the underside of Judaism. But its surface is beautiful. I love, I ardently love this gifted people who have survived every kind of persecution and misfortune solely by virtue of their intellectual strength—a rare, if not unique phenomenon in history.

He carefully copied his article and sent it to the editors of *Russkii Evrei*. He was extremely disillusioned when the editor returned the manuscript several days later, explaining that the novel was unsuitable for publication: there were interesting ideas in it, but it lacked a plot.

In addition to being hard up the Dubnov brothers also had to contend with the complications caused by their illegal status. An attempt to move to lodgings in the center of the city belonging to a fellow countryman, a minor speculator who had contacts in the police, led to the arrest of both brothers on suspicion of murder. During the interrogation it came out that the young men were living in the capital without a permit, and they were ordered to return to their own province on pain of deportation. Vladimir quickly left for their hometown, where he would be called up for compulsory military service, but his younger brother reentered the usual realm of hardships for a Jew without rights. These hardships did not destroy his energy, however. "I am as cheerful and as enthusiastic as before," he writes to the Freidlin sisters. "I still despise faintheartedness and despair and I am ready to struggle against anyone or anything whatever. I have been mulling things over a good deal recently. All these sorry events have given my world view a more vivid coloring. My heart still seethes with indignation but I am afraid of no one."

Dubnov obtained forged permit papers and immersed himself in reading materials for the cycle of historical articles he had conceived. He was working at fever pitch; he wanted to express everything that had accumulated in his soul from the day that the *kheyder* boy had rebelled against the dispute about the the egg laid by a hen on the Sabbath. In the winter of 1880 he writes:

> I rush about my room, and I think with such fervor that I have decidedly forgotten the whole world. These are serious, impassioned thoughts, which are, perhaps, fated to appear in print on the pages of one journal or another.

Now I am in a very whirlpool of ideas which give me no peace. I must speak out. Otherwise I would not have undertaken this work.

It was a blizzard-swept winter evening when the author of the dire tirades against rabbinicism set off, shivering from cold in his summer coat, for the editorial office of the weekly journal *Razsvet* for a meeting about the article. Yakov Rosenfeld, the editor of the journal, was troubled by the aspiring author's radicalism and tried to convince him that the article was anti-national in tendency and therefore unacceptable to a journal struggling against the national indifferentism of the Jewish intelligentsia. The other Jewish periodical proved more accommodating: the manuscript was accepted for publication with cuts.

Exciting plans for future work crowded into the young journalist's brain. And suddenly he realized that he had completely forgotten one of his main purposes in coming to the city: to obtain the high school graduation certificate necessary for admittance to the university. The school books appeared on the table again. "Oh, how tired I am of these interminable preparations for examinations," he writes to his friends. "Four years of perpetual wandering and an anxious life, four years of failures, disappointments and setbacks are making themselves felt now. I have already had it up to here, but I have to keep my patience until May. . . ."

Circumstances were hardly conducive to poring over textbooks. At twilight one gray evening in March the landlady knocked on the door of Dubnov's wretched room: the tsar had been killed in a street near Nevskii Prospekt, and the tradesmen in the Haymarket were threatening to get even with the students. The good-natured woman advised her lodger not to leave the house: he looked too much like a "nihilist." The young man was shaken; the next morning he dashed over to a fellow Jewish student's lodgings, where a group of young men had gathered and were excitedly discussing the latest events. Rumors of mass arrests filtered through the city; the faces of the passersby reading the official bulletins were blank and apprehensive. Dubnov was in no mood for the "wisdom" of textbook fare in those alarming days. He forced himself to go through the lessons again, but his thoughts were far away. April brought news of pogroms against the Jews in the South and of the new tsar's manifesto, announcing an era of reaction. The atmosphere in the country became more oppressive, and it occurred to Dubnov more and more frequently that only abroad would he be able to concentrate on studying in peace. The news that *Russkii Evrei* had finally published his article wrenched Simon from these gloomy reflections. *The Book of My Life* describes the event thus:

In the middle of April 1881, a young man with a newly printed copy of the weekly journal in his hands came out of the house . . . where the editorial office of *Russkii Evrei* was housed. The first installment of his first long article, "Some Moments in the History of the Evolution of Jewish Thought," was printed there. The young writer turned onto the Fontanka embankment and, as he walked, kept looking at the precious lines of his literary first-born with the same joyful emotion with which a young mother examines the features of her newborn infant. It seemed to the budding writer that he was called upon to bring Russian Jewry a new word, the gospel of free thought.

The festive feeling which had seized the aspiring man of letters did not last long: notification of the coming examinations brought him back to the tedium of the everyday. On the day of the examination the adult "extern," with heavy heart and dull head, took his place on the school bench beside the young gymnasium boys. The mathematics teacher dictated several problems. Incomprehensible numbers swam before his eyes on the white page; there was not one idea in his brain. Dubnov got up, handed the examiner the sheet of paper covered with crossings-out, and said that he was in no state to solve the problem. The teacher reminded him that the oral examination could mend matters, but young Dubnov decided not to go back to the gymnasium again.

He writes in his memoirs:

> I returned to my small room on the fifth floor of the big, dark house . . . and began to think. Poverty, worries, the alarming political situation, cramming and premature literary work—all this had prevented me from taking an elementary examination. What now? Put off the examinations for another year? But immediately an inner protest swelled within me. It was time to put an end to the hardships of an "extern" chasing after a graduation certificate. True, without that slip of paper it was impossible to get near the university, but surely it was not impossible to obtain a university education at home, an even broader education, in line with Comte's and Spencer's classification of the sciences? . . . After all, my idols Mill and Spencer never completed their higher education. . . . And so there grew in me a decision which scarcely impeded my intellectual development . . . yet which condemned me to all the miseries of a Jew without rights and without the status of an accredited member of the intelligentsia. Perhaps that too was necessary: that the Jewish writer should not enjoy the privileges of a diploma but should suffer on an equal footing with the Jewish masses.

All photographs courtesy Archives of the YIVO Institute for Jewish Research.

Simon Dubnov and Ida Freidlin, St. Petersburg, 1883.

Odessa, 1913.

Left to right: Alter Druyanow, Hayyim Nahman Bialik, Dubnov, Sh. Y. Abramovich, and Yehoshua Hana Rawnitzki, Odessa, 1913.

Dubnov packing his library in preparation for moving from St. Petersburg to Berlin, 1922.

Ida and Simon Dubnov, Reinerz, 1930.

Berlin [Reinerz?], 1930.

Dubnov (first row, center) with members of YIVO's Historians' Circle at the Institute's Tenth Anniversary Conference, Vilna, 1935.

Riga, 1937.

6

The Preacher of Free Thought

The intellectual labors filling Simon's life took two directions—self-education and literary work. Every day on a table in the Public Library, next to a lamp with a green shade, a stack of books would pile up—the writings of French and English philosophers and materials from the Judaica section. The young journalist was reading a great deal of history; but at that time he was ruled not so much by the instinct of a historian as by the temperament of a political writer: in the facts of the past he sought above all for analogies to the present and confirmation of his own ideas and interests. Two paths lay before him in the history of the Jewish people, which he originally identified with the history of Judaism: the path taken by Rabbi Akiba, one of the founders of the rabbinate, and the path taken by the heretic Elisha Akher, a preacher of free thought. And inexorably the idea arose: if such men as Elisha, Uriel Da Costa, and Spinoza had been the predominant element in Jewry, they would, perhaps, have been burned during the Age of the Inquisition, not as Jews but as thinkers like Giordano Bruno and Galileo, heralds of ideas which had advanced mankind.

Dubnov tried to develop these ideas in the existing Russian-Jewish press intended for the small circle of readers whose association with Russian culture had not led them into the camp of assimilation. It was a singular milieu: at the end of the last century a type of man of two cultures, a type unknown in Western Europe, surfaced among the Jewish intelligentsia in the Russian Empire, the nation with the greatest concentration of Jews. The relative weights of the two cultural influences did not always balance, but instances of harmonious coexistence were not uncommon. The radically inclined Jewish intelligentsia declaimed the poetry of Nekrasov[10] and Frug,[11] the bards of Russian and Jewish populism, with equally intense feeling. The pogroms at the beginning of 1881 forced many of those who had recently assimilated to turn back to Jewry; thus new audiences for the Russian-Jewish journals came into being. The overall stance of these journals—the weeklies *Razsvet* and *Russkii Evrei* and the monthly *Voskhod*—was a vague, purely empirical nationalism of the early *Haskalah* variety, often with a touch of Palestinophilia. The majority of the contributors treated the burning issues of the day with extreme caution, not wishing to antagonize either the captious official censorship or conservative Jewish circles.

More than once, Dubnov, who considered himself a direct heir of Elisha Akher and Da Costa, had to fight for what seemed to him the most essential passages of his articles. Avoiding general issues, the editors of the journals vied with one another in suggesting to their refractory contributor "innocent" topics from the realm of literature or foreign news. But he preferred to choose his own topics. When the wave of Jewish emigration from Russia swelled under the influence of the pogroms, and the direction of the emigration became an issue, the young journalist hotly defended in the pages of *Razsvet* a project to establish Jewish agricultural colonies in the United States. To his great dismay Lilienblum, the writer whose autobiography had once seemed a virtual credo of Enlightenment to the young *maskil*, came out emphatically in favor of Palestinophilia in the same journal shortly thereafter.

The era when Simon Dubnov began his literary career was a time of crisis for Jewish culture. Hebrew literature, which had played such a large role in the *Haskalah* period, was losing readers; the well-known Hebrew poet Judah Leib Gordon asked sadly in his verses, "For whom do I labor?" and finally crossed over to the ranks of the contributors to *Voskhod*. Russian-Jewish literature had its own circle of readers but was inaccessible to the broad masses. Yiddish, then called *zhargon*, was still in the process of formation. Only the entrance of the Jewish masses into the arena of history made it an instrument of a developing national culture. But the first signs of the future renaissance were already beginning to emerge in the eighties. Young Dubnov, whole-heartedly committed to Russian-Jewish journalism, was sympathetic to a plan for publishing a weekly journal in Yiddish. In an unsigned article entitled "The People's Yiddish Newspaper" (*Razsvet*, 1881, No. 35) he campaigned fiercely for creating serious journalism in the *zhargon* for which nationalists and cosmopolitans alike had such disdain. "The main task," he writes in the article, "of a Jewish people's paper must be to conduct a serious, not flippant—as it has been hitherto—discussion . . . of social issues." And the new organ, *Di yidishe folksblat*, did attract fresh, young, literary talents: among its contributors were Sholem Aleichem,[12] Frug, and Spector.[13]

Dubnov still felt isolated among the Russian-Jewish intelligentsia. The men with whom he worked possessed neither broad vision nor genuine élan in thought or deed. He recalls this in *The Book of My Life*:

> In my letters I complained of moral and intellectual isolation. This was explained by the fact that I had been drawn into the circle of specifically Jewish problems while I was increasingly gripped by more general, "eternal" questions. . . . I was the youngest in my circle; Frug was my only peer, and world problems interested him very little. . . . I was in a phase . . . of sharply rejecting

received dogma, but I was constantly searching for new "scientific dogmas".
. . . I considered myself only a temporary contributor to Jewish literature
and was obsessed with great plans in the realm of general historico-philosoph-
ical literature. I spent long hours in the Public Library, reading the complete
works of Diderot and Condorcet, my favorite eighteenth-century thinkers,
with a view to writing detailed monographs on them eventually.

The yeshiva student's old "bibliomania" reemerged in an even more
acute form. One could often encounter the swarthy, dark-eyed youth excitedly rummaging around in chaotic piles of books in the dusty shops of
the second-hand booksellers under the arches of the old market. The antiquarians, experienced psychologists, knew how to profit from the weakness of their frequent customer; a significant part of his meager literary
earnings found its way into the pockets of their greasy, padded jackets,
while he rushed home with his precious load: Börne's collected works or
an old edition of *Buch der Lieder*.

The even flow of working days was interrupted by a summons to his
native province for military service. Extreme short-sightedness saved Dubnov from a soldier's life, which he found repugnant. But he did not return
to the capital immediately. The winter of 1881–1882 he spent in his native
town occupied by his favorite work, reading Montesquieu, Rousseau, Mill,
and Comte. Learning English gave Dubnov the opportunity to read some
of his teachers in the original, and he reread the treatise *On Liberty* with
the same feeling with which a true believer reads the Holy Scriptures.
He relates in his memoirs,

> I was living in Mstislavl then, near the main avenue, in a house resembling
> a long barn, in the middle of a large courtyard covered with snow. My small
> room had a separate entrance and a low window, which opened into snow-
> drifts. The girl who was later to become my wife came to see me: the older
> of my two friends, the Freidlin sisters. We fell in love with one another after
> three years of close friendship. As the blizzards howled that memorable winter
> we abandoned ourselves to dreams of our future life together, of working to-
> gether, of moving to St. Petersburg and then Paris, and transforming our
> path of thorns into a smooth and joyful one.

The mail came, bringing into his cell, half-buried beneath the snow,
the Russian-Jewish journals reflecting the confusion gripping the intelligentsia circles. Under the influence of growing anti-Semitism, the Palestinophile movement gathered strength. Vladimir Dubnov, too, joined and
decided to go to Palestine. His younger brother did not share these sentiments. Distressed by *Razsvet's* direction Simon sent the journal an acerbic
article with the title "What Next?" The starting point of the article was
a principle set forth by Börne: "He who wishes to act for the good of
the Jews must merge his actions with demands for freedom in general."

The editor angrily declared that such an article could only play into the hands of the enemies of the Jewish people and refused to print it.

Dubnov's disagreement with the editorial policy of *Razsvet* continued even after his return to St. Petersburg. He had to go back to neutral subjects again: a series of articles about the Jewish pogroms in Bogdan Khmelnitskii's time appeared in the journal under the pseudonym S. Mstislavskii. But the journal was already in its last days and ended its existence shortly thereafter. It was a heavy blow for the young journalist, who had to hunt frantically for other sources of livelihood.

The financial question became even more acute when Ida Freidlin left her parents' home without any means of subsistence and arrived in the capital. A sharp disagreement with her mother had precipitated her departure. Her mother, a domineering woman, considered the girl's aspirations to independence and higher education a youthful whim. Moreover, the prospect of her daughter marrying a pauper with a reputation in the town as a freethinker frightened her. The poor mother did not suspect the worst: the young people could not formalize their relationship because civil marriage was not recognized by Russian law and a religious ceremony seemed incompatible with the convictions of a preacher of free thought.

Penury and the hardships caused by their illegal status tarnished the joy of the couple's first months of life together. For a while the police left Dubnov in peace, for he was registered as a domestic servant in the employ of a St. Petersburg lawyer. Ida registered falsely as an employee in a sewing workshop and then entered a midwifery course. When he later recalled this period of his life, Simon observed that the forces Schiller called the mainsprings of life dominated then: love and hunger. Another problem hounded the young man besides financial worries: how to combine "individual happiness" with serving an ideal. The problem of the right to happiness might seem incomprehensible to people of a different time, but it played a large role in the life of the ascetic young people brought up on radical Russian journalism. It was a singular generation: they naïvely polarized "individual happiness" and the struggle for the good of humanity, and saw no contradiction between the egocentrism of the "critically thinking individual" and the altruistic postulates of serving the people. Vladimir Solovev once formulated the paradoxical credo of the men of the seventies with good-natured irony: "Man is descended from a monkey, therefore let us give up our lives for our kin."

Dubnov was a typical child of his time, with its idealism, its rigorous moralism, and its logical inconsistency. He writes in his memoirs,

> I was torn between "life for an ideal," as the phrase went, and the heavy cares of making a living. Such moments in one's quest for one's path in life, the labor pangs of individual self-determination, are most dangerous in early youth: they are accompanied by fits of depression, and in my notes dating to that time I find unmistakable signs of that condition in my own notes.

Work was the best medicine for spiritual travail. In the autumn of 1882 the harsh period of unemployment in the young writer's life ended. He became a permanent contributor to the largest Russian-Jewish periodical, *Voskhod*. From that time forward the monthly journal rarely appeared without one of his articles; for a quarter of a century his literary career was associated with the periodical on which a whole generation of the intelligentsia was brought up. Dubnov regularly published articles on historical, literary, and social and political subjects in *Voskhod* under his own name, the initials S. D. D., and various pseudonyms—Criticus, S. Mstislavlskii, and Externus.

Dubnov made his debut in the journal with a long piece on Sabbatai Zevi and the pseudo-Messianic movement, written under the influence of Graetz. The young historian approached the subject in his own way, however. He contrasted the mystic-adventurer to his contemporary Spinoza, an ideal "critically thinking individual"; the Jews of that time were to be reproached for following a man who drew them into the "realm of ignorance and darkness," and for anathematizing the philosopher who showed them the path of true progress. The success of the article encouraged Dubnov to study another Messianic-mystical movement, Frankism. He was drawn to this subject because he saw in it a protest against the assumption by the rabbinical tradition of an unhealthy form under the impact of historical circumstances.

Starting in January 1883, long critical articles or surveys of current Jewish literature in three languages began to appear regularly in *Voskhod* under the name Criticus. In accordance with the traditions of Russian criticism, the articles also touched on philosophical and social problems. Their author vehemently attacked hack writing and dilettantism in an attempt to wean budding writers, especially those writing in Hebrew, away from the bad habits of pretentiousness and turgidity, and convert them to "European" clarity. Whatever he wrote about, the central question was always the one which stirred him most, the battle with hidebound tradition. In the heat of polemics the preacher of free thought did not notice the contradictions undermining his argument: the call for religious reform, although radical in itself, was at odds with the philosophy of positivism, which rejected all religion as a mere relic of the theological phase of thought. Dubnov realized his inconsistency only many years later; in his younger years the desire to express at last the ideas he had cherished and suffered for, even though they did not constitute a coherent system of thought, dominated everything else. An attempt to expound them before a non-Jewish audience failed: the editor of a liberal Russian paper, an assimilated Jew, approved of the contents of the article attacking prejudice and fanaticism but considered it unsuitable for his own publication.

At that time Pinsker's pamphlet "Auto-Emancipation" was the subject of heated discussion in Jewish circles. Its author, a rabid nationalist and a Palestinophile, sharply criticized those elements of Jewry who considered the civil emancipation of the Jews and cultural renewal in a European spirit the most important task. Dubnov offered a heated rebuttal in the article "What Kind of Emancipation Do Jews Need?" He castigated the hypertrophy of ritual and argued that the ritualistic system of Judaism destroyed the principles of pure faith and ethics and reinforced the segregation of the Jews from other peoples. Polemicizing with the Palestinophiles, he asserted that the national idea was a transitional phase on the way to the idea of the unity of all mankind; Pinsker's "nationalization" was necessarily and diametrically opposed to "humanization." The article contained considerable polemical passion, but this did not trouble the editor of *Voskhod*, Adolph Landau, a man of a practical bent who had a foretaste of a *succès de scandale* and a rise in circulation. The relations between the young enthusiast who had, not so long ago, refused "to profane" his literary labor by accepting payment, and the hard-headed and rather coarse "master" of the journal, who put material interests first, were very strained. Dubnov was quite unable to reconcile himself to the fact that the contributors to the journal, particularly the newcomers, had to remind the editor repeatedly about remitting payment for an article that had already appeared in print. The appeals to the editor so distressed the shy and self-regarding young journalist that day after day he put off the inevitable visit to the office of the journal, despite bitter want.

While Simon became increasingly absorbed in his work, Ida was diligently preparing to enroll in the Medical Institute. At first the young couple lived in different rooms in the same house, but at the beginning of 1883 they decided to move in together. They intended to regularize their relationship abroad, where they planned to go and study at the first opportunity. Simon remembers those distant years in *The Book of My Life*, "It was a very daring step at that time not only with respect to our families in the provinces but also with respect to our social circle in St. Petersburg; but when it was a question of remaining true to my convictions there were no obstacles for me."

What did the shy, gentle girl, who unhesitatingly took up the burden of being an unmarried woman in the conservative milieu of the last century, think of her companion's uncompromising attitude? She did not demur: having fallen in love deeply and forever, she firmly resolved to be the faithful and staunch companion of a man who had wholly devoted himself to the service of an idea. Endowed with a great store of strength and spiritual health, Ida looked calmly into the future: the prospect of deprivation, want, and the daily grind of work did not frighten her. In those years of youth she could not have guessed that to be the wife of a toiler who had dedicated his life to the fulfilment of a vow would be no easy task even in the best of circumstances, for all creative work is demanding and despotic. Becoming accustomed to living in the shadow of another's life was probably accomplished with no small effort, for she had inherited an independent nature from her mother. But as the years passed self-denial became second nature to Ida Dubnov; in it she found satisfaction and the meaning of existence. The secret bitterness which inevitably accumulates on the bedrock of long self-denial did not undermine her will but only strengthened her rigorous moralism. There came a time in Dubnov's mature years when rebellion against the unswerving asceticism of his youth flared up in his soul. But his companion never once doubted that the essence of life lay in the discharge of duty dictated by deep feeling.

7

At the Crossroads

"I am a lover of humanity, a democrat and an atheist," intoned the slender young man with a thick mane of dark hair as he paced up and down his room. The words he was repeating belonged to his new favorite, the English poet Shelley. The young man was in a state of great excitement: he was writing an article called "The Last Word of Condemned Jewry." The article, describing the government's policy toward Jews, was timed to coincide with an investigation of the Jewish question by a special commission. Insisting on full civil emancipation for the Jews, Dubnov emphasized the humanitarian nature of this demand: "The Jews are persecuted, and this should be sufficient cause for anyone with a heart to fight for them. . . . One need not be a Jewish nationalist or have any other feeling for Jews except the feeling a man has for the suffering of other men." At the request of the editor of *Voskhod* the essay was signed with the unknown pseudonym Externus. Adolph Landau was seriously alarmed by collective and individual protests to the young journalist's recent sharp polemics against conservative Jewish circles.

When he had finished the article on civil emancipation, Dubnov began to prepare a memorandum on the legal position of Jews in Russia. Based on painstaking research into the sources, it was destined for the government commission, but it disappeared without a trace in the private archive of one of St. Petersburg's Jewish community leaders.

Some months filled with intensive and absorbing literary work passed, and Dubnov felt the need to immerse himself in study again. His dream of the "domestic university" was rekindled. Half of the fee he had received for his official memorandum went to purchase a scholar's library, carefully selected for methodical study. It was clear that it would be easier to carry out this program in the peace and quiet of the provinces than in the harsh conditions of the capital. It proved necessary for Simon and Ida to legalize their relationship in connection with their plan to return to Mstislavl. In the presence of several casual witnesses, a dejected young man in a thread-bare jacket placed a ring on the finger of an embarassed young woman and quickly muttered the marriage vows. The next day Ida Dubnov, with a new name on her passport, left for their hometown to look for lodgings.

Spring was in full bloom when the "prodigal son" returned home. He writes in his memoirs:

> I drove up to a small, wooden house with a vegetable plot and a garden, with flowers gaily smiling in the windows. My wife met me on the porch in a shining halo of sunlight and led me into two spotlessly clean rooms with the modest furniture of a Russian petit-bourgeois dwelling. . . . It was a bright time in our life, something like the honeymoon we had not had in gloomy Petersburg. For a short time we made our nest in this Russian house, where inquisitive eyes could not spy on our religious conduct. . . . But the rumors and slanders continued about town. A lad who did not come to the synagogue even on the Sabbath and who did not observe religious customs was an unusual phenomenon in that pious community.

Life proceeded quietly in the comfortable house on the edge of town. The bookcase near the desk sagged beneath the weight of books: works of philosophy were wedged against books of poetry. Two portraits of Mill and Shelley in a single frame—the stern profile of the thinker and the inspired face of the visionary in an aureole of pale curls—symbolized the union of philosophy and poetry. On the top shelf stood Goethe's *Faust* and slim volumes of the lyrical poetry of Byron and Victor Hugo. They were Dubnov's true friends, the companions of his solitary reflections. The young positivist also read contemporary prose with delight. In the middle of reading Turgenev's "An Unhappy Girl," he suddenly flung himself face down on the pillow and began to weep. Above all the other Russian classics he placed Tolstoy, whom he revered throughout his life.

A family event was soon expected—the birth of a child. A row of books on education and child psychology appeared on the study shelves. The father-to-be wanted to create for his child the conditions that he himself had lacked. He reread the chapters in Mill's *Autobiography* describing his childhood years. Meanwhile he and Ida had to move into a large house belonging to Simon's mother-in-law, the widow Freidlin. It was not easy for the heretic to adjust to living with relatives. The rooms appointed for the young couple were completely separate from the floor occupied by the mistress of the house; the taciturn bookworm appeared in the common dining room only at meal times. This produced an atmosphere of alienation but averted open conflict.

Simon's eighty-year old grandfather Bentsion was still alive and continued to teach at the synagogue. His grandson's articles were inaccessible to him, but vague echoes of the arguments conducted in the pages of the Hebrew press found their way even to him. Meyer-Yakov Dubnov, who read the paper *Ha-Meliz* during his travels, gently chided his son in his letters for going too far in his polemics and compromising the glorious name of Dubnov. A critical moment was approaching, the autumn High Holidays. Simon relates in *The Book of My Life*,

> One day my grandfather summoned me. . . . He asked where I intended to pray on the Holy Days. Trying to spare his religious feeling as much as possible, I replied that I had not yet decided, that I did not even have a tallis, which is essential for a married man. In answer to his question "Why not?" I replied that these garments were laid down not by the Torah but in the Oral Law. . . . My grandfather's tall figure seemed to shrink, his head dropped on his chest. . . . For several minutes there was a heavy silence. Suddenly he stopped before me and said in a penetrating voice, which rang with infinite sorrow, "Simon, the time will come when you will say with the prophet Hosea, 'I will go and return to my first husband,/For it was better with me than now. . . .'"

These words, pronounced in the sad, traditional chant, rang in his grandson's ears for a long time. But when the holidays of Rosh Hashanah and Yom Kippur came and the old man robed in white stepped before the pulpit like a cantor, his grandson remained in his study among his heretical books. *The Book of My Life* says,

> From the autumn of 1884, the following picture could be seen in the quiet, provincial town: on two parallel streets grandfather and grandson sat in their booklined studies. One cultivated the wisdom of the Talmud and the rabbis and transmitted it to his listeners, the other plunged with equal zeal into the new wisdom of the age and had his own distant, but more numerous audience. . . . Both lived like the Nazarenes, obedient to strict vows, each with his own understanding of life, intellectually different, ethically identical.

Young Dubnov's conduct drew sharp criticism within the Jewish community. Hostile stares followed him when he strolled with his cane along the main avenue on the Sabbath; the street urchins shouted "Heretic!" after him. But he set to work zealously to accomplish his university plan, based on Comte's classification of the sciences. The program included the natural sciences, philosophy, history, and sociology. His working day had to last no less than thirteen hours. The hermit shut himself up in his spacious study, the room which had once housed the Freidlin sisters' library, and which was now the home of his own library. Such books as Mill's *Logic*, Schlosser's *World History*, and Spencer's *Sociology* and a number of books on the history of philosophy opened up new horizons and deepened conceptions of the world which were already firmly established in his mind. But sometimes he felt sad at the thought that he had no one with whom to share the discoveries born of prolific reading. "How many times," says an entry in his dairy, "has the philosopher's impassioned Eureka echoed within these four empty walls! If a joy shared is a joy doubled then a thought shared is a thought multiplied. But such good fortune falls to the lot of very few."

However, Dubnov had to interrupt his studies in the "domestic university" for his current literary work. He returned to a subject which never ceased to excite him: educational reform. A new article devoted to this question was permeated with the same spirit as his former discussions of religious reform, but its tone was less sharp. In it he pointed to a singular phenomenon: a distant descendant, coming across materials on a *kheyder* education might think that three million Russian Jews were training all the male children in theology. Urging the necessity of abolishing the *khadorim* and replacing them with secular schools offering a general education, the author concluded with words shot through with heartfelt pain:

> The entire length and breadth of the Pale is dotted with thousands of children's prisons. A great crime is committed there: a massacre of innocents, the murdering of the spirit and the flesh. From them come exhausted, pale creatures. These unfortunate little men have known no childhood. The openness of fields, the freshness of meadows, the heights of blue skies are unknown to them. Between four walls, in a stifling atmosphere, under debilitating mental strain, beneath the rod of an ignoramus, their best childhood years trickle away. There the monstrous Babylonian wisdom is violently hammered into their infant minds. They are taught nothing of the real world, or nature, or life, and everything about the world beyond the grave, death, commandments, heaven and hell.

The editor of *Voskhod* was extremely disconcerted when he received this article. He was afraid of new protests from the representatives of the St. Petersburg Jewish community, who were already enraged by the refractory journalist's recent attacks. For a long time the manuscript lay in his files. Finally it was printed with substantial cuts and an editorial disclaimer. Instead of a signature the editor wrote D.S., the author's initial in reverse.

Having poured out his bitterness, Dubnov again immersed himself in study. But the constant strain fatally affected his eyesight; his eyes became so inflamed that he was obliged to stop reading. His family read aloud to him for hours on end but this could not satisfy the insatiable bookworm. One night pandemonium broke out in the house; then long, anxious hours of waiting dragged by until at last the midwife proudly showed the distraught young father a little red bundle tightly swaddled. It was a girl whom they decided to name Sophie. The following days were joyless. Exhausted by the difficult birth, the young mother lay motionless in the bedroom, from which came the child's pitiful whimpering. Meanwhile the head of the family sat in his study, the shutters closed to keep out the sun on the doctor's advice, and reflected on his own illness and his precarious financial position. He was very reluctant to tie himself down as a permanent contributor to *Voskhod*, turning his literary work into a source of livelihood and making himself dependent on the whims of the business-minded editor, but the arrival of a child imposed new duties on him.

Some time later Simon's sight improved, but his plan of study was already disrupted. The house was more lively now: his brother Vladimir had returned from Palestine, unable to endure the arduous, back-breaking work on the land. Heated arguments about nationalism and cosmopolitanism began, but there were already signs of a mental breakdown in the younger brother's expressions. The melancholia which had gnawed at him in the lonely hours of meditation in his dim room ate even deeper into his soul. In an attempt to crush it he tried to occupy himself with physical work, putting into practice the Tolstoy plan of "a simple life," which had lately become especially dear to him. A carpenter's lathe was set up on the glassed-in veranda, arousing the indignation of the neighbors looking through the windows. In addition to his reputation as a freethinker, Simon was now considered a crank. Carpentry was soon replaced by bookbinding, and a row of books in new, simple bindings smelling of glue appeared on the high shelves lining the walls. But even physical labor did not alleviate his misery:

> Something had snapped in my soul, a kind of crack had opened in my world view and anxiety poured in. Just as doubts in faith once arose in me, so now doubts in the omnipotence of reason were born. Positivism, which blocked all my thinking with toll gates, had begun to press in on me; my intellectual organism had outgrown a suit that was now too tight.

In Dubnov's life inner restlessness was always connected with a need to change his surroundings. Toward the end of summer the wanderer set off for the capital again, taking with him a large supply of books. He immediately sensed a change in the social climate there. Alexander III religiously obeyed the call of that ideologue of reaction, K. Leontiev, "to freeze Russia." The Russian-Jewish press was in decline. Only *Voskhod* still appeared, but over it hung the Damocles sword of the censor, who often made harsh demands of the editor. Moreover, articles containing sharp criticism of Jewish tradition had done the journal's reputation considerable harm. Nevertheless, Adolph Landau offered Dubnov work in the historical and critical sections on his return from the provinces. Criticus' surveys began to appear in the pages of *Voskhod* again, noting each significant development in Jewish literature. The critic wrote with special feeling about Franzos, the chronicler of life in a small Galician Jewish town. A new note could be heard in this article on poor, backward, provincial life, a note of gentle resignation. Dubnov felt that there were no righteous and no guilty men in this life. The article concluded with a lyrical address to the reader: "It seems as though after long wanderings you have returned once more to your native home, you have seen familiar places, images close to your heart . . . and have understood everything: the past and the present, the meaning of both the one and the other and the connection between them."

As before, historical subjects attracted Dubnov. He agonized over the question of what to write about: the Encyclopedists and Condorcet's theory of perfectibility, or Jewish mysticism and the Cabala. For a while the young historian's attention was taken by a modern Dante, the obscure Jewish poet Immanuil Romi, the nature of whose gifts recalled Heine's. An article on Mommsen[14] was devoted to a serious historical problem. The author criticized the bias of this well-known historian, who condemned the national uprising of ancient Judea. Instead Dubnov tried to rehabilitate the reputation of the Zealots struggling for independence and, in part, the reputation of the Pharisees, who had tried to create a bulwark against assimilation. In the way he posed the question one can sense a clear turn from cosmopolitanism toward new concepts.

The attacks of eye disease which recurred from time to time severely hampered Dubnov's literary work. And, as in Mstislavl, forced idleness roused him to reflection, bringing on an ideological crisis. About this time the entries in his diary become more frequent and detailed. In one of them he notes the four phases through which he had passed in his quest for a complete world view: orthodoxy, reform, deism, and positivism. Now, as he entered a new phase, the diarist observes:

> The nature of my skepticism is not yet entirely clear. In general its underpin-
> nings are purely emotional. Its essential features are the following: a thirst
> for faith which cannot be satisfied by a wholly positivistic "religion of man";
> cheerless thoughts on the inscrutability of the most important mysteries of
> existence, which assail the mind despite the prohibitions of positivism; doubt
> of the moral progress of mankind.

When such moods overwhelmed the young writer he was drawn to the subject of "Job and Ecclesiastes, Pessimism and Skepticism in the Bible." Pacing up and down in his room, he recalled lines he had read in his childhood to the mournful howling of the autumn wind in the days of Succos, or he repeated Byron's verse:

> Count o'er the joys thine hours have seen,
> Count o'er thy days from anguish free,
> And know, whatever thou hast been,
> 'Tis something better not to be.[15]

"I subjected my entire world view to scrutiny" he recalls in *The Book of My Life*, "I was in the power of a 'fear of the void,' which overwhelmed me in the interval between one part of a full life and another. . . ."

The consciousness of his spiritual isolation weighed increasingly heavily on him. Frug's constant companionship, as in former years, was not entirely satisfying. By that time Frug had become popular for his melodious, formally unpretentious poetry on national and biblical themes. Dubnov gladly listened to him and could recite many of his verses by heart and with enthusiasm, but he avoided conversation about the "accursed questions." Much more interesting as a conversationalist was the young Akim Flekser, who later became very well known as a religious philosopher and art critic under the name Volynskii.[16] The student's small cell often rang with impassioned voices, as the young men argued themselves hoarse over the relative merits of English or German philosophy. Flekser fiercely defended Hegelianism, which his opponent, a faithful disciple of Mill, called "cobwebs of the brain." When they had done arguing the two talkers would settle down to study jurisprudence peaceably together: Flekser was preparing for the final examinations for the Law Faculty, and together they worked their way through the course of study, which Dubnov had included in his program for the "domestic university."

The summer months spent in the bosom of his family in Mstislavl rested Dubnov's soul and his eyes. In a little house with a garden outside the town, two infants now wailed, a second daughter, Olga, having been born in the spring during her father's absence. Dubnov's wife; her sister, Fanny; and Vladimir Dubnov took turns reading books and journals aloud to their tired visitor from the capital. The brothers again spent a good deal of time together. They took walks in the environs of the town, argued in an amicable manner, and occasionally called on their grandfather Bentsion.

As before, the inhabitants of the *shulhoyf* looked sourly at the pale, slight man in spectacles, muttering after him that God had punished him with blindness for his grievous sins. But the freethinker about whom they were so distressed tapped his cane absently on the boards of the sidewalk and pondered his forthcoming articles: a discussion of Börne, whom he called a new kind of Marrano, and the cycle "A General Survey of the History of Jewish Literature." He was to express for the first time in this article the idea that two principles run parallel through the entire history of Jewish literature: the national and the universal. The fact that he emphasized not so much the struggle of these two principles as their interaction was a sign of the change in the author's historical concepts. A new path had opened before the young historian.

8

History Was Revealed to Me

In the evenings when the babies were asleep, and cool, fragrant air wafted in from the garden, Simon and Ida sat on the porch of the house on the edge of town and quietly talked over their plans for the future. Simon's work as a writer required his presence in the capital, but he could not bring himself to sentence his family to an illegal existence there. Lately the police had been ruthlessly driving everyone with forged papers out of St. Petersburg. Dubnov decided to take the straight and narrow path and apply for permission to reside in the capital as a writer. In the autumn he left for St. Petersburg.

An endless rigmarole ensued. His application was denied. The Police Department made a short but explicit notation in his passport: he had to leave in twenty-four hours. His friends advised him not to give up, to find other opportunities. Meanwhile Simon had to tramp about the suburbs, spending the night illegally with relatives or in the editorial office of *Voskhod*, among packages of books and papers. After two months of a nomad's existence the possessor of the "wolf's passport"[17] was obliged to return to his native backwater.

> I felt that the birth pangs of my self-determination were coming to an end
> . . . that I was finally about to fix on one of the many plans of activity pulling me
> in so many different directions. The twenty-seventh year of my life was a deci-
> sive moment. Until then my thoughts were of vast humanistic literary projects,
> although I was in fact working in Jewish literature. . . . My eye disease . . .
> gave me the opportunity for deeper reflection. I became convinced that a pro-
> cess of self-limitation was necessary for truly creative work . . .that my path
> to the universal lay through precisely that realm of the national in which I
> was already working. . . . It became clear to me that . . . the general knowl-
> edge I had gained and my universal aspirations might bear fruitful results when
> combined with the treasures of Jewish knowledge I had unearthed and the
> national ideals still to be defined. My interest in the important issues of Jewish
> history dates from that time. It led me from the broadly conceived *History of
> Hasidism* to the plan for a complete history of the Jews of Eastern Europe and
> ultimately to the even broader design for a world history of the Jewish people.

As he turned the pages of a slim volume of Victor Hugo, Dubnov lighted on lines which seemed a genuine revelation. The French writer wrote in his customary, lofty and rhetorical tone: "History was revealed to me and I understood the law of the development of generations, searching for God and bearing the Holy Ark, ascending the great staircase step by step." For Simon Dubnov these words described the process going on within him: history was leading him out of a period of grave doubt, pessimism, and resignation onto the broad avenue of creative work.

At the time the disciple of Mill and Spencer was scarcely likely to wonder why he was so strongly drawn to the subject of Hasidism. He first experienced this attraction in his youth, and it lasted almost until the end of his life. It was not easily explained as a historian's simple curiosity about an under-researched era. Already at the dawn of his career, Dubnov sensed in the pseudo-messianism of Sabbatai Zevi and Frank a perversion of the protest against the entrenched rabbinic authority which was the dominant element of his youth. Now he found the same protest in a far more mature and profound form in the Hasidism of the Baal-Shem-Tov and his immediate disciples. It was not mysticism—alien as it was to a descendant of the *misnagdim*—but the romanticism of a great national movement which fired the imagination of a seeker who felt a sudden chill amid the sober formulas of positivism. During the preparatory work his attention was drawn to the figure of the visionary Moses Luzzato, "in whose soul darkness and light, the night of the Cabala and the dawn of the renaissance, had fought." In the hours of his solitary walks along the muddy banks of the Vekhra, Dubnov pondered an article devoted to this poet. A path led straight from Luzzato to Israel Baal-Shem-Tov (the Besht). "Henceforth," writes the future historian of the Hasidic movement, "the shades of the Besht and other founders of Hasidism never left me."

From time to time the literary surveys which appeared regularly in *Voskhod* distracted Dubnov from his historical work. The prognoses he made then were by no means all borne out. Criticus' attachment to the strict realism fostered by Russian criticism did not allow him to divine a future great writer in the author of *Monish*;[18] the form of Peretz's early works seemed mannered and pretentious. On the other hand, Dubnov immediately sensed the indubitable talent in *Dos meserl* (The Penknife), a modest tale by Sholem Aleichem, a writer as yet unknown. Sholem Aleichem himself later acknowledged that the generous review in *Voskhod* encouraged his literary career at a time when he was still uncertain of his own powers and of the possibility of creating anything significant in his national language.

Dubnov continued to follow the growth of political reaction in the peace and quiet of the provinces. "A terrible, vile time!" he notes in his diary. "If I were physically healthy and single I'd be off to America for good. I'd rather chop wood in a land of liberty than be a writer in a land of tyranny, slavery, and despotism." And a month later: "Sometimes the energy born of indignation awakens in me, and then I become capable of great deeds: I could fight despotism, I would fight for my own injured people, for the freedom that has been trampled under foot, for the rights of man, until I dropped in battle. . . . But such moments are very rare, usually my heart is overflowing with impotent grief."

The summer of 1887 was the first and the last that Simon spent with his father. Meyer-Yakov Dubnov left his work and returned home with a serious lung disease. He used the money he received on being discharged to realize an old dream and built a little house of his own. On the day of the housewarming, which fell on the eve of the High Holy Days, the faces of Meyer-Yakov and Sheyne, two toilers worn down by life, shone with quiet joy. Only their son's absence from the synagogue on Rosh Hashanah clouded their joy. Shortly afterward Simon's father fell gravely ill.

On the day of Yom Kippur he lay in bed whispering the words of a prayer incessantly, and tears streamed down his hollow cheeks. He looked at me with forgiving eyes as I stood beside his bed as though . . . he was already praying for the forgiveness of my erring soul. Several days later . . . he died. They knocked on my window at dawn to bring me the news. I found my father on the floor beneath a black cloth, two candles burning at the head of the bier. My wailing mother and my weeping sisters were beside him. I sat next to them on the floor, an orphan among orphans. . . . The outward calm of my grandfather, who had lost his only son, struck many people, but one had only to look hard at the old man to see that he was inwardly shattered. . . . At midday . . . we walked behind the coffin bearers at the head of the funeral procession. My grandfather's figure moved among us like a living symbol of grief, wordlessly conveying the mysteries of death and eternity. At that moment it was as though a great magnet was drawing me toward that towering rock of faith and at the cemetery, beside my father's newly filled grave, I and my brother recited the mourner's Kaddish together; for me it was the first and the last time.

When Simon recovered from the blow, he returned to his manuscripts. He gradually came to the conviction that he would have to make a number of trips to gather materials for the history of Hasidism. A visit to Warsaw proved particularly fruitful. The noise and bustle of the mercantile Jewish quarter almost stunned the recluse, but he quickly set to work. It was particularly pleasant working in the quiet library attached to the large synagogue, where an aged librarian searched out old books on Hasidism for the stranger. The bibliophile spent hours on end rummaging through piles of old books in the dusty, dimly lit shops of the second-hand booksellers. The Hasidic antiquarians in their long robes stared suspiciously and uncomprehendingly at the young man in a short jacket who showed an interest in the writings of the *tsadikim*. Dubnov was able to obtain a number of rare books of old anti-Hasidic literature and make valuable extracts from primary sources. These were the first deposits in the archive which was to become the foundation of the future history of Hasidism. Indeed, it was not only the yellowed pages of books which revealed the mysteries of the Hasidic way of life. Living people told him much of interest—the writer Mordecai Spector, who had visited the rabbinical "courts" of the Ukraine, and Nahum Sokolow, the editor of Ha- Zefirah.[19] The young historian met with a warm welcome among the Jewish men of letters in Warsaw; he became especially intimate with the gentle, delicate Jacob Dineson,[20] the author of popular tales in Yiddish. They had lively conversations on literary and social subjects for long hours in the evenings, and in one of their conversations Dineson owned that he had imagined Criticus to be far more forbidding and distant.

When the wanderer returned home a new member of the family was being rocked in the cradle, his newborn son, Yakov. There were now three children in their cramped lodgings, and the young mother went to no small trouble to create the atmosphere necessary for Simon's concentrated and demanding literary work. The family was living from hand to mouth. The editor of Voskhod paid meanly and irregularly, ignoring his contributor's requests for payment. Dubnov's eye disease prevented him from considering other sources of income. But all discomforts were forgotten at his desk. While the nurse was hushing the baby with a doleful Belorussian song on the other side of the wall, the young historian was excitedly thinking about how to apply Renan's[21] methods to the Besht's biography. In 1888 "An Introduction to the History of Hasidism" began to appear in Voskhod. The pages in which Dubnov spoke of the religious pantheism of the founder of Hasidism, his solitary life in the Carpathian Mountains, and his repugnance for rabbinical formalism were written with particular animation. In The History of Hasidism, which appeared forty years later, the author deleted many of the lyrical passages in the interests of scholarly objectivity, but at the time they were particularly dear to him.

Dubnov's youthful passion for books and the company of like-minded thinkers continued to thrive even in his years of maturity; only its subjects changed. Now Renan and Tolstoy became the "rulers of my thoughts." The writer shared a common spiritual evolution with Renan: a Catholic seminary student, the brilliant French thinker had turned from dogmatic theology to scientific philosophy, and from that to the study of religious movements. Under the cover of philosophical skepticism a longing for the lost faith of his youth lived in his soul. Dubnov writes in The Book of My Life,

This drew me to Renan . . . and also to Tolstoy as the creator of an ethical God. . . . At that time I was deeply moved by reading manuscript copies of Tolstoy's A Confession and What I Believe, books banned by the censor. I was, of course, painfully struck by his attacks on science and social activism, and troubled . . . by the principle of "non-resistance to evil," but the general tenor . . . was akin to my own mood. I was irresistibly drawn to the depth of the true believer's soul plumbed by the artist and thinker.

The mind of the positivist standing at the crossroads combined in a very distinctive way the melancholy refinement of the heir to centuries of culture with the moral maximalism of one of the greatest sons of a young people which had only relatively recently stepped to the forefront of Europe's spiritual life.

Soon the great humanist's disciple was to show his predilection for action. Malicious rumors about Tolstoy's anti-Semitism appeared in print; a satirical feuilleton written by some hack proved to be their source. It was not hard for Dubnov to refute the slander in the weekly *Khronika Voskhoda*: quotations from the tract *What I Believe* clearly proved that Tolstoy's attitude to Jews was of the same standard as his ethical teaching. The author of the *Khronika* article also quoted from Tolstoy's conversations with his Jewish teacher, the Moscow rabbi Minor. More than once the great writer had expressed horror and indignation that men brought up on the Gospels were taking part in Jewish pogroms. Soon after, a refutation of the slanderous rumors by Tolstoy himself appeared in the same paper, *Khronika*, where the writer reaffirmed his opinion that his teachings were incompatible with national and racial hatred, and declared that he could not understand how a thinking man could be an anti-Semite.

His journalistic work did not allow Dubnov to concentrate on his large historical topic. He had to work under constant nervous strain; when his eyes were tired he applied himself to his bookbinding tools or went out for a walk with his older daughter. The rare visitors to the deserted avenue were accustomed to meeting this inseparable pair on the wettest and frostiest days: a swarthy man in spectacles and a high fur hat with a red-cheeked little girl, round as a ball in a dark blue fur coat and muff. Because he had decided to educate his daughter according to Mill's system, Dubnov tried to instill in her brain the rudiments of natural science during their walks, but he quickly became bored and began to recite his favorite poems with passion. It is difficult to say whether a popularization of the laws of nature interested the child, but she listened to the rhythms of the incomprehensible poems with indubitable pleasure and even repeated individual lines.

Dubnov maintained an extensive correspondence at this time. One of his most frequent correspondents was Sholem Aleichem. Only now did Dubnov learn the real name of his literary colleague. Sholem Aleichem related his plans and complained of the contempt in which many writers held their native language. Even Frug, who wrote verses and feuilletons in Yiddish himself, at the same time ridiculed the language in *Khronika Voskhoda*. Under the influence of this correspondence Dubnov wrote an article for *Voskhod* on "*zhargon* [i.e., Yiddish] literature," in which he showed that the everyday language of the Jewish masses had an indisputable right to become an instrument of literature because trilingualism was imposed on Jews by history. In a footnote the editor of *Voskhod* said that *zhargon* anthologies were usually full of "all kinds of rubbish." Nevertheless, he continued to print regular surveys of Yiddish literature in his journal.

The feeling that society was living in a Dark Age continued to trouble Dubnov. One of the entries in his diary reads:

> I am perpetually depressed by the consciousness that it is my lot to live in an era of the most terrible reaction, the end of which is not yet in sight. The trampling underfoot of all idealistic aspirations, the rule of brute force, the reign of the military and police, the persecution of thought and hounding of conscience. . . . The anniversary of the greatest historical event (the French Revolution) is approaching but half of Europe stands ready to meet it with contempt and bayonets at the ready.

On the eve of the anniversary of 1889 the need to steep himself in the atmosphere of those heroic years seized the young historian's soul, and he feverishly set to work on a lengthy article, "The Great French Revolution and the Jews."

The article appeared in *Voskhod*, signed "Mstislavlskii." The editor deleted the word "great" from the title to avoid arousing the censor's suspicions that the author was proclaiming revolution. "Nevertheless," says *The Book of My Life*, "the revolutionary thrust pervaded the entire exposition in the lengthy quotations from the speeches of the National Assembly and of the Paris Commune orators who came out in defense of Jewish emancipation. I succeeded in putting out a good deal of political propaganda under the cloak of history."

After each diversion Simon returned to his favorite subject. A cycle of articles called "The Rise of *Tsadikism*" appeared in *Voskhod*. The next series of studies, published from 1890 to 1891, bore the title "History of the Hasidic Schism." These articles were written with great enthusiasm. "Never before had I felt the joys and torments of creative work to such a degree as in those long months of labor in my provincial solitude. There was no time to abandon myself to individual sorrow or world problems."

The deeper Dubnov delved into the study of the religious movements of the eighteenth century, the wider his horizons became. A new, vast plan took shape in his brain—the collection of materials for a history of the Jews in Poland and Russia over the course of the centuries. The discoveries made by Vladimir Dubnov in the Mstislavl community archives led to the idea of collecting *pinkeysim* (community chronicles) in other places as well. This task, which exceeded the resources of a single individual, could only be realized through a public organization—a historical society. To work within such a society became the young historian's dream. He realized that it required the atmosphere of a large cultural center, and his need to escape the stifling backwater became increasingly urgent. However, new attempts to settle in the capital met with one failure after another. At the same time he learned that a fund had been set up in the southern university town of Odessa, under the aegis of one of the Jewish communal organizations, for work on the history of the Russian Jews. Odessa was a cultural backwater compared to St. Petersburg, but the opportunities for scholarly and literary work were much wider there than in a small, out-of-the-way town in Belorussia. Dubnov decided to make one last attempt to move to St. Petersburg, and, in the event of failure, to go south.

Shortly before his departure an incident in Mstislavl stirred up that sleepy backwater. The scourge of reaction, growing stronger each year, was felt in all corners of the country; hand in hand with it went further loss of rights for Jews. The police authorities in a number of towns in the Pale of Settlement began claiming that Jews were behaving defiantly and not showing proper respect for government officials. Dembovetskii, the governor of Mogilev, ordered the police under his command to see that Jews remove their caps and in general conduct themselves respectfully on meeting government officials. When Prince Meshcherskii, a high-ranking official in Mstislavl, received the memorandum from the authorities, he summoned the representatives of the Jewish community and rudely demanded that they root out "disrespect to the government" from among themselves and threatened them with corporal punishment in the event of disobedience. This insolent declaration incensed the town's Jewish population. When Dubnov learned that the offensive words had met with no protest on the part of the representatives, who were taken aback by the insult, he organized a new deputation, but Meshcherskii was "unavailable." A sharp article in *Khronika Voskhoda* made the crude conduct of the Mstislavl authorities public. Many Russian newspapers, even the conservative ones, reprinted it; and news of the scandal reached beyond the Russian border.

The literary campaign led by Dubnov greatly improved his reputation among the local Jewish population. On the eve of his final departure from his native town, the apostate received amnesty. One of the most virulent of the former fanatics who had considered the young historian a certain heretic, quoted a talmudic aphorism: "And there are those who will attain the kingdom of heaven in one hour." The heretic was especially touched by the warm sympathy shown by his grandfather Bentsion, who already had one foot in the grave. In *The Book of My Life* he recalls the scene with emotion:

The old man of eighty-five years, almost blind now, was sitting at the table. His white head resting on his palm seemed lost in visions of the century he had seen. The old man's face lit up with joy when he heard my voice. Quietly my grandfather's words flowed forth, "I have heard, Simon, that you have done a good deed, you have defended the honor of Israel. They say of you, 'and there are those who will attain the kingdom of heaven in one hour,' but I think that in your heart you were never a stranger to our people. May

God grant that you work to His greater glory!" Deeply moved, we said our farewells—forever. Grandfather Bentsion died several months later.

The summer of 1890 was the last the Dubnovs spent in their native town. On doctors' advice Simon went to Kiev to cure his weak eyes and spent several weeks in a suburban dacha with Sholem Aleichem's family. It was the first time the literary colleagues had met after long years of correspondence. The double life his confrère led, divided between the desk and the stock exchange, seemed strange to a working writer who had spent his youth in want and in intense mental toil. The differences in their characters and outward circumstances did not, however, prevent their becoming close friends. During their walks along the paths of a fragrant pine forest, they had endless conversations on literary subjects, and on the eve of Dubnov's departure they vowed to meet again in exactly ten years.

The petitions of a number of influential people, including the editor of *Voskhod*, to allow Dubnov, as a permanent contributor to the journal, to reside in St. Petersburg came to naught. The Mstislavl authorities, to whom the police in the capital turned for information, depicted the initiator of the recent campaign against anti-Semitism as politically unreliable.

Dubnov decided to move to Odessa. In the gray days of October the coachman's jolting cart carried a young woman and three young children bundled up in shawls and blankets, fearfully huddled together, over roads washed out by autumn rains. The head of the family was waiting for them in Mogilev. There they boarded a small steamer going South.

9

The Odessa Literary Circle

Dubnov had grown accustomed to wandering. Often, a quiet country lane on the outskirts of an unfamiliar town or a view along a distant avenue touched his soul as would a favorite tune and became part of the unique background of his spiritual life. For this dreamy northerner Odessa could not become "the city of his soul." The scorching summer sun beat down, and the stinging winter wind blew in from the sea mercilessly. On sultry nights the scent of the acacias was suffocating. The tumultuous, multilingual crowd was too motley and too raucous. But Dubnov came to love this city because he was fated to spend the noontide of his life here, the time of true maturity, when the storms of youth had died down and a straight, broad path had opened.

Subsequently, he came to the conclusion that the most salient feature of this period was the ultimate triumph of "historicism," which came in the wake of both its stormy antithesis and its melancholy resignation. He writes in *The Book of My Life*,

> In historicism I found a counterpoise to religious and philosophical dogmatism. . . . I reasoned this way: I am an agnostic in religion and philosophy, . . . but I can know how mankind has lived . . . and what paths mankind has followed searching for truth and justice; I have lost my belief in individual immortality, but history teaches me that there is collective immortality and . . . that the study of the past of the Jewish people can connect me to something eternal. . . . Historicism . . . led me out of the narrow circle of individual problems into the open space of social problems, less deep but more urgent. . . . Then the path lay open to a national synthesis in which I would have to combine the best elements of the old thesis and the new antithesis—Jewish and universal ideals, the national and the humanistic.

Leaving for the South, Dubnov did not expect to find the conditions for scholarly work which the capital could offer. But Odessa was a major Jewish center; the local intelligentsia were stirred up by the changes taking place in the Jewish community. Dubnov was given the opportunity to participate directly in the shaping of new ideas. In this new phase of his wanderings he found what he had long dreamed of: a circle of friends whose company enriched his mind and spurred him toward a new awareness of the past and the present. None of the members of the Odessa literary fraternity shared all the stages of the journey that had brought the autodidact and individualist to the idea of nationhood. No one was as susceptible as he to the influences of Russian literature and West European philosophy, but each one was passionately seeking a way out of the morass of Jewish life warped by disfranchisement. And if an amicable polemic arose between the writers, its effect was to deepen and clarify the controversial issue.

The Dubnovs settled on the edge of the city. At the end of their street lay a vacant lot, and beyond that the ground sloped down to the sea. The dusty street, paved with uneven cobblestones, baked in the fierce heat of summer and lay deep in snowdrifts in winter. The windows of their apartment looked onto a large courtyard ringing from morning to night with the shouts of children. The Dubnov children often joined the rowdy games; at home they were required to observe the strictest silence so as not to disturb their father.

The study was the brightest and most spacious room in the apartment.

The walls were lined with high bookshelves made of walnut-stained pine and crammed with books, sometimes two rows deep. They were arranged in a particular order so that at any time their owner could immediately find any book he might need. An especially large shelf was allotted to the Judaica section. On another, in densely packed rows, stood slender volumes of the European poets, most of them in old, mouse-eaten covers. These books, rescued from the dust of antiquarian bookshops in St. Petersburg and bought at the cost of many weeks of undernourishment, were reread often; individual lines were often underlined excitedly in colored pencil. The small, oval-shaped portraits of Heine, Börne, Byron, and Shelley hung in carved frames above the wide desk, where exemplary order reigned. When he was working, Dubnov liked to pace up and down the narrow strip of colorful carpeting as he thought things out and honed a phrase. If the work was going smoothly he would hum under his breath, switching unexpectedly from a doleful synagogue melody to a Russian folk song.

The arrangement and the colors of the furniture evidently answered the inner needs of the master of the house. Later it might have seemed that the Odessa study was transported in its entirety to Vilna, St. Petersburg, Berlin, and Riga. At every stop in his wanderings the disposition of the objects remained unchanged. The spartanly furnished room was not only a place of work. Long conversations with a constant stream of visitors were held on a sofa near a little round table. Only when the circle of friends was gathered in force did the hospitable mistress of the house set the table in the half-lit, modest dining room and place beneath the hanging kerosene lamp a huge bowl piled with fragrant homemade pastries and a steaming samovar.

The most colorful figure in the Odessa literary circle was Sholem Yankev Abramovich, otherwise known as Mendele Mokher Sforim. The two writers' first encounter, the beginning of a friendship lasting nearly thirty years, took place shortly after Dubnov's arrival in Odessa. Abramovich, who was about sixty then, ran a *talmud-torah* and lived on the school premises in a poor, remote section of the city. His apartment exuded gloom. The massive dark furniture seemed to have taken root in the floor, and the heavy, dusty draperies gave off the bitter smell of mothballs. That odor presided over the vast, cold rooms. It emanated from the gray flannel smock of the mistress of the house, a silent, wrinkled old woman with an eternally swollen cheek. It saturated even the hard, mint-flavored cakes which inevitably accompanied the tea. Against the background of drab, colorless wallpaper the master of the house, with his hawk's profile beneath a shock of silvered hair, his sharp, piercing eyes, and his quick movements, seemed like a large bird of prey locked in a cage. The guest was struck by the idiosyncrasy of his host's brilliant, picturesque, paradoxical speech, abounding in leaps, digressions, and surprises. Dubnov writes in his memoirs,

What originally drew us together was that neither of us belonged to any camp, and both of us were free from the influences of the various factions. Also, Abramovich was convinced by my reviews of current literature how highly I valued his work in both our languages. . . . A private conversation with Abramovich always gave me great pleasure, although . . . he did not believe in conversations of less than three or four hours and, in addition, was enamored of the monologue form. For me, a systematizer, conversation with a man bound to no system, but improvising original thoughts in the process of talking, was instructive in the highest degree. Abramovich always had his own approach to every question; he compelled his companion, aspiring to breadth of vision, to plunge into the depths of the problem. . . . As a result the question would be deepened and illuminated from a new and unforeseen angle.

At his get-togethers with friends the old writer could actually hold forth only on one subject at a time. One day it was an unexpected interpretation of a passage he had just read in the Bible (he usually began his working day by reading a fragment from the Bible); another time it was a colorful anecdote about something he had just seen. Making his way through the entire city on his way to the Dubnovs' he would invariably linger in the large market square, jammed with carts. His keen eye would pick out some striking human figure from the seething throng or the sagging back of an emaciated dray horse with its ribs sticking out. He would enter his friends' house bursting with new impressions, overflowing with inner excitement, often to find Dubnov engaged in conversation. With an impatient gesture he would dismiss the usual subject—bitter complaints over the administration's arbitrary rule and anti-Semitism—and, without looking at anyone, he would start telling the story of some nag he had just seen, its bony back striped with welts and its suffering, eloquent eyes. Those around him would involuntarily fall silent, subdued by the hypnotic power of his artistic improvisation. Mendele was an improvisator at public gatherings as well. Once when his listeners caught him contradicting himself and confronted him with speeches he had given on two successive occasions, he muttered angrily, "Am I really obliged to hold the same opinion every Saturday?"

Dubnov, who had been accustomed to strict mental discipline since early youth, was fascinated by Abramovich's intuition and keen powers of observation, but there were many gaps in their friendship. The philosophical reflection and the quest for a comprehensive world view, which dominated the rebellious *maskil* in his austere youth, were alien to his older colleague. Fortunately there was a man in the Odessa circle who had studied English philosophy and who combined the rationalism of the Rabbis with the rationalism of the Encyclopedists—Ahad Ha-Am (Osher Ginzberg).

The friendship between Dubnov and Ahad-Ha-Am, based on genuine spiritual affinity and lasting until the latter's death, did not start immediately, but was preceded by a lively polemic. The first article written by Dubnov in Odessa bore the title "The Eternal and the Ephemeral Ideals of Jewry." In it he juxtaposed two books: a collection of articles by French scholars about the historical mission of the Jewish people and the almanac *Kavveret* (Beehive), put out by a group of Odessa Palestinophiles with the participation of Ahad Ha-Am and Lilienblum. Dubnov pointed to a glaring contradiction: While the French scholars' attention was riveted to the "eternal" and universal ideals of the Prophets, the "homegrown nationalists" of Odessa, whose torches "burn no brighter than a penny candle," never ventured beyond the bounds of narrowly practical matters. Lilienblum drew especially sharp criticism in calling for the preservation of that part of Jewish culture embodied in the codes of religious laws. The ardent freethinker in Dubnov was roused, and he inquired ironically, "Exactly when did Lilienblum begin to think of Joseph Caro's *Shulhan Arukh*[22] as the criterion of true Judaism?" His polemic with Ahad Ha-Am bore a more peaceful stamp. In this debate Dubnov first put forward the idea of "spiritual nationalism," which was later developed in detail in *Letters on Old and New Jewry*.

Ahad Ha-Am replied with the article "Slavery in Freedom," which marked the beginning of his literary reputation. Subjecting the French anthology to close analysis, he pointed to traces of internalized slavery in the ideology of Western Jews who sought justification for their existence in the historical mission of Judaism because they did not feel themselves members of a living Jewish nation.

He and Dubnov first met in 1891. Ahad Ha-Am immediately impressed his interlocutor with his powerful, lucid intellect. In the course of conversation it became clear that he was well acquainted with the theory and practice of Hasidism, since he had grown up among Ukrainian Hasidim and was married to the granddaughter of a *tsadik* of the Shneerson family. Along with great Jewish erudition Osher Ginzberg possessed a solid liberal education; he had read European writers in their original languages. He turned out to be an adherent of the English evolutionary school in philosophy, and this facilitated a *rapprochement* between the writers. They did not, however, become good friends right away: Dubnov was initially troubled by his new acquaintance's membership in the closed order *Bney Moyshe* and by the ambiance of the tea-drinking sessions at Ahad Ha-Am's, which reminded him of the gatherings at a Hasidic rabbi's court. Genuine friendship between the literary colleagues, based on shared intellectual interests and spiritual aspirations, only blossomed several years later. Narrow practicality, against which the author of the article about the "eternal ideals" had unleashed the thunder of his polemic, was alien to Ahad Ha-Am. In fact, in his article "Not This Way" he warned those of his camp against excessive involvement with "small deeds." Ahad Ha-Am, progeny of a devoutly Hasidic family, was an extreme rationalist. His faith in the power of reason was unshakable and absolute, and was combined with moral rigor. Moving along a straight and solitary path, he seemed immune to temptations. This stamped his features with puritanical severity and melancholy. Still, renunciation of simple, earthly pleasures is accomplished at a price even when it is achieved without apparent effort. Dubnov set great store by his new friend's intellect and moral purity but could not reconcile himself to his organic indifference to nature, poetry, music, the play of colors. There was something of the purity and icy calm of mountain peaks surrounding this man with a philosopher's high brow and spare, deliberate movements.

A small circle composed of people more or less involved with literature gradually began to assemble more regularly. The gatherings took place on Saturdays, most often at the Dubnovs' or Abramoviches'. Ten to twelve people would gather around the tea table beneath the hanging lamp. Abramovich's silvery mane would toss above his sharp, hawklike profile as he underlined his figures of speech with an abrupt gesture. There was Ben-Ammi (Rabinowicz),[23] a short, nearsighted man, prickly as a hedgehog, who was a mediocre Russian-Jewish fiction writer and a fanatical nationalist. His love for his people took the form of hatred of everything not Jewish. He would become overheated in arguments and, twitching all over, bump into those sitting next to him. Calm and taciturn, Yehoshua Hana Rawnitzki,[24] a writer, pedagogue, and Hebraist, listened intently to the arguments and now and then inserted a carefully thought-out word into the impassioned debate. Ahad Ha-Am would listen in silence and then rise from his seat, a glass of tea in his hand. His longish face, with its sharp features, seemed impassive as his voice kept an even tone. Gesturing monotonously up and down, he looked as if he were hammering his arguments into the brains of his listeners. Dubnov was incapable of speaking without emotion. He became inspired by the contact with other peoples' thoughts and was happy for the chance to express his own cherished ideas on the destinies of his people and mankind, which had accumulated in the long hours of solitary reflection. Actually, in this assemblage of people differing in temperament, way of life, and mode of thinking, every speech was a monologue.

Listening intently to the conversation was a young, fair-haired woman with a tired face and work-worn hands. Ida followed none of the speakers blindly and did not always agree even with her husband's impassioned tirades; but she would weigh the arguments critically and notice logical incongruities. Her life, filled with heavy daily chores and household worries, left her little leisure for self-education, reading, or intellectual training, but she was accustomed to grasping a great deal intuitively. And the most sensitive members of the literary circle knew and appreciated this.

In the summer months the circle took up residence in the outskirts of Odessa. The Dubnov family spent the first summer in Lüstdorf, a German colony on the shore of the Black Sea, in a modest house with a thatched roof and walls made of packed earth. The newcomers from the North never ceased admiring the magnificence of southern colors, the dense, burning blue of the waves against the dazzling gold of the sandy shore. They had no cause to complain of isolation, as some close neighbors turned out unexpectedly to be old friends: Sholem Aleichem, who had to leave Kiev with his family after going bankrupt; and Frug, who had been deprived of the right to live in the capital. Abramovich and Rawnitzki often came to visit, and there were walks and excursions. Many years later Dubnov was to recall those days with affection:

> The breakers echoed all along the seashore, and further inland the deep still-ness of late summer hung over fields and gardens and vineyards, a time when the caress of the southern sun, only recently scorching hot and now gentle and soothing, could be felt in the luminous air. We used to walk to the neigh-boring estate of the vintner Sh———, and sit in his garden among the vines . . . and we would return home, that is, to my little dacha, with a large jug of new wine.

One especially memorable evening is described in *The Book of My Life*:

> We sat in the arbor in our yard, we drank wine, talked convivially, and sang folk songs late into the night. Abramovich was inexhaustible in his reminis-cences and his original discourses; Frug sang a Hasidic parody splendidly; Ben-Ammi, who was in a peaceful mood that evening, sang a Hasidic *nign* with a profoundly sad melody, and then we all repeated it in chorus. Jewish folk songs echoed through the air of the sleeping German colony, and the lapping of the waves on the seashore accompanied us. We all felt so good that night, all of us, sorrowful, preoccupied, weighed down by our own and our people's grief. . . .

Occasionally Sholem Aleichem, subdued and saddened, would look in on the little house in Lüstdorf. He was agonizing over his loved ones: his family, accustomed to comfort, were now living in a small, damp, half-dark dacha. Between visits the two writers exchanged mock epistles written in a specially contrived hybrid of Yiddish and Hebrew. It was laughter through tears; life weighed heavily on both correspondents. At such times friendly contact was especially valued, for it helped prevent being overwhelmed by depression.

10

The Spirit of the Past

Within the four walls of Dubnov's study, amid piles of books and manuscripts, a mystery came to pass; by persistent effort the young historian resurrected the spirits of the past. They rose up from the paragraphs of the Code of Laws, from the dusty chronicles of the *kahals*, from the folios kept in the archives. The work was well under way; his imagination had already sketched the outline of the future building. As he gathered materials and made extracts, he drew up a plan for the activity of a future historical society. He dreamed of collaborative research and a collective of enthusiasts. The treatise "On the Study of Jewish History" began with a quotation from Cicero—"Not to know history means always to be a child" —and called for the creation of such a collective.

In the introduction Dubnov observed that if a conscious attitude toward the future is dictated by practical expediency, then the need to establish the laws of phenomena impels us toward the study of the past. Furthermore, he averred, historical consciousness is the foundation of the Jewish national idea because Jews, deprived of a nation's material characteristics, are held together primarily by their common historical fate. The lengthy essay contained a survey of the development of Jewish scholarship in Europe, an outline of the plan for a history of the Jews in Poland and Russia, a detailed classification of printed and manuscript materials, and a plan for the prospective work of a historical society.

Dubnov was writing his new piece in a state of great elation, despite unfavorable external circumstances. His family was living from hand to mouth. Their first lodgings in the unfamiliar town proved cold and damp. Nervous exhaustion combined with physical weakness sometimes obliged Simon to interrupt his writing. On one such day of forced idleness, he notes in his diary: "The more I write, the more I divine the grandeur of the idea to which I am prepared to give my whole life. The work is complicated; it demands immense effort. But all the physical torments it causes me are nothing compared to the spiritual delight to be derived from it."

The strain of work proved so acute, however, that despite the family's penury, Dubnov had to cut back his contributions to *Voskhod* and give up the critical surveys. "I am ill," he declares in a letter to his editor, "that is the word which must answer all your questions." This letter was never sent. Unexpected news came; on the orders of the authorities *Voskhod* had been temporarily closed down for "its extremely harmful orientation." The censor's cup of patience had finally overflowed with the publication of Abramovich's *Di klyatshe*.[25]

The closing of the journal, Dubnov's only source of subsistence, was both a moral and a financial blow. However, depression did not prevent him from finishing "On the Study of Jewish History." His diary entry for 2 April 1891 reads, "I have finished my long piece. In the last chapters the words poured forth without restraint, ardent and full of conviction. At times it seemed as though I were writing my own spiritual testament." Having finished the essay with nowhere to print it, Dubnov became engrossed in a manuscript on the history of Hasidism he had received from Poland. Immersion in the past distracted him from his serious financial worries and his fears for the Jewish community. Russian Jews were experiencing dark days. The expulsion of Jews from Moscow and the pogrom atmosphere in a number of southern towns created a climate in which it was difficult to preserve his spiritual equilibrium.

During the summer in the seaside village the luxuriance of southern nature and walks with friends once again healed Simon's tormented soul. Some of the chapters from the cycle "History of the Hasidic Schism" were written on a simple table made of boards in the secluded arbor, where warm sunbeams filtered through the climbing ivy. But worry persisted. It was not easy for a family of five to live on the mere pittance advanced by the editor of the closed journal. A modest subsidy from the Literary Fund, to which the unemployed writer turned with a request for help, was soon spent. In the autumn the family moved to new lodgings not far from their former home. In Simon's diary for September 1891 we find the short entry, "Installed in new lodgings—whether to live or die I don't know. . . . There's nothing to live on."

Several months later publication of *Voskhod* was resumed. Following the six-month hiatus, the editor put out a large anthology; Simon's essay "On the Study of Jewish History" opened the volume. It appeared simultaneously in St. Petersburg in the form of a substantial pamphlet. Dubnov, who had worked as a journalist for ten years, held his first small book in his hands with emotion. The pamphlet was a success. The restrained passion permeating each line infected many readers. In response to the author's call, circles were formed in St. Petersburg and Moscow for the purpose of gathering materials on the history of East European Jewry. Soon the St. Petersburg circle formally became the Historical-Ethnographic Commission and was affiliated with one of the Jewish cultural and philanthropic societies. Under current police conditions one could not even think of creating an autonomous historical society. Inspired by success, Dubnov published in *Voskhod* an address to the Jewish community at large, calling on them to make voluntary contributions. Soon he began to receive materials from unknown correspondents in far-flung corners of the country. He hid them, with great enthusiasm, in a special drawer of his desk; these were the bricks for the foundation on which the monumental structure of the history of the Jews of Eastern Europe was to be erected.

Work was going at fever pitch when news of Graetz's death came. It was a shock for Dubnov, who considered the late historiographer his teacher. A commission by the editor of *Voskhod* to write a full-length article about the late historian answered a deep spiritual need. When Dubnov began to read through Graetz's remarkable work, volume by volume, a picture of the singular historical path of the Jewish people unrolled before him in all its grandeur, and he gasped at the immensity of the task which lay ahead.

An entry in his diary for 1 January 1892 reads: "My purpose in life has been made clear: the popularization of the historical knowledge of Jewry with a special emphasis on the history of Russian Jews. I have become a 'missionary of history.' For the sake of this purpose I have renounced literary criticism and journalism." The piece on Graetz, written in this exalted mood, took the form of a lengthy treatise. It was printed in consecutive issues of *Voskhod* in 1892 under the title "The Historiographer of Jewry." Outlining the contents of each separate volume in detail, the author took issue with several of Graetz's ideas. He also came to the defense of the favorite writers of his youth: Elisha Akher, Da Costa, Spinoza, and even the heroines of the Berlin salons,[26] whose exodus from Jewry he explained as the "springtime flood" of the revolutionary era. While Graetz did not seem faultless to him, Dubnov valued his teacher highly as a herald of the idea of the spiritual nation, although not the form in which it later crystalized. Elated, he thought of carrying on the late historian's work on the history of East European Jewry. The realization of this plan hinged on the efforts Graetz had already made in collecting materials. Dubnov decided to develop that work in various directions. At Rawnitzki's suggestion he wrote an article for the collection *Pardes*, analogous in content to the treatise "On the Study of History" and addressed to readers of Hebrew. This article also came out as a separate pamphlet. In *The Book of My Life* he recalls,

> While I was writing it, I received news of my grandfather Bentsion's death in Mstislavl. A local correspondent, one of his students, sent me an obituary with a description of the funeral for the eighty-five year old man. I buried him in my soul with deep emotion. I recalled my childhood and early youth, the more recent tragic clash between Akiba and Akher in the quiet of a provincial town, our final reconciliation and our peaceful farewell. . . . And on the title page I dedicated the pamphlet "To the memory of a man who dwelled in the tent of the Torah all the days of his life." I felt then that I was indebted to that hero of the spirit who bequeathed to me his attachment to the "tent of the Torah," albeit a completely different, wider and freer Torah. I felt the need to dedicate to my grandfather's memory this short work in the "sacred" language which he was the first to teach me. . . . Even now I am

grateful to Rawnitzki for wedding me once more to my first-loved, national language.

At Dubnov's suggestion the Odessa committee of the Society for the Promotion of Enlightenment among Jews of Russia decided to publish an abridged version of Graetz's three-volume *History of the Jews* in Russian translation; the initiator of this project undertook the translation of a number of chapters and the editing of the whole. This did not prevent him from working on Hasidism. In the summer of 1892, in a rustic cottage near a suburban railroad station, the most dramatic chapter of the Hasidic epic, "A *Tsadik* in the St. Petersburg Fortress," was written. Here Dubnov reconstructed the story of Zalman Shneerson's arrest on the basis of scanty data, a picture later confirmed by documents found in the State Archives. When he had finished this chapter, he set to work on the introduction to the translation of Graetz, entitling his essay "What Is Jewish History?"

The translucent days of a southern "Indian summer" arrived. Spider webs floated above the vines, and sea winds rustled the leaves of the yellowing acacia bushes. As he wandered past empty dachas, Dubnov recited his favorite verses by Tiutchev[27] about the autumn "days of crystal" and pondered the essay which was to formulate his credo.

I wanted to give a synthesis of our historical experience and to establish the national ideology flowing from it. The entire study was permeated by extreme spiritualism. . . . By way of a motto I quoted Pascal's words that the continuity of Jewish history equals the continuity of the history of all mankind and characterized Jews as "the most historical people". . . . I defined the content of Jewish history strictly idealistically: the story of a people—of believers—in the first half, and the story of a people—thinkers and ascetics—in the second half. The foundation of the national idea was "historical consciousness," this spiritual territory of the Diaspora.

This concept made it possible for Dubnov, a recent critic of rabbinism, to find historical justification for the Talmud, which was now presented as a huge arsenal where the spiritual armaments of a spiritual nation were kept.

"Yesterday evening I finished the introduction," an entry in his diary says, "much energy has been expended on the work. And I think I have achieved my goal of formulating a historical philosophy and a historical credo, albeit on a small scale." To this last line he added some time later, "A philosophy? No. A credo? Yes." This addendum was made in a period of self-criticism when Dubnov had come to understand that his past attempt at a synthesis could be called "a poetry of history" rather than a philosophy.

The Book of My Life observes that the "historicist lyricism" set out in essay form pleased readers not so much by its learning as by its emotional resonance. Subsequently the study "What Is Jewish History?" enjoyed great popularity in the West; it was reprinted twice in German translation and also came out in English and American editions.

The introduction, suffused by deep national feeling, found no approval among the circle of men who had undertaken to publish Graetz's *History of the Jews*. A majority of the members of the Committee of Enlightenment objected to the emphasis placed on the idea of a spiritual nation; they were also afraid that the young historian's impassioned, hortatory manner would provoke the censor's displeasure. The arguments dragged on and on. Finally, seeing no possibility of reaching an agreement, Dubnov resigned his duties as editor. In any event, Graetz's work was not fated to appear in print. The censor sent the first volume, which had already been printed, to the ecclesiastical censor, who saw a departure from tradition in the free interpretation of biblical passages and declared that the entire edition must be destroyed. That decision was confirmed by the notorious Procurator of the Holy Synod, Pobedonostsev, one of the pillars of reaction. Petitions were of no avail; five thousand copies of the banned book were committed to the flames. However, Dubnov considered himself Graetz's heir and did not give up his plan to popularize Jewish history. Some time later he realized this plan, but in a different form.

11

Workd and Dayd

Dubnov's working day began between eight and nine o'clock in the morning. The tightly closed door separated him from the noise of the children, the clatter of cooking, and domestic bustle. He worked especially intensively in the morning hours; then, according to his strictly observed daily routine, he went for a walk. But even during the walk—mainly along the avenues of the nearby seaside park—his thoughts would return persistently to the manuscript he had left at home, and jottings in precise, round letters appeared in the pages of his notebook.

However hard Dubnov tried to isolate himself from daily life, he did not always succeed. The indigent writer could not permit himself the luxury of complete immersion in learning. He was more keenly aware than ever before of the burden of endless scrimping and uncertainty about the next day. Accustomed to deprivation from his earliest years, he was not afraid for himself. However, concern about his wife and small children weighed heavily on his soul and forced him to fight even more tenaciously than in former years with the editor, who took advantage of his monopoly over the Russian-Jewish press. An entry in his diary in October 1892 is full of sadness: "To live by literary work alone, cleaving to my sacred purposes, putting my soul into every piece—that would be a triumph akin to martyrdom. It often seems to me that I cannot endure it and that I will collapse in the ruins of my work, without having done even a part of that which constitutes the meaning of my life."

Finally, exasperated by his boss's stubbornness, Dubnov revolted and went on strike. Breaking off work at *Voskhod*, he began to consider a plan for a periodical where he could systematically publish the results of his research along with papers by other writers. His writer friends were sympathetic to the idea but none of the wealthy Odessa patrons would agree to subsidize a new literary enterprise. Moreover, on learning of local conditions, Dubnov came to the conclusion that "the Odessa censor was not far removed from the Inquisition."

Simon had to end the strike when his five-year-old son fell seriously ill, and money was urgently needed for his care. In January 1893 he reached a new agreement with the editor of *Voskhod*. Dubnov was to continue his contributions in full, including the criticism column. His monthly salary was set at one hundred roubles; the money barely sufficed to keep a family of five.

Having paid his due to the worries about getting his daily bread, the hermit shut himself up in his cell again. A voluminous correspondence told of his progress in collecting materials. With a feeling of relief he buried himself in reading manuscripts. But there was no escape from everyday life for a wife and mother. Each day brought Ida new money worries. She accepted this hard lot with the same outward calm as generations of her foremothers, who had cleared the path to the Torah for their husbands with their unremitting toil, energy, and self-denial; but her physical strength was sapped by endless grappling with want. Ida Dubnov withered and dried up before her time. Sleepless nights ringed her eyes with dark shadows; bitter lines framed her tightly pressed lips. While her husband was deep in the study of an ancient *pinkes*, an unpaid grocer's bill or a hole in her small son's shoe stared her in the face.

Ida's working day began in the dull half-light of morning, while the children were still asleep. Late into evening the lamp illuminated her head with its wispy, ash-gray hair, bent over a pile of torn stockings and linen. Life was uncomfortable, difficult, bumpy as a ride over ruts and potholes —the stove, stoked with damp wood, smoked; the kerosene lamp with a crooked wick gave off fumes; the peasant maid rudely banged at the door, with little respect for the penniless "masters"; her children coughed in the cold house. But late at night, when the house was sunk in sleep, the head of the family tidily arranged his manuscript, sheet by sheet, and hid it in a drawer of his desk. Then they both went off to their own room, where Ida read aloud to him from the latest issues of journals, contemporary Russian novels, and volume after volume of Emile Zola's novel-chronicles. And then they talked in whispers about what they had read, about the children, whose characters were becoming more and more distinctive, about the day's impressions. Sometimes they made plans for the future, always returning to the project for a trip, just the two of them, to some solitary spot suffused with peace, fragrance, and sunlight. And a luminous mirage of rest shimmered before the exhausted couple at the end of the day.

So the days passed. Simon, immersed in sources for eight centuries of the history of the Jews of Eastern Europe, was composing a chronology of events. He shared the results of his research with the readers of *Voskhod* in a special column called "Historical Report." The series of articles on Hasidism, published over the course of six years, was now finished. Their author dreamed of making use of the new material accumulated in those years and publishing a large work, but there was neither time nor means for that.

As he was writing his "Report," Dubnov endeavored to enliven the dry material and make it accessible to the ordinary reader. He had no use for the narrow professionalism of scientific facts addressed only to experts. In the introduction to this new cycle of articles, to be published over several years, he distanced himself from "scholars with a limited intellectual horizon, who strive to turn the most vital of all sciences . . . into a museum mummy." "History," he writes, "is the learning of the people, for the people, and therefore it cannot be a narrowly professional science. . . . We work for the goal of the people's self-knowledge." "The most vital of all sciences" ruled the young historian's soul not only by virtue of its cognitive and ideological function. The animation of the past by creative imagination provided an outlet for that secret need which had dwelled in him from his early years and tried, unsuccessfully, to find expression in the unfinished poems scattered through the pages of his diary.

Dubnov had to interrupt his historical work to write the surveys of current literature. In 1893 he began to publish a series of articles called "The Literature of the Time of Troubles." He pointed to indications of new forms of national self-determination appearing in Jewish journalism. Ahad Ha-Am's initiative in trying to create an ideology of Neo-Palestinism seemed the most significant. At the basis of this ideology lay the idea that Palestine could not be transformed into a true sanctuary for the Jews, but must become a spiritual center of Jewry. Ahad Ha-Am was covertly polemicizing with the theses of the essay "On the Study of History" by warning against being overly involved in the past of the people at the expense of the future.

Such covert polemics between the friends were not uncommon. Only about four years later did they expand into open combat between spiritual Zionism and Autonomism.

If his polemics with the father of spiritual Zionism were restrained, Dubnov gave free rein to his emotionalism whenever he was forced to come out against reactionary ideologues like B. Javitz, who hysterically howled "Back to the ghetto!" and demanded the repudiation of Europeanism and a return to the fold of Rabbinical Orthodoxy. This polemic, in which the term "spiritual nation" appeared more and more frequently, did not satisfy Dubnov. More than once he felt the need to elaborate his opinions, the fruit of his study of Jewish history, in more detail. "I realize," he writes in September 1893, "that my synthesis is too short and too compressed. I dream of developing it by applying it not only to the past but also to the present in the series 'Letters on Old and New Jewry.' This subject has long preoccupied me, but I must wait."

During the time which is referred to in Dubnov's autobiography as the "period of synthesis," the union of the historian seeking truth and the journalist seeking justice was finally forged in the writer's soul. The temperament of the social activist needed wider, more sustained, and direct contact with people than that which satisfied the closeted scholar. Hence, Dubnov was obliged to leave the bounds of his narrow literary circle. The doors of his book-lined study were flung wide open to new people, mainly young men. With his characteristic methodicalness, he allotted regular hours for conversation with his visitors, including them in his daily working schedule.

The most frequent visitors to the Dubnov's house at that time were the young externs of obscure social origin, recent graduates of the *khadorim* and the yeshivas. These young men had left their homes and condemned themselves to hunger and cold not only for the sake of knowledge; they were trying to escape the lethargy of provincial existence. As he looked at these skinny, ragged youths wiping their battered shoes in the hall with embarassment, Simon Dubnov remembered the trying, hungry times in Dvinsk and Smolensk. As one of the writers who joined a committee in order to help these autodidacts, he really understood these young men and experienced their emotions. The externs interested Abramovich very little; his artist's curiosity drew him only to fully-formed, "finished" people. The splenetic Ben-Ammi looked at the voluntary martyrs of learning and muttered angrily, "When these lads pick up an arithmetic book they read on the first page, 'There is no God.'" Dubnov understood that his shy visitors came to see him not only for material but also for spiritual aid, and he had long conversations with them about the meaning of life and serving the people.

Some of the new people were also encountered in another setting. In the spring of 1894 Dubnov gave several lectures in Kharkov before a large audience of members of the intelligentsia. He set out the theory of cultural-historical nationalism coherently for the first time. "I began," he writes in his autobiography, "by defining nationality as collective individuality. . . . Then I spoke of the four stages of the Jewish national idea, from primitive racial unity, through state and religious unity, to contemporary cultural unity in a free national union." In conclusion he developed the idea that contemporary Jewry was passing from the thesis of tradition, through the antithesis of assimilation, toward a synthesis of progressive national ideology. The lecture sparked a substantive debate. Even livelier was an exchange of opinions at a colloquium organized by students and young people of different ideological orientations. Objections were raised in various quarters. Some found a national ideal without Palestine too abstract, others rejected the very idea of struggling for national self-preservation, promoting instead social struggle and participation in the all-Russian revolutionary movement.

Sometime later, similar colloquia were organized in Odessa, too. Despite being overburdened with literary work, Dubnov considered constant association with the wavering, searching young people a duty. "I feel that at such a time I cannot fulfil my duties toward the people by literary work alone . . . it is necessary to rouse thinking men, let them support and rescue the spirit of the people." A plan for organizing a historical and literary student circle was proposed, but the pressures of work prevented Dubnov from participating in the young people's gatherings. Meanwhile the members of the circle dispersed; some joined the Zionist party, which had just drafted its constitution at the the First Zionist Congress in Basle; others joined the newly formed Bund.[28]

Every detail and every aspect of the concepts on which the colloquia had focused were developed in articles published in *Voskhod*. Dubnov maintained that the idea of building cultural centers in the Diaspora was practicable. Its supporters would work with whatever already existed, and they would continue to spin and weave the centuries-old thread of Jewish history while the Zionists were creating a utopian ideal of a new Judea. The spiritual territory created by history was more real than a nonexistent physical territory.

Simon's contribution to public life did not prevent him from continuing to gather new materials. Vladimir Dubnov was his most loyal assistant in this task. Traveling frequently to Odessa from the neighboring town where he lived and worked as a schoolteacher, Vladimir diligently rummaged through the town library and made extracts from ancient Russian publications. The younger brother shared his literary plans with the older and always found a sensitive reception. A failure in his personal life, Vladimir knew how to enter wholeheartedly into the involvements of those close to him, helping them disinterestedly and selflessly. Simon valued that quality, and the days his brother spent in his house in serious conversation or playing with the children he considered among the best times of his life in Odessa.

In discussing their work plans, the brothers often returned to the question of whether there was any point in working in any particular area of history while there was still no general survey of Jewish history in Russian. The attempt to translate Graetz had collapsed. Along with Graetz's massive work there were now more modest studies from the West, for example Dr. Samuel Bäck's short *History of the Jewish People* and a two-volume survey by Marcus Brann, a professor at the Breslau seminary. Both books needed revising: Bäck was too elementary, while Brann reduced the history of the Jewish people to the history of rabbinical learning. Dubnov finally decided to publish a one-volume, condensed survey of Jewish history to be based on the work of both scholars. But the more involved he became in the work, the stronger became his desire to abandon this confining format and compose a history from primary sources and specialized monographs. The scope of the book grew, and the material had to be presented in two volumes instead of one. When the book came out, Ahad Ha-Am observed that the names of the German scholars were really the pseudonyms of the real author.

As he worked diligently at this compilation Dubnov tried to snatch time for original research. Studies on ritual murder trials and on the Jews in Poland during the Reformation were based on new materials. An article on Frankism published in *Voskhod* in 1896 was a significantly revised version of work Dubnov had done in his youth. It was becoming clear to the attentive reader how far the writer had developed since 1883. Dozens of enticing new subjects thronged his brain, but there was not enough time for them; printing a two-volume work presented typographical and distributional problems. Dubnov was obliged to recognize that he was unequal to these practical tasks. Nor were his financial expectations fulfilled, as the low price of the book cut the author's honorarium to a minimum. Two years of intensive work had still not freed him from acute financial worries and had seriously undermined his health. He writes in his autobiography,

> Attacks of dizziness, oscillation between nervous excitement and depression, and a kind of feeble listlessness, all this testified to a deep nervous disorder and the need for prolonged rest. I felt so drained of strength that I could not even manage a research trip across the Pale of Settlement which I had envisioned by way of a rest after completing the main work.

Finally he decided to take advantage of a small grant awarded by the Society for Enlightenment in consideration of his fifteen years of literary activity, and seek a cure. On the eve of his journey abroad, Dubnov went off to his native town for several weeks.

12

Between Journalism and Poetry

> One moment more—the fairy tale
> is gone,
> And again the soul is filled with the
> possible. . . .
> —Afanasy Afansevich Fet

Dubnov's native town greeted the wanderer with soft patches of sunlight amid the new greenery along the town avenue, with the singing of birds in the branches of the old maples. After seven years of separation it was a great joy to breathe the slow northern spring with its pungent fresh smells. His mother came out onto the porch, aged and wizened, in a baggy, black jacket. She dissolved into tears as, with wrinkled hands, she embraced her pale son and her rosy-cheeked granddaughter. Simon's friendly sisters, middle-aged now, smiled shyly at the visitors. The rooms were small and cozy, with rugs laid neatly on the floor and windows flung open to the tender shoots growing in the garden. But the visitor could not sit at home once he had arrived. He was burning with impatience to see and show his daughter the places connected with his childhood memories. With deep emotion he entered the local *beys-medresh*, where in years gone by he had chanted texts from the Bible and the Talmud and later recited Lebensohn's poetry. The spirits of the past accompanied him everywhere. He wrote in his diary,

> I look, I experience and I recall, and I sense something infinitely sad but at the same time infinitely heart-warming in the quiet, drowsy life of this Jewish kingdom which . . . cannot be destroyed by any persecutions or pogroms. I was at the *shulhoyf*: the same pitiful houses, ragged children in the streets, sleepy women dozing on the steps of their little shops, the same mournful voices from the *khadorim* and the yeshivas.

The carefree summer days flew by in walks and unhurried conversations with Dubnov's family and the few childhood friends who had remained in this provincial backwater. The Dubnov sisters ran a small library; there Simon drew a battered and much-read volume of Turgenev from a row of books in worn bindings. Seated on the little garden bench, the tired man lifted his face to the warm breeze. Golden bees droned softly in the bushes, and his twelve-year-old daughter read aloud lines drenched in the fragrance of timid spring.

The journey abroad, the first of Dubnov's life, offered new and un-dreamed of sights. Galicia—with its ancient Jewish quarters and its nests of Hasidism, where the past still lived in the houses and in the people who kept their traditional appearance—was the gateway to the West. The traveler passed through Zloczów, Zbaraz, and other historic centers of Ha-sidism. In the forests and mountain ravines flashing by the train window he seemed to see the spirits of the first *tsadikim* praying and gathering medicinal herbs in the mountain valleys. These spirits melted away in the dazzling glitter of the sun on the snows of the Alpine peaks. A Swiss neuropathologist diagnosed symptoms of brain exhaustion in Dubnov and prescribed living in the mountains and a regime of complete rest.

Dubnov settled in Itliberg, high above Zurich, in the middle of a pine forest. Luminous, resinous stillness surrounded him, and the sharp, snow-covered peaks, outlined against a sky touched with pink, shut in the hori-zon and blocked the path to care and worry. A fairy-tale life began: the mountain train with cog wheels climbed like a cat along the crags, ripples washed across lakes in unearthly colors, waterfalls foamed down rocky ledges, valleys glittered green, bottomless chasms gaped suddenly beneath rickety little bridges. A relative and old friend, Robert Zaichik—a Zurich professor, an aesthete attracted to Catholicism and familiar with Nietzsche and the Renaissance—proved an excellent guide through Switzerland. The arguments he and Dubnov had during their walks touched on eternal ques-tions and were peaceful; they did not disturb the magnificent calm of nature.

French Switzerland—with its vineyards, tiny houses, and the deep-azure lakes—breathed gentle enchantment over the visitor. In quiet Neu-châtel, in the foothills of the forest-clad Jura, Dubnov said to his compan-ion, "This is where I would like to spend all my days in thought and work." From distant Switzerland he brought to his unsettling, anxious life in Odessa a dream of uniting work with the contemplation of nature; henceforth that dream never left him.

Returning to Odessa was like waking from a wonderful dream. Personal worries and community troubles immediately clamored for at-tention. The year 1897 opened a new era in the life of Russian Jewry. Zion-ist circles had sprung up in many towns, basing their activities on the Basle program.[29] The Jewish Social Democratic Party, the "Bund," was founded at the same time. In these circumstances Dubnov felt a compelling need to systematize the ideas he had once formulated in his Kharkov lec-tures and in conversations with Odessa students. This was the origin of the series of articles written over five years and called "Letters on Old and New Jewry." Dubnov later characterized that five-year period as one of national-humanistic synthesis, which finally defined his concept of the past and his attitude toward contemporary problems.

Heated quarrels now broke out constantly at the meetings of the literary circle. A group of Zionists who attacked Ahad Ha-Am for criticizing Herzl's vision of political Zionism[30] were particularly unruly. Dubnov listened to these arguments and was confirmed in his belief that the time had come to examine the national question in all its ramifications. The first two Letters were written in October and November 1897. An attentive reader could have discerned notes of remorse in the introduction, which spoke of the necessity of reexamining old opinions: "Each man should declare with complete sincerity what lessons he has drawn from past mistakes and what corrections he has been able to make in his world view; he should not take pride in persisting in mistakes . . . that force a man to profess outwardly a faith he has rejected in his soul." Dubnov also insisted that in discussing the Jewish question it was necessary to proceed not only on the basis of present circumstances but also from all the accumulated data of the past. The first Letter defined nationalism as collective individualism. Dubnov's other basic thesis was the proposition that factors of race and state were less essential in the development of nationality than spiritual and cultural-historical ones. The clearest proof of this was the Jewish "spiritual nation," which manifested a stubborn will to live though it rested neither on territory nor on state machinery.

The second Letter appeared at the beginning of 1898 and met resistance from both wings of the Jewish community. It directly raised the question of assimilation, which Dubnov declared not only theoretically inadequate but also morally defective in condoning "desertion of the besieged camp." All the Zionists could offer to counter the assimilation process was the slogan "Let's go home!" Opposing that solution of the Jewish question, the Letter posited the Jewish people's historical right to the European lands where it had dwelled since the fall of the Roman Empire. For the first time in Jewish writings the demand for civic equality was linked to the postulate of "national rights."

The views set forth in the first Letters became the subject of discussion in various groups and in the press. Ahad Ha-Am subjected the theses of "Dubnovism" to detailed analysis in a number of articles published in the journal *Ha-Shilo'ah*. The third Letter, "Spiritual Nationalism and Zionism," was a reply partly to the literary and partly to the oral polemic. Dubnov objected to the assertion that Jewish nationalism necessarily led to Zionism and declared: "I do not have to be a Palestinophile to be a Jew." The fanaticism of "the heathen of nationalism" (as he called the extreme political Zionists) provoked serious misgivings in him. If the choice offered was one between Palestine or the destruction of Jewry, disillusionment with Zionism would inevitably lead to assimilation.

It was difficult for Dubnov to engage in scholarly work in the tense atmosphere of public bickering. As before, everyday cares absorbed a good deal of energy. The family's financial position remained precarious; Dubnov's work at *Voskhod* did not guarantee a living wage. Simon considered other possibilities of earning money, such as writing for the local daily press, but found them unacceptable. Finally he took Abramovich's advice and decided to put together a textbook of Jewish history, for which there would be a steady demand. Without any real enthusiasm, but with his customary energy and methodical approach, he set to work. The textbook justified the hopes pinned on it; the family's financial position improved somewhat over the next few years.

Dubnov's adolescent children required more attention than before. On the eve of his first child's entry into the world, Simon had diligently prepared himself for the role of a father by reading a stack of books on pedagogy. He had set to work with great zeal to practice the precepts of the English psychologists. The birth of a second daughter and then a son had coincided with a period of depression brought on by unsuccessful attempts to settle in the capital and a serious eye disease. The main burden of caring for the new members of the family fell on their mother. The children were totally dissimilar: Olga grew up a boisterous, healthy, rosy-cheeked girl, a leader of noisy games; Yasha was an earnest, self-possessed little boy, always occupied with some work or other. Both children entered the gymnasium early. The older daughter, Sophie, stayed at home until the age of fourteen; her father taught her himself, ignoring the school curriculum. Enthusiastically he taught her the Bible, world history, and literature, trying to instill in her a love of what he valued himself. A love of poetry drew father and daughter especially close together. There was an established family custom of reading poetry one evening a week. Books were piled up on the dining table under the hanging lamp: Pushkin, Lermontov, Nekrasov, Tiutchev, Fet.[31] The nearly forty-year-old man with graying hair and the young girl, intoxicated with the music of poetry, forgot everything else in the world. Ida sat at the table with her sewing or knitting and looked askance at the initiator of these poetic orgies: "What next! Turning a girl's head with love poetry, indeed!"

The next morning would find Dubnov at his customary work. By the summer of 1898 he had finished the first part of the textbook and went to Polesia to see Marcus Kagan, a friend from his youth. The spacious house on the banks of the Sozh River stood next to a sawmill. The regular screeching of saws and the cries of the raftsmen poured in through the low window of the writer's room. Dubnov felt at ease, surrounded by the large, patriarchal, hospitable family. During table talk the friends often returned to that distant time when they had both approached literature with trembling hearts. Dubnov wandered for hours without getting tired through mossy glades, sometimes alone, sometimes in the company of chattering children and their young teacher, Vera G., a gentle, melancholy, reticent girl. In those intoxicating days of languorous heat he responded to the familiar landscape in a new and special way. Never before had such a strong longing for joy and harmony filled the ascetic toiler's soul.

Each day I walked into the pine forest, which rose like a high wall beyond the rye field adjoining our courtyard. . . . I entered . . . the jaws of the forest as though entering the semi-darkness of a sacred temple, and walked between colonnades of pines to a steep descent to a meadow beyond which the smooth surface of the river glittered in the sunlight. And along with the cult of nature, my ideal of a harmony of physical and intellectual labor was reborn. I worked in the carpentry shop at the sawmill.

A distant upheaval took place in his rigorously ordered, work-filled life. Youth, with its romantic dreams and its "Turgenevian" moods, was behind him. His life had taken shape, but suddenly, in moonlit nights over the quiet Sozh and sunlit noontides fragrant with the aroma of pine needles, rebellion against extreme intellectualism and asceticism flared up. This rebellion passed away, as did the writer's "midsummer night's dream" in the Polesia retreat. A secret longing, which was not soon stilled, and an aspiration to unite the cult of nature with the cult of history remained. "Since then," he writes in *The Book of My Life*, "I have been powerfully drawn to that amalgam of pantheism and historicism, which gave me spiritual support on the next stage of my journey through the gathering social storms."

When Dubnov returned to Odessa he wandered through the hot, dusty streets as though he had come from another world. Partisan disputes swirled around him; the young people insistently demanded the continuation of the "Letters on Old and New Jewry." To quell his longing Dubnov again buried himself in the history of Hasidism and wrote a long introduction to the future major study, entitled "The Social and Spiritual Life of Jews in Poland in the Eighteenth Century." In this study he described Hasidism as a teaching from which one becomes "darker of head and lighter of heart" (Heine's words on love). As Dubnov worked on the article he found himself in an exalted "Hasidic" mood. But the prose of life exacted its due; next came work on the second part of the textbook.

13

Thoughts on Old and New Jewry

In the spring of 1894, after a year-long interval, Dubnov again felt the need to enter the battle of ideas being fought all about him and returned to the "Letters." The immediate impetus was the Dreyfus affair,[32] which had unmasked the bestial face of French chauvinism. The activities of the anti-Dreyfus clique inevitably raised the question of the moral and political evaluation of different brands of nationalism. The new Letter was devoted to this problem. Its author insisted on making a strict distinction between aggressive and defensive nationalism, between national egoism and national individualism. He claimed that confusing the different forms of nationalism was as great an error as putting Hus,[33] who was burned for his faith, and Torquemada,[34] who burned others for his faith, in the same category. Vindicating the ethical value of the national idea as it was correctly understood, he described the assimilation process as moral capitulation; such idealists of assimilation as Riesser[35] and Lazarus[36] were exceptions to the general rule.

The main target of the fourth Letter was the extremism of political Zionism as expressed in the speeches of Max Nordau,[37] one of the leaders of the movement, and the author of the sensational *Degeneration*. When he went over to the Zionist camp, he began indiscriminately accusing public figures in the Diaspora of servility, of being ready, in the words of the Latin aphorism, "to lose the meaning of life for the sake of life." His shallow disregard of historical conditions appeared to Dubnov to be a kind of "inner assimilation"; he called Zionists of Nordau's type "contingent nationalists." Dubnov encapsulated the difference between the three main currents of Jewry in a brief formula: the assimilationists considered Jews a nation of the past; the political Zionists, a nation of the future; and the supporters of "spiritual nationalism," not only a nation of the past and of the future, but also a nation of the present. The editor of *Voskhod* did not share his long-time contributor's views and furnished his essay, as he had done on more than one occasion, with a disclaimer.

Russian-Jewish journalism enjoyed a period of renewed vitality in the second half of the nineties. *Voskhod* had passed into the hands of a group of young, mainly pronationalist literati. Another periodical, *Budushchnost'*,[38] had also appeared and attempted to reflect the different currents of Jewish opinion evenhandedly. Dubnov gave in to persistent requests and wrote an article for the new journal, "Changing Trends in Russian-Jewish Journalism," drawing up a balance sheet of the past forty years. He outlined the development and elaboration of the ideas of Enlightenment and equality up to the time when these ideas culminated in the humanitarian-national synthesis.

The article's principal theses provided the basis for a public lecture, and they were then debated at length at public discussions. The arguments, which became fractious at times, greatly distressed old Abramovich, who disliked polemic. He emphasized his neutrality and his "nonparty" stance, repeating firmly, "I am neither an assimilationist nor a nationalist, simply a Jew." Such ideological neutrality was incomprehensible to the author of the "Letters," who was fighting a battle on two fronts. The debate with the Zionists was conducted mainly in print. Objections of a different kind were more frequently raised at public meetings. People with close ties to Russian culture and society reproached the speaker for trying to wrench the Jews out of the surrounding society. The apostle of "spiritual nationalism" answered them with great fervor. Without even realizing it, Dubnov was battling his former self, the youthful enthusiast who had read Buckle and declared himself a cosmopolite.

Toward the end of a year devoted to journalism, Dubnov began to yearn for historical work. An anthology containing a large selection of valuable material published by the St. Petersburg Historical-Ethnographic Committee gave him great pleasure. Maxim Vinaver,[39] the chairman of the committee, who had recently become prominent as a gifted jurist and a public figure, sent the book to Dubnov. Vinaver said that the essay "On the Study of History," published in *Voskhod* eight years before, had been the impetus for the collection. In the introduction the editors stated that by studying historical documents the young members of the intelligentsia would come in contact with "Mother Earth" and "gain that steadiness and self-sufficiency which gives life its inestimable value." Dubnov was elated by these assertions: "They have justified my recent appeal to the intelligentsia to become one with the people through the study of history; I sensed the growth of a new intelligentsia risen from the people, an intelligentsia with whom I would soon be destined to work in literature and in public life."

In November 1899 the American publishers Funk and Wagnalls proposed that Dubnov respond to a questionnaire about the historical role of the creator of Christianity. His response set out a concept developed by analogy with early Hasidism. Dubnov asserted that research into the Besht's activities was the key to understanding the teachings of Jesus. Both men—Jesus of Nazareth and Israel Baal-Shem-Tov of Podolia—had rebelled against religious rigidity and formalism; both had turned to the common man with their preachings and put faith above law. Jesus spoke to his contemporaries in the grip of political passions about the "kingdom of God within us"; the Besht had inspired his followers, who had become dispirited by the failure of the Sabbatian movement, by preaching that the persecuted Diaspora Jew could attain spiritual bliss through communion with God. Dubnov expressed his conviction that under different historical circumstances "Jesus would have become the creator that the Besht later became, of religious pietism *within* Judaism. . . . But the teachings of Jesus went beyond the bounds of Judaism and subsequently became contaminated by foreign, pagan elements." The Jews, struggling to preserve their nation, could not accept his teachings. The Zealots did not want to give up the political struggle, or the Pharisees national discipline.

Two years later, at the request of the initiators of the inquiry, Dubnov answered a question on the attitude of contemporary Jews toward the figure of Jesus. He stated once more that he considered Jesus a Jewish prophet who had propounded his teachings to fellow Jews at the same time that Paul was trying to convert the heathen. The progressive Jewish intelligentsia, he asserted, saw in Jesus one of the best sons of the people, a herald of love and forgiveness. But it was difficult to ask historical objectivity of the ordinary Jew, who was in no position to forget that his forefathers had for centuries been the victims of cruel reprisals perpetrated in the name of Jesus.

Dubnov spent the winter of 1899–1900 at work on a long monograph, *The Inner Life of the Jews in Poland and Lithuania in the Sixteenth Century*. He wanted to draw a picture of Jewish life in the age of the greatest flowering of the Polish-Lithuanian center, based on primary sources (rabbinical responsa and the community *pinkeysim*). He spent long hours among ancient folios, winnowing the grains of daily life from the chaff of the convoluted casuistry of rabbinical edicts and impassioned synagogue sermons. But soon he had to interrupt this greatly satisfying work, for a new edition of *World History of the Jewish People* awaited. Dubnov decided to add to the first two volumes a third which would be devoted to the biblical period and based on the latest findings of biblical research.

An entry in his diary in February 1900 speaks of his future plans:

Today as Ida and I were sunning ourselves in the park, I dreamed about my future activity. Here are my dreams. 1900–1901—publish the revised edition of the *World History of the Jewish People*. . .; 1902—*History of Hasidism*; 1903–1904—a collection of my critical essays; 1905—selected historical monographs; and 1906, on the twenty-fifth anniversary of my literary activity, turn to the *History of the Russian Jews*. The second twenty-five years of labor must be devoted to that work. In 1906 we will also move to a little house with a garden and a vegetable plot in some corner of Polesia. There I will occupy myself for half the day with historical work and for the other half with manual labor and gardening. To live out the remainder of my life with Nature and History, in the wheat field of God and on the heights of creativity—that is my sole desire.

The dream of work in the bosom of nature never left him. The notes for the biblical volume of the *History* were written in the park, on a hill planted with cypress trees. In the summer, in his favorite corner of Polesia, Dubnov worked diligently at a table knocked together from planks, by a window looking out onto a wide, green forest glade. In the evenings, during his walks with Marcus Kagan, the master of the house, and Ahad Ha-Am, who was also spending the summer in the wilds of Polesia, he shared his ideas on the latest methods of Bible study. The result of this work was a new volume of the *History*, which appeared at the end of 1900.

An entry made during the New Year of 1901 was born of anxious reflections:

> We are entering the twentieth century. What will it bring us, mankind in general and Jews in particular? Judging by the history of the last decades of the past century, one might think that mankind is entering a new Middle Ages, what with the horrors of war and national struggle, and the destruction of the highest ethical principles in politics and private life. But I do not want to believe in such overgeneralizations. The current, vile wave of reaction must bring a counterreaction. The eighteenth century was the age of intellectual revolutions, the nineteenth century—the age of political revolutions and scientific and intellectual progress. The twentieth century must bring a moral revolution. An ethical revolution in the conscience of the majority, now corrupted by the growth of materialistic culture at the expense of spiritual culture, must take place.

Intense work in his study prevented Dubnov from examining more carefully what was going on around him. When he made his prognosis for the immediate future, he overlooked the growth of the revolutionary movement. Meanwhile signs of social dissatisfaction became increasingly visible. In the winter and spring of 1901 the unrest found an outlet in mass student demonstrations and strikes. The response from on high was vicious police repression and harassment of the independent press. Within the Jewish community the growth of national consciousness paralleled the spread of revolutionary sympathies. In Odessa, considered one of the most active Jewish centers, a process of differentiation among the intelligentsia became apparent. The recent theoretical discussions betwen nationalists and assimilationists at meetings of the Society of Enlightenment led to open conflict in connection with the practical question of a program for national Jewish schools subsidized by the Society. Dubnov reluctantly found himself in the middle of a battle raging around the question of national education.

In the mid-nineties a cohesive group had sprung from within the Society, demanding greater emphasis on teaching Jewish history and literature and Hebrew. The aim of this group was to create a new kind of school, one with a distinctively national orientation. The Society's executive committee still adhered to the principle of Russian schooling for Jewish children. In response to the opposition's demand it declared that nationalist education was incompatible with a general European education. A bitter confrontation erupted at the next general meeting, in the spring of 1901. Distressed by the acrimonious polemics and attacks of a personal nature, Dubnov tried in vain to shift the discussion to questions of principle. He objected to the distinction between the "Jewish" and the "universal" element in instruction:

> Not one living nation makes such a distinction; for the universal is always attained through the national, and if we do not have the option of teaching in the national *language*, we must at least strengthen the national *content* of the curriculum. For a nation in Diaspora, isn't a national education a surrogate for territory? The school must be a shield against the assimilationist influence of society and not only a purveyor of "useful information." It has moral and spiritual as well as utilitarian tasks.

There was an uproar in the community and the press in the wake of this meeting. It was the beginning of that movement which Dubnov dubbed a Kulturkampf. The Zionists and the nationalists united to form the Committee of Nationalization, which set itself the task of fighting to strengthen the national element in Jewish social institutions and, above all, in schools. The followers of Ahad Ha-Am occupied the center of the organization; the political Zionists and the "Dubnovists" occupied the extreme wings.

Speaking at meetings took up a great deal of Dubnov's time and energy. Nevertheless, he finished the third part of the textbook, devoted to the Middle Ages and the modern period in good time. This part of the textbook was banned in the schools because its contents incurred the censor's displeasure. The author was accused of "trying . . . to highlight the virtues of Jews and play down . . . the dark side of their activities, which explain the enmity of other races toward them." The bureaucratic censors were particularly troubled by the chapters containing criticism of governmental measures with respect to Jews. The censor's ban wrecked the writer's plans. The first two parts of the textbook had been adopted for use in the schools, but the third had not, and only a few teachers used it, in secret.

Dubnov was accustomed to bearing practical setbacks stoically. He was far more upset by the thought that his incidental work meant postponing the long-planned, major undertaking indefinitely. Nevertheless he did not think it right to turn his back on attempts to popularize Jewish history. When a Jewish Encyclopedia in English began to come out in America he considered it his duty to assist the new publication and fulfilled the obligations of consulting editor for a number of years.

In the summer of 1901 the Dubnovs left the dust of Bazarnaia Street and moved into a small, isolated house with a garden on a quiet side street by the sea; the blue of the sea sparkled through green trees. Worn out by the strain of work and the city tumult, Simon put his library and archive in order and went first to Polesia and then to his native town. He immediately realized how much the sleepy, Jewish backwater had changed over the past few years. Political arguments seethed everywhere, and on his arrival he was besieged by visitors craving to exchange ideas. The changes in his family circle were less noticeable. The modest house in which his family lived seemed to have decayed even more and to have sunk deeper into the ground. His mother was sad and coughed continuously, nor were his taciturn, aging sisters happy. Low-key conversations about the perpetual lack of money, about dead and living relatives, took place around the samovar. When Simon bade his mother farewell the old woman wept bitterly, as though she sensed that this was their last meeting. She died soon after, of the same illness which had taken her husband to the grave. When Simon left Mstislavl he did not suspect that he had seen his mother and his native town for the last time.

On his return to Odessa he threw himself into journalism again. He had to finish the theoretical part of the "Letters" and move on to more topical matters. In these autumn days he wrote the article "A Divided and a United National Party" (*Voskhod*, 1901, No. 11) in his spacious study, in which he could hear the distant murmur of the sea. The subject was dictated by the activities of the recently formed Committee of Nationalization. Dubnov was convinced that a single national party embracing the various factions was essential. He feared that, as a result of Zionist separatism, the energies needed to help the millions of Jews would be channeled entirely into the creation of a sanctuary for a small segment of the people.

In the next Letter, entitled "Autonomism, the Basis of a National Program" (*Voskhod*, 1901, No. 12), the central idea of the cycle of essays as a whole was formulated. In articulating the principle of "cultural-national autonomy," Dubnov concretized for the first time his vague demand for "national rights," which had been proclaimed three years earlier. In connection with the new concept he further developed his favorite idea of the dialectical triad in more detail. He saw the nineteenth century as the century of the war against the national-religious thesis, which had isolated Jews from the outside world and stifled individual freedom for centuries. The emergence of the individual Jew, as a protest against the despotism of the collective, was the antithesis which marked this century. The protest proved one-sided, however, for in humanizing the Jew, it also denationalized him. The establishment of a harmony between humanism and nationalism was to be the twentieth century's task. In this century Jews were to know themselves as a cultural, historical, freely self-determining nation. The national community would encompass religious Jews as well as nonbelievers; it would become a self-governing entity. Such a secularized community would be a more effective instrument of national unification than the traditional community, which automatically excluded the free-thinking intelligentsia. The union of autonomous communities in each country and an "International Jewish Union of Communities" would become the highest representative bodies of a nation scattered throughout different countries.

When Dubnov formulated his concept of "autonomism" he did not then know of the recently published work of the Austrian Social Democrat Renner-Springer, creator of the theory of "personal autonomy" for nonterritorial nations.[40] "I arrived," he writes in *The Book of My Life*, "completely independently at the same solution to the same question which was later, after the World War, formulated still more simply: the autonomy of national minorities. It goes without saying that this system is predicated on international recognition of the Jews as a living, single, worldwide nationality."

Dubnov went still further in spelling out the idea of national autonomy in his next article, devoted to the problem of national education (*Voskhod*, 1902, No. 1). Drawing his examples from the life of contemporary Western Jews, he showed the deep, spiritual duality of those who belonged to Jewry by birth but to another people by education and culture. This duality had lately become particularly agonizing as a result of the growth of anti-Semitic sentiment in many countries in Europe. To the author of the "Letters" the only way out of this abnormal situation was for the younger generation to substitute cultural nationality for "blood" nationality so that the universal could be perceived through the national. He puts it thus: "The old school, the *kheyder* and the yeshiva, produces only the Jew; the new school produces the rootless 'man'; the school to come must form the Jew and the man simultaneously." Building on this principle Dubnov proposed a radical reform of the *kheyder* by introducing general subjects into its curriculum, and simultaneously reforming instruction in the elementary schools in a national spirit. Initially the "Letters" did not touch on the question of the language of instruction; but when the "Letters" came out in a separate volume after the 1905 Revolution, the author inserted in the chapter on national education a demand for "equal rights for the people's living language."

The principles set out in this chapter were developed by Dubnov in a paper read at a meeting of the members of the Society of Enlightenment in May 1902. Ahad Ha-Am supported the speaker, asserting that a school which alienated its pupils from their native culture was committing an act of moral annihilation. Both speeches were delivered in calm, restrained tones but unleashed a storm of opposition in the packed hall. The debate assumed such an impassioned character that a representative of the police closed the meeting before the motion could be put to a vote.

The unexpected acrimony of the ideological polemic profoundly discouraged Dubnov; he plunged into his historical work for a long period. He was assailed more and more frequently by doubts about whether his chosen path was correct. He writes in his diary,

I realize with sadness that I am being drawn deeper and deeper into social strife, to the detriment of my main work. Now and then I snatch time from history for journalism, and from the latter, time for direct social activity. It is impossible to be so fragmented. It washes the mind blank, it depersonalizes it. The twenty-second year of my literary life is passing and I have more than twenty-five years of work still to do.

14

Farewell to the South

The literary circle, formed at the beginning of the nineties and gradually enlarged by new members, became the nucleus of the Committee of Nationalization, of which Dubnov was chairman. Its meetings took place in the writer's home, in his spacious study with windows looking onto the garden. Some of his new colleagues became family friends—energetic and sociable Meir Dizengoff, later the mayor of Tel Aviv; the young rabbi Chaim Tchernowitz, a man of broad theological and philosophical culture; Hayyim Nahman Bialik,[41] who had recently moved to Odessa. At first glance Bialik gave the impression of being a phlegmatic man. Stout, moon-faced, and taciturn, he usually withdrew into a distant corner and appeared absorbed in thought during the meetings. The young poet's verses, which appeared in the magazine *Ha-Shilo'ah*, were striking even then in their blend of inner strength and deep, restrained tenderness, but probably few read them with more delight than Dubnov, himself a frustrated poet. He clearly grasped the originality of Bialik's gift long before he was able to appreciate his singular personality. The new member of the Odessa circle did not lend himself to easy classification. In contrast to his older colleagues, Bialik was not a bookish man at the dawn of his literary career and disliked conversations on literary subjects; there were rumors that he spent a lot of time playing with ragged urchins in the dusty yard of his house, and that he lay alone for hours on the rocky seashore beneath the scorching rays of the sun. Abramovich, who stubbornly emphasized his own idiosyncrasies, was closer to him in spirit than anyone else, and the two writers would often drop in at the Dubnovs' together.

The Committee of Nationalization chose the social club Beseda as their permanent base of operations. Its lectures and papers attracted large audiences; even Dubnov, who usually preferred the written to the spoken word, often appeared in the capacity of speaker. His colleagues complained that he was reluctant to leave his study for the rostrum, but he explained that written propaganda reached a larger audience than speeches.

Voskhod published the "Letters" without cuts, but the editors' attitude toward the author's ideological stance remained unclear. More than once Dubnov felt the need to talk matters over with the journal's new proprietors; it would not be difficult, or so he thought, to find a common discourse. In the spring of 1902 he went to St. Petersburg.

The North met the visitor with a cool wind off the Neva. It was the month of May, and twilight clothed the city in a blue haze. Almost twenty years had passed since the young dreamer had wandered along the granite embankment, gazing into the watery depths as well as into the depths of his own soul—rebellious, searching, dissatisfied. Now a man who had attained maturity strode thoughtfully through the streets of St. Petersburg. He had found the meaning and the purpose of his existence. The past lay open before him; life's path seemed as straight as the main avenue streaming like a ribbon into the distance. But longing, a vague, regretful longing for his youth rose from the bottom of his soul in the jagged twilight of the white nights.

Meetings with people prevented Dubnov from surrendering to memories. His month-long stay in the capital passed in conversations and arguments with old and new acquaintances. He scrutinized the generation of journalists and public figures who had appeared on the scene in his absence. The difference between St. Petersburg and Odessa was very striking: the intellectual level was higher and the horizons wider in the capital, but Dubnov sadly observed that the local activists lacked the innocent enthusiasm of the Odessans. He rarely met with any sympathy for his opinions in the literary world. L. Sev, the chief editor of *Voskhod*, a man with a broad philosophical education, absolutely rejected a national program in education as well as other areas of cultural life. His ideal, formed under the influence of Herman Cohen,[42] was an ideological syncretism, an organic fusion of the elements of Russian and Jewish culture. The other members of the editorial board were more nationalistic, but their general attitude to the ideology of the "Letters" could be characterized as "friendly neutrality." Having given the participant in the Odessa Kulturkampf the opportunity to develop his notions, the editors refused to come out in favor of the campaign for national education. An article written by Dubnov in the heat of editorial arguments (*Voskhod*, 1902, Nos. 3–6) was remarkable for its fervent tone: "Henceforth, national education is a battle cry; it is a shibboleth by which one may distinguish the orientation of any given group. Not one people . . . in the world can find in its experience such a monstrous instance where the intelligentsia pits universal values against its own national values." To those who expressed dislike of his phrase "national intelligentsia" he declared: "As long as assimilationism exists nationalization must also exist."

Despite disagreement over principles, friendly relations were established between Dubnov and the editors of *Voskhod*. The editors decided to publish a revised edition of the three-volume *History* as a supplement to the journal. Freedom from worrying about publication and arguing with the censor was a great relief to Dubnov, but he realized that it would be difficult to supervise the publication of a large work in St. Petersburg while living in the far South. The old pull of the North reasserted itself. Family plans coincided with literary plans; his daughters had graduated from the gymnasium and were dreaming of university in the capital. However, Dubnov did not want to renew the degrading petitioning to obtain right of residence in the city. He began to think of moving to Vilna, near the capital. He was weary of the public bickering in the Odessa community; it frequently occurred to him that in a new setting he would find it easier to devote himself wholly to his scholarly work. Reality was to shatter that illusion, however, for it was in the "Jerusalem of Lithuania" that Dubnov was to witness the stormy times of revolution.

He returned to Odessa and plunged into the usual atmosphere. During receiving hours his home on the quiet seaside street was besieged by visitors eager to talk about the subjects he had touched on in his recent political articles. One unexpected guest was a glib stranger who called himself Y. Volin and claimed he was the representative of the Jewish Independent Workers' Party, founded in Minsk.* Volin was in Odessa trying to forge a link with the Committee of Nationalization, but he failed completely. When the Committee learned the true nature of his activities they categorically refused to have any dealings with him. The hope of enlisting Dubnov's help testified to Volin's extreme political naïveté. Though he did not suspect his guest's clandestine connections, Dubnov firmly rejected any program which gave precedence to economic over political struggle.

The next Letter (*Voskhod*, 1902, Nos. 11–12), called "The Intelligentsia in Disarray," was a reply to a lengthy discussion of the national question recently published by M. Margulies, one of the leaders of the Odessa Jewish community. Dubnov's opponent reminded him, among other things, of the "sins of his youth"—the articles written in his rebellious freethinking period. Dubnov replied with a quotation from Victor Hugo: "The horizon may change, marquis, but not the heart. Nothing has changed within me, but everything without. The eyes are the same, but they see another sky."

Intensive work on the *History* filled the last winter Dubnov spent in Odessa. He felt great satisfaction when his study "What Is Jewish History?"

---

*This name was full of irony: the "independents" were completely dependent on Zubatov, the notorious chief of the secret police, who attempted to splinter the growing workers' movement with their help.

appeared in America in a translation by Henrietta Szold.* But bitter thoughts immediately welled up. For a long time he had attempted to revise and publish in pamphlet form the article into which he had put so much spiritual ardor, but thus far he had not been able to do so. Meanwhile other work, planned long ago, was still awaiting its turn. In March 1903 melancholy lines appear in his diary: "My strength is waning, life is waning, more and more frequently one reckons up how much time is left to live. Major works are being postponed for decades. . . ."

Spring came and Dubnov arranged to go to Vilna to prepare for the move. But all his personal plans were unexpectedly overshadowed by the news of a bloody pogrom in Kishinev.

On 7 April 1903 a large audience gathered at the Beseda Club to hear the young Zionist activist Vladimir Jabotinsky.[43] The talented journalist, who had recently become a fierce supporter of Herzl, gave a speech picturing the Jews of the Diaspora as a ghost people wandering over the crossroads of the world, filling those around them with terror and loathing. Those feelings would disappear, the orator declared, only when the Jews became a normal, territorial nation. Dubnov listened to the fiery tirade ringing from the rostrum with a heavy heart. He was thinking, was it really so necessary to instill in the wavering Jewish intelligentsia terror in the face of their own national shadow? In the intermission he was pacing alone about the wide foyer when distraught voices and bitter weeping suddenly attracted his attention. Refugees from Kishinev who had escaped the massacre had brought word of the horrors they had just survived.

Soon the terrible truth became clear: for three days a cruel pogrom had raged in the town under the eyes of the police and, here and there, with their participation. The massacre was inspired from on high and carried out by the lower classes of the populace. The details related by witnesses froze one's blood. The Kishinev tragedy thrust all the problems of the Jewish community into the background for a while. When people recovered from the shock, they felt the need to respond to what had happened. Above all, it seemed essential to tell the world the truth about the horrors of the pogrom. Dubnov proposed creating an information clearinghouse which would collect materials and disseminate them abroad. The plan met with general approval, and Bialik was sent to Kishinev. The fruit of his journey was not only an abundance of factual material, quickly written up by Dubnov and sent abroad, but also the shattering images of Bialik's famous poem, filled with anger, pain, and burning shame.[44]

The Kishinev outbreak created an atmosphere of fear: the Damocles sword of pogroms hung over the entire Pale of Settlement. The most active members of the Jewish community were conscious of the necessity for self-defense. The Odessa writers' group debated at length the text of an

---

*Jewish History. An Essay in the Philosophy of History (Philadelphia, 1903).

appeal to the Jewish populace to offer armed resistance to aggressors. The appeal, written by Ahad Ha-Am in Hebrew (for conspiratorial reasons), was signed by an anonymous "group of writers" and sent to the official representatives of the Jewish community. It did not, however, reach a wider audience. The self-defense groups which organized rapidly in a number of towns were born of the Jewish population at large, not in writers' studies. They became a concern of the workers' movement, one of the acts of revolutionary struggle.

When the turmoil caused by the Kishinev pogrom had died down somewhat, and Dubnov, now in Vilna, had plunged into the twilight of twisting medieval side streets and ancient synagogues, a longing for literary work was rekindled in his soul. How wonderful it would be, he thought, to resurrect the past in a setting where each stone spoke of bygone days. But all those around him were living in the present. The Jewish community had been shaken to the very core: there were signs of ferment, especially among the young. Dubnov was drawn into endless conversations with people of different persuasions; some urged emigration, others intensification of the struggle with the government. He himself tried to articulate the feelings that gripped him in the article "A Historic Moment," which provoked sharp conflict between the editors of *Voskhod* and the censor. Never in all the long years of his career had the writer of the "Letters" felt such anger at the control by bureaucratic blockheads as he did in the days when those lines, breathing pain, were written. The article began:

> Once again we are witnessing events which prove that history is cyclical rather than linear. The martyrology of Jewry has now come full circle, from the massacre of Uman to the massacre at Kishinev, from 1768 to 1903.[45] Twenty years ago, we who believed in the line of steady progress, saw for the first time in perplexity and horror how sharply that "straight" line of recent history had bent and taken a direction leading us back to the starting point, to the dark past. The circle has now closed, the starting point and the end point are one. . . . Yet we were more prepared, psychologically, for this latest blow dealt us. . . . The twenty years we have witnessed bequeathed to us the great watchword: 'national self-help.' "

National self-help must, in the author's opinion, move in two directions: the struggle for civil and national-cultural rights in all countries where Jews live, and the creation of a new center of Jewry by way of organized, mass emigration to America.

The article had to be printed in an abridged version because of censorship. Two years later Dubnov returned to the subject of self-help and self-defense in the introduction to a German edition of the *Letters*, translated by Dr. Friedlaender, under the title *Die Grundlagen des National-Judentums* (Berlin: Jüdischer Verlag, 69 S. 8).

Dubnov left the South in the middle of summer. He wandered through the park and along the seashore, bidding farewell to the places where he had pondered so many ideas in solitude. He wanted to say goodbye to his friends quietly, in a small group, but was obliged to give way to their insistence. More than thirty people were present at his farewell party. *The Book of My Life* gives this account:

> The speeches rang with the sorrow of separation, particularly Abramovich's speech. He talked of the first years of our shared lives in Odessa, when there were no official "meetings" with . . . irksome discussions, but rather, amicable conversations about the higher questions of life and literature. In some speeches I detected a note of gentle reproach that I was leaving Odessa in the heat the battle. Greatly moved, I replied in my speech that our community life had entered a new and stormy stage. I too was drawn into the battle, but another duty to our people called me—the duty of a historian—and I was sailing for a quieter haven.

Several days later two people in a railway carriage exchanged memories of the autumn evening when they arrived in Odessa with their small children. Thirteen years in the tumultuous southern town had left their mark: a thick streak of gray had appeared in Dubnov's hair, and the web of wrinkles under Ida's eyes told of their difficult life. And yet, as they were leaving the city which claimed a part of their souls, they were sad. Later, when Dubnov took stock of the Odessa period he wrote:

> We experienced a great deal of hardship but there was much that was bright and good. . . . The Odessa period was the warm noontide of my life. It was still long before nightfall, but the best years of my life were then behind me. The family nest was moving to a new place, where it would soon be deserted, for the fledglings had grown wings and were about to fly away in different directions. . . . I was leaving the warm South, the warm sea, friends, and comrades-in-arms. . . . Searching for peace for my weary soul and quiet for my scholarly work I changed the *place*. Alas, I could not change the *time*. And the years of life to come coincided with an era of social storms. . . .

15

In the "Jerusalem of Lithuania"

From the balcony of the Dubnovs' new apartment there was a view of the roofs of small, low houses and the bell towers of medieval Catholic churches. On the horizon green forests encircled the ancient city. A wide street descended steeply to the noise and filth of the marketplace, but the far end stopped at fragrant, green woods of pine.

While a carpenter fitted high shelves to the walls of the study, the long years of work at his desk passed before Dubnov's eyes. The family nest was becoming empty. His older daughter had gone away to university in the capital, his younger daughter to a nearby provincial town to finish her studies at the gymnasium. Later, in *The Book of My Life* he recalled: "It was the first period of separation in our family, joyful for the young ones, sad for the old. There was a feeling that a single organism was disintegrating, that the link between the generations was being broken."

The sadness which permeates the pages of the diary relating to this time was not caused solely by the flight of the young birds from the nest. Sophie's acceptance in the Women's Free University, a difficult achievement for a Jewish girl because of the *numerus clausus*,[46] was considered a great accomplishment by her family. Her father was the most pleased, for in his youth a university education had been an unattainable ideal. But there was a secret fear mixed with the joy. The words about the broken link between the generations provide the key to understanding that fear. It was not the physical but the spiritual break with his children, going off to some incomprehensible life of their own, which depressed Dubnov. He had dreamed of a unanimity of thought within the confines of his own family and harmonious friendship between the older and younger generations within the larger Jewish community.

Dubnov's entire youth had been spent beneath the banner of the struggle with the "patriarchs," the bearers of centuries-old tradition. Having eschewed negation and arrived at a national-humanistic synthesis, he firmly believed that the new structure of ideas would be embraced by the young. "We were certain," he writes in his memoirs, "that the younger generation would use our synthesis . . . born in pain and suffering, as the basis for the further development of their own world view." The objectivism of the chronicler, accustomed to perceiving the change of ideas from one generation to the next, betrayed the writer when he found himself in the camp of the "patriarchs." A rationalist in theory, Dubnov was always ruled by feeling in practice; and when the amalgam of individualism and spiritualistic nationalism, born in the cells of the *maskilim*, proved unable to answer the questionings of a generation flung by the will of history into the very thick of mass movements, he experienced bitter disillusionment.

Social differentiation could be felt more keenly in Vilna, an old center of Jewish culture, than in Odessa. Dubnov scrutinized the new currents and new people with interest. He willingly accepted a proposal by several representatives of the local Bund organization to discuss together a number of controversial ideological issues. Their conversation took place in the Dubnovs' apartment in the presence of Ahad Ha-Am, who was visiting Vilna at the time. The details of Dubnov's first meeting with active members of the revolutionary underground are given in his memoirs:

> On the appointed evening . . . four or five men who gave only aliases came one by one into my study. . . .* I received my mysterious guests with great foreboding. The pale intellectual faces of these men, bearing the stamp of political martyrdom, predisposed me toward them. Our conversation was conducted quietly. Ahad Ha-Am took virtually no part in it; he only listened intently, sitting on the couch and smoking incessantly. He had considered any agreement impossible beforehand, and the Bundists obviously placed no hopes in him. Toward the end . . . I summarized our disagreement in two basic points: As a historian I could not share the doctrine of historical materialism, which was, in my opinion, contradicted by the evidence of Jewish history in particular. As a political commentator I found intensified class struggle among Jews incompatible with national struggle at a time when our people as a whole was facing destruction and should therefore defend itself collectively against the common enemy. It was clear we could not agree. . . . We parted peacefully, having defined our differences, which were as yet theoretical.

Two days after this conversation an event occurred which could serve as a commentary on that time. Gomel, one of the centers of the Jewish workers' movement, became the stage for a pogrom. Here, however, circumstances differed from those in Kishinev. The instigators of the pogrom were met by armed resistance from the workers' self-defense detachments. The men whom Dubnov had reproached for cutting themselves off from the people proved heroic fighters for their people's cause at this difficult time.

The news from Gomel inflamed an unhealed wound. An entry in Dubnov's diary bears the traces of spiritual turmoil: "There is no peace. The work falls from my hands. I want to cry out with pain, rip the veil from this abyss of evil. So much for calm scholarly work! My soul is in torment. . . . In Vilna it's the same as in Odessa. There is no escaping the common woe. . . ." The author's experiences were reflected in the chapters of *World*

*S. Gozhanskii-Lonu and V. Aizenshtat-Iudin were undoubtedly among the Bund representatives.

History of the Jewish People written at that time. Describing a pogrom in Alexandria, Dubnov saw pictures of Kishinev and Gomel before him; in his imagination the figure of the deranged Caligula fused with the figure of Nicholas II. This parallelism of past and present is characteristic of all Dubnov's later work, including the ten-volume *History*, where the journalist's fervor frequently disturbs the calm pace of the historical narrative.

The chapters devoted to the heroic struggle of Judaic patriots and Roman warriors were written with great élan at the beginning of 1904. Next came the complicated question of Christianity. Dubnov expressed his conviction that early Christianity grew out of the Essenic movement, that it was a protest of the individual against the strict discipline of the national collective, a protest which was bound to reach beyond the limits of the national religion.

The sounds of other battles broke into the quiet of Dubnov's study in Vilna, which was haunted by the ghosts of the Zealots and Roman military commanders: the guns of the Russo-Japanese War thundered in the Far East. Blow after blow rained down on the despotic regime, and Dubnov saw this as punishment for its crimes. The death of Plehve, one of the pillars of reaction, from a terrorist bomb was also accepted as an act of historical justice.[47] In his diary Dubnov posed the question: Are we now standing on the threshold of a turning point in history, as we were after the Sevastopol Campaign preceding the Age of the Great Reforms?[48] A sixth sense told him that what was in the air was not reform but revolution.

In those troubling days Dubnov felt a particularly acute need for association with like-minded people. He did not succeed in creating a literary circle in Vilna, but quite a few of the visitors to the Dubnovs' home came from the nationally minded intelligentsia. Occasionally old *maskilim*, a type still found in the "Jerusalem of Lithuania," would pay them a visit. Lively conversations on current events were the order of the day, as tea was served in the bright, cozy dining room. The Zionist activists Shmariia Levin and the Goldberg brothers were the most frequent guests. Sometimes arguments broke out at these get-togethers—for Dubnov was, as before, critical of the excesses of political Zionism—but this did not hinder amicable association based on a common approach to many contemporary problems and on shared social activities.

In the summer of 1904 Dubnov spent several weeks at his forest retreat in Polesia, and then went to a remote town in the Mogilev province to see his uncle Ber Dubnov. Torpor and disarray reigned over the small town. Fear of mobilization augmented the emigration fever. The guest brooded a good deal in the small, idyllic country house with flower beds beneath the windows. He writes in his diary,

> I thought about future labors; they are the milestones of my remaining years.
> I will soon be forty-four. . . . But I see no personal joys before me, no realized
> ideals, no hopes achieved. . . . The pale glimmer of dawn may yet break

in public life, but I will not live to see the full dawn. And one thing remains: to finish my life's work, the work on the past for the sake of the future, and . . . go in peace like the plowman from his field. And on this August evening, in this God-forsaken corner of the world, I hear a voice—"Enough of your labors! It is time to look at life more calmly, from the standpoint of eternity. Take your stand at your furrow and cultivate it, put your ardent soul wholly into your work, look there for that which personal life has not given you, and when the One who sent you here summons you, go and say, 'I am ready, I have done my work.'"

Dubnov recalls those days in *The Book of My Life*: "Little did I think when I made that vow that I already stood at the threshold of mighty revolutions which would fill the second half of my earthly wanderings with greater troubles than ever before, and that I would have to fight hard for the right to work peacefully . . . 'in my furrow'. . . ."

When he returned to Vilna at the end of August, his friends met him at the station with news they had just received: the liberal Prince Sviatopolk Mirskii had been appointed Minister of the Interior. The appointment appeared to indicate the government's readiness to make concessions in the wake of defeats. Dubnov poured all his energy into fulfilling the vow made that summer evening in the Belorussian backwater. He spent all autumn and part of the winter working intensely to complete the second volume of the *History*, which was devoted to the Middle Ages. During the days when drunken new recruits broke windows in the towns of the Pale and tore open Jewish featherbeds, he described the raids organized by the Crusaders. "History repeats itself," he writes in his diary, "a time of madness. . . . What next? It is impossible to find oblivion in the contemplation of history now: the sounds of the past and the present are merging in one terrible chord. The day's anxieties, newspapers, conversations, evening guests, visitors from afar—all this transports me from the hell of the past to the hell of the present."

Each day the tension grew; the signs of impending change multiplied. The tsar's coarse response to hints at a constitution in the liberal *zemstvo* conclaves had a sobering effect, even on the moderate monarchists. The regime's prestige was clearly falling. At the end of 1904 Dubnov wrote: "They rudely shoved aside reform with the help of society and, in doing so, left the solution of the problem to revolution." Reality confirmed these words. Revolution stood at the door.

16

Year of Revolution

The beginning of the year of revolution found Dubnov in the depths of the Middle Ages. He was finishing the second volume of the *History* when news came that the military had fired indiscriminately into a procession of thousands of workers taking a petition to the tsar. The guns turned on the peaceful demonstrators shot the autocracy's prestige to pieces. A high voltage current ripped through the country from end to end. The discontent accumulated over the years rose to the surface. The floundering government declared its intention of convening an advisory parliament and permitting its subjects to appeal to the supreme authority with collective petitions. In effect this meant instituting the freedom of assembly, which opposition factions had sought for so long.

The wave of revolution swelled to a great height in the towns and villages of the Pale. The many years of underground work had found fertile soil there. Double oppression awakened a keen sense of protest in the Jewish masses. While the mobilization of forces for a revolutionary assault on the bastions of autocracy was under way in the lower echelons of society, a peaceful assault of petitions was being readied at the higher level of the intelligentsia. Conferences of social activists to discuss the demands to be made of the government took place in all the major centers. In the Jewish world the weakening of the powers which had organized the recent pogroms was welcomed from a national perspective as well, and the prospect of fighting for equal rights invigorated the community. Dubnov shared the general enthusiasm as a citizen and as a Jew. The time had come, he believed, to realize his youthful, libertarian impulse to fight for the principles of full national rights formulated in his mature political articles. These principles were, however, disputed by many in his milieu. There was no consensus in the higher echelons of the Jewish community regarding the scope of specifically Jewish demands or the methods for fighting for them. A petition composed in St. Petersburg in circles close to the influential Jewish philanthropist Baron Günzburg[49] seemed unsatisfactory to the plebeian writer: "I did not care for the tone of the petition, which, instead of demanding our rights and justice, argued that Jews were useful to the state and their persecution harmful to it. I insisted at length . . . that we should appear before the government now as accusers, not as the accused." A draft drawn up by a group of young democratic intelligentsia seemed more appropriate to Dubnov, and he proposed that it be accepted with the addition of some paragraphs of his own, which set forth national demands.

In the spring a well-attended conference of representatives of the legal Jewish social organizations convened in Vilna. Delegates traveled from all corners of Russia and represented all shades and varieties of political opinion. They agreed that it was essential to create an organization for the purpose of fighting for the rights of the Jewish population. A group of attorneys from the capital, who had recently brilliantly defended the heroes of the Gomel self-defense movement, took the initiative. Maxim Vinaver, a prominent Petersburg jurist and one of the founders of the Constitutional Democratic Party, was elected leader of the group. Dubnov had corresponded with him for many years about the affairs of the Historical-Ethnographic Commission. Their meeting at the Vilna conference was the beginning of many years of collaboration. While Dubnov sometimes disagreed with Vinaver about matters of national politics, he invariably valued Vinaver's intellect, his gift for words, and his organizing abilities. Clarity and discipline of thought were qualities which Dubnov, with his strong emotionality, always admired. Vinaver reminded him a little of Ahad Ha-Am. But whereas the arguments of the architect of spiritual Zionism were of a speculative, abstract nature, the Petersburg party leader's thought led directly to action. Despite differences in their views and casts of mind, in the years to come Dubnov and Vinaver were to be linked by a strong and meaningful friendship.

Dubnov also had many points of contact with left-wing representatives at the conference: the militant democrat Leon Bramson,[50] subsequently the leader of the Trudovik group in the Duma, and the Kiev lawyer Mark Ratner[51] of the Socialist-Revolutionaries. When Dubnov's paper on the new organization's national program became the subject of lively debate, the young Kiev activist showed himself a staunch supporter of the program. The paper argued that it was necessary to obtain not only full civil and political rights but also autonomy for the kahals, as well as recognition of Yiddish and the national school system. Dubnov expressed the hope that the organization set up by the conference would eventually broaden its scope and become a vehicle for implementing the postulates of national-cultural autonomy.

Dubnov's recent Odessa opponents of the "Letters" were sharply critical of the paper. They rejected the very term "national rights," calling attention to the fact that not one of the champions of emancipation in the West had made such a demand. The speaker's hope that the Zionists would give him their support did not materialize. The idea of national-cultural autonomy in the Diaspora elicited no enthusiasm in Zionist circles. Nevertheless they voted unanimously for the motion put forth by Dubnov demanding the "implementation of the civil, political, and national rights of the Jewish people in Russia." Indeed, even Vinaver's group, which disputed several of the paper's theses, voted for it. Intransigent members of the opposition were few in number.

The new organization needed a name. Dubnov supported the radical wing, which proposed to call it the League for the Struggle for Equality for Jews, but the word "struggle" alarmed some of the delegates. A "learned Jew" from the province of Vilna squawked in horror: "It'll be another Bund!" After a long debate they decided to call the new organization the Union for the Attainment of Equal Rights for the Jewish People in Russia. This ponderous name allowed the members of the Union to be spoken of ironically as "attainers."

Dubnov was elected to the Executive Board. He writes in his memoirs: "I willingly accepted election to an organization founded on the idea of national struggle for emancipation. For the first time I saw my ideas embodied in the program of a political union, and I hoped that they would spring to life with the success of the liberation movement."

In the spring and summer of 1905 a wave of pogroms organized by the Black Hundreds,[52] with the help of the police and, to some extent, the military, swept over the Pale. The government took cruel revenge against the Jews for their mass participation in the revolutionary movement. Persistent rumors were circulating that the Jews would not be permitted to take part in the upcoming elections to the first Russian parliament. The Union for Equal Rights decided to respond to the authorities' policy of blatantly encouraging pogroms and to the rumored restrictions of election rights. Dubnov wrote two declarations fiercely protesting government policy. He wrote them in a state of great agitation, putting aside his regular literary work to do so. The summer spent in a country dacha on the banks of the Viljia brought no calm: he keenly felt the discord between his personal work and the surrounding circumstances. "How my weary soul craves calm," he writes on 3 June. "I would have liked to rest a little and then complete my historical work. . . . But to write history at a time of revolution in Russia, amid barricades and the thunder of gunfire—how is it possible?"

In the quiet of the countryside the first fragments of Dubnov's autobiography were born unexpectedly. "My flight into the deep waters of the past, away from the storms of the present, was strange," he writes in *The Book of My Life*, "but I experienced many such moments subsequently, and I am convinced that it is precisely in times of revolutionary crises that the storm-tossed soul seeks shelter in recollecting the past and finds safety by means of integrating its experiences. . . ."

In August the tsar's manifesto on the advisory Duma appeared. Dubnov was skeptical:

Yesterday's manifesto can hardly satisfy anyone. What kind of constitution can it be which is promulgated in the absence of prior guarantees of freedom of assembly and freedom of the press, in the complete absence of even the

most rudimentary legality, under conditions of martial law and naked terror. . .? All the same one must work and agitate. . . .

In the stormy circumstances of 1905 Dubnov was drawn to work on
the period of emancipation in the West. He wanted to show his contemporaries how their forebears had struggled for their rights in the Age of Revolution. In the autumn he set to work with great zeal on the third volume
of the *History*, hastening to reach the end of the eighteenth century. He
was proud of having managed, "standing on the volcano of the present,
to peer into the past and depict it." But soon the volcano began to spew
hot lava—the October days had arrived.

The general strike changed the face of the country. Humdrum life was
replaced by a fantastic reality. Vilna, the ancient city of three nationalities,
was transmuted in the fire of revolution. Its twisting side streets and
squares paved with sharp cobblestones were thronged with dense crowds
from morning to night; incessant meetings went on in every public building. On 16 October a shot rang out near the governor's carriage, as it cut
through the crowds on the wide avenue. No one was hurt but police and
soldiers fired a volley into the unarmed crowd. When the screams of the
wounded rang out and dead bodies lay in the street, a murmur of indignation ran through the town. The following day the entire adult population
of Vilna took part in the funerals of the fallen. For the first time in his
life Dubnov was swept by the current of events from the quiet of his study
and drawn into the noisy streets.

At noon on that overcast autumn day he walked behind a hearse as
a member of the delegation from the Union for Equal Rights, holding a
mourning banner which displayed a revolutionary slogan. The town was
in the hands of the people. Some invisible hand removed the police from
their posts and brought the soldiers back to the barracks. A member of
the local Bund committee, the writer Devenishskii-Vaiter, nicknamed the
"revolutionary police chief of Vilna," effectively led a procession of thousands as it moved slowly through the shuttered, narrow streets.

The next morning the jangling of the doorbell echoed through the Dubnovs' apartment. Friends pushed into his study shouting "Constitution!"
A new manifesto had been promulgated promising full civil liberties and
a full-fledged parliament. Dubnov was again drawn into the street. At
the crossroads he met a journalist with whom he had worked in the
Russian-Jewish press at the beginning of the eighties, and the old colleagues embraced in a burst of high spirits. The euphoria was short-lived,
however. Several days later the sounds of gunshots and the groans of the
wounded were heard through the open windows: the keepers of public
order had returned to their posts. And soon dreadful news began to arrive
from various parts of the country. Immediately after the promulgation of
the manifesto the authorities had sent bands of Black Hundreds into the

streets for bloody reprisals against the progressive intelligentsia and the Jews.

When rumors spread that a massacre was being planned in Vilna as well, the local community organizations decided to offer fierce resistance to the Black Hundreds. Armed self-defense groups sprang up. Dubnov wrote a declaration beginning with the words: "Rumors of a pogrom being prepared against the Jews are spreading through the town. We, the representatives of different parties and unions of the town of Vilna, express our deep indignation at these secret instigations. We give warning that the slightest attempt at a pogrom will meet with the most vigorous resistance on the part of our united forces." The declaration was signed by twelve organizations of which only three were Jewish. Among the signatures were those of the Union of Railway Workers and various organizations of professional intelligentsia. The public declaration succeeded in forestalling the reactionary bands.

The anxiety-filled days weighed heavily on Dubnov. Personal emotions —his younger daughter and son, relatives and friends were then living in battered Odessa—were submerged in the common grief. His diary entry for 31 October reads:

My heart is breaking, I have no strength to bear the horrors of which one reads, hears and speaks every hour of the day. . . . I wanted to write, to shout, but my hands fall useless before a pile of corpses. Groaning and lamentation hang over all Jewry; an individual voice will not be heard. But I will try all the same. I am not capable of any other work. I have dropped everything, all I do from early morning 'til late at night is feed on the poison of newspaper reports.

In the middle of November the first chapters of the cycle *The Moral of Terrible Days* were written. For the first time their author was able to speak freely, without the control of the censor, of everything that had accumulated in his soul over the long years. He read one of the chapters at a crowded memorial service on 17 November, thirty days after the death of the victims of the pogrom week. His ringing words were a moving requiem.

17

The Moral of Terrible Days

Soon after the memorial gathering Dubnov went to the capital to take part in the second Congress of the Union for Equal Rights.

> In Petersburg I fell into a boiling cauldron. The capital was seething with the hundreds of meetings and conferences, the thousands of delegates from all ends of Russia, the rumbling of the old revolutionary underground risen to the surface of public life. . . . More than once the cold November wind slapped the flushed faces of people emerging from the overheated atmosphere of meetings into the wet streets of Petersburg.

The nervousness apparent in the debates was only partly explained by the fact that many attending the Congress had witnessed the recent pogroms. The events of those stormy days enhanced the popularity of national sentiments. A motion enthusiastically adopted called for an All-Russian Jewish National Assembly to "establish, in accordance with the will of the entire Jewish population, the forms and principles of national self-determination and lay the foundations for its internal organization." Dubnov, the ideologue of cultural-national autonomy, considered the acceptance of the motion he had introduced a genuine victory: "It was the second, more specific endorsement of my theory of autonomism after its overall endorsement at the first Congress." On the other hand, the general political part of the paper, containing a proposal to adopt the Constitutional Democratic Party's program as the Congress's platform, drew objections from left-wing delegates. Countering these attacks in print, Dubnov claimed that he advanced the "Cadet" platform as a minimum program only and mainly to disassociate himself from right-wing elements.

Dubnov's general political views finally crystallized at this time. In his maturity he remained in essence true to the rationalistic individualism of his youth. The crisis, of which many of his diary entries speak, did not affect the foundations of his world view. The transition from cosmopolitanism to nationalism was accomplished without a major upset because the autodidact-*maskil's* cosmopolitanism was a derivative phenomenon. It was fed less by feeling than by the influence of sociophilosophical conceptions popular in progressive circles. Dubnov kept much of the ideological baggage of his youth. He turned his back on Buckle but remained faithful to Mill. His moderate, English version of individualism, alien to the extremes of Stirnerian anarchism,[53] evolved into classical sociopolitical liberalism with all the intrinsic features of that current: a critical attitude toward Marxism, emphasis on the primacy of political over economic demands, and rejection of radical "Jacobinism." Dubnov fortified his views by references to history. This required no particular effort, for history usually teaches men what they require of it. He was firmly convinced that "political revolution must precede socioeconomic revolution, for it is necessary to win freedom first in order to fight for the emancipation of the proletariat in a free democratic state. To attempt both political and social revolution at the same time would be to doom both." And, in his opinion, a general political program should be implemented by means of gradual reform. "I thought anxiously about the possibility of the collapse of the 1905 revolution," he writes in his memoirs. "Demands for a republic were premature, since the evolution of Russian society had only reached the stage of constitutional monarchy."

These thoughts were repeated more than once in the cycle of articles published in *Voskhod* under the general title *The Moral of Terrible Days*. Two articles in the cycle appeared soon after the Congress: "Slavery in the Midst of Revolution" and "National or Class Politics?" Here Dubnov vented the feelings which had stirred him during the past year. He asserted that "Jewish revolutionaries in the ranks of the Russian Socialist Parties and even in the Jewish Workers' Party, the Bund, come out exclusively with general political or class slogans and not with national demands, as the Poles, the Finns, and other oppressed nationalities have done." As a result "the Jewish revolutionary protest is lost in the general Russian protest. . . . The anger of the most oppressed and insulted of nations cannot be heard in it." Dubnov attributed this phenomenon to the influence of assimilated members of the intelligentsia who belonged to the Party. He was completely unable to reconcile himself to the fact that the Bund refused to join the Union for Equal Rights. In his opinion a Jewish party had no right to play class politics to the detriment of general national politics, and, by doing so, "undermine the besieged camp from within." There were frequent heated arguments on these subjects in his family circle. Echoes can be heard in several passages of *The Moral of Terrible Days*. In a later edition the author deleted some occasional abrasive passages, penned in the heat of polemics.

The last chapter of the cycle was devoted to the subject of "planned emigration." The Jewish pogroms following on the heels of the Revolution again increased the attractions of crossing the ocean; this obliged Dubnov to return to an issue which had long concerned him deeply. In December 1905 he writes:

> We are standing on a volcano which has already swallowed tens of thousands of Jewish victims, and the crater is still smoking. . . . People are gripped

by great confusion. . . . The great mass of refugees has taken the old path out of the Russian Egypt . . . to the promised land of America. . . . And now, as Russia, about to become a land of freedom, has not ceased to be a land of pogroms, our eternal wanderer will once again cross the ocean. . . . And there is one more land, the native land of our forebears, lit by the rays of our distant national youth. Longing hearts strain toward it . . . but longing has not yet turned into strong will. . . . The Diaspora will never disappear but . . . the creation of even a small national-spiritual center in the historical cradle of Jewry is a noble task.

In the days these lines were written the Revolution was nearing its demise. In a last bright flare the glow of the tragic Moscow insurrection lit up the country before it sank into darkness. Dubnov was unable to work; laying his manuscript aside, he paced restlessly up and down his study, beset by anxiety. Yehuda Novakovsky,[54] a young yeshiva student who belonged to the Sejmists[55] (he later became an active Bolshevik), lived nearby and often looked in on the Dubnovs in the evenings. Neither host nor guest felt like talking. They listened to the howling of the wind and the logs crackling in the stove and gave themselves up to the power of dark forebodings. Sometimes, to break the silence, the young talmudist chanted in a soft, slightly tremulous voice. He intoned a song about an old question which is asked in every century and remains unanswered. The doleful chant told better than any words could of the bitterness filling the heart to overflowing.

On the eve of the new year Dubnov forced himself to return to work. The last chapters of the third volume of the *History* were written at a feverish pace, for the author was eager to reach the age of the French Revolution. He sent the chapters to the editors of *Voskhod* with a letter to the reader. The letter said that continuation of the work was indefinitely postponed. "It is difficult to write history at a time when one should be making history, when the flood of life sweeps violently into the chronicler's study."

The diary entry on 31 January reads: "Another month has gone by . . . amid the triumph of executioners soaking Russia in blood after the disastrous Moscow insurrection. You hear and read constantly of arrests, searches, executions. . . ." Several days later he goes on: "I've no strength to endure this orgy of reaction. One waits for the search, . . . for incarceration. There is talk of proscription lists at the disposal of local authorities on which my name and the names of other public figures appear."

However, Dubnov was determined not to give in to depression. A new Union Congress was approaching; it had to work out a campaign in connection with the elections to the Duma. Ahad Ha-Am had arrived from Odessa and joined the Vilna delegation bound for St. Petersburg; the friends met under new political circumstances. The Congress was stormy and apprehensive. Many delegates had lost faith in the prospect of establishing a free parliament in an atmosphere of reaction and proposed boycotting the elections. These tendencies were particularly strong on the left wing. Dubnov campaigned vigorously for participation in the elections, insisting that an oppositional Duma was a far more effective means of fighting reaction than a boycott of parliamentary activities.

When the time came to consider the question of alliances with the various political parties, Dubnov insisted on the inadmissibility of negotiating with parties to the right of the Constitutional Democrats. He was greatly distressed by the defection of his old colleague Ahad Ha-Am, who declared with his characteristic forthrightness that Jews had no business with general political programs but ought to consider national interests only. His declaration stemmed not from any tendency toward compromise but from a peculiar atrophy of civic feeling. Ahad Ha-Am lived in a voluntary spiritual ghetto and felt a stranger in the country where he had been born and spent the greater part of his life, in contrast to his more emotional colleague, who experienced his link with his native land as a living bond.

The Congress gave Dubnov great satisfaction: almost all his proposals concerning the general political and national platform were accepted by a significant majority: "I worked hard, taking part in sessions as a member of the presidium from early morning 'til late at night. How wearing those sessions were, but how much spiritual élan and faith in a bright future animated them!"

Political passions were seething everywhere. When Dubnov appeared at the editorial office of *Voskhod*, he had to fight a fierce battle with the editor over *The Moral of Terrible Days*. A new acquaintance, Sh. An-sky (Rapaport),[56] who had recently returned from abroad, took part in the dispute. Despite disagreements, the two writers had a great deal in common. They had both emerged from the rebellion of *Haskalah*, and both had formed their world views under the influence of progressive Russian literature. In one of the latest issues of *Voskhod*, An-sky—who combined Russian and Jewish populism idiosyncratically—took up the defense of the Jewish revolutionaries whom the author of *The Moral* had accused of being estranged from their people. Dubnov replied with the article "On the Supremacy of National Politics in the Life of an Oppressed Nationality." He declared that he did not deny the *legitimacy* of class struggle but rather the *predominance* of class politics in a people who were the object of persecution. The essence of the article can be summarized as follows: A single national policy must become the surrogate for territorial unity for a nation which, existing in the Diaspora, faces the threat of dissolution within the surrounding territorial nations. If the ruling peoples can turn national policy into a weapon of oppression, it can be a means of self-defense for minorities.

Spring passed in the fever of the election campaign. Pre-election meetings were held in a stormy atmosphere. Representatives of the left-wing parties had been obliged to go underground once more, and they frequently tried to use legal outlets to agitate for a boycott of the Duma, which often led to police intervention. Dubnov's colleagues insisted that he run for parliament in Vilna, but he flatly refused. When the elections were over he wholeheartedly welcomed the election of his friend, the energetic Zionist activist Shmariia Levin.

Dubnov responded to the convocation of the Duma with elation: "Two melodies sing in my soul," he wrote in his diary, "the quiet music of flowering nature and the marching strains of a new Russia. . . . At noon the newspapers arrive, one throws oneself on them and greedily gobbles up the news. . . . The confrontational stance of the majority of the Duma, the readiness to fight for freedom is clear. . . ." Remembering this phase of his life in his autobiography, he observes: "Only the men of my generation who, for a quarter of a century, in the chains of slavery, dreamed of a constitution and a Constitutional Assembly, can understand the festive mood of the spring of 1906, when the weary soul thirsted for faith in the new Russia and, within it, for the renewal of Jewry."

In the quiet of the country Dubnov cheerfully settled down to work consonant with what he was witnessing. Before him lay the task of finishing the revision of his monograph on the emancipation of the Jews, mutilated by the carping censor of the eighties. He decided to expand the study and print it in pamphlet form. The work went forward rapidly. One of the May entries in his diary reads:

> History, nature, politics. This evening, after two weeks of sustained work, I finished the *Emancipation*, a very different piece now from what it was in 1889. The reader will be struck immediately by how much experience and reflection have broadened the author's outlook in seventeen years. A work of the mind and the pen in the stillness . . . of this enchanted retreat . . . to the distant sounds of politics brought daily by the newspapers—all this produced an intricate scale. . . . In the morning the speeches . . . in the Paris National Assembly or the Commune of 1789–91; in the evenings speeches . . . in the Russian Duma, and, in the interim, the soothing murmurs of pine trees, the pond, the fields.

The pamphlet soon appeared and had a large circulation;* its author promptly set to work revising the "Letters" and other political articles published in periodicals over the past ten years. The time had come, he thought, to systematize the scattered material and publish it as a separate book. Reading new works on the national question confirmed the correctness of the ideas which formed the basis of the "Letters." He writes in his diary,

> I am pleased that my views of the nation as a spiritual or cultural entity coincide with the predominant trend of modern scholarship. Even my autonomism

---

The Emancipation of the Jews During the Great French Revolution 1789–1791, Izdatel'stvo Pravda, 74pp., 1906.

in many ways resembles Springer's (Renner's) theory of personal autonomy; I have only now become acquainted with his work. An independent process of thought led me to much that is now accepted, but also to much that has not yet been acknowledged and which emerges, I believe, from the entire evolution of Jewish history.

The news of a pogrom in Bialystok and the dissolution of the Duma was a stunning blow. "On 9 July," Dubnov writes in his diary, "the shattering news of the dismissal of the Duma broke into my room. The pen fell from my hand. This miracle was born in such travail—how hard to lose it at a moment when it was our sole support. . . . The labor of Sisyphus must begin again. . . ."

The idea of moving to the capital had not left Dubnov. His scholarly as well as his public activities urgently required it. He wished to believe that, in the circumstances of the postrevolutionary period, it would be easier than in former years to realize the dream of his youth. The immediate impetus to change his place of residence was a proposal to lecture at the St. Petersburg Free University directed by Professor Lesgaft.[57] Dubnov had long dreamed of constant association with young people and immediately agreed.

The news came that the Faculty of Social Sciences had officially confirmed Dubnov's appointment as lecturer on his birthday in September. An entry in his diary reflects the doubts which arose on the eve of his departure: "Do I have the strength for this labor, O God? Shouldn't I really go abroad after twenty-five years of service . . . and consecrate the remainder of my life there to my beloved historical work. . . ? But another voice says, 'Stay, go to the Russian capital and take up the maximum load, seethe, burn until you burn out.' And I shall go."

In the middle of September 1906 Simon and Ida Dubnov left Vilna. They had not put down any deep roots in this city where political storms had overtaken them, but the memory of the twisting medieval streets and the deserted green banks of the Vilija long lingered in Simon's soul. He declined a farewell banquet in his honor. He was in no mood for banquets in so troubled and anxious a time. He went to face the "second Petersburg" period with frayed nerves but ready to put all the strength of his heart and mind into scholarly and public labor.

18

Back in St. Petersburg

The Dubnovs' apartment on a quiet side street was dark and uncomfortable, with windows opening onto a grimy, blind wall. This was the district of old houses, narrow alleys, and murky canals under hump-backed bridges which brought back memories of the writer's youth. Much had changed in over twenty years: the editor Landau had died, and the journal into which Dubnov had put so much effort and intensity of thought and feeling had recently ceased to exist. His old colleague Frug had taken refuge somewhere on the far edge of town, and both the content and the slow, ponderous rhythms of his poems, devoted to the modern world, spoke of hopelessness and resignation. Dubnov had changed least of all during these years: his eyes still burned with their youthful gleam beneath a graying mane of hair, and he gave himself to his literary and public work with his old ardor. He still had a passion for the beauty of nature, and he still recited his favorite poems. But reality, becoming more complicated by the day, often gave rise to bitter bewilderment.

His university activities, which Dubnov approached with great enthusiasm, proved short-lived. The Free University of Professor Lesgaft—a brilliant scholar, a brave public figure and a democrat—was the most progressive university in St. Petersburg. It attracted an array of talented, radical professors, and the majority of the students were young people who sympathized with the revolutionary movement. In view of the young people's keen interest in social questions, the new lecturer decided to teach a course on the recent history of the Jews, beginning with the French Revolution. However, the faculty advised him to keep to the chronological order and begin the program with the biblical period. To prepare his lectures Dubnov sat long hours in the Asian Museum at the Academy of Sciences, reading a monograph on the recently discovered *Codex Hammurabi*[58] and rereading the works of the leading German Bible scholars. The introductory lecture attracted a large audience. Dubnov drew attention to the Free University's initiative as the first Russian university to create a Department of Jewish History in the Faculty of Social Sciences. He developed his sociological conception of Jewish history and concluded with a few words about free historical research in a free country. The young people received the new professor warmly but when he began to give his lectures it became clear that very few of the students had even a superficial acquaintance with the Bible, and more of them were Christian than Jewish. What Dubnov had feared had come to pass—in the tense, postrevolutionary atmosphere Bible criticism and the latest discoveries in the history of the Ancient East interested only a narrow circle of specialists. The lectures became seminar sessions, and soon even these were discontinued when the Free University was closed on government orders. It had come to the attention of the Police Department that illegal organizations were meeting in its lecture halls.

The Free University was one of numerous hotbeds of social ferment. The immense city lived an intense, feverish life, as though all the energy of the inert, sleepy countryside was concentrated within its limits. Political life bubbled up at secret and open meetings, in university auditoriums, in legal societies, and in countless small circles. It was not only the modern Jacobins, insisting on pushing the revolution further, who came to blows with the "Girondists" of various factions. Vehement arguments flared up around questions of philosophy, religion, and art. Never had the pulse of the capital's literary and theater life beaten so furiously; never had the foreboding of impending cataclysm been so evident. Dubnov could not help sensing the restlessness in the air. He could no longer indulge in the illusion of isolation within the four walls of his study; it became only too clear that there was no escape from the life seething around him, and in fact he did not even wish to escape it. But at times, in moments of solitary meditation, a disturbing question arose: would life escape him?

Dubnov entered his Petersburg period with great hopes. Physical incapacities—the fruits of intensive work and the hard struggle for existence —were behind him. His old plan of settling in the capital had at last been realized, if imperfectly (his residence permit was only temporary). The acuteness of financial worries had lessened—his textbook was reprinted every year and became the basis of the family's modest budget. But all this was insufficient for spiritual equilibrium.

Dubnov felt no symptoms of advancing age. The mood of resignation was alien to him, but all the more keenly did he feel his discord with the contemporary world. In his youth he had had to waste much energy in overcoming external obstacles, but there were no dissonances in his inner life. The ethos of the age—its idealistic love of the people, which had often grown into Jewish populism among the young *maskilim*, its sober, rationalistic philosophy, its taste for realism—all this was comprehensible, and as dear to him as his own. Much had changed in a quarter of a century. The political situation had become more complex with the appearance of new powers. Marxism, asserting the primacy of material existence over consciousness, had attained great power over men's minds. At the same time the higher echelons of the intelligentsia were gravitating toward mysticism and the irrational. In literature uneasy forebodings had exploded the classical canons. The disciple of Comte and Mill was not at home in the new age. Intellectual disquiet increased his personal pain, gnawing like a worm at his heart. The new, tangled, complex life was the life of his children.

Now only Dubnov's oldest child, a university student, lived with her parents. Sucked into the whirlpool of the capital, she was rarely at home. As the writer wandered through his silent, empty dwelling he sometimes went to her desk. Beside the small Bible, which he had given her and which they both considered a "talisman," lay the latest philosophical and literary anthologies and the verse of modern poets. These books were alien to him. The poetry was especially bewildering; it seemed mannered and convoluted. He shut the book, muttering in annoyance, "Decadence." And in his memory rose the enjoyable, cozy evenings beneath the hanging kerosene lamp, devoted to Lermontov, Nekrasov, Fet.

Ida also remembered the old days with a sigh. She often wanted the impossible: to hear her children's ringing voices and the patter of tiny feet once again, to resurrect days which had been hard and wearisome but filled with activity. The children had grown up long ago and were far away. Her son was in Odessa, doing well in mathematics and, by all accounts, taking an active part in the student movement. He wrote regularly, but briefly and laconically. Her daughter Olga had left the university and moved to Vilna to be with her husband, a worker and autodidact who had climbed out of the peasant class. In the evenings, as the Dubnovs drank tea in the gloomy dining room, silence now reigned, disturbed only by the hissing of the samovar and the rustling of newspapers. With a bitter sense of their loneliness the aging couple avoided talking of what pained them.

Simon found relief in putting his archive in order. The manuscripts lying in even rows in neatly labeled packets were lasting, unchanging; this was where the meaning of existence lay. The briefcase hanging over the table bore the telling inscription: *Scripta.manent* (What is written remains). It was not easy to leave the study, where he breathed freely and thought well, for noisy and verbose meetings. But Dubnov felt he had no right to absent himself from them, the more so since the elections to the second Duma were approaching. It was the last public campaign undertaken by the Union for Equal Rights. The recently formed organization was obviously foundering; the first breach was made by the Zionists, who included the ideas formulated by the Union in their program at the Helsingfors convention but decided to implement them only under their own party banner. This moved Vinaver's group to break away and issue a sharp denunciation of "programmatic emigrants." His organization borrowed only one plank from the Union's broad national program—the general principle of self-determination. At the same time the Jewish Democratic Group, which adopted a more radical position on general political questions, coalesced. Dubnov and like-minded thinkers remained Union "patriots" longer than the others, but they finally formed an association called the Folkspartey. The broad, national tasks which this new organization set itself contrasted with its extremely limited opportunities for political action; it played a genuinely significant role only in the sphere of Jewish culture. From the small circle of nationalist enthusiasts, convinced that the center of gravity of the Jewish question lay in the Diaspora, came the moving spirits of societies which undertook the study of Jewish history, literature, music, and folklore. The role of these societies was particularly great in the main centers of the Pale, where they became genuine loci of cultural renaissance. Many years later, in independent Poland, the Folkspartey was transformed into a mass movement.

The program of the new association was drafted by Dubnov and printed in two St. Petersburg publications, *Razsvet* (1907, No. 2), and *Der fraynd* (No. 35), the daily newspaper in Yiddish. He writes in *The Book of My Life*,

> This article represented the distilled essence of everything I had thought through in the last two years. Our path was clearly marked. We should continue the struggle for emancipation into which we had plunged with the anger of the insulted and the passion of martyrs; we should struggle as a single Jewish nation scattered among various nation-states. . . . Otherwise, we might win civil rights for ourselves, but we would not be saved from national death.

He observed in conclusion that the Folkspartey aspired to unite all of the nation's progressive forces.

The article provoked a lively polemic. Vinaver's journal reproached the new party's founders for going the way of the Zionists. Dubnov answered his opponents in the columns of *Der fraynd* (Nos. 42–43). For the first time he wrote in Yiddish and was pleasantly surprised when he discovered that this language presented him with no difficulties. "As I wrote," he says in his diary, "a warm current flowed to my heart: *mame-loshn*. . . ." Dubnov wrote an article for the same paper focusing on the emigration question, and finally came to the conclusion that the language of his childhood, which had been perfected in the literature of the last few years, was sufficiently supple to convey the most varied nuances of thought.

The collapse of the Union for Equal Rights, which had existed for all of two years, was a blow to Dubnov, who had believed that the organization was destined to implement many of his most cherished ideas. Now he felt the need to assemble and print the articles, scattered through back issues of the journals, in which he had formulated those ideas. He returned to the work he had begun in the country outside Vilna: a painstaking systematization of his thoughts taking stock of the stormy decade. The work was completed in the spring of 1907, the articles filling a substantial volume. In the introduction he gave a short description of the recently completed process of differentiation among Jewish political groupings. He assigned his own ideology the middle ground between the extreme wings, foreseeing that he would be attacked both from the right and from the left.

Despite the varied and, at times, incidental nature of his work, Dubnov never ceased dreaming of immersing himself in a large-scale project. The notion of an isolated retreat, in the silence of which the voices of the past would be heard more clearly than in the tumult of a big city, became ever more insistently intertwined with the idea of such a project. Fate helped him find such a retreat in nearby Finland, a land of forests and lakes—a neglected estate belonging to well-to-do St. Petersburg relatives. During the very first summer Dubnov spent in Linka, he felt the charm of the stern yet tender northern nature. The same pantheistic ecstasy, which had gripped his soul in the forests of Polesia, was reborn. An entry in his diary for August 1907 reads: "I have just finished praying in my own synagogue. Early in the morning I went into the forest, the sun smiling through tears of rain or dew, and for a few moments . . . my soul prayed in words familiar to it since childhood. . . . Holy martyrs of 1903–1906! I pray for you here, deep in a Finnish forest, humming in tears *"El male rahamim."*

The Finnish retreat became for Dubnov a place of concentrated, joyful, and wholly undisturbed labor for many years. Preparations for departure began as early as May. The banging of a hammer echoed through the hall: humming his favorite airs, Dubnov would carefully arrange his manuscripts and books in large, wooden crates and nail them shut. When he and Ida reached the estate, the slow northern spring breathed the scent of cherry blossoms upon them, and the day, riotous with the chirping of birds, flowed into the silvery, enchanted twilight of the white nights. Then the summer days arrived, thick with acrid, torpid heat. It was good working in the green stillness; there were delightful walks along paths slippery with pine needles, winding between mosses and heathers. In the evenings convivial conversations took place around the samovar on the comfortable veranda of the spacious manor. The hospitable owners, Dubnov's cousin Roza Emanuil and her husband, often reminisced about those distant years when a young, shy, provincial boy dreaming of a literary career came to their house for the first time.

In the summer of 1907 disturbing news broke the quiet of the estate: the second Duma had been dissolved and the election laws changed by order of the tsar. Dubnov thought of the future with trepidation in the hours of his solitary walks. A thought nagged at his brain: would it not be wiser, in a time of ever-growing reaction, to leave the tumult of aimless meetings, settle in some quiet corner of Finland, and devote himself wholly to his major work? Simon and Ida Dubnov discussed this plan many times but could not reach a decision. When they returned to the city, the writer petitioned for an extension of his residence permit. The Ministry replied that permission could only be given for one year at a time. This uncertain situation troubled Simon, who dreamed of a settled life. When he moved to the university district in the autumn of 1907, he wrote in his diary:

I must settle once and for all in one place, even if it has to be on this academic island of the Neva, and live out the remainder of my days here in uninterrupted work. . . . If I could grow accustomed to this political volcano it would be possible . . . to give myself to scholarly work . . . in this clean, quiet suburb of Petersburg, and each summer heal my weary soul in the air of Finland.

At the time the author of these lines did not foresee that all his attempts at a quiet, settled life would be wrecked, one after the other, by the cruel storms of history.

19

Unity in Variety

In his St. Petersburg period a great variety of literary and social functions fell to Dubnov, who dreamt of concentrating on his main work. These functions met his inner needs, but combining them demanded a strenuous effort. When, at the end of 1907, a move was made to publish a Jewish Encyclopedia in Russian, Dubnov did not immediately decide to join the editorial board; participation in such a huge scholarly undertaking threatened to destroy his large-scale work. Recognizing, however, that the new cultural enterprise deserved support, he agreed to edit the section devoted to the European period of Jewish history. The publisher was not satisfied by this. He insisted that Dubnov take on the editing of the publication as a whole, and threatened that his refusal could wreck the entire undertaking. This virtual ultimatum perturbed Dubnov; an entry in his diary for February 1908 reflects serious doubts. He was reluctant "to sell myself for a handsome annual salary of five thousand rubles" (which was significantly larger than his usual earnings) and to postpone his forthcoming major works until the distant future.

> Never have I accepted financially seductive proposals, preferring poverty and work I love to riches and work I dislike. But an encyclopedia is not a disagreeable project, and without me, it may indeed come to naught. . . . What should I do? Should I sacrifice five years of the few remaining to me, when as it is I am afraid of dying without completing my *magnum opus*?"

Finally, after three days of cogitation in the stillness of the Finnish villa, buried in snowdrifts, Dubnov decided to turn down a proposal which would have meant years of financial security.

Organizing the new scholarly enterprise proved an extremely complicated matter. Pedantically strict with himself and others, Dubnov could not reconcile himself to superficial dilettantism, but there were few serious scholars among his fellow contributors. Not infrequently he had to rewrite articles practically from scratch and pepper the proofs with correction marks. The intense work left no room for even a short respite. And in the winter of 1907–1908 yet another enterprise needing support claimed his services. It was a program of courses in Jewish studies launched by a group of St. Petersburg intelligentsia headed by Baron Günzburg. Dubnov was much attracted by the idea, but the organizational meeting, which took place in the Baron's apartment, had a dampening effect. "The whole thing," he writes in his diary, "is confined in the straitjacket of the Baron's private undertaking, complete with stodgy professors, among whom I am supposed to occupy the chair of history." The initiators of the new school thought up a ponderous academic name, Courses in Oriental Studies, counting on allaying the government's suspicions by this ruse. Among Dubnov's students were a number from institutions of higher learning. The majority, however, were provincial autodidacts, yeshiva students who possessed wide talmudic erudition but an extremely limited stock of general knowledge. They were plebeian, idealistic young men, thirsting for enlightenment. Dubnov easily found a common language with them, but the tenor of the program did not satisfy him. Here, too, the pseudoscientific approach and dilettantism, with which he had to contend so often in editing the articles for the *Encyclopedia*, prevented the enterprise from meeting the requisite standards. Especially galling was the fact that the materials for his prospective large-scale work still lay untouched at the bottom of the capacious drawers of his desk. There was not even enough time for journalism. Polemical articles written about the *Letters on Old and New Jewry*—Klausner's[59] article in the journal *Ha-Shilo'ah* and Chaim Zhitlowsky's[60] article in the collection *Serp*—went unanswered.

In the spring of 1908 Ahad Ha-Am came to the capital to bid his old friend farewell on the eve of departure for London. An entry in Dubnov's diary speaks of this meeting: "a second day of pouring forth our souls, sad conversations about the disintegration of our small literary family, about personal and national sorrows, everything which moves and pains us. . . . A whole phase of life, which started in 1891, ends with this separation." As they bade each other farewell on the deck of the steamer bound for Stockholm, the friends had no presentiment that they were seeing each other for the last time. For the next nineteen years, they were destined to meet only in thought, in literature, and in friendly correspondence.

In his summer retreat the dream of independent creative work revived with new strength in the writer's soul. Dubnov had moved into an ancient two-story house on the very edge of the district. As he relates in his autobiography,

Beneath my balcony was spread a colorful field of clover. Beyond it lay the lake's smooth expanse; serried rows of pines, firs, and birches pressed in on either side of the house. I remember summer evenings when, from the vantage point of the balcony, I followed the slow dying of the light of sunset for hours, and sensed the coming of the white night in the sudden hush in the leaves rustling in the tree tops and in the mysterious light over the lake.

When in these idyllic surroundings, he took stock of his experiences during the noisy, wearisome winter, Dubnov came to the conclusion that participation in the *Encyclopedia*, even in a limited capacity, was incompatible with work on his monumental opus. "My head is full of ideas for my coming labor," he writes at the end of the summer. "Before me lies a stack of notes and plans, and I feel that I can and must draw a vivid picture of the recent evolution of Jewry." In his study overlooking the lake he sketched a plan of his activity for the next thirteen years.

On his return to the city he immersed himself in work. A lengthy introduction was to give a picture of the life of world Jewry on the eve of the nineteenth century. But it was not easy for Dubnov to closet himself within the four walls of his study. The cultural life of the capital was in full swing. Political reaction could not drive the country's awakened energies underground. The right of assembly won by the Revolution made it possible for a group of Jewish journalists of various persuasions to obtain legal status for the Jewish Literary Society. In the inaugural speech at the Society's crowded constituent meeting, which took place in October 1908, Dubnov called for renewed commitment to cultural activity, reminding his audience that "in an era of reaction literature has a duty to stand guard and prepare for a new embrace of social responsibility." The meeting touched on the language question, which had been much discussed since the Czernowitz Conference, where Yiddish had been recognized as a national language, along with Hebrew.[61] A number of later meetings of the Society were devoted to detailed discussions of the Czernowitz resolutions. As usual Dubnov defended his familiar conception of equal rights for three languages:

I was obliged to defend the rights of the Russian language in our literature against the Yiddishists and the Hebraists, by demonstrating that it was impossible to take away the cultural tool of vast segments of the Jewish intelligentsia who speak and read in Russian. I allowed that the Russian and the Hebrew languages were not of equal value in a national sense, but they must be recognized as having equal rights as cultural instruments.

The Petersburg Literary Society became the seedbed for Jewish culture. Branches sprang up in many towns in the Pale, and within two years their number had grown to one hundred. Sociopolitical as well as literary questions were discussed at the meetings, but the government smelled sedition only three years later. In 1911 Stolypin[62] closed down the Jewish cultural organizations, along with Polish and Ukrainian societies. In the early days of the Literary Society Dubnov was an active participant in its well-attended gatherings, but soon another organization, even closer to his own spirit and purposes, diverted his attention.

In the autumn of 1908 Maxim Vinaver succeeded in obtaining permission to turn the modest, narrowly specialized Historical-Ethnographic Commission into a Society with broad prerogatives. Dubnov was asked to sit on the constituent committee. The formation of a new center of learning belatedly fulfilled an appeal the young contributor to *Voskhod* had once made to the Jewish intelligentsia at large. Despite being overburdened with work, Dubnov considered it wrong to refuse to take part in a project for which he had so fervently campaigned in his youth. There was a series of meetings at Vinaver's home. Their initiator declared: "The Revolution tore us away from the historical work we began in the nineties; now the time has come to resume it."

Dubnov delivered the introductory speech at the first meeting. He was usually restrained as a public speaker, but this time he was unable to resist a personal and emotional note.

> At this solemn moment, a feeling of joy mixed with sorrow moves me. I rejoice that at last an institution designed to satisfy the vital demands of our national life has come into being. I grieve that it has arisen so late, that the Jewish people as a whole have only now obtained what smaller groups of Jews in the West have long possessed. At this moment I cannot help but remember . . . the first call to found a Jewish Historical Society. It has taken seventeen years for our youthful dream to be realized at last.

Vinaver, the chairman of the meeting, observed in a cordial response that the appearance of the pamphlet *On the Study of Jewish History* had wakened many young St. Petersburg intelligentsia, brought up on Russian literature, to an interest in the past of their people and the sense of a connection to them. Under the impress of this meeting Dubnov wrote in his diary:

> It opened this evening, the Historical Society, a project I outlined in early spring 1891. . . . Before us lies an immense labor: the collection and publication of materials, the publication of a trimonthly journal and individual books, lectures, and papers. . . . If this were seventeen years ago, how I would have thrown myself into it, how much I would have done! A thirty-year-old dream has been realized at the age of forty-eight—is it too late?

At the beginning of December Dubnov began a series of lectures in the new Society's seminar, "The Process of Humanization and Nationalization in Recent Jewish History." He developed a number of arguments to support the idea that establishing harmony between humanism and nationalism was one of the most important tasks bequeathed by the nineteenth to the twentieth century. The lecture sparked a heated debate which went on for two evenings. From that time forth Dubnov was often the one to initiate discussions on historical and political subjects. He was familiar with most of the objections from former oral and literary debates, but now he often faced opponents with wide general, as well as Jewish, erudition. The level of the meetings was high; some of the papers were the result of independent research. Dubnov did not regret that he had to tear himself away from his own work for the sake of the Society, where he acted as vice-chairman (Vinaver was chairman). He rejoiced in each successful paper and the lively exchange of views, but he considered the publication of a trimonthly scholarly journal the most important aspect of the Society's activities.

The year 1909 opened a new era in Russian-Jewish journalism. After a lull, two journals appeared almost simultaneously: the scholarly *Evreiskaia Starina* (Jewish Antiquity) and the literary and political *Evreiskii Mir* (Jewish World). Dubnov participated actively in both. After the closing of *Voskhod*, to which his literary career was linked for many years, he had longed for a journalistic platform and dreamed of a periodical which would have more ideological integrity than its eclectic predecessor. He believed such a journal should propound the national-progressive ideology upheld by the Folkspartey. When a group of social activists received permission to publish a monthly journal in 1909 and invited Dubnov to join the editorial board, he agreed without hesitation. The editorial board was a coalition. It included Zionists, representatives of the People's and the Democratic groups, and two delegates from the Folkspartey (Dubnov and Sh. An-sky). The middle ground between the diverse currents corresponded with the orientation of the Folkspartey, so Dubnov had to play a leading role on the editorial board and calm the passions roused by the discussion of the monthly reviews of current events.

Abramovich, Peretz, and Frug published work in the literary pages of the new journal. Dubnov contributed to the early issues a lengthy introduction to recent history, entitled "Humanization and Nationalization," and an excerpt from the cycle called *Reflections on the Eternal People*, signed with the pseudonym Historicus. The excerpt harks back to his favorite notion that, for the freethinker, a faith historically anchored in the immortality of the people can replace faith in individual immortality. The writer wanted to develop this thesis in more detail, but had no time. Meanwhile, the need to commit to paper ideas which had emerged in the "margins" of his major works became more acute as the years passed. He realized this long-time dream only shortly before his death, in the stillness of the Baltic forests, when he included fragments of his reflections in his autobiography (the third volume of *The Book of My Life*).

Despite the fact that a Zionist representative sat on the editorial board of *Evreiskii Mir*, the journal was savagely attacked by the Zionist weekly journal *Razsvet*. The editor of this publication, Abraham Idelson, spoke ironically in one of his articles of the activities of such Diaspora organizations as the Literary and Historical Society and the Courses in Oriental Studies. Dubnov immediately responded with an article entitled "Nihilism or Anarchism?" It was signed with a pseudonym and roundly condemned the disrespect for cultural values shown by "negators of the Diaspora," who embraced a longing for Zion as the only legitimate part of a rich historic legacy. When the secret of the pseudonym was revealed, *Razsvet* answered the criticism by boycotting the literary and social enterprises in which Dubnov played a leading role.

When he recalled this distasteful episode in his autobiography, Dubnov compared the intolerance of these opponents to his "truly courteous" public dispute with Ahad Ha-Am on the same subject—the meaning of the Diaspora.

The dispute was a continuation of years of polemics in print, at the lectern, and among his circle of friends. An article entitled "The Negation of the Diaspora," written by Ahad Ha-Am in his habitual laconic and brilliant style, appeared in the journal *Ha-Shilo'ah*. It was a belated reply to one of the "Letters on Old and New Jewry." The author of the Letters had once reproached the followers of Ahad Ha-Am for their inconsistency. He averred that the recognition of Palestine as a spiritual center combined quite naturally with the theory of autonomism in the Diaspora. In "The Negation of the Diaspora," Ahad Ha-Am declared that he had not ignored the past or present Diaspora, but that he found it a distorted form of the people's life. Dubnov did not consider the argument at an end and expressed his objections in "The Affirmation of the Diaspora" (*Evreiskii Mir*, 1909, Vol. 5). He maintained that those who recognize the historical necessity of the Diaspora must strive for the normalization of Jewish life with the help of the instrumentalities granted to national minorities by modern legal consciousness. The theoretical monism of spiritual Zionism should give way to an actual dualism. On this basis he went on to observe that the opponents of *zhargon* disdained a powerful instrument of Jewish autonomy in the Diaspora—the everyday language of seven million people—and that by doing so they were committing a grave sin. "Ahad Ha-Am's essay and my reply," he writes in *The Book of My Life*, "were peaceful dialogue rather than polemic."

The existence of *Evreiskii Mir* gave Dubnov the opportunity to return, from time to time, to the stimulating problematic of the Letters; but his favorite child was *Evreiskaia Starina*, the Historical-Ethnographic Society's trimonthly journal, which he edited from the first to the last line.

Dubnov adumbrated the purpose of the new publication in an introductory article, stating that the initiators of *Starina* aspired to create a particular kind of journal. While remaining rigorously scholarly, it was to move the reader to "historical reflection which would not take him away from life but lead him into its depths, passing through old Jewry to new Jewry." The journal was mainly devoted to the history and ethnography of Polish and Russian Jews, the least-studied area in Jewish historical scholarship.

The regular collaboration of the Polish-Jewish historians Meir Balaban,[63] Moses Schorr,[64] and Ignacy Schiper[65] was a valuable resource. Julius Hessen[66] wrote at length on the history of Russian Jews; Mark Wischnitzer,[67] an active member of the Historical-Ethnographic Society, was responsible for a permanent section on bibliography, and An-sky worked on problems of folklore. The editor himself published articles and notes in almost every issue, and also regularly published materials from his own archive in the section "Documents and Reports." Joyfully he watched the laying of the foundation of scholarly research and raw materials on which the structure of the history of East European Jewry was to be erected. Dubnov was so absorbed in this work that he did not even find time to keep his diary. The number of entries might serve as a measure of his inward peace. He went running to his diary mainly at those moments when anxiety crept into his soul, when physical and spiritual weariness engendered fear that he would not succeed in completing the plan of work which constituted the meaning of his life. And when, on 20 April 1909, he took the cherished notebook from its drawer after a three-month interval, the following lines appeared:

> Life is full, you are doing your favorite work, you are realizing your youthful ideal. But why is it that I am not only physically exhausted but my soul is weary and the clamor "No! That is not it!" does not abate? I am supplying the Historical Society and a historical journal with enough material to last Jewish historiography for the next half century. But isn't it too late for me? I'm giving up the remainder of my life to the accumulation of historical material and lose hope of participating in the actual work of building. Such self-sacrifice might seem reasonable if I saw a host of builders and creators following in my footsteps. But where are they? And meanwhile even at *Starina*, I alone have to bear the burden of editorial drudgery. . . .

The oft-repeated thought that the thread of life might suddenly snap was engendered not by a fear of death but by the consciousness of the magnitude of the task Dubnov had set himself. On Rosh Hashanah 1909 he prayed amid the purple and gold of the northern autumn that he would yet "be given the time to finish my beloved work before quitting the world." He carved the date, 3 September 1909, into the bark of a birch tree; he cut off a sliver of the bark when he left Finland several years later and even in Riga he kept it in his desk drawer.

Editorial work not only took up a great deal of time but was also a source of perpetual irritation. The censor kept a careful watch on both Russian-Jewish journals, and denunciations by the reactionary press reinforced his watchfulness. *Evreiskii Mir* was financially unstable, and the editorial board decided to turn it into a political weekly. Dubnov approved of the decision but he was obliged to withdraw as editor because of lack of time. As it was, the journal was not destined to live long. It soon closed in the absence of strong community support.

At the end of 1909 Dubnov finally decided to give up many of his literary and social responsibilities for the sake of working on his multivolume book. As he prepared to set to work he suddenly felt a pang of longing for old friends and the town where he had spent his years of maturity. He decided to visit Odessa.

20

At Work on the Magnum Opus

On the night of 1 January 1910 Dubnov was in Odessa visiting relatives and gave himself up to memories. He writes in his diary,

> At this very moment the new year is born in the old city where almost half my literary life was spent. I have met old friends and acquaintances. . . . The day before yesterday we strolled together through the park. But this evening I wandered alone through a district I remember well. . . . The ill-lit streets were quiet and deserted, but I could clearly make out the silhouettes of familiar houses. Before me rushed the years 1891–1903, and the ghosts of the past walked beside me, whispering of former impulses, of the last period of my youth, with its inner crises and outer struggles. Now I wander here as in a graveyard. . . . The city has grown old; it is deserted, as though shrouded in deep mourning since the bloody days of October. I walk through the streets and often think: this pavement here ran red with the blood of my brothers, over there the heroes of the self-defense movement were executed by soldiers protecting bullies and murderers. This city, once so radiant and effervescent, is now muted by those bloody ghosts. . . .

Abramovich was delighted to see his old friend. The seventy-five-year-old writer had recently returned from a lecture tour in Lithuania and Poland, where he had been noisily fêted. He was lively, in excellent spirits and spoke of his journey and his immediate literary plans with great animation. Dubnov found Bialik and Rawnitzki with him; the thread of the conversation broken six years ago was picked up again. The writers had founded the Moriah publishing house and tried hard to persuade Dubnov to begin writing in Hebrew. He promised to make every effort to publish a Hebrew translation of the *History* at the same time as the original.

The social climate had changed in recent years. The question of national education occupied the minds of the Odessans as it had before, yet the disputes were no longer between nationalists and assimilationists but between Hebraists and Yiddishists. Dubnov tried to stay away from their noisy gatherings. He was in an elegiac mood and spent hours wandering through the park, always with his diary. On 4 January he observes: "I am writing on a small hill, beside the pillar where I used to sit in former years, pondering my work, reading and dreaming. It seems only yesterday that I was here, and not six years ago." He was drawn down a deserted side street to a two-story house with a garden. Within those walls, which now sheltered strangers, his former life—work, reflection, and a secret, heart-rending longing—still seemed to dwell. Another abandoned nest next door, where Ahad Ha-Am had lived in bygone years, stirred many memories.

Dubnov spent his last evening in Odessa with a circle of friends. By the middle of January he was back in St. Petersburg.

> I have come back to my own world. I have been sitting at my desk for eight days now. . . . I tear myself away only for dinner, walks, and sleep. I have plunged into the second millennium of the pre-Christian era. I am radically reworking the ancient history of the Jews for the new edition. I work with enthusiasm, knowing that I am creating something new on the foundation of all the thinking and lecturing I have done in recent years.

Another entry reads: "I am true to my vow. I lead a life dedicated to historiography. I tear myself away only for a few days to read manuscripts for *Starina* and, on Saturdays, to prepare and give lectures on medieval history for the Courses in Oriental Studies." The thought that he was at last advancing along the "highway of my life's task" gave him particular satisfaction.

At the annual meeting of the Historical-Ethnographic Society in February 1910 Dubnov read a paper entitled "The Current State of Jewish Historiography." Here he set out his sociological conception of Jewish history and proposed a new periodization scheme. These ideas were developed several months later in the introduction to the new edition of the *World History of the Jewish People*.

His work was going especially well now in the quiet of Finland, and his enthusiasm sometimes reached a pitch of ecstasy. At one such moment he writes:

> God is so near to me. He is within me, in my every impulse towards eternity, in my every intense spiritual striving. . . . Thus must a servant of the spirit live. . . . So lived my grandfather Bentsion, and so I too have lived from the time when grandfather and grandson, in two parallel streets in Mstislavl,

labored in the quiet of their libraries, each in his own way seeking the Eternal.
. . . You are so near to me, my kinsman's soul, hovering, perhaps, over me
now—no, living in me in another reincarnation.

At such times Dubnov thought that his grandfather's prophecy of the
grandson's return had come to pass. He writes in his autobiography,

I returned, although without dogma and without ritual, to the Source of the
Spirit which nurtured us both. . . . I repeated my favorite verse of the psalm
which had imbued my grandfather's life and my own life with meaning: "One
thing have I asked of the Lord, that will I seek after:/ That I may dwell in
the house of the Lord all the days of my life." I always understood those words
in the sense of unbroken spiritual creativity.

Dubnov was in Finland on his fiftieth birthday, working on the chapters
on ancient history. As he wandered along the lake shore he suddenly recalled the Bible verse: "In this year of commemoration each man must
return to his own land." The words seemed symbolic: he really had returned, in his fiftieth year, to "his own land," to the territory of history.
He was now deeply absorbed in revising the chapter "The Rise of Christianity," which he had had to abridge in the earlier edition because of
the censor. "The entire chapter," he says in his autobiography, "is built
on the antinomy of Christian individualism and Judaic nationalism, which
reached the heights of world tragedy at the time of Judea's rebellion against
the Roman giant. The concluding pages of this chapter, which have been
revised several times, reverberated with deep feeling. . . ."
When he had finished the large volume Dubnov allowed himself to
pause for breath. He gave a lecture, "Past and Present in Jewish Journalism," at a crowded meeting of the Literary Society. He involuntarily recalled how he had taken stock of forty years in the life of the Russian-
Jewish press at a meeting in Odessa eleven years earlier. Much had
changed over the past few years. Previously, the paper's thesis had been
hotly disputed by the supporters of assimilation. Now the same objections
were raised by the representatives of the nationally inclined youth, Hebraists and Yiddishists, who considered Russian-Jewish journalism an anachronism. Dubnov's response to his new opponents was contained in his
concluding remarks:

It is impossible to ignore the fact that the Russian language has been the primary, sometimes the only, instrument of culture for a significant part of the
Jewish intelligentsia. The fanatics in favor of monolingualism should remember that at various times Maimonides, Mendelssohn, Graetz, and many others wrote in "foreign" tongues. Are these men to be placed outside Jewish
literature?

It was at this time that Dubnov's thoughts, riveted to historical questions, turned unexpectedly to one of the idols of his youth: the tragic death of Tolstoy, who had taken up the wanderer's staff in advanced old age, shook all of Russian's intellectual community. Dubnov recalls in his diary how he had almost become a real Tolstoyan during his hermit's life in Mstislavl, so dear to him had been the thinker of Iasnaia Poliana, the preacher of the "simple life." His youthful attachment had weakened, but he always retained an admiration for the man who had turned from a pagan cult of physical beauty and strength to Judeo-Christian moralism. Dubnov made this idea the basis of a lecture devoted to Tolstoy given at the Courses in Oriental Studies. Then he developed it in an article published in the journal *Ha-Shilo'ah* (1911, No. 25).

The beginning of 1911 passed in revising the plan of the *Recent History*. The preparatory period always seemed the most creative to Dubnov. In his autobiography he writes,

> It is then that the skeleton of the history is constructed, the material is organized, . . . the eras take shape, each with its own profile and functions in the process of the growth and development of the social organism. Thus my periodization scheme for recent Jewish history was created: the era of the first emancipation and the first reaction, the era of the second emancipation and the second reaction. I connected . . . this alternation of periods in political life to the successive processes of assimilation and nationalization in the cultural dynamic and to their various manifestations in Western and Eastern Europe.

The entire scheme was laid out in the theoretical introduction to the *Recent History of the Jewish People*. The first chapter of the book depicted the process of the struggle for emancipation in France in the Age of Revolution and the Empire. This was the third, extended treatment of a subject which had first attracted Dubnov's attention back in 1889.

As he prepared the chapters on the nineteenth century for publication, Dubnov decided to make use of materials he had worked up for lectures at the Courses. The lectures had attracted a large audience. Dubnov derived immense satisfaction from his association with the young people prepared to overcome penury and hardships, engendered by the lack of civic rights, for the sake of learning. The government was trying with even greater persistence than before to bar the path to education for these autodidacts. Dubnov wrote bitterly of this in a political article beginning with the words: "The Jewish extern is dead. . . ." While he was writing these lines, news came from Odessa of new repressive measures directed at students, in which Jewish students suffered particularly. Yakov Dubnov was among those arrested; several months later he was exiled to Bessarabia under police supervision.

In the spring of 1911 Peretz visited the capital. The arrival of one of the literary masters was a great event for the Jewish community of St. Petersburg. Dubnov, however, saw no cause for celebration, as relations between the writers remained strained. Peretz was clearly unable to forget Criticus' sharp opinion about *Monish*, while Dubnov thought the visitor's demeanor both arrogant and pretentious. It was possible, in fact, that their mutual antipathy was an echo of the old dispute between *misnagdim* and Hasidim. This antipathy came into the open at a banquet arranged by the Literary Society in the guest's honor and resulted in a public clash which marred the occasion. When Dubnov had finished his speech about "the unity and duality of the Yiddish language," Peretz protested against the fact that the speech was delivered in Russian. Insulted by the guest's rude outburst, Dubnov immediately left the banquet.

After a hard, tiring winter Dubnov took great pleasure in the summer solitude of his beloved retreat, a new cottage with freshly planed planks still smelling of pine resin. But the peaceful flow of country life was soon disturbed. Ida Dubnov had felt unwell during the winter. She endured inexplicable pain with her habitual stoicism. Her condition deteriorated in Finland. The doctors diagnosed cancer of the stomach, the disease which had taken her mother to the grave. One hope remained: immediate surgery. Two days after the consultation the Dubnovs left for Berlin. The surgeon's skill saved the patient's life, but her convalescence was extremely slow.

Dubnov spent the difficult days while his wife's fate was being decided with a cultivated and hospitable family. He stayed at the home of Manefa Frevil-Abramovich, Abramovich's daughter-in-law, who lived in Berlin with her daughter and her aviator son, Vsevolod, whose aquiline profile put one in mind of his grandfather. Manefa was the daughter of a Russified French aristocrat, an unusual and gifted woman who had lived an eventful life. Manefa made every effort to distract Dubnov from his worries. She talked to him for hours on end of her meetings with Turgenev, Savina,[68] and other prominent persons.

The Dubnovs stayed in Berlin almost until the end of the summer. Every day Simon went straight from the clinic to the town library. He was studying the materials for the next chapters of the *Recent History*, books and pamphlets published in the eighteenth century.

> I was enthralled by those gray pages where the embers of dead passions still glowed. As I returned home through the Zoo I searched for the villa I'd read about, where the beautiful Henrietta Herz[69] had once lived, and the avenues along which Dorothy Mendelssohn,[70] . . . the Schlegel brothers, and the Humboldts[71] had walked to her salon. . . . I wanted to find a justification for old sins in the "green noise" of spring,[72] in the heady aroma of romanticism, in the hopes for the brotherhood of man. . . . In my thoughts I was living in late eighteenth century Berlin. . . .

Dubnov's meditation on the past was disturbed by voices from the present: news came from Russia that the government had closed the Jewish Literary Society in the capital as well as all its provincial branches.

August was nearly over when the doctors decided that Ida could return home. The surgeon's skill had accomplished a miracle but the strength of the resilient and hard-working woman had been undermined by the terrible disease. At the remote Finland station an old woman, frail and bent, with ash-gray hair at her temples and hollow cheeks got off the train.

Finland greeted the new arrivals with a dense, fragrant, August stillness and the early gold of birches and maples. Simon was about to pick up the thread of his interrupted work when the mail brought official notification that the Ministry of the Interior had denied his application to extend his stay in the capital. The functionary to whom he turned for an explanation churlishly declared that he was under no obligation to inform Dubnov of the motives behind government decisions. A bulging file of documents with the inscription "S. Dubnov Case" lay in full view on the table. Later it transpired that an agent of the political police had infiltrated the audience at the Courses in Oriental Studies and shadowed the "unreliable" lecturer who permitted himself to criticize government policy.

Thanks to the intervention of influential people, Dubnov's residence permit was extended. When he returned to the capital, his comrades in the Folkspartey were impatiently awaiting his arrival. The organization, which included new members from the Socialist-Revolutionaries and the Sejmists, changed its name to United National Group. Changes were also made in its program with Dubnov's assistance. The political platform of the Constitutional Democratic Party ceased to be considered binding. The paragraphs touching on the autonomy of the internal life of Jewry were broadened. The new program laid down the following propositions: instruction in Jewish schools must be conducted in the students' native language, at least in the primary schools. While not including religion in the sphere of its activities, the Group considered people who had formally repudiated the Jewish religion and entered other denominations to have repudiated their nationality as well. Sympathizing with the systematic colonization of Palestine, the Group was prepared to "support all expedient steps designed to facilitate Jewish emigration to Palestine and adjacent countries." Dubnov took an active part in formulating these propositions and devoted his later political writings to elaborating and defending them.

21

On the Eve of War

At the beginning of 1912 Dubnov resumed his work on the nineteenth century, firmly resolved to complete it. For the next two years he was to relive mentally the history of that stormy century, stage by stage. The chapters on the Polish and Lithuanian Jews were systematically published in *Evreiskaia Starina*. From time to time Dubnov tore himself from his work for an article or a lecture. In the monthly *Di yidishe velt* (1912, No. 1), the reorganized Folkspartey's periodical, he published an article entitled "After the Thirty-Year War," an account of the government's war against the Jews. He put forward the idea that years of persecution had neither killed national feeling nor led to assimilation. The people's power of resistance had increased. Suffering was a spur to fight for equal rights, to fortify economic and cultural positions, and to create new centers in America and Palestine simultaneously. "Do you think," the writer asks, "that only heroes can save the people? No, martyrs do so too, suffering for the people so that their children and grandchildren can be heroes, so that the hidden energy of the former will be transformed into the open energy of the latter." The article ended with a call to fight faint-hearted desertion of the besieged camp.

At that time there was a wave of indignation over the staging, by reactionary circles, of the Beilis affair, involving a Kiev Jew accused of the murder of a Christian boy for ritual purposes.[73] The Historical Society thought it timely to use strictly factual data to shed light on the criminal machinations of the instigators of such trials in the past. Dubnov published several articles in *Starina* on the history of blood libel in Poland and Russia. A number of papers devoted to this topic were read at the Society's meetings. Korolenko,[74] who had recently signed a protest by Russian writers against the ritual accusations, happened to be among those present at one of the meetings. He answered the chairman's words of welcome by stating his conviction that the struggle against racial prejudice was a writer's plain duty and not a meritorious act. Dubnov notes this incident in his autobiography. He long remembered this noble statement by one of the finest members of the Russian intelligentsia.

Dubnov's chapters on the assimilation movement among the German Jews in the period of the so-called Berlin salons were written during the summer on the high balcony overlooking a field of pink clover. Memories floated into his mind as he contemplated the historical past. "The passion for reform in my youth," he writes in his autobiography, "lay trembling under the surgeon's knife of scholarly criticism, in the light of a new world view, which justified the reform of Judaism only as a renewal and not as a destruction of national culture." The chapter on Börne and Heine was written with particular emotion. As he pondered anew the dramatic fates of his youthful favorites, the tribune and the poet, Dubnov clearly felt the immensity of the distance separating him from that impassioned youth who, at the end of the seventies, had formed his political opinions under the influence of Börne's essays and who had been enraptured by Heine's romantic skepticism. Now, with pain in his heart, he had to condemn them both for leaving their persecuted people.

The summer of 1912 was the last that Dubnov spent in Linka. The owner of the estate, an old friend of the Dubnov family, died, and the romantic estate passed into other hands. During his solitary walks Dubnov bade a silent farewell to his favorite spots. More and more he thought that work was really possible only in the quiet of the country, but he knew that he was in no position to part with the Historical Society, the journal, the Courses, and the libraries of the capital.

As he wandered along forest paths, prodding mossy roots with the tip of his heavy cane, Dubnov kept asking himself if it wasn't time to begin writing part of his work in Hebrew, the language of his early youth? However, when his old friends Rawnitzki and Bialik produced numerous reasons in their letters for using Hebrew, Dubnov jokingly replied that it was not at all easy to divorce a "foreign-born" wife after she had borne him a whole pack of children. Then, in a more serious vein, he insisted once again that content, not language, defined a writer's cultural-national allegiance. In accord with this principle Dubnov refused to write an autobiographical note for the *Dictionary of Russian Writers* compiled by Semyon Vengerov;[75] he considered himself a Jewish, not a Russian, writer.

In the autumn the Dubnovs moved into a bright, cozy apartment on the Peterburg Side. Winter and spring were spent working on the era of the second emancipation (1848–1881). As he strolled through the quiet, snowy streets, Simon mulled over the new chapters: "I was enthralled by a completely new subject, the picture of the era whose end coincided with the youth of my generation." The work expanded to such an extent that he had to end the volume with the eighties. He intended to devote the next volume to the period 1881–1905. He thought anxiously of the threat which the censor's crude interference was likely to pose to chapters so close to the present day.

As he worked on the manuscript Dubnov found time to read numerous newspapers and journals, and carefully kept up with current events. He was troubled by the mass exodus of educated young people into Christianity. Every year, before the start of the academic year, many school graduates converted in order to enter the university. A nationalist group proposed that Dubnov compose an appeal to the Jewish community, urging it to oppose a mass exodus from Jewry motivated by considerations of personal gain. The writer fulfilled the commission he was given, but the text of the appeal presented to the Committee seemed too blunt to its majority. It provoked a lively exchange when it was published in the Jewish press under the title "Exodus."*

Preparations for printing that latest volume of *The Recent History* filled the summer of 1913, which was spent in a modest Finnish dacha. In his moments of relaxation, Dubnov rocked his six-month-old, dark-eyed grandson in the baby carriage. The child was the son of his older daughter; she was temporarily in the capital filing petitions on behalf of her husband, who had been arrested. Reading proofs had to be interrupted in order to write a topical article, "The Sources of the Ritual Lie," a historical and psychological analysis of the blood libel. The influential paper *Rech'* refused to print it, fearing reprisals. The paper *Den'* did print the article (1913, No. 256) and paid for its daring—the editor was sentenced by the court to a year's imprisonment.

The book, the result of two years' work, came out in November 1913. As Dubnov held the book, redolent with printer's ink, he felt not only satisfaction but immense weariness. In December he and Ida went to Odessa to rest. They undertook the journey suddenly, obeying a vague impulse; a presentiment of impending historical cataclysm brought a desire to see old friends once more.

In Odessa the Dubnovs immediately encountered a gregarious circle of friends. The local Literary Society had arranged a Hanukkah party with the participation of Abramovich, Frug, and Bialik, and the travel-weary guests from the capital were greeted joyfully. Several days later Abramovich's birthday was solemnly celebrated in his old apartment next to the *talmud-torah*. The eighty-three-year-old guest of honor cheerfully scattered paradoxes and assured those present that he would not yield to God a single year of the maximum life span—one hundred and twenty years. "I saw Abramovich almost every day," recalls Dubnov, describing his stay in Odessa. "We picked up the thread of our former, long conversations."

Dubnov long remembered an evening arranged in his honor by the Literary Society. This time he did not raise his usual objections to a "banquet," as though he foresaw that such an evening would never be repeated. About fifty people gathered in a small restaurant. The guest of honor was seated between Frug, the companion of his youth, and Abramovich, the friend of his mature years. The former's speech tried to resurrect the distant years when the two shy, young provincials lodged next to each other in miserable, furnished rooms. The poet recalled that, time and again, he would return late at night from drinking with friends to find his neighbor buried in a book. In his speech of acknowledgment Dubnov

*Novyi Voskhod, 1913, No. 29; Razsvet, No. 29.

observed that it was no accident that they, the writers of the middle generation, were seated at the table between grandfather Mendele and grandson
Bialik. "At that gathering," he writes, "Frug and I symbolized the early
renaissance of Russian-Jewish literature among the Hebraists and the Yiddishists, both of whom urged me in their speeches into their camps. The
language question . . . injected a dissonant note into an evening of memories. . . ."

Several days later there was a well-attended colloquium on the topic
"The Question of the Literary Language in the History of Judaism." Dubnov used a number of historical examples to show that the linguistic dualism or pluralism of Jewish literature had existed in virtually every period,
and that this ability of the national culture to use any instrument should
be seen as one of its strengths. The recent nationalist movement had ef-
fected a shift of power within this trilingual literature; it had enhanced
the significance of Hebrew in some circles and Yiddish in others, but it
had in no way removed the need for literature in Russian. In summing
up Dubnov declared: "The dogma of the unity of a culture expressed in
various languages must correspond to the unity of a people scattered in
the Diaspora." This formula proved unacceptable to the majority of the
audience. Bialik was the main opponent on the Hebraist side, Merezhin[76]
among the Yiddishists.

Three weeks of relaxation spent in conversations and get-togethers flew
by quickly. Dubnov had long arguments with the militant anti-Yiddishist
Klauzner, the editor of *Ha-Shilo'ah*, and also with the "iron chancellor"
of Zionism, Usishkin.[77] There was almost no time left for walks, and only
on the eve of his departure did Dubnov visit the hill where the plan for
his great historical work was first conceived. He jotted down in his diary:
"light frost, mist over the sea, . . . if I could only sit for hours here and
remember thirteen years of life, relive them again. . . ." When he left
he broke a twig off a cypress bush. This relic of Odessa was preserved
for many years between the pages of his cherished notebook.

The twenty-fifth anniversary of Ahad Ha-Am's literary career was approaching. When Dubnov returned to St. Petersburg he wrote an article
called "The Negation and Affirmation of the Diaspora in Ahad Ha-Am's
Thought" for a Festschrift issue of *Ha-Shilo'ah* (1914, No. XXX, pp. 206–
210). The article summarized an argument which had lasted a quarter
of a century. More than once over those years Dubnov had tried to demonstrate that the conflict between spiritual Zionism and autonomism was
based on a misunderstanding, because these currents were essentially two
sides of the same coin on which was etched "the renewal of the majority
of the nation in Diaspora and of its minority in Zion."

Dubnov's next project was a new edition of the *World History*. According
to his original plan it was to have consisted of five volumes, but it soon
became clear that the plan would have to be significantly expanded. Meanwhile his energy was being squandered on short pieces, meetings, and

a whole series of public lectures—on Ahad Ha-Am's work, the language question, and Hasidism. The diary entry for 4 March complains: "I am not living my own life, it is not a concentrated life but a fragmented one. . . . I still have not taken up the main work, and I speak with myself briefly and rarely. And yet I am the sort of person who speaks little with people and much with his own soul." Touching the native soil of history restored his usual ebullience. Some time later he writes with a feeling of satisfaction: "I am reading hundreds of pages of new researches to correct and supplement twenty or thirty pages of my own text. The new excavations in the East give biblical tales more solid, historical underpinnings."

Now and then the voices of the contemporary world penetrated the world of ancient legends. Some Petersburg intelligentsia came up with the idea of founding a university in Western Europe, primarily for young people deprived of access to higher education. At the same time a few public figures were discussing this scheme in the capital. Usishkin's proposal at a Zionist conference to found a university in Jerusalem was greeted with a storm of applause. A vehement polemic began in print between the "negators of the Diaspora" and the opponents of "the Torah of Zion" concept. Dubnov protested against the acrimony of the debate, asserting that the European and the Palestinian plans could be implemented simultaneously.

Shortly before the war Sholem Aleichem arrived in St. Petersburg from Switzerland. The meeting with his old friend after a ten-year separation moved Dubnov:

> A picture is clearly fixed in my memory . . . of a sunny May day when we sat on the balcony of an elegant hotel, . . . a sea of people surged below . . . while we . . . were recalling the summers in Boiarka in 1890 and Lüstdorf in 1891. Sholem Aleichem told me then he was writing his autobiography, where our meetings in literature and life would be chronicled. He told me of the beauty and peace of Lausanne, and I averred that I would have been happy to write my historical work in that town. . . . Little did we think then that we were chatting for the last time, that we were "confessing" to one another on the eve of a lasting separation.

Three weeks later alarming events forced Sholem Aleichem to leave Russia. Two years later came news of his death in New York.

When Simon and Ida Dubnov went away to rest at the Finnish spa of Nodendal in the summer of 1914, storm clouds were already gathering on the horizon of Europe. Soon news came from St. Petersburg of the streetcar workers' strike, which coincided with the arrival of the French president, Poincaré. Every day Dubnov's fears grew. The entries in his diary, very frequent at this time, reflected the writer's inner turmoil: forebodings of disaster alternated with hopes that the war would bring a revolution in Russia. He writes in his diary, "We have the psychology of prisoners who welcome the fire which burns down the prison, though it may destroy them too. Let my soul die with the Philistines!"[78] On 2 August he notes: "Germany has declared war on Russia in response to the mobilization. . . . Finland is under martial law. . . . In our town of Nodendal the panic reached its peak today. . . . I am among the calm and reserve judgment, although the horror of the coming slaughter of peoples and the horror of Europe's self-destruction numbs the mind. . . ."

22

The Thunder of Guns

The Dubnovs returned from the shores of Finland to the capital squeezed into a stuffy railway carriage overflowing with anxious passengers. Military trains rushed past them. Young recruits shouted, "Goodbye!" The reply came ringing back, "God bless you!" A fellow passenger, a well-known ethnographer, observed: "The times of great events are upon us, one should keep a record." Dubnov had already decided that his diary must be turned into a political chronicle from now on and register facts rather than moods and reflections. But he could not prevent himself from evaluating these facts and probably did not even try to.

The first entry after his arrival in St. Petersburg reads:

Yesterday's emergency meeting of the Duma. Patriotic exclamations thundered forth in the declarations of party and national minority representatives. The Jewish representative's speech was pathetic, it was so timid that the right wing applauded. . . . There was much to be ashamed of in last week's Jewish street demonstrations in Petersburg, with genuflections before the monument of Alexander III. . . . I can think of nothing except world disaster paving the way for an upheaval of historic proportions. The defeat of Germany, that spider of militarism weaving its web over all Europe, will bring deliverance to the world. The combined victory of Russia, France, and England is not likely to encourage reaction in Russia—on the contrary, the atmosphere can only be cleansed. But meanwhile, meanwhile—"the red death," carnage, the destruction of culture and desolation of the soul.

The war brought a burst of patriotism in some circles of the Jewish intelligentsia in the capital. Dubnov reminded them that duties were inseparable from rights; that Jews, who could be mobilized on a par with the rest of the citizens, must demand equal rights for themselves in other areas of life. The time had come, he asserted, when it was necessary to declare, for all to hear, that the Jews are fighting for a future free Russia. He developed these ideas at the meetings of a new organization, made up of the representatives of various Jewish parties, for the purpose of defending the Jewish population from the military authorities' arbitrary exercise of power. The organization, named the Political Conference, gathered materials concerning persecutions of Jews in the zone at the front. News from the towns and villages of the Pale, together with the stories of refugees from Western Europe were disheartening. Dubnov wrote in his diary, "I want to believe in the renewal of mankind after the war, but meanwhile we confront growing bestiality and savagery among even the most civilized peoples. Exiles from Germany, who come through Sweden and Finland daily, tell horrifying tales of German atrocities."

It was difficult to escape into the past away from the troubles of the present. "Where can I find the peace necessary for my work?" he asks in perplexity, "How can I settle down to the work necessary for peace and spiritual equilibrium? A vicious circle!" With a heavy heart Dubnov wrote the following lines in his voluminous notebook, a diary which covered four years: "Hearing of the horrors of war I close this book of notes. . . . I stand troubled before the tomb of the past and the riddle of the immediate future. A great crisis is brewing in the history of the world and in the history of my people. I will continue the chronicle of a single life interwoven with the life of the nation, past and present."

Soon after, much affected by reports about the devastation of the Jewish population in the battle zone, Dubnov wrote, "Yesterday evening a second conference to assist war victims. The sheer immensity of the task staggers us. How can we save nearly half the population of the Pale, fleeing and devastated, from death by starvation? Political aid is unlikely." When a delegation of Jewish community leaders tried to obtain permission for the refugees to enter towns lying outside the Pale the chairman of the Council of Ministers was astonished: "Where do you Jews get such optimism?" At the same time the Minister for Education declared that any hopes for changes in denominational restrictions were idle. "That is how they talk to us," observes Dubnov, "at a time when thousands of our brothers lie on the fields of Poland, Volynia, Podolia, slain in battles for Russia."

He forced himself to return to his work by an immense effort of will. He kept remembering that in his youth he, like Börne, had condemned Goethe for sitting undisturbed at his books during the Battle of Jena. "Now," he acknowledges in his diary, "I look at the matter more sagaciously. If for Goethe . . . learning was . . . a profound need of the soul, then that story can only reveal the grandeur of a spirit standing *above* the fates of men. However, I would find such heights too chilling."

The attitude of the military authorities to the Jews worsened every month. The official pretext for repressive measures was a rumor, started by anti-Semitic propaganda, that many Jews on the western border had an "Austrian orientation" and were helping the enemy. While representatives of the community in the capital fought in endless conferences over the texts of protest resolutions, the military authorities, enraged by defeats, dealt mercilessly with Jewish hostages. A sense of impotence lacerated Dubnov's heart as he shuttled frantically between scholarship and political activities, between the past and the present.

In September 1914 Dubnov reached fifty-four years of age. He writes in his diary: "Fifty-four years behind me. Already fifty-four? Only fifty-four? Here's a double-edged question. Much has been done, but there is still more to be accomplished." On his birthday he felt an acute need to resurrect the past. He wandered in a drizzle—a short, gray-bearded man in a broad-brimmed hat—through the gray streets of the merchant quarter, seeking traces of his youth. He lingered briefly before an old yellow house where he had lived in the mid-eighties, and then strode over a humpbacked bridge toward a gloomy building which had once housed the editorial office of *Voskhod*. How many times had he run up that steep staircase, full of excitment, with a manuscript sticking out of his pocket, the words of which had fired his brain in sleepless nights. Thirty years had passed since then—what years they had been!

The day which began elegaically ended, as usual, in a noisy meeting. And the next morning an entry appeared in his diary: "endless debates, unimplemented decisions—necessary work, but so much energy wasted. . . . Am I to seethe in the daily strife, reading newspapers in the morning, attending meetings in the evening, and in the middle of the day, between two hells, write history?"

Not only inner uncertainty prevented Dubnov from immersing himself in the past. The war dealt a heavy blow to scholarly work. *Evreiskaia Starina* lost its Poland-based contributors, who had provided a wealth of valuable material. The editor tried to fill the gap with letters and documents from his own archive. Disaster threatened his own large plans. The publication of the revised volume of ancient history was shelved; it also proved necessary to give up editions of the *Recent History* in Hebrew and German. "Life under siege conditions," says Dubnov in his diary. "The income from my publications has ceased. The booksellers won't pay. We must live on our small savings. Our links to the outside world are almost cut."

The documents gathered by the Committee for war relief painted a devastating picture. Dubnov spent long hours reading pages containing the dry documentation of facts. He wanted to inform wide circles of readers about the situation and to vent his anger and grief, but the military censorship prevented this. "I want to cry out, but it is impossible to speak even in a whisper, in hints," he writes on 19 December 1914. "I am preoccupied by a plan for a series of short articles to be called *Inter Arma*." The first article in this series, entitled "Rights and Duties," soon appeared in *Novyi Voskhod* (1915, No. 1). Criticizing a speech by one of the representatives of the Jewish community, Dubnov writes: "They advise the most under-privileged people not to think during wartime . . . about that simple act of civic justice which, by the dictate of conscience, ought to follow the present war and which is at least one hundred years overdue. . . . This is likely to create an image of the Jew as one ready to go into battle with the brand of eternal slavery, like a Helot."[79]

Another series of articles followed the first; the censor made several cuts (*Novyi Voskhod*, Nos. 2, 3, 4, 5, 6). The lines breathe pain: "They speak of the tragedy of Poland, whose sons are fighting in the armies of three states. But what can be said of the tragedy of a nation whose children shed their blood in the armies of eight states, of which five are on one side and three on the other?"

This idea, which runs throughout the *Inter Arma* cycle, introducing a note of optimism, was uttered for the first time in the article cited above. Dubnov was convinced that the Jewish question would enter a new phase, an international phase, as a result of the World War. A long article on the prospects of the war deals particularly clearly with this question.* Dubnov took as his starting point the declaration of the Entente powers about the "freedom of small nations," and predicted the creation of new states after the war as well as the possibility of securing the rights of national minorities through international treaties.

A sense of the link between history and the present never left Dubnov. He described this link in one of the lectures at the Courses in Oriental Studies. "The essence of historicism lies in apprehending the past with the immediacy of the current moment and in thinking of the contemporary world historically." He kept his distaste for "dead learning" throughout his career. It reasserted itself with particular vigor when he had to visit the venerable historian Harkavy[80] on behalf of the Historical-Ethnographic Society. The decrepit host, whose apartment lay deep in the dust of old folios, greeted the delegate rather coolly. He had not forgotten that thirty years earlier the young, sharp-tongued critic had spoken of him as the personification of arid, soulless learning. Now that critic was ready to reaffirm his previous description. "How lifeless everything was there," he writes in his diary. "A mummy of history, entombed among books and papers in his home, his vault. . . . He and I do not speak the same language, for me history is a bubbling spring of life, struggle, creativity, and a guide to a world view. . . ."

*"The Jewish Question from the Prospect of the World War," *National Problems*, 1915, No. 2.

"Living history" led Dubnov by the hand while he was drafting an outline of the history of the Jews in Poland and Russia for an American publisher. As he worked on the vast, unmined material for this study, he decided that he had to make the monumental labor, the *World History of the Jewish People*, his life's task. The history of Eastern Jewry, originally conceived of as a separate monograph, must become part of this work. And he was asking fate for one thing only—to live long enough to bring the work to completion.

The news of defeats at the front caused great fear at home. Anti-Semitism, fed by poisonous rumors, grew in this atmosphere; but at the same time resistance to it quickened in the circles of the progressive intelligentsia. Dubnov noted in his diary Leonid Andreev's fervent protest against the racial persecutions which dishonored Russia. In 1915 the League to Combat Anti-Semitism was founded on the initiative of Maxim Gorky,[81] Andreev,[82] and Fedor Sologub.[83] The League's crowded first meeting, opened by Gorky's impassioned speech, made a profound impression on Dubnov. The militant notes sounded in many of the speeches gave him great satisfaction. Such bold criticism of the government was impossible in the press, which was fettered by the iron band of censorship. The *Inter Arma* cycle was never completed. The military censor closed *Novyi Voskhod* and then the other Russian-Jewish journals.

Dubnov's passion for political polemic found an outlet in the new pages of the *World History*. Dubnov was now working on the concluding chapters. At the height of the government's anti-Semitic campaign his attention was drawn once again to the autocratic regime's "Thirty-Year War" against the Jews, a subject he had touched on before, and he gave it a thorough treatment. Writing had a calming effect. "I sit in the quiet of my study," reads the entry for 1 August 1915, "and compose a chronology of the era since 1881 on the basis of the periodicals. My youth was interwoven with the beginning of that era and my entire life with the sequel to it. I cannot do this work without stirring up personal memories."

Physical conditions noticeably deteriorated as time passed. Food shortages, high prices, and a labor shortage were severely felt in Russia. Sometimes it seemed strange to Dubnov that, despite all these difficulties and the terrible news from the front, life went on, and that "we are still able to meet at the Committee of the Historical Society and discuss historical subjects and literary enterprises (a meeting at Gorky's about a Jewish national anthology), and that I am editing *Starina*."

In November 1915 a letter came from the long silent Ahad Ha-Am in London. Despite his habitual reserved tone one could feel he was deeply shaken by the war. "At the center of world conscience," he wrote, "I have become convinced that this conscience is a fiction." It was a cry from the soul of a man with high moral standards, stunned by the orgy of brutal instincts. Dubnov's article "*De profundis*" was a response to this tragic letter. The writer asserted with his characteristic optimism that world conscience must awaken after the atrocious bloodshed. Otherwise mankind would have lost the meaning of life. But it was precisely that growing sense of the meaninglessness of human existence which gnawed like a worm at Ahad Ha-Am's mind.

However galling his dependence on the censor was to Dubnov, he could not renounce journalism completely. The sketch "The Story of a Jewish Soldier" (*Evreiskaia Nedelia*, No. 11) was the deathbed confession of a long-suffering World War infantryman who had been the victim of the government's anti-Semitic policy in peacetime. Only the first chapter of this topical prose poem appeared in print; the rest were banned. Gorky, on whom it made a deep impression, tried to publish it in the journal *Letopis'*, but the military censor was immovable. Dubnov very much wanted to publish a piece invested with so much anger and pain outside Russia, but he was unable to send the manuscript abroad.

Although the atmosphere of the worldwide carnage blunted the impact of social and literary losses, Dubnov felt the death of each of his contemporaries in literature as a heavy personal blow. The news of Sholem Aleichem's death in America in 1916 hit him hard. Perhaps only now did he really understand how much wisdom lay hidden in that "humane simplicity" which a diary entry describes as his late friend's distinguishing characteristic. "Never did I think, . . . considering all the differences in our characters, that I would recall our meetings with such deep emotion," Dubnov acknowledged, as he worked on a memoir for *Evreiskaia Starina*.

Several days after Sholem Aleichem's death he received a letter from Frug, who was confined to his deathbed. Enclosed in the envelope were poems which spoke of his farewell to life. His agonizing pain dragged on for several months. When news of the poet's death arrived, Dubnov devoted to him a chapter of the memoirs in *Starina* and a paper at the Historical-Ethnographic Society. His heart was still aching from this loss when the mail brought a sad missive from Ahad Ha-Am, fraught with ominous forebodings. Several passages in the letter sounded like a spiritual testament. Ahad Ha-Am made an unexpected request of his old friend: "When I die, try to defend my memory from all those vulgar eulogies, oral and written. . . . You might publish a notice . . . that, as an old and close friend, you are certain that the 'deceased' was opposed to all noisy display of feeling." Dubnov could not keep back his tears when he read these lines. The same day he wrote in his diary: "People, meetings, shared joy and grief . . . weave the cloth of life. At first the cloth keeps growing thicker, more and more new threads are woven into it, . . . then death begins to pull the threads, one by one, out of the cloth, it draws out one, then another. You feel the gradual unraveling of the cloth, the threads in your soul snap. Your circle, your generation dies. . . ."

In the autumn of 1916 one more trial fell to the writer's lot. His son, Yakov, fell gravely ill with a disease which almost destroyed his young body. Simon reached his fifty-sixth birthday "amid sad thoughts that the end of life was approaching and that my life's task was far from completed, amid the collapse of Jewish culture and the higher spiritual values." Cheerful lines appeared in his diary less and less frequently. He did not lose faith that after the war Jewish life would be reconstructed on the principle of "a nation among nations," but he was troubled by the thought that he would be unable to take part in that process.

The year 1917 began in an atmosphere of confusion and fear. Rasputin, the evil genius of the dynasty, was murdered in a palace in St. Petersburg one blizzard-swept night, almost on the threshold of the new year, and many took his death to portend the end of the monarchy. Life became more difficult every day. St. Petersburg was starving. Long lines of women formed in front of the bakers' shops at night, and now and then an ominous rumbling swept along the lines like the cruel wind off the Neva. An entry in Dubnov's diary made almost on the eve of the March Revolution reads: "They broke into the bread shops and demanded bread in the town today. The factories are on strike. . . . At such times in past years there has been a Purim feast, lively conversations—now there's dead silence, deserted streets. All the words have been spoken, the dying are duly silent. . . . We are in the kingdom of death—the death of people, eras, cultures."

23

The Great Upheaval

From days of war, from days of freedom
A bloody reflection shines on faces.
—A. Blok

In the frosty March days of 1917, the "days that shook the world," Dubnov lay ill with a severe case of influenza. Bits of news from the street tore like a whirlwind into his clouded brain, each more incredible than the last. The absence of newspapers—the town was in the grip of a strike

—heightened the anxiety. As soon as his temperature began to fall the patient was drawn to his diary. The brief, almost daily entries became a necessity in those anxious times. They were, contrary to his original intention, not the notes of a chronicler, but the cry of a man trying to find his bearings in the middle of a storm. Like the vast majority of the representatives of the oppositional intelligentsia, Dubnov, who had for decades been calling for revolution, was now stunned when he came face to face with the unleashed elements. The diary reflected his confusion. In its pages the joy of deliverance from a hated regime alternated with terror in the face of anarchy. With the passage of time terror became the dominant note. The encounter of the two deadly whirlwinds—war and revolution—prompted ominous forebodings.

An entry made at the beginning of March reads: "the papers haven't come out, the streetcars aren't running. The strike is taking on the dimensions of the 1905 strike. . . . No one knows what the Duma decided yesterday. . . . Not one Mirabeau among the moderates, not one Danton among the extremists." The next day his doubts had dissipated: "No, it's not a rebellion but a real revolution. . . . Four guard regiments have risen, seized the arsenal and seem to be distributing weapons to the populace. . . . A great historical moment has come. Will society prove too small for it?"

Although his strength was slow in returning after his illness, Dubnov could not stay at home. Winding a warm muffler around his neck, he would venture out into the wide, snow-covered avenue. Trucks flying the red flag roared by with bayonets sticking out: detachments of soldiers and sailors who had joined the revolution were driving about the city, eliminating the remaining pockets of policemen. Now and then the heavy rattle of gunfire issued from rooftops and attic windows. The last defenders of the old order were sniping from under cover. Gunfire became an everyday occurrence, but it did not disturb Dubnov. He did not quicken his pace, and lingered at the fences and pillars plastered with white posters. Passersby, old women in shawls and streetsellers, often gathered around him and, in a hoarse voice, weak from illness, he would read them the manifestos of the Provisional Government and the appeals of the Soviet of Soldiers and Workers Deputies. When he returned home he rushed to pen lines charged with feeling in his notebook: "My soul overflows with the grandeur of the moment," he wrote, "1905 deceived us; perhaps 1917 won't. And if it does? Then there is no salvation for Russia."

One of the entries reads:

There is something strange in this revolution, as there is in the weather now —spring sun and harsh winter cold. Light but no warmth. Is it that terrible events are brewing at the front or that revolution and counterrevolution may be tied all too quickly into a bloody knot in the thick of the army and the peasantry? I don't know, but I feel uneasy. All is well, it would seem; equal rights have rained down on us; we have apparently obtained everything we

fought for for decades and the vile police state has been overthrown. . . .
We congratulated one another last night . . . at the meeting . . . and resolved
to send a message of congratulation to the Provisional Government and the
Soviet of Workers' Deputies, but there was no elation. . . . The nightmare
of war is strangling the revolution.

The first night of Passover, which Dubnov was accustomed to spending
with friends, passed strangely that year:

Between seven and eight in the evening I went into my library. Through the
window a full Passover moon gazed at me. As I began singing sad synagogue
airs through my tears, memories of the past welled up. . . . My cherished
dreams have come to pass, but I will soon be fifty-seven, and worlds are
collapsing in a great cataclysm. . . . After the deluge the reconstruction of
life will begin from the ground up, . . . but my strength is failing, and I
still have to complete my life's work and fulfill my vow.

Dubnov felt a sense of satisfaction when he succeeded in extracting from
the censor's office two manuscripts confiscated during the war—"The
Story of a Jewish Soldier" (this piece quickly appeared in *Evreiskaia Nedelia*,
Nos. 19–23) and a monograph about Jews during the reign of Nicholas
II, which was intended for an American publisher. After a long break he
resumed work on the *World History*. At the beginning of May he observes:

I have been writing about Christianity in the first centuries, the Gospels and
Revelations. . . . But life is seething all around me: the Revolution continues.
. . . The 1 May parades, mass rallies. Workers demonstrated against the Provisional Government all day yesterday. . . . The antinomy of revolution and
war becomes more and more terrible. . . . I need to go simultaneously into
the apocalypse of the second century and that of 1917. Can this be the "end
of time"? The boundary between the old era and the new?

Often, as he returned home from meetings in the silvery twilight of
the white nights, Dubnov came upon long lines at the bread shops. The
agitated city never rested even late at night. Not far from the house where
the Dubnovs lived, small groups of soldiers and sailors gathered under
the balcony of a white house recently occupied by a well-known ballerina.
They were waiting for a short, broad-shouldered man with a large bald
patch to appear on the balcony and speak in simple, direct language about
what mattered most—bread, land, peace. Dubnov anxiously watched
these political street rallies in the luminous twilight of the northern night
and tried to guess what they foreshadowed. The next morning he was
gone again into the distant past for six or seven hours.

At the beginning of the summer he notes: "The continuation of the war
threatens the further spread of anarchy, hunger, and epidemics. A separate
cease-fire would mean a break with the Allies and the total collapse of
the government. A vicious circle is strangling Russia." He spoke about

the exceptional complexity of the historical situation at a political meeting called by representatives of the Jewish community. In this speech he put forward the idea that the spread of anarchy was due not only to the war but also to a disproportionate growth of the class struggle, which was incompatible with the nature of a revolution designed to accomplish political transformation.

The summer months were spent in a quiet corner of Estonia. Dubnov was hoping to restore his strength after his long illness. He sought respite from turmoil by listening to the noise of the sea and the carefree romping of his little grandsons, but there was no escape from war and revolution. The news of the July uprising particularly disturbed him. "The war is destroying the revolution, the revolution is destroying the war," he writes under the immediate impression of reports from the capital. "It is possible we will end both in the same way—badly."

The question of combining scholarly and community work had always troubled Dubnov, and it became particularly urgent at this time of crisis. An entry made at the beginning of August speaks of this:

> The morning mist shrouds the forest. I am sitting on the balcony. . . . I lapse into thoughts with which I have been preoccupied lately. I am deciding what to do with the remainder of my life. Should I sacrifice it to political strife . . . and submerge myself in the new wave of social activism, or should I "leave the world" and fulfil my vow to complete my life's work? In the first case, upon returning to Petersburg, I would have to enter the whirlpool of political activity, speak at meetings, organize the Folkspartey, attend the Jewish Congress, run for election to the Constituent Assembly, and boil for years in the all-Russian cauldron. . . . It would mean changing my life plan . . . and leaving the whole edifice unfinished. But if I do not choose this self-sacrifice then a sacrifice of another sort is needed. I would have to break with everything around me, . . . shut myself away in the midst of the storm and weave the thread of history from the fourth century to our day. . . . Following that path I will preserve my spiritual integrity.

As though troubled by this prospect he adds several lines later: "Giving up political activity I am not giving up intense political thought which will be expressed in political criticism on the most important issues."

As soon as Dubnov returned to the capital he was sucked into the whirlpool of events. Once again resolutions made in solitude proved ephemeral on confronting reality. It was difficult to shut oneself up in a study when Kornilov's[84] troops, the first regular army of the counterrevolution, stood outside the capital. After that threat was eliminated and the siege was lifted, Dubnov found himself in a circle of like-minded people impatiently awaiting his return. The Executive Committee of the Folkspartey, now called the Yidishe Folkspartey, insisted that the organization's main ideologue should assume leadership during the crisis. At the beginning of October Dubnov writes:

From the depths of the centuries I have again emerged . . . onto a battlefield.
. . . War is everywhere: at the fronts, the war between the Baltic fleet and
the Provisional Government, rebellions and pogroms in many parts of Russia.
The real war is going on at the Democratic Convention, where the splintered
parties of Russian democracy are fighting one another. The Bolsheviks have
conquered the streets. . . . Hunger, excesses, the German advance on Dvinsk,
official warnings of a possible Zeppelin attack on Petersburg.

In such circumstances the frenetic work of the Jewish social organizations
seemed at times like childish games near the crater of a volcano. "Yesterday
I finally refused to run for the Constituent Assembly," Dubnov reports.
"I look at this election dance and think, 'Children, can't you see that the
house is on fire?'" And several days later: "Until the thirst for peace parch-
ing every throat is quenched, the horrors in Russia will grow. But everyone
thinks constantly of peace and no one dares to talk about it in public
except the Bolsheviks. . . ."

In October the Provisional Soviet of the Russian Republic was convened.
It was a surrogate parliament that was soon to transfer its functions to
the Constituent Assembly. Dubnov was skeptical of the value of the institution's activities: "Trite patriotic speeches about fighting the enemy, which
the orators themselves don't believe possible."

It was clear no government could increase the battle readiness of an
army which did not want to fight. Meanwhile life became harder every
day; the populace of the capital, cut off from the grain-producing areas
by the revolution, felt the shortage of food acutely. "There are days," observes Dubnov, "when Ida, harassed by worry and toil, cannot even get
bread after standing in lines for a long time."

Dubnov made haste to escape into the peace and quiet of his study,
away from the streets with their instant rallies, lines before the cooperative
shops, and the swift, harsh lynchings of "enemies of the people," streets
which daily became more incomprehensible, violent, and terrifying. A distant time was brought to life in his imagination, a time when a group
of talmudic scholars tried to forge an iron enclosure of laws and moral
codes for a people without territory. One dark, autumn night as he was
finishing a chapter on the early Talmud period, the silence was shattered
by gunfire from the cruiser *Aurora* firing on the Winter Palace.[85]

24

Into the Whirlpool

Revolution is a clot of sorrow accumulated over hundreds of years.
—Victor Hugo

The revolution deepened—therein lay its inexorable logic. While prominent jurists closeted in their studies painstakingly polished the paragraphs of election statutes, files of men with wind-burned faces, in worn overcoats —the tatters of the disintegrating front—trudged from west to east over the dusty and muddy roads of the immense country. They were met by a smoky glow hanging over gentry estates: the peasants were settling the land question without waiting for the Constituent Assembly. Revolution swept across the country, bringing in its wake fires, ransacking of wine cellars, and merciless lynch mobs of sailors and soldiers avenging years of grievances. In the whirlpool of events utopians and realists changed roles: the former insisted that, in that poor and backward country, revolution must be moderate and gradual; the latter instinctively sensed that "in hutted, stolid Russia"[86] there was no power which could contain the elemental rebellion. And when reality began to rain blow after blow on the utopians, their indignation knew no bounds.

Dubnov belonged to the utopians. His entire life's philosophy made this inevitable. He was shaken when the revolution, of which he had dreamed since his early youth, when he declaimed Victor Hugo's fiery tirades, proved more terrible at close quarters than through the prism of history. The stirring speeches of the Girondists could conceal the cruel reality of the September massacres from posterity, but it was more difficult to turn away from the reality embodied in rough street justice and starvation bread rations. To Dubnov the rationalist, a disciple of Comte and Mill, the poet's felicitous line promptly picked up by the street, "we will fan the world fire to the grief of all bourzhooys,"[87] was the apotheosis of the destructive elemental principle in which he saw the greatest danger for humanity. As he read of the horrors of war Dubnov comforted himself with the thought that reason would ultimately triumph. He considered the revolutionary period preceding October as an unavoidable struggle between the spirit of order and the spirit of chaos. But when the Petersburg garrison, which had toppled the autocracy eight months before, toppled the Provisional Government, the very ground shook beneath his feet. It was not fear for himself which dictated the embittered lines in his diary. A writer who lived by his own labor was not threatened by the loss of his livelihood under a socialist revolution. Something else frightened him —loss of faith in the redemptive power of revolutionary upheaval.

As always in the difficult times of his life, work gave him resilience and strength. Three days after the October Revolution his diary reads,

> I wrote . . . today about the ancient school systems. I have ceased to marvel at this capacity for working on a volcano: don't people eat, and drink, and sleep on the battlefield? When spiritual food has become the same daily necessity as physical food, you take it, even on a volcano. . . . And for me historical work is both food and air without which I would suffocate. There is no merit to it, it is simply the soul's act of self-preservation.

And several days later:

> There is famine in Petersburg. And blood is already flowing in Moscow. The Kremlin and the center of the town have been sacked. Kaledin's[88] Cossacks have seized control of the South and are marching on Moscow. . . . Each day I save a couple of hours for work. I steep myself in the literature of *Aggadah* and *Midrash*—it warms the soul.

Worries about daily bread depressed Dubnov and sometimes dragged him away from his work, but they weighed most heavily on his wife. From early morning until late at night the frail, sickly woman strained every nerve to fight hunger and cold. The hours she spent standing in lines, often to no purpose, particularly exhausted her. While Ida racked her brains to make dinner from pitiful substitutes for food, such lines as these appeared in Simon's diary: "On the island of learning, where I seek shelter from the storm, the work of the mind is as active as ever. I am reading and examining dozens of volumes of new or previously unobtainable sources. The scope of the *History* is expanding, I feel a heady sense of accomplishment, and the sadness of an architect destined to build in the midst of general destruction."

The time came for the elections to the Constituent Assembly. Dubnov voted for the Constitutional Democrats. He did not always approve of their party's tactics, but he considered that it rose above class struggle and that its leaders were men of a European cast of mind. In conversation with Vinaver he had once compared them to the Girondists; now this description could be seen as an ominous prophecy.

News of the Balfour Declaration burst unexpectedly on Dubnov from afar. In his diary he was skeptical:

The Zionists rejoice, but isn't it premature? They are already talking in their newspapers about the "Jewish state," they are planning celebrations as in the days of Sabbatai Zevi. It is a new drug, but the awakening will be dreadful. I rejoice in the English Declaration as a recognition of the Jewish nation, but their motives are less than admirable (an enticement for the Jews, like Bonaparte's proclamation in 1799), and the consequences are problematic. . . . It would be good to have one's own, quiet, historical retreat, or even the hope of it, in these terrible times. . . . Blessed are the believers!

Dubnov felt lonely at times despite meetings with his circle of friends. This feeling grew stronger when news of Abramovich's death arrived at the beginning of December. Dubnov writes in his diary,

An old man of eighty-five has passed away, and the brightest thread from the summer of my existence has been torn out of my life. And now, on a harsh winter night in the northern capital, amid the conflagration of the civil war, I mourn both for the death of my friend and the memory of the years in Odessa when I communed with that powerful mind. I remember my first meeting with A[bramovich] in November 1890, and the long conversations over thirteen years, our shared meditations.

Visions of the past, lit by the southern sun, pursued Dubnov as he waited in line to receive his rations in a biting wind off the Neva. And during the Christmas season, when the capital was smothering in snowdrifts, he wrote a memoir of his old friend as though in a fever. He had to write in his overcoat: the kerosene lamp smoked; his numb hand moved over the paper with difficulty. But an inner fire warmed his soul. The memoir, dictated by deep feeling, appeared first in an abridged version in Yiddish (a pamphlet from the series *Fun tsayt tsu tsayt*) and then in full, in Russian, in the collection *Safrut*.

The dissolution of the Constituent Assembly in January 1918 was a heavy blow to Dubnov; the All-Russian parliament seemed the only way out of the political impasse. He was overwhelmed by a sense of hopelessness. The exciting prospect of a Jewish Congress—the first step toward realizing the idea of cultural-national autonomy—began to seem illusory, meaningless. He gave way to pessimism in a public speech on the subject "The Current Situation and the Jewish Congress." His main opponent at the meeting was the Deputy Commissioner for Jewish Affairs, who declared that in his youth he had considered Dubnov his "spiritual father," but that after ten years' political experience in jail, he was convinced that the place for Jews was in the ranks of the most uncompromising fighters for the revolution.

Events at the front took a tragic turn. The Germans were advancing on the capital. Dubnov witnessed the collapse of Russia and the loss of the border lands with deep pain: "This is a vivisection of my people too," he wrote, "six million Jews chopped into six pieces."

At the beginning of 1918 the Soviet of the People's Commissars was transferred to Moscow, and the former capital was turned into the "Northern Commune" ruled by Zinoviev.[89] The supply of goods dwindled each day. Bread rations were allotted according to categories. Dubnov was originally assigned to the category of people allotted an eighth of a pound of bread a day. Hunger drove the inhabitants of the Northern Commune south and west, to the grain-producing provinces. Friends tried to persuade the Dubnovs to leave the doomed city, but Simon would not hear of it. He was chained to his desk. In March he finished the third volume of the *World History*, on which he had been working for a year and a half. "Working conditions are incredible," he states in his diary, "war plus revolution plus dictatorship. . . . I have been writing at full steam lately. . . ." More than once he thought of undertaking a Hebrew translation of his largest work, but such a labor would require several years.

> Strange thoughts! The world is dying, there's civil war in Russia, bloody fighting has broken out again in the West . . . and I think of my own historical works! Isn't that strange? No, it only bears witness to the immortality of the Spirit and its resilience. . . . We are like Archimedes at the conquest of Syracuse: *"Noli tangere circulos meos!"*[90] It's not indifference, on the contrary— it's the result of extreme responsiveness, which forces us to seek salvation in the Spirit, in what is indestructible amid the destructible.

In April, at a meeting of the Jewish National Council, a body carrying out the function of the Congress, which could not be held because of the civil war, Dubnov delivered an impassioned speech. He condemned the political fragmentation of Jewry, which had prevented the Congress from being organized when there was still time, and pointed out that other nationalities, even backward ones, had preceded the Jews in creating their own organs of self-government. The National Council was a stillborn institution. Soon after its establishment Dubnov notes in his diary: "Yesterday's meeting—petty, flabby, poorly attended; passions flare up only in party bickering. Everyone has given up."

The rebirth of *Evreiskaia Starina* after a prolonged interruption was an unexpected ray of light in a hopeless situation. The task of publishing a large annual anthology lay ahead. Once again a pile of manuscripts appeared on Dubnov's desk. When his eyes tired he would go off to the nearby city park, which grew more and more quiet, gloomy, and desolate. Every day one could meet in its deserted paths a lean, gray-haired man in a baggy, faded jacket, a slim volume of Hugo peeping from his pocket. Sometimes he appeared in the company of two pale, dark-eyed little boys with whom he held lively conversations. At the end of August the walks with his grandsons ceased. Hunger forced his daughter's family to move to Poland. The silence which reigned in their apartment after the children had gone depressed its occupants. The news of a wave of terror in retaliation for an attempt on Lenin's life depressed them further. Bitter, lonely moments gave rise to a wish to leave Russia. Here is a typical diary entry:

> I went to the Botanical Gardens. Sat on a bench, looked at the fallen leaves, . . . I thought: I can still go on living somehow in the midst of hunger, cold . . . and terror as long as the link to the past, the integrity of my soul, is not broken. But if they break into my dwelling and take away the fruit of years of labor—the manuscript of the *History*—and seize my diaries of thirty-three years, they will take away part of my soul, they will destroy the meaning and the integrity of my life. As I walked home by the linden avenue on the bank of the Neva, I wondered: Go or stay?

Dubnov was tormented by the thought that there was no one to bequeath his spiritual testament to. "There's no use," says his diary, "in entrusting to others the completion of an unfinished building, the plan of which I will take with me to the grave." To finish the building while it was still possible—this was the only impetus to live. Dubnov knew no rest. Before he had finished editing *Starina* he set to work on the article "What Should We Do at the World Congress?" It came out in pamphlet form (in the series *Fun tsayt tsu tsayt*, No. 2) and focused on the idea of waging a struggle for the right of the Jewish national minority at the coming World Peace Congress.

Despite interruptions, Dubnov's work on his *magnum opus* progressed. In the autumn of 1918 his diet improved somewhat (he was reassigned from the third to the first category and began to receive three-eighths of a pound of bread a day) but the fuel shortage remained a vexatious problem. He often had to abandon his work and chop up furniture to stoke the stove.

A Palestine newspaper report that the foundations of a Jewish university had been laid in Jerusalem was like news from another world. The organizer of this triumph was Dubnov's old friend Marcus Kagan, the hospitable host at the dacha in Polesia, the memory of which was etched forever on the writer's soul. Dubnov drank in the voices from the distant past carrying him away from daily hardship. "I remembered a time long past," he writes in his diary, "I dreamed of a journey to Palestine in two or three years when I will have finished my main life's work according to the vow I made long ago. And, who knows, perhaps my historical homeland will enchant me, perhaps the new university will claim me, perhaps the song of Judea will soothe a weary son of the Diaspora."

This mood proved fleeting. Dubnov buried himself in the time of the Crusades. His working day began in the morning gray, by the dim light of a kerosene lamp, and ended late at night. The past sheltered the writer from the present, and the only piece of news to bring him back to the contemporary world and make his heart beat with hope was the report of the cessation of four years of slaughter.

25

An Island amid the Elements

By 1919 Russia was in the throes of a savage civil war. Incessant fighting raged all over the country. Kolchak[91] in the East and Denikin[92] in the South tried to crush the Red Army in an iron ring; Iudenich[93] stood at the approaches to the northern capital, and Haidamak[94] bands added to the bloody chaos in the Ukraine. The trickle of supplies and fuel condemned the population of the capital to a cave-like existence. Dubnov's study seemed an island amid storms, but each day it became more difficult to work on this island. Here is a typical entry from his diary:

> I rose early in the morning, dressed, pulled on my overcoat, galoshes, and cap (the room was 7 degrees [centigrade]) and sat at the desk. Wrote with frozen fingers about the Dominicans and the French Inquisition of the XIII century. Had something to eat at 10, looked through the paper, and went to the district Soviet's Fuel Department to get a requisition for wood. Found myself in line with hundreds of people winding down the back stairs of a huge house. . . . I stood two hours in a crush of unhappy, worried people and, like hundreds of others, went away empty-handed: the stuff ran out before our turn. . . . Walked home feeling depressed, bought one and a half pounds of bread on the way. . . . Some good fortune as well as sorrow in our courtyard. A friend did us a good turn and sent about two cords of wood on a cart. . . . Dusk fell. I sat down, tired, to the work I'd interrupted, finished the paragraph, and now I sit and think. We are "fortunate": we'll be able to heat the kitchen (I carried several heavy bundles of wood upstairs myself) and poor Ida won't have to freeze or run off to other people's kitchens. . . . We are wasting away from cold more than from hunger.

The enormous increase in expenses—prices at the free market shot up every day—exhausted the writer's modest savings. Dubnov had to devote part of the time scheduled for his main work to extraneous jobs. He accepted a proposal from the Commissariat of Education to edit a bibliographical guide to Russian-Jewish literature. Grinberg, Lunacharskii's[95] energetic assistant, obtained a substantial grant in support of the Historical Society. The Jewish People's University, where lectures were given in Russian and Hebrew, was also founded on his initiative. Dubnov became one of the professors; courses were also taught by Michael[96] and Joseph Kulisher,[97] Israel Zinberg,[98] and Aaron Steinberg.[99] When a number of research commissions were set up under the aegis of the Commissariat of Education, Dubnov participated in editing the collection *Materials for a History of Anti-Jewish Pogroms* and later sat on a commission on ritual murder trials.

All this work slowed the pace of writing the *History* but the main obstacle was the external dislocation. Sometimes it was necessary to abandon an unfinished chapter and hurry off to a nearby wooden building designated for demolition by the municipal authorities; that was how the inhabitants of the Northern Commune obtained fuel. Dubnov would return home half dead, dragging dirty, rotting planks with difficulty. The intolerable hardships increased his intellectual anxiety:

> Last week I delivered the opening address at the Jewish People's University. . . . A sad opening. I spoke of the present crisis in which it is difficult to discern whether we are moving toward a new age of culture or toward the twilight. I spoke of the new civilian militarism emerging at the very moment of the triumph of international pacifism and the idea of the League of Nations. I called for learning from Jewish history. Further lectures are planned, but to whom to give them, and what and how to give them is still unclear to me. . . .

In his hours of loneliness Dubnov pondered anew questions which had long preoccupied him and attempted to take stock. In the summer of 1919 he wrote,

> I often think about my own attitude toward the Palestine question and Zionism over the decades. Not long ago I explained in the Zionist *Khronika* that I consider it a nationalist's duty to pay the *shekel ha-geulah*,[100] on the condition that he participates in the all-Jewish Congress, rather than the Party Congress, on the rebirth of Palestine. Only now is it becoming clear that Eretz Israel can be a haven, as in the time of ancient Judea, for part of the nation only— and then only after decades of formidable toil—and the Diaspora will still remain with all its alarming problems.

In a postscript couched in Hebrew, he spoke of his desire to visit Palestine on the completion of his *magnum opus*, but sadly added that in all likelihood he was destined to end his days in the wilderness and, before his death, hear the words "You shall not enter the promised land. . . ."

In the autumn the town was transformed into a military encampment. Iudenich's troops were advancing on Kronstadt. Everywhere feverish preparations for defense were being made. The circles hostile to the new regime secretly rejoiced at the successes of the White Armies. However, reports that the victories of the "Volunteers"[101] were almost always accompanied by pogroms troubled many people. When news of the atrocities committed by Mamontov's Cossack troops reached the capital, Dubnov observed, "'The saviours' have shown their true colors. . . ."

Iudenich's attacks were repulsed, but the northern capital remained cut off from the rest of the country. Dubnov tried to create the conditions necessary for work. He joined the study to the kitchen so as to be a little closer to the source of heat—a small cast-iron stove, the *burzhooyka*, which in the absence of firewood was fueled with furniture and sometimes with the less-important books. In the constant war on two fronts—cold and hunger—the body did not always emerge victorious. Dubnov began to experience spells of dizziness, and his feet would swell. A ten-pound bag of rye flour, which turned up unexpectedly in the library cupboard, seemed an extraordinary stroke of luck under these conditions; one could stop agonizing about food for two whole weeks. Despite these worries, which cast a pall over everyday life, Dubnov's spiritual strength seemed inexhaustible. In an entry on 18 November 1919 he says:

> I write with a shaking hand, it has still not recovered from the daily chore of chopping wood with a blunt axe. The mood for prayer has not left me even today; it saves my soul from freezing. Unhappy are those who do not know how to pray in the difficult moments, mundane people, without an inner God, chained to the earth, lacking wings to rise above its horrors!

Toward the beginning of 1920 the civil war began to subside. The armies of Kolchak, Denikin, Iudenich, and Petliura were beaten. In the heat of battle the Ukrainian "separatists" and the representatives of the "White Movement," mouthing republican and democratic slogans, revealed their true natures. Jewish pogroms took on unheard-of proportions; the Ukraine presented the most terrible picture. The actions of the new Haidamak army strikingly resembled those of the seventeenth- and eighteenth-century Haidamaks. Dubnov concluded bitterly that men had not become more humane with the passage of time.

The physical conditions of life changed for the better in 1920. The Commission for the Amelioration of Scholars' Living Conditions, founded on Gorky's initiative, was a godsend to a large number of scholars. Dubnov was included in the category of people entitled to "academic rations," an additional quantity of flour, fat, and sugar. The distribution center for rations was located in a distant part of town. One had to cross almost the entire city, lugging a sack of provisions on one's back or dragging them on a child's sled. On 8 February this entry appears in Dubnov's diary: "This week . . . we have eaten our fill of bread for the first time. . . . I record this event in my diary after more than two years of going hungry." In the summer Dubnov was given the chance to spend two weeks in a rest home for writers and scholars in a large suburban dacha. The house was overflowing with emaciated, irascible people, and there was no question of privacy, but the guest rested from worry and physical exertions. When he returned home he took up his interrupted work with redoubled energy.

He was now keeping his diary regularly, almost every day, giving free rein to the bitterness which found no other outlet. Occasional lyrical notes inspired by a chance meeting or the loss of a close friend appear in the diary. Any contact with the past induced a painful, oppressive sadness. The news of the death of Sh. An-sky, Dubnov's comrade-in-arms for many years, stirred a host of memories. The unexpected visit of an old Mstislavl friend, a former *maskil* with whom Dubnov had read Lilienblum's *Hatte'ot Ne'urim* at the end of the eighties, brought to the surface a still deeper stratum of the past. That visitor had remembered Ida Dubnov as a blooming, vivacious girl. Now, as she returned from the shop with an empty basket, she was a stooped woman with ash-gray hair, chilled to the bone and all in tears. She had stood for three hours in a line for kerosene—in vain. But in Simon's imagination rose a winter evening long ago, when a youth and a girl picked their way through the snowdrifts of Mstislavl's main street, their young, excited voices ringing through the frosty stillness.

As the multivolume *History* neared the end, Dubnov was increasingly troubled by the thought of what would happen to it now. It was obviously unthinkable to print such an immense work during a time of general devastation. Dubnov worked on the final chapters with particular passion. He spent whole days at the desk and rejoined the outside world only on Sundays, when he visited the university. Those were his days to meet friends and official visitors dropping by the university reception hall. One day a chance visitor handed him a letter from Ahad Ha-Am, quite unexpected after three years of silence. It transpired that his old friend had been ill with neurasthenia for fifteen months and considered himself an invalid. His letter spoke of an imminent move to Palestine.

News of the thriving publishing industry in Berlin appeared in the newspapers which came from abroad. Some of the publishers tried to come to an arrangement with Dubnov, but he refused to discuss it, considering the printing of a large work impossible in the author's absence. It was becoming clear that in order to accomplish his life's chief task he would have to move to Western Europe. As he strode through the dimly lit streets of the deserted city he was laying his plans: He would finish his work, publish it in Berlin, and then go to Palestine for several months. But his dreams hit a major snag; obtaining an exit visa appeared problematic. Soon, however, the plan to emigrate took concrete form. The Jewish National Council in Kovno petitioned through the Lithuanian ambassador for Dubnov to be given permission to move to Lithuania to lecture at Kovno University.

Dubnov wrote the last chapters of the *History* to the grim sounds of cannon in the days of the Kronstadt uprising. The political situation deeply disturbed him, and his wish to leave became increasingly insistent. Meanwhile, as the Lithuanian ambassador's petition remained unanswered, Dubnov had the idea of sending a letter to Lenin through Gorky. It was to contain the following reasoning: since the theory of historical materialism had become official dogma in Soviet Russia, the opportunity to leave for another country should be available to scholars who did not accept the dogma. But the letter was never sent. Friends advised Dubnov to arm himself with patience and wait for the official reply.

The forty-year anniversary of Dubnov's literary career was approaching. He usually shunned honors, but this time, aware that this encounter might be the last, he willingly accepted a proposal to meet with friends, readers, and students. He spent the day of the celebration in a state of spiritual elation. For the first time in four years, lines permeated with joyful excitement appeared in his diary. On 29 April he writes,

> Yesterday was a very special day. A radiant morning. I answered Ida's good wishes by expressing my gratitude for helping me bear the burden of life for almost forty years. Tears choked me when I said that if she had not maintained her resolve to bear deprivation and want, I could not have endured so many sacrifices for the sake of fulfilling a spiritual vow. . . . I took off the shelf two books, once precious but which had long lain untouched: Comte's *Philosophy of Positivism* and Mill's *On Liberty*, which became my Bible in 1881. I read the notes in the margins, the underlined passages, and reminisced a great deal. Toward midday the anniversary committee arrived with their congratulations. I was not expecting them, and my crowded study barely accommodated all those who came. Toward six in the evening they sent for me and Ida . . . and we attended a gala at the Jewish university—a large assembly, noisy and excited. M. K. had come from Moscow; he brought a sheaf of letters and congratulations, as well as two volumes of the German translation of my *Recent History of the Jews*, printed in Berlin in 1920, which particularly pleased me.

Dubnov answered his numerous well-wishers in a long speech:

> I spoke of my joy in seeing again at this gathering those who would once come together so often for papers, debates, and late-evening sessions, and who in recent years had been separated and dispersed. . . . I recalled the day of 15 April 1881 and my first iconoclastic article, where I had tried to present Jewish history from the point of view of Elisha Akher, and how from that time forward I had studied the tortuous course of Jewish history, first through others' eyes and then with my own eyes . . . and how I had just finished my main work, only to see book publishing lie in ruins. . . . I spoke of the generation of the forty-year period, "the generation of the wilderness," but with Sinai and great national-cultural achievements, and I spoke of the oldest Jewish international, which would yet save us after the world deluge. I spoke with passion but clearly and crisply in the keen silence of the hall, where deep sighs could be heard now and then. . . . We parted at midnight, moved but renewed, as it were, by the encounter, the sharing of our experiences, and the proud challenge . . . clear to all.

The anniversary celebration was the summation of a forty-year career. The congratulations which came from various corners of the world gave Dubnov great pleasure. Strangers wrote of following his articles in *Voskhod* and how they had learned from Dubnov's writings, and many declared that they still considered themselves his students. The same notes were sounded in the speeches at a crowded banquet arranged at the beginning of May. The speakers underscored the influence of the "Letters on Old and New Jewry" on their world views. One of those present made clear that he was a militant Communist but declared that he and many others of like mind accepted the concept of cultural autonomy. The guest of honor answered these speeches with deep emotion:

> I spoke of a fissure in the Jewish world which runs through the heart of our generation, of the agonies accompanying the dislocation of the historical centers of the Diaspora. . . . The air was heavy with sadness and the pain of separation, and of the disintegration of the Petersburg center. My heart ached, I wanted to turn away and weep on the grave of the past.

In moments such as these Dubnov was often tempted to immerse himself in the past and work on his memoirs, but each time he came back to this thought: I must bring the history of my people to its conclusion, then it will be time to take up my own life.

Despite the uncertainty of his situation, Dubnov actively prepared for departure. He was occupied in putting his massive archive in order when he received a farewell letter from Bialik, who was about to leave for Palestine with a group of Odessa writers. The letter was warm and full of sorrow. "One more word of good wishes—and a tear will fall," the poet wrote, but he ended with encouraging words about meeting soon.

The question of the fate of his books and archive greatly troubled Dubnov. He found it hard to accept the partial dismantling of the library he had so lovingly assembled over many years. The ghosts of four decades of his life rose up as he compiled a catalogue. Neither was it easy to part with letters. "I could not raise my hand to do it," he writes in his diary. "I could not bring myself to destroy the graves where so many emotions, the sorrows and the joys of two generations, lie buried. . . ." Yet another matter troubled him: if the manuscripts to be taken out of the country were to be subjected to inspection then the diaries of the last few years could fall into the censor's hands. Dubnov decided to place part of his archive and library at the disposal of the Jewish National Council in Lithuania, as the foundation of a future collection, and sent them to the Lithuanian embassy; he decided to take with him only what was essential for his scholarly work or of particular sentimental value.

In considering the Lithuanian ambassador's petition the authorities sought the expert advice of the Deputy Commissar of Education, Professor Pokrovskii.[102] When Dubnov learned of this he addressed a letter of appeal to Pokrovskii as a professional colleague. He did not expect an encouraging response from a Marxist historian notorious for following the party line, but Pokrovskii's report turned out to be entirely favorable. The matter had reached the last stage: the final decision rested with the All-Russian Cheka.[103] Dubnov's opinions were well known to that body since he had openly and repeatedly expressed his criticism of Bolshevism in print and at meetings. This fact made him very apprehensive. He was also worried because he was a native of Belorussia and not of Lithuania.

The process of parting with his homeland lasted several months. In August 1921 Dubnov bade farewell to the Historical-Ethnographic Society. He resigned the duties of chairman and handed the editor's portfolio of *Starina* over to the Committee. The idleness associated with waiting for a visa hung heavily on his hands, but he had a happy idea during one of his bouts of depression. Now that the *History* was finished, the time for his memoirs had come. He disappeared wholly into the distant past. "I forget myself in writing the memoirs of my childhood," he writes on 8 August, "I make an effort to write. Otherwise my soul could not endure the agony of waiting and the constant worry."And several weeks later: "I am preparing to write the chapter . . . about 1882–84, and I am settling down now to read the materials—the letters I have saved. The reading moves me, but the writing itself much less so. I write of myself as though of a stranger. . . . The main emphasis now is on the process of the development of my ideas in the antithesis stage." When Dubnov recalled that time later he claimed that a "psychic cure" saved him.

Once an unexpected ring at the door interrupted him as he was reading the yellowed pages of an old notebook. On the doorstep stood his daughter Olga, who had come from Siberia with her two adolescent sons. Father and daughter had not seen each other since 1907, but they met as though they had parted only yesterday. Olga and her children moved in with her parents, and the boys quickly became fast friends with their grandfather.

In the autumn of 1921 the publishing cooperative Kadima expressed its readiness to publish several of the last chapters of the *History* in pamphlet form. The chapters passed the civilian and the military censorship and appeared in print without any changes. The pamphlet, entitled *The Jews in the Reign of Nikolas II*, was wretchedly printed, but the writer was troubled less by the shoddy, gray paper than by the new spelling system.[104]

At the end of February Kovno University officially confirmed Dubnov's appointment as professor of Jewish history. This news increased his impatience. Several weeks later the long-awaited exit permit arrived. Now the emigrant worried only for the safety of his archive, but here, too, he met with favorable circumstances. The baggage inspection took place at his home. The clerk dispatched by the authorities, a student in the Department of History and Philology, was overcome by respect for the master of the house when he saw the ten bulging paper folders, the original manuscript of the *History*. Beneath the folders was a layer of ancient documents and, hidden at the very bottom of the trunk, lay the seditious diaries. The young censor was much interested by the author and his monumental work and brought the conversation around to historical subjects. Then he beckoned the customs official aside and arranged for the trunk containing the manuscripts to be sealed. Dubnov breathed a sigh of relief.

All that remained was to say farewell to a few close friends and the town where so much had happened to him. The last meeting with his students was very moving. Dubnov had lectured at his own house throughout the winter of 1922. Students had come to him from all parts of the town, picking their way precariously through the snowdrifts and slipping over the icy cobblestones. The study he had recently converted into a kitchen now became a lecture hall during the hours in which he taught his course in recent history. His farewell lecture was devoted to the future prospects of the new centers of Jewry forming in Poland and the Baltic states.

The last entries in Dubnov's diary before his departure were mostly hurried and laconic. Their author felt he was already on his way. The last entry, made 22 April, reads:

> A clear day, the study is flooded with sunlight, but there is none of the former, gentle sorrow of parting in my soul. . . . Yesterday . . . I saw the old familiar places: *Voskhod's* former headquarters in the Bolshoi Theater Square, the dilapidated house by the Troitskaia church, a haven in 1884. But I rode on by, weighed down by a prisoner's worries, and the gentle sadness of parting shriveled beneath their icy breath. . . . But all the same, if this is my last entry in Petersburg I would like to bid a warm farewell to this "city of cold and darkness and longing" to which I first came almost forty years ago. Then there were "many thoughts in my head, much fire in my heart." Now there is still much of both, but of a different kind. The thoughts of dawn have become the thoughts of sunset, the fire of youth, the low-burning fire of old age with the glitter of cold eternity. Sunset is often more beautiful than the morning dawn. Am I destined for such a sunset after a day of storms? Can I recover from the blows of recent years sufficiently to finish at sunset the work begun at dawn?

The next day, 23 April 1922, Simon and Ida Dubnov left Russia.

26

Meeting the West

The battered, creaking train rattled loudly west. The carriage was filthy and the upholstered seats were torn but the passengers, two aging people with tired faces, did not notice. They could not tear themselves away from the window, as waterlogged meadows, barely touched by the first blades of spring grass, flashed by. The monotonous clanking of the wheels told them over and over that they were seeing the humble Russian plain under a low, gray sky for the last time.

The sorrow of parting mingled with the joy of freedom. The train carried the emigrés out of a country which, in Pushkin's words, reared up under the iron bit of history. The spectacle frightened them; they unequivocally refused to march in step with the stern young era, which had swept away the coziness of scholarly retreats and destroyed the only forms of existence that held for them the possibility of both work and rest. Now, as they changed countries, they changed eras. They were turning back from the twentieth to the nineteenth century.

The very first meeting with the West brought a breath of the old life. In Riga, which had become the capital of the small nation of Latvia, the Dubnovs were met at the station by a delegation from the Jewish community bearing flowers and greetings, and they immediately plunged into the thick of gregarious, provincial hospitality. There was no end to the conversations at a brightly lit table, around the steaming samovar. And when children began to recite Frug and Bialik at a school festivity, the guest in a clumsy, homespun *tolstovka* stealthily wiped away a tear. He felt like a man who had returned to his home after a long and arduous separation.

The Dubnovs went on from Riga to Kovno. The modest-sized town of a western borderland of the Russian Empire, with its ill-paved streets and unpainted, provincial houses, had not yet accustomed itself to its role as a capital. The new arrivals had dreamed of European comfort and were taken aback by the cramped housing, the lack of culture, and the absence of rudimentary conveniences. The political climate of a small country, where the intoxication induced by the unexpected bestowal of statehood spawned unbridled chauvinism, was not inviting. Many professors at the new university did not conceal their displeasure at the establishment of a Department of Jewish History. Dubnov faced a difficult dilemma. He considered himself duty-bound to show his gratitude somehow to the country which had given him citizenship. On the other hand, living conditions in the Lithuanian capital seemed ill suited to realizing his large-scale scholarly and literary plans. The letters of this period reflect the doubts plaguing him. "I had thought," he writes in the middle of May to a fellow historian, Elias Tcherikower, "of moving to Berlin for the sake of publishing my books—the most important reason for my 'exodus'—but meantime the Jewish Department in the Lithuanian university keeps me in Kovno."

At the end of May the Dubnovs went to Brezen, a small resort near Danzig. They moved into a comfortable summer house by the sea with their daughter's family. Simon took childlike pleasure in the quiet, the communion with nature, and walks with his grandsons, nine-year-old Alia and seven-year-old Vitia, whom he had greatly missed in his Petersburg solitude. The sun-drenched days flowed quietly by. The murmur of the Baltic waves poured through the open windows of the veranda. A distant lighthouse gleamed like a tiny star in the evenings, and the damp salt breeze blew gently in his face, washing turmoil and bitterness from his soul. New books and journals from all over piled up on a small round table near the couch. Dubnov had not seen any new foreign publications for a long time and read avidly. *In Polish Woods*, a historical novel by Opatoshu,[105] had a special appeal. "The deep sense of history which permeates your book is so dear to me," he writes to the author in America. "The robust figures of the Jews from the Ukrainian villages, the bonds linking dozens of generations, the atmosphere of the Kotsker Hasidim, which has long interested me, the Polish-Jewish romance of that era, it is all so full of life and so unlike our own reality."

His letter was the beginning of a friendly correspondence between the two writers, who immediately felt drawn to one another. More than once in his letters Dubnov praises Opatoshu's wholesome, realistic manner and compares it to the phenomenon in Jewish literature, which in exasperation he had labeled once-and-for-all as "decadence."

The summer spent in the company of nature, his family, and books could have been a real holiday for Dubnov had he not been hounded by the uncertainty of his plans. Publishers besieged him with proposals to bring out all or parts of the *World History* in Russian, German, Hebrew, and Yiddish. He spent long hours at his desk, immersed in personal and business correspondence. The renewal of connections with friends, ideological comrades-in-arms, and fellow historians, which had been broken by the historical cataclysm, gave him great joy. On 15 May he writes to Mark Wischnitzer, a long-time collaborator in the Historical-Ethnographic Society and *Starina*: "I am seeking out lost friends and rejoice when I hear they are alive, working and weaving the broken thread."

Publication of the ten volumes of the *World History* was the main task at hand. As it took concrete shape, the attractions of a professional career in Lithuania paled. Dubnov understood the immensity of the work yet to be done. Pedantically demanding of himself, he was accustomed to subjecting every line he wrote to close scrutiny. New editions of books already in print were always accompanied by fundamental revisions and additions as well as a painstaking polishing of prose. He tirelessly reworked and refined the text, battling the typesetters right down to the last proof sheet. No wonder the prospect of a final revision of his beloved work conquered all hesitations. Dubnov definitely decided to resign from his chair for good and sent a lengthy letter to Kovno explaining his decision. He cut the Gordian knot with a sense of relief. Now, as he wandered along the deserted beach, he could dream freely of wholly uninterrupted work on manuscripts and proofs. In the damp sea breeze he could almost smell the fresh printer's ink tickling his nostrils pleasantly. Relaxing in a deep armchair on the veranda among books and papers, his wife contemplated a scene of domestic comfort and quiet in the setting of a large cosmopolitan city.

On 5 September the Dubnovs went to Berlin. They moved into furnished rooms in one wing of a house. The windows looked out on a small front yard, but it was not easy to realize their dream of domestic comfort. Orderliness and neatness, a striking contrast to Russian poverty, proved inadequate for creating the cozy home of which the tired wanderers dreamed. They arrived during a housing crisis and were obliged to take furnished rooms cheek by jowl with people alien in temperament, pedantically petty, and somewhat xenophobic. The petit-bourgeois milieu depressed Dubnov, and he repeatedly complained in letters and personal conversations of the "campaign of terror waged by German landladies." He began to dream of a modest house of his own in one of the quiet green suburbs, but securing a property required an ample sum. The financial question therefore assumed extreme urgency. Creating the conditions essential to accomplishing his life's task hinged on its resolution.

Every day proof sheets piled up on his desk. The *Recent History* was coming off the presses apace. It was appearing in its complete and final form for the first time. The introduction, written back in 1914, emphasized that the author was applying a method which "examines the different aspects of the life of the people—political, socioeconomic and cultural-spiritual—against the background of the evolution of the national character, its growth and decline." Dubnov deemed it essential to remind the reader once more of the difference between his conception and the approach of such historians as Graetz,[106] Jost,[107] and Philippson,[108] who had reduced the history of the people to the history of Judaism.

As in former years a hankering after journalism occasionally intruded upon scholarly work. Time and again Dubnov felt the need to speak his mind on current affairs. On one such occasion he thought of making public certain extracts from his diaries. Publishing his diaries of many years in their entirety seemed premature to him. He sent Elias Tcherikower extracts relating to the years 1917–1918, explaining that he had selected from an immense quantity of material only what was typical of the mood of the active segment of the Jewish intelligentsia. He was simultaneously negotiating for the publication of selected extracts in the American *Forverts* (*Jewish Daily Forward*).

The year 1923, spent in the quiet suburb of Lichtenrad, brought Dubnov great satisfaction. His book *The Jews in Russian and Western Europe in the Age of Anti-Semitic Reaction* was printed by a private press in Moscow. The Berlin publishing house Grani[109] brought out the three-volume *Recent History*; a Yiddish translation of the first volume was issued by the same press; and it appeared simultaneously in Hebrew at the Moriah Press in Palestine. Dubnov interrupted his scrutiny of proof sheets for a while and plunged into writing the article "The Third Haidamak Massacre" for inclusion in the anthology *Anti-Semitism and Pogroms in the Ukraine*, edited by Tcherikower.

Dubnov had fought depression in freezing and starving Petersburg at the beginning of the twenties by nurturing the hope that the world, thrown out of joint by four years of bloody slaughter, would regain its equilibrium after the war. The socialist revolution and the concomitant chaos and dislocation would remain a phenomenon confined within the borders of one country. What he actually found in the West—intellectual confusion, economic crisis, and increasing national conflict—provided meagre nourishment for his illusions, but his irrepressible optimism compelled him to believe in the stability of transient forms created by postwar reality and in the magic power of paragraphs in democratic constitutions. To nourish these illusions in Germany was most difficult of all. The country had been bled white by the prolonged war effort and battered by the Peace of Versailles. The revolution had stopped at a halfway mark. The dissatisfaction of the masses had been subdued, but from time to time it gave intimations of its existence in ominous flareups. By the early twenties a grave economic crisis had befallen the country. When inflation took on monstrous proportions and long lines of sullen, darkly muttering people grew in front of food shops, Dubnov felt uneasy. In a letter to Opatoshu dated 7 January 1923, his anxiety breaks out in unexpectedly bitter foreboding:

> We are suffering now along with Germany, and perhaps we will yet be made to suffer by Germany. . . . The situation is very difficult and I am feeling very low, particularly after the recent breakdown of the Paris Conference. . . . But, were it not for all these worries, I would be pleased with my present work. It goes well and advances rapidly, without snags.

Inflation brought an epidemic of bankruptcies. Several publishing houses were financially unstable, and new plans for an edition of the *History* were in jeopardy. The current situation bred doubts about the viability of the political structures created in Germany after the collapse of the old regime. This sense of instability prevented Simon and Ida Dubnov from feeling that they had at last reached a quiet haven after long, hard years, and it cast a shadow over a life so strictly subordinated to a design. In many respects Berlin justified the hopes they placed on it: the high degree of civilization and comfort, combined with the peace and quiet of the picturesque suburbs, offered an ideal setting for scholarly work. The vast public and university libraries and the rich collection belonging to the Jewish community were at Simon's disposal. For her part, Ida valued the comforts of Western European life, which lightened her household chores and allowed her to devote several hours a day to copying the newly revised chapters of the *History* or reading periodicals.

An even greater boon than physical comfort was the opportunity for constant association with kindred spirits. In the German capital, a center of Russian-Jewish emigration in the twenties, Dubnov found what had been granted him long ago in the Odessa years: a small circle of close friends, an intimate atmosphere, and the joy of a fruitful exchange of ideas. His new friends Elias Tcherikower,[110] Jacob and Liya Leshchinsky,[111] the brothers Aaron and Isaac Steinberg,[112] and Daniel Charney[113] and his wife were a generation younger than Dubnov but he did not feel the difference in age; the feeling of being old was unknown to him. All those with whom he now worked and spent his leisure hours had been nourished, to a greater or lesser degree, on Russian culture and combined it with ardent national feeling, great Jewish erudition, and genuine commitment to Jewish communal life and learning. All this bred mutual affinity and encouraged frequent meetings, discussion of urgent questions, and personal and social prospects. Not infrequently Dubnov turned to his friends for practical advice as well. Despite his energy and persistence in implementing literary plans, he could be as helpless as a child in practical matters, especially so in a foreign land; like many bookish men he swung easily from excessive confidence to extreme pessimism at the prospect of failure. Competent, friendly assistance was essential to restore his lost equilibrium.

Communion with close friends became a substantial part of his active, work-filled life in Berlin. Meetings took place either tête-à-tête or in a small, tightly knit circle around a cozy tea table; sometimes the Dubnovs spent the evenings in larger gatherings of friends. When Simon went away to the shore or up into the mountains, he took care that contact with his friends not be curtailed. If he had not been able to organize a joint holiday, he devoted much of his time to correspondence. His letters, those written in a light, jocular tone as well as the more businesslike ones, almost always reflected his public concerns, for Dubnov was accustomed to sharing his doubts and apprehensions with his friends. And reality was not sparing in alarming warnings, which injected dissonant notes into the harmony of the calm sunset of his life, devoted to his beloved work.

27

Fulfilling the Vow

From his youth Dubnov had been accustomed to stilling inner turmoil by work, and he did just that in the days of crisis battering Germany. The events of that troubled time did not long disturb his inner equilibrium. The dark rumblings in the working-class districts did not penetrate the suburban villas. No grim figures of the unemployed could be seen in the wide green avenues along which the writer took his daily walk, as erect as in former years, still wearing his inevitable, old-fashioned hat. After long wanderings the Dubnovs settled for several years in spacious, sunlit lodgings on a quiet side street. The high windows of the study looked into green treetops. Simon paced cheerfully back and forth over the slightly worn, antique carpet along the bookshelves. The books on these shelves, the faithful companions of his life's wanderings, seemed to him a link between past and present. He rarely left his retreat and then only when absolutely necessary. He was wholly absorbed in preparing his monumental work for publication and customarily declined participating in local social organizations. Yet he willingly joined the Jewish Scientific Society, which was founded in 1924, bringing together scholars from East and West. Aaron Steinberg, David Koigen, Ismar Elbogen, Gotthold Weil, and Mark and Rachel Wischnitzer were the most active members of the Society. Dubnov formed friendships with some of these new acquaintances, including the philosopher Koigen.

Life, subordinated to the strict rhythms of work, was cast in a firm, complete mold. Its content became the fulfilment of Dubnov's most important vow. In 1925 *World History of the Jewish People* in German translation began coming off the presses at Jüdischer Verlag. The Russian edition had stopped at the fifth volume. The author comforted himself with the thought that German, the classical language of historiography, would facilitate the book's dissemination in various countries of the world. Exceptional good fortune befell him. Aaron Steinberg, a young scholar recently arrived from Russia, undertook the translation of the book and proved a master of the subject as well as an excellent stylist.

The ten-volume work aroused great interest. Within the first few months subscriptions had exceeded the wildest speculations of the publisher and the author. The letters in which Dubnov reported on the publication of the first volumes were exuberant. At the beginning of the winter of 1926 he wrote to Opatoshu that he would now be chained to his desk for a long time to come, for the publisher was counting on putting out a substantial volume every four months. Even the summer brought no respite. Dubnov had to toil over proofs for hours on end at the seaside resort of Albeck. A Yiddish translation of the *Recent History* was being printed at the same time by the Warsaw publishers Kultur-lige. When Dubnov did tear himself away from his correction-strewn proofs, he recalled the modest embryo of the *History*, which had appeared thirty years earlier.

Ida Dubnov did not look so far back. Still fresh in her mind were their last years in St. Petersburg, when she had typed hundreds of pages with weak, freezing fingers and a feeling of hopelessness in her soul. The dream which then seemed unrealizable had now become reality.

The first volume opened with a short foreword, followed by a longer introduction formulating Dubnov's historical credo. The foreword pointed out that the present work was the result of decades of research. The articles and historical reports which appeared in periodicals in the eighties and nineties were the foundation of the monumental building. The building itself had been constructed over seven years, from 1914 to 1921, in a time of terrible political storms. Only in the mid-twenties had it proved possible to consider bringing out the *History*. Much new material had accumulated between the beginning of the work and its publication, and the last versions of a number of chapters differed significantly from the original redactions.

The introduction to the German edition of the *History* contains the definitive and succinct formulation of the author's basic views. The historian's task, Dubnov asserts, consists of establishing the organic connection between the separate links of the historical process. Hitherto, the theological tradition had been the main obstacle to fulfilling this task. It had encumbered the biblical period in particular, and even the creators of Bible criticism had been unable to free themselves of it completely. The light shed by historians on a later period, the Middle Ages, was also that of a lopsided spiritualism. It was considered indisputable that a people deprived of territory could manifest activity only in the sphere of spiritual life, remaining the passive object of history in all other domains. In accordance with this principle, Zunz and Graetz reduced the history of the people in Diaspora to a survey of its writings—a fact clearly demonstrated by the periodization scheme they established, notably a division into the Talmudic, Gaonic, Rabbinic, and Enlightenment periods. Against this orientation Dubnov set forth his own bio-sociological concept. He claimed that the Jewish people, guided as they were by the instinct of national self-preservation, had been the active creators of their fate not only during the period of statehood but all along their historical path. During the long centuries of dispersion they invariably acted as a nation and not as a religious community. This tightly knit national entity had struggled for autonomous forms of existence, creating its own organs of self-government (the

Exilarchs, the Gaonim, the legislative synods in Babylon, the communal delegates in Spain, the *kahal* and *vaad* of Poland and Lithuania[114]) in the countries where their greatest numbers were concentrated. At the present time the idea of autonomism, which inspired the Jewish national movement, found support in the principle of equal rights for national minorities, which was an integral part of contemporary legal consciousness.

The nature of Jewish historiography was determined, Dubnov asserted, by having originated at the peak of assimilation. The corollary that the Jews were not a nation but a religious group identified the history of the people with the history of Judaism. Even such an independent-minded historian as Graetz could not bring himself to break with this tradition. Dubnov declared that the time had come for a reassessment of values: the secularization of the Jewish national idea required the secularization of historiography and its emancipation from the fetters of spiritual dogma. According to the new conception of history, the national entity and its origin, growth, and struggle for existence must become the axis of history. Jewry came into existence as a nation, Dubnov maintained, in the era of its first political crisis (the Babylonian exile). The second catastrophe created new forms of preserving national unity through the medium of autonomous organs. The *History* lays down the principle that Judaism was created in the image and the likeness of the social environment in which the Jewish people lived, rather than the other way around. Once this principle was established, the reexamination of obsolete views of such phenomena in Jewish history as the Age of Prophets, the Pharisees, Christianity, and the Talmud must follow. Condemning the neglect of economics displayed in the works of the spiritualist historians, Dubnov reminds his reader that the life of the people is shaped by the interaction of several factors.

He acknowledges that in his own first works he was himself indebted to the theological tradition, and that it had taken a good deal of time to free himself from the influence of Zunz and Graetz. As he explored the idea of autonomism in his political writings he had gradually reached the conviction that all the centuries of Jewish historical experience confirmed this idea. A new periodization scheme resulted from this new conception, one according to which the history of the period of statehood can be divided into stages on a political basis and the history of the Diaspora on a geographical basis. Dubnov divided all history into an Eastern and a Western period. In the Western period hegemony moved gradually from one center to another (Spain, northern France, Germany, Poland, and Russia). In recent decades two new centers had arisen, America and Palestine.

Dubnov saw some symbolism in the fact that his major work was fated to appear in the cradle of Jewish historiography and Bible criticism. Even as he polemicized with his predecessors, he valued them highly and considered them his teachers.

The last volume of the *History* came out in the autumn of 1929 and was celebrated with elation among a circle of friends. A number of variations were rung on the theme that now, having completed his life's work, Dubnov had the right to a prolonged rest. "Rest?" He was astonished. "What rest can there be if the baby which came into the world forty years ago has not yet had its turn?" He reminded his friends that back in his youth he had started gathering materials for a history of Hasidism. The result of this work has been the series of articles in *Voskhod*, which shared with the Russian-Jewish reader that broad religio-social movement that had sprung from the depths of the people's life. As the articles on Hasidism appeared (1883–1892), the writer's archive was replenished with new sources, and the outlines of a lengthy monograph began to take shape in his imagination. The realization of his youthful dream was postponed from year to year, however, because of large-scale works; according to his rigorous blueprint the *History of Hasidism* was to follow directly after the *World History*. Dubnov decided to write his new work in Hebrew. It would be more convenient to quote the material he wished to cite, namely Hasidic and *misnagdic* texts, in the original. But it was not technical-literary considerations that dictated this decision, which surprised many readers. Dubnov had long thought of writing one of his major works in the ancient national language, and Ahad Ha-Am had made him promise that the *History of Hasidism* would be that work.

A slender volume in Yiddish appeared almost at the same time as the last volume of the *History*. The anthology *From Zhargon to Yiddish*, which came out in Vilna in 1929, contained a number of literary memoirs written concurrently with the *magnum opus* in the interval between 1916 and 1928, primarily the result of emotional promptings. These literary portraits, originally scattered in periodicals, were united by the notion of the growing significance of Yiddish and profound reverence for the memory of the pioneers of the people's literature. As Dubnov reread his old articles, he felt the need to perform still another duty of which he had been vaguely aware for many years. In an article which appeared in 1886, Criticus acknowledged that he had approached Judah Leib Gordon's *zhargon* verse with some bias. He had not believed that true poetry was possible in a language poor in nuance and lacking codified grammatical forms. Two years later, influenced by his acquaintance with the work of Sholem Aleichem and Spector, the young journalist overcame those doubts. In his subsequent critical surveys he noted a new phenomenon in Jewish life: the emergence of a genuine people's literature meeting the needs of the broad masses to a greater degree than did literature in either Russian or Hebrew. He tried to convince the opponents of *zhargon*, who decried its poverty, that literature of social realism could only be written in the people's everyday language, with all its vividness and color and its inimitable intonations. Reality confirmed the bold prognosis disputed by the majority of Russian-Jewish journalists in the eighties. And when Dubnov came to take stock of his life and times he felt the need to chart the path leading from *zhargon* to Yiddish.

The introduction to the anthology notes the profound changes in the life of contemporary Jewry. The ancient language of liturgy and writing had become the language of everyday speech in Palestine, while *zhargon*, considered the stepchild of culture, had become the language of literature, journalism, and scholarship in Eastern Europe and America.

> The new generation should realize that forty or fifty years ago neither Mendele nor Sholem Aleichem nor anyone else among the representatives of *zhargon* literature dreamed that a time would come when Yiddish might rival Hebrew and even the more sophisticated languages in schools, literature, journalism, and scholarship. They had not dreamed that the "language of the common people" would turn so rapidly into a full-blown national medium. The Yiddish Scientific Institute . . . along with numerous researches in history, economics, philology, ethnography, and folklore—what an incredible fantasy would such a prospect have seemed to us in those days! And yet this has come to pass before our very eyes, and it is only the beginning!
>
> One must beware of linguistic chauvinism however. . . . It is impossible to deny the permanent significance of both the ancient . . . national language and the languages of Europe and America, which have indeed become the instrument of culture for different segments of our people. But it is our duty to recognize . . . the flowering of the people's language in the lands with the greatest concentration of Jews.

The men associated with the literary renaissance pass by in a colorful procession: the publisher Alexander Zederbaum, a typical rationalist *maskil* of the eighties, the initiator of a popular *zhargon* newspaper for those "poor in spirit" to whom the "serious" Russian and Hebrew publications were inaccessible; the writer Mordecai Spector, a pioneer who fought the disdain for the "language of the common people" which was deeply ingrained in the intelligentsia; the romantic *maskil* Dineson, author of naïvely sentimental tales. Abramovich (Mendele), Sholem Aleichem, and Frug occupy the central place in the book. Dubnov's affinity for Sholem Aleichem, as the memoir devoted to him clearly shows, owed a great deal to their common battle for the people's language. The letters of the young Jewish fiction writer included in the collection repeatedly emphasize that Criticus alone in Russian-Jewish journalism championed the rights of the poor *zhargon* and defended it from attacks. From shared opinions grew a friendship which was sustained for many years by correspondence and infrequent meetings. The long years of closeness with Abramovich were marked by still greater emotional richness. The memoir, written immediately after the death of Dubnov's old friend, recreates the atmosphere of their intimate and enriching association. Dubnov was always to remember how masterfully Mendele had read lyrical passages of his own works, and how he had once said, "I too am a historian, but of a singular kind. When you reach the history of the nineteenth century you will have to make use of my work." Abramovich's letters to his younger colleague were suffused with heartfelt warmth. Probably few would have considered the stern and imperious "grandfather of Yiddish literature" capable of such effusion. In sketching the portraits of his friends Dubnov knew how to find the soft, human features, and thus he creates a mood of warmth and intimacy. The lines devoted to Frug, the companion of his youth who lived a difficult and luckless life, are suffused with deep sorrow.

Having paid his due to personal memories, Dubnov plunged into work on the *History of Hasidism*. Dusty, yellowed manuscripts were pulled out of the drawers. With emotion he examined the writings in which the voice of the ages reverberated. The heir to generations of *misnagdim*, who had kept faith with Spencer and Mill, was unable to resist the strange fascination of the mystical movement born in his people's years of travail. He had to deal with new and still unexamined materials. In the introduction to the Yiddish edition, which was published in Vilna at almost the same time as the original, he writes:

> I had to gather the building materials, dig in the sand, knead the clay, fashion the bricks, and then build according to a definite architectural design. I made use of all the Hasidic writings, dogma as well as legends, trying to find a system in the tangle of the various Hasidic "teachings" and uncover the grains of truth in naïve folk legends. I searched for verification of the data in the materials which have come down to us from *misnagidic* literature. . . . That way I was able to link the statics of Hasidism with its dynamics. . . .

After the enthusiastic pioneer had cleared the path for researchers with his first articles in *Voskhod*, monographs on Hasidism began to appear systematizing the immense quantities of legendary and historical materials. Dubnov particularly valued the work of Martin Buber,[115] who had produced finely stylized versions of Hasidic legends and the aphorisms of *tsadikim*. However, the new researches went no further than organizing the raw material. Their authors succeeded in dislodging the superficial image of Hasidism fostered by the *Haskalah* as a hotbed of ignorance and reaction, but a depiction of the historical process was not part of their project. Dubnov was the first to approach Hasidism as a dynamic popular movement and to reveal its social roots:

> The main aim of my book is to integrate the Hasidic movement into the chain of events of Jewish history, to illuminate its social origins and consequences, to find a place for it in the evolution of our culture. I brought the history up to 1815, to the moment when the battle between Hasidism and the *misnagdic* ideology ends and the battle between Hasidism and the *Haskalah* begins. At that time the creative period of Hasidism comes to an end, and the movement as a whole is turning into down-to-earth *tsadikism*. . . . This was the beginning of the era of decline.

The author faced a dual task. Establishing the ideological genesis of Hasidism defined the movement's place in the process of the spiritual evolution of Jewry, while analysis of the social conditions located it within the framework of a definite era. In this light the battle between Hasidism and rabbinism appeared to be the latest form of the tension between the individual and the national principle which runs throughout the entire history of the people, dying down only to flare up again. Dubnov considered its culmination to be the rise of Christianity, which grew out of the Essenic movement and proclaimed the primacy of the individual over the collective, the man over the nation. In that crucial period the Pharisees and their followers, the creators of the Talmud, became the leaders of the people. The long-subdued quarrel flared up again in the middle of the eighteenth century, when the collapse of Messianic expectations, the Haidamak pogrom, bloody reprisals, poverty, and disfranchisement brought the great masses of Eastern Jewry to despair. Neither ritual nor talmudic widsom nor the mystical formulas of the cabalists, which were accessible only to the initiated, provided a way out of the impasse. Then a powerful and original religious movement arose in the lower depths of the people. "Hasidism," writes Dubnov, "was not a reformation which affected the foundations of religion and its offshoots. It aspired to transform not faith but the essence of the religious credo, when it placed feeling above reason, fusion with God above knowledge of God, the truth of the heart above the truth of books." This movement absorbed elements of cabalistic mysticism, bringing them closer to the level of the ordinary man. In a dark, transitional era it raised the morale of the persecuted Jew, creating the sense of spiritual freedom in an atmosphere of physical persecution.

Dubnov divided the history of Hasidism into four periods: (1) the era of the emergence of the movement led by the Besht and of the first clashes with rabbinism (1740–1781); (2) the period of the growth of Hasidism in Eastern Europe, the formation of the dynasties of *tsadikim*, and the final schism (1782–1815); (3) the period of the consolidation of *tsadikism* and the struggle with the *Haskalah* (1815–1870); (4) the period of the movement's decline. The chapters featuring the figure of the Besht, enveloped in a lyrical mist, and the dramatic figure of the Vilna Gaon[116] were especially compelling. Enthusiasm turned a scholarly work strewn with footnotes and references into a historical drama of many acts, which the reader follows breathlessly.

28

The Golden Autumn

In the initial days of autumn comes
A fleet, enchanted time.
 —Fedor Ivanovich Tiutchev

The autumn of life is not always a period of waning powers. Special breadth and clarity of thought are often vouchsafed men of great spiritual intensity in their late years. No wonder Dubnov loved to recite Tiutchev's poem about crystal, luminous autumn. He belonged to those lucky few upon whom fate bestows "a fleet, enchanted time" of calm and self-assured maturity in the sunset of their days. By that time, thoughts that had been in his mind for years had finally crystallized, and the spiritual storms had abated. The hesitations, doubts, and fears that he would not bring his well-laid plans to completion had vanished. Financial worries had ceased to harass him. Dubnov was now contemplating the bygone years through a luminous mist. A lyrical tenderness veiled the images of the past and drew him irresistibly to memories.

He remembered the Odessa period of his life with special affection. He maintained a regular correspondence with old friends who had settled in Palestine. Lately the letters had been full of anxiety; Ahad Ha-Am's health had noticeably deteriorated. Ahad Ha-am rarely wrote himself, and news of his death came in 1927. Dubnov interrupted his work for a time. He wanted to pause before his past and resurrect in thought the course of their many years of friendship. Under the impact of this loss he became more keenly aware than ever before of the depth and fruitfulness of the intellectual communion with his ideological ally-opponent, of the singularity of a friendship, the emotional intensity of which seemed, if anything, enhanced by disagreements in matters of principle.

As he mourned the loss, Dubnov sorted through the letters and old journals he had kept. He reread lines written by Ahad Ha-Am in the early days of their friendship in the context of a polemic about West European Jewry. "I may as well admit," the then editor of *Ha-Shilo'ah* had written, "that spiritual nationalists, such as there are, are dear to me. After all, it is not unanimity in practical activity that matters, but common spiritual roots, . . . for this is what forges the most intimate and the most durable link." Dubnov had insisted in a number of articles that the contradictions between spiritual nationalism and spiritual Zionism were apparent rather than real. Ahad Ha-Am did not always agree, but both in their private conversations and in correspondence he emphasized with touching insistence not what divided the friends but what united them. The language question was one of the main bones of contention; the formula of "the equal rights of three languages" was unacceptable to this abstract thinker and staunch theoretician of Zionism. It was characteristic of Ahad Ha-Am that he was more intolerant of *zhargon* than he was of the Russian language. The dispute flared up particularly fiercely after the Czernowitz Conference. In the summer of 1909 Ahad Ha-Am wrote bitterly:

> I am not surprised at what you write . . . about *zhargon*. After all, it is a direct corollary of the theory of autonomism. Without *zhargon* we have no national spoken language, and what autonomy could there be without schools teaching in the national language? Forgive my candor: I am certain that deep in your heart you have no better an opinion of *zhargon* than I, . . . but autonomism makes this obligatory.

After the appearance of an article by Vladimir Medem[117] in *Evreiskii Mir*, expounding the essence of cultural-national autonomy, Ahad Ha-Am warns Dubnov, the editor of the journal:

> You must understand where this can lead us. After all, he is logically correct. If *zhargon* is the basis of national life, then there can be no single people but many peoples. . . . I want to remind you that I foresaw the danger of national disintegration twenty years ago but . . . I came to other conclusions. This is what the difference between a "Hebrew" Jewry and a *"zhargon"* Jewry consists in. . . .

The letters Dubnov was reading often voiced regret at the fact that the publication of the *History of Hasidism* was being put off from year to year. In 1908 Ahad Ha-Am wrote in excitement,

> You will understand how I rejoiced at the news that your new work will be published simultaneously in Russian and Hebrew. I assume that you will write the Hebrew version yourself rather than relying on a translator, who could scarcely do justice to your style. Write and tell me if this is so, for the day when this . . . book appears will be a time of celebration for our hapless literature.

In 1917 he returned to the same subject.

> I . . . repeat: should you add but this book to the treasure-house of our national literature, it would survive, I assure you, all your works written in a foreign

language. Can't you see for yourself what the fate of our literature in foreign languages will be? You will say that the book can be translated, but knowing your style I don't doubt that the work written by you in Hebrew is one which will immortalize your name. . . . A translation, even the very finest, can usually render only the content and not the spirit of a literary work. . . .

The thought that Ahad Ha-Am had not been fated to live to see the appearance of the book on Hasidism now weighed heavily on Dubnov. An article devoted to the memory of his late friend in *Ha-Olam*, a journal published in Palestine, expressed his sorrow:

He could have become the Rambam of our generation. I regret that he could not realize his intention to give us a modern *More Nevukhim*.[118] . . . Only a few knew that Ahad Ha-Am dreamed all his life of creating such a synthetic work. . . . Daily cares prevented him from giving himself to his beloved work, and then a war began which shook that champion of truth and justice to the very bottom of his soul. While Ahad Ha-Am was with us we knew that fate did not neglect a generation of which such a man was part. Now we are orphaned. . . . A titan of the spirit has fallen, . . . the source of light has gone out, our teacher has left us. . . .

As he was revising and preparing his large works for the printer, Dubnov still found time for political and scholarly articles intended for publication in periodicals. For the first time in many years the rivalry between journalism and history gave way to peaceful coexistence. Dubnov wrote a great deal in Yiddish in those years, contributing to the New York daily newspaper *Tog* (political articles, extracts from his diaries, chapters from his memoirs), the New York *Forverts* (a series of articles on pogroms), the Riga publications *Frimorgn* and *Dos folk*, the Kovno *Folksblat*, and the Warsaw *Literarishe bleter*. The articles in Hebrew were published in the journals *Ha-Olam*, *Ha-Aretz* and *Ha-Tekufah*. Works of a purely scholarly nature appeared from time to time in the publications of the Yiddish Scientific Institute[119] and the *Jewish Lexicon*, which came out in German.

Dubnov experienced the past and the present with the same intensity. He was moved by Schwarzbard's[120] attempt on the life of Petliura,[121] the former head of the Ukrainian government (1926). It raised the bloody ghosts of recent pogroms and the distant Haidamaks. In an appeal addressed to the Ukrainian democratic intelligentsia, Dubnov urged them to understand the motives behind the terrorist act and insisted that it was their elementary duty to tear out the tenacious roots of racial hatred from the consciousness of the Ukrainian people.

In August 1927 Dubnov went to Zurich to attend a conference on the defense of the rights of Jewish minorities. Representatives of two parties, the Zionists and the Folkists, and delegates from a number of influential social organizations took part in the conference. Dubnov was elected to the presidium and read a paper entitled "The Struggle for the Rights of the Jewish People, Past and Present." The basic stance of the paper, published in the Jewish press (*Tog*, August 1927) can be summarized thus: The struggle of the Jews for their rights has always been connected with revolutionary upheavals. This struggle proceeded along two paths, the Western and the Eastern. The postulates of equal rights were promulgated for the first time during the French Revolution. At that time, when the concept of a "cultural nation" was still unknown, those fighting for emancipation declared that the Jews were a part of the ruling nation, i.e., the French people. Gabriel Riesser also put forward the same concept with respect to German Jews at the time of the 1848 revolution. Eastern Jewry had taken a different path and, during the Revolution of 1905, proclaimed the necessity of defending not only civic but also national rights. In 1917 the principle of national-cultural autonomy was clearly articulated. Its realization was to become the task of the All-Russian Jewish Congress. The October Revolution and its economic and political consequences put an end to plans for the autonomization of Jewish life in Russia. The Jewish minorities in a number of countries in Eastern Europe—Poland, the Baltic republics, the Balkan states—had become the bearers of the principle of autonomy in recent years. Even while, within their respective countries, they were fighting for their national rights, they had the possibility of appealing in each individual case to the authority of the League of Nations. The authority of this supreme international body was at present the sole guarantee of implementing the national demands of the Jewish people.

The paper concluded with a pessimistic evaluation of the future of Soviet Jewry. It drew a rebuttal from Cherviakov, the chairman of the Belorussian Soviet People's Commissariat, who observed in his speech at the Congress of Jewish Farmers that Jews enjoyed wider rights in the Soviet Union than anywhere else, and they did not suffer from anti-Semitism as their fellow Jews did in Poland and Lithuania. Dubnov returned to this question in another article (*Tog*, April 1928). Rights for Jews to equal those of other citizens, he asserted, could not compensate for the losses inflicted on the Jewish population by the elimination of the trading activities which played a dominant role in the economic life of the people. The development of a national culture was unthinkable under conditions of poverty.

Shortly afterward Dubnov had another opportunity to renew direct contact with his native land. The inauguration of a Department of Yiddish Language and Literature at Kiev University was to take place in 1928. Representatives of Jewish scholarship, including several scholars living abroad, were invited to the ceremony. Dubnov was surprised to receive an official invitation. In a letter he thanked Kiev University for the attention and welcomed the creation of a center of Jewish scholarship in the Ukraine. He expressed the wish that lecturers and students would be allowed to work in an atmosphere of political freedom, for without freedom, scholarly activity was unthinkable.

In the political articles of the Berlin period, which recall the "Letters" stylistically, new notes occasionally sounded. Dubnov now appraised the Balfour Declaration, of which he had once been skeptical, as a major event in the life of the people, and said so in the article "A Party and a National Concern," published in the collection *Svershenie* (Berlin, 1925). Its basic idea was that from the moment the Declaration was made, the creation of a "national home" in Palestine had been a concern for Jews the world over. All those who viewed the Palestine center as one of the foci of Jewry's global autonomization should take part in building it, along with card-carrying Zionists. The tragedy of the situation lay in the fact that the "national home" in Palestine had the support of no more than a sixth of the population. The task for the immediate future was to increase the size of the Jewish minority in the country and to strengthen its cultural and economic position. At the same time it was essential to keep firmly in mind that Zion was more important than Zionism, and that a small real "home," accommodating a portion of the people, had a larger significance than the ephemeral palaces of a future state. Dubnov disliked Jabotinsky's militarism: "There are," he asserted, "more effective means of fighting for one's rights than with a weapon which cuts both ways."

The enthusiasm aroused by these new prospects did not prevent Dubnov from expounding the doctrine of autonomism with his customary vigor. In an article contributed to a Festschrift honoring Chaim Zhitlowsky (1929), Dubnov congratulated him on being the first socialist to speak of Jewish national rights and regretted that a public figure so akin to him in spirit had not stated with sufficient clarity the principle of autonomy in his own national program.

Emotional notes sounded in all of Dubnov's articles of the Berlin period. Whether he was writing of the need to investigate new developments in Jewish economics or of the times of the Haidamak, the impassioned voice of the political writer could always be heard. An article in *Literarishe bleter*, 1929, on the significance of the Yiddish Scientific Institute, written to coincide with the convocation of its first conference, was a spirited affirmation. From the moment the Jewish academy of sciences was founded in 1925 Dubnov had been its loyal friend and supporter. He noted with pleasure that the scope of its activities expanded yearly and viewed the development and enrichment of Yiddish, which served as the link connecting different parts of the Jewish people, as one of the Institute's principal tasks. "Under present circumstances," he maintained, "Yiddish, as the language of the renaissance in Jewish scholarship, had become a 'historical necessity.' In the course of our history various languages have been the language of cultural revival along with our ancient national languages, be they Greek, Arabic, or German. . . . The time of the language in which the majority of our people speak is now upon us."

At that beginning of 1930 Dubnov had to interrupt his work for a while and pack up his archive. The Dubnovs were about to move to another apartment, this time their very own. The new lodgings had been picked out long before. During his walks Dubnov had often strolled down a quiet side street where a house in the modern style stood among ivy-clad private residences. With its flat roof and wide rectangular windows, the house was a pleasure to behold. It had a bright, polished look; in the sun it gleamed with varnish, glass, and metal. But when the books were arranged and the portraits in their faded frames hung in the light, cozy study, the feel of Odessa, Vilna, and St. Petersburg—the atmosphere which accompanied the occupant of the study in all his wanderings—pervaded the "modern" Berlin house.

When the sun was not too hot he worked on the flat cement roof, furnished with plain but comfortable garden furniture. The wind carried the scent of roses from a neighboring garden, the voices of children playing below, and the distant, muted sounds of a calm and orderly life. Several chapters of his memoirs were written with particular zest against this background. But now and then Dubnov would lay down his pen. A stream of bicyclists would come tearing along the glaring asphalt road toward the newsstand on the corner, and from up above he could see broad-shouldered, fair-haired young toughs in brown shirts tossing bundles of newspapers to the vendor. It happened that Dubnov ran into these youths as he walked down to get an evening paper. They scowled at his gray beard, his wide-brimmed hat, his Semitic nose. Headlines drunk with hatred screamed from those pages, and the frenzied shouts, brown shirts, and bull necks cast an ominous shadow on the landscape of a golden autumn.

29

Seventieth Birthday

On a high shelf among the tightly packed rows of books, ten large volumes in dark bindings with gilt engraved spines stood out: they were Dubnov's *magnum opus*, which had demanded the utmost dedication and exertion. The *History* received its due acclaim. Letters from friends scattered across the globe, responses from anonymous readers, and the reviews of experts all bore witness to this. The leading scholars in the West, such as Hugo Gressman and Fritz Beyer, commented in their reviews on the Russian-Jewish historian's phenomenal energy, his erudition, and his originality in handling the primary sources. Ismar Elbogen spoke with the greatest praise of the organization of the *History*. The author was pleased by the gratifying reviews of experts, but he was even more pleased by the responses of ordinary readers who delved into their people's past, searching for a path to the future. Indeed, it was for them that the multivolumed work was intended.

Dubnov was to reach his seventieth birthday in September 1930. The date coincided with the fiftieth anniversary of his literary career. Chronological landmarks usually spur one to look back on one's life, but Dubnov had no need of such a spur. He had long been working on his memoirs, analyzing his own life and that of the whole era. The excerpts he had read to friends provoked a lively exchange of views, and the author decided to read the chapters regularly in his circle. He had no peer among his listeners. Maria Reinus was older than the others. She was a talented doctor, a person of great intelligence and deep culture who had, in her youth, stepped out of the atmosphere of the *Haskalah* straight into socialism. She brought a distinctive tone to the amicable conversations, adding finely observed touches to the portrayal of the era she had known.

While Dubnov steeped himself in the recent past, his friends, like-minded thinkers, and colleagues were planning to honor his seventieth birthday in a manner worthy of it. They decided to set up a special fund in his name for publication of a Jewish encyclopedia. A group of historians were at work on a substantial anthology, *Festschrift zu Simon Dubnows siebzigsten Geburtstag*, edited by Ismar Elbogen, Mark Wischnitzer, and Josef Meisl. The massive tome contained a number of studies in the history of Western and Eastern Jewry. The collection opened with a warm, brief tribute. Articles by Elbogen and Aaron Steinberg were devoted to a description of the man they were honoring. The German scholar showed that Dubnov had taken Graetz's place in Jewish historiography, and that he had significantly expanded the scope of investigation with the help of new methods and recently discovered materials. Steinberg analyzed the historian's philosophical and historical views, and expounded the idea that the cornerstone of Jewish historiography was the notion of the singular character of Jewry's historical path. In this connection he cited Nicholai Berdiaev,[122] who had maintained that the fact of the Jewish people's existence, inexplicable in terms of historical materialism, was an exceptional phenomenon in the history of mankind. The article showed that Dubnov shared Berdiaev's conception. Despite Dubnov's attraction to positivism and his break with the metaphysical tradition, his historiography rested on the conviction that at the core of the people's life lay a spiritual principle, namely, the will to national affirmation.

A chronological bibliography of Dubnov's writings over fifty years was compiled by Josef Meisl and printed at the end of the anthology; it was a valuable anniversary gift. The long path leading from a youthful contribution to the journal *Russkii Evrei* to the article published in 1930 in the Berlin *Jewish Lexicon* was recorded accurately for the first time in an index containing approximately seven hundred titles (including translations into foreign languages). The bibliography was no mean achievement and became an indispensable tool in studying Dubnov's literary legacy, a significant part of which was scattered in periodical publications.

Representatives of Jewish scholarship and the Jewish community began to plan an anniversary celebration. Rumors of it reached Dubnov and he decided to decline any official ceremonials. The delegates from the Jewish community, who came to his home in their best suits and gleaming top hats on the day of the anniversary, were startled when the tiny gray-haired woman who opened the door muttered in some confusion that the guest of honor had left Berlin for several days. Even greater was their astonishment when they went outside and saw two people on the flat roof of the low house playing catch with happy cries—a five-year-old boy and an agile, swarthy man with flowing silver hair, the man the public was awaiting so impatiently at the anniversary celebration.

The five-year-old friend was the first visitor to whom the doors of the Dubnovs' home were flung open that day. In the evening their guests, all friends, seated the lady of the house, as the guest of honor, in a deep armchair and bustled cheerfully about the tea table. The mood was festive. The light wine, the honored host's favorite songs, and the many toasts —some emotional, others humorous—made him feel a little tipsy.

The entire Jewish press marked the writer's seventieth birthday, and every aspect of his career was subjected to analysis. The authors of these articles affirmed in unison that Dubnov had blazed new paths in historiography and journalism. In *Literarishe bleter* Tcherikower reviewed his work of half a century and attempted to trace the deep, emotional roots which insured harmony between the historian and the political commentator. From his youth, wrote Tcherikower, ardent national feeling had dwelled in the rebellious positivist's soul, and, as a result, the transition from cosmopolitanism to nationalism was almost painless. His interest in historical subjects sprang from his concern with the fate of Jewry, for Dubnov was seeking in the past the strength which could help his people survive in vicissitude. For him the pivot of the historical process was not abstract Judaism but the living, concrete nation. In this lay his originality as a historian. All of modern Jewish historiography sprang from the soil of scholarly research he had plowed and liberated from the fetters of tradition.

In *Zukunft* Jacob Leshchinsky described the new paths Dubnov had charted in the realm of social thought. He considered "Letters on Old and New Jewry," which had appeared almost at the same time as the first Zionist Congress and the founding of the Bund, one of the major events in the life of Jewry. The author of the Letters became the creator of a new Diaspora nationalism, which pitted faith in the inexhaustible creative powers of the people against the aristocratic skepticism of the followers of Ahad Ha-Am. It was a democratic and active nationalism which arose against the backdrop of a mass revolutionary movement. It did not urge the Jews into a spiritual ghetto but demanded that they fight for their rights side by side with other peoples. The Letters were of immense significance, declared Leshchinsky, for the entire progressive Russian-Jewish intelligentsia. The world view of the opponents of Dubnovism as well as that of his followers was formed under their influence.

The young Marxist historian Raphael Mahler recapitulated his older colleague's career, with particular emphasis on questions of historiography. He observed that the theological tradition had been created by the assimilated German-Jewish intelligentsia, whereas Dubnov's secularized historiography emerged as the fruit of an era of revolutionary ferment and cultural renaissance among the broad masses of East European Jewry. The author of the *World History* became the first genuine chronicler of the Jewish people. He had not succeeded, however, in discarding certain habits of dogmatic thinking. He tried to enclose the endless variety of historical phenomena within the framework of an abstract schema, whereby the history of mankind was represented as an arena for the interaction of two principles: humanization and nationalization. In Mahler's opinion, this schema suffered from artificiality. Nevertheless, its creator, who followed Lavrov[123] in emphasizing the influence of the historical environment on the formation of ideas, was far more empirical than Ahad Ha-Am, a strict Hegelian and disciple of Krochmal, who had viewed the ethical ideals of Judaism as the unchangeable fundament, given once for all time, of the spiritual life of the people.

Among the articles devoted to Dubnov's career the one by Sh. Niger in *Zukunft* stood out. To the literary critic, Dubnov was above all "a man with a mission." His cast of mind, his steady, concentrated gaze, even his firm, clear handwriting spoke of the essence of his character—an abiding sense of purpose: "Here is a life which knows where it is going and why. A clear, full life. A man who entered life with his mission, remained faithful to it and will evidently remain so to the end of his days," writes Niger, seeing the gaze directed unswervingly into the future as the distinctive feature of Dubnov the historian. Not for nothing was the attention of the young contributor to *Voskhod* fixed on the dynamic, critical periods: Hasidism, Sabbateanism, the flowering of autonomism—these were the subjects into which he plunged with the involvement and passion of a contemporary. As Niger maintains,

> Dubnov approached past generations not as men do when they visit the graves of their ancestors out of piety. Like the pious Jewish women of old he went to the cemetery to "rouse the dead." He turned to them for solace, he demanded help, he asked for advice. The object of his quest was not what had died, but what was still living . . . because he searched in the past for the key to the future.

Along with anniversary articles the journals published congratulations from various cultural organizations. A collective letter from the fellow members of the Yiddish Scientific Institute gave Dubnov particular pleasure. More than once in past years he had spoken in his diary of the danger that the research work he had begun would find no one to continue it and die away. Now representatives of young Jewish scholarship addressed the seventy-year-old historian, declaring openly: "We see in you the founder of the Eastern European current in Jewish scholarship which . . . our Scientific Institute is destined to continue and develop. You taught us to draw knowledge and inspiration from the very depths of the people's life, . . . to search in the past for the materials with which to build the future." In this congratulatory message, as well as in a letter from the editorial board of the *Literarishe bleter*, special mention was made of Dubnov's role in the struggle for the rights of the people's language.

The anniversary celebration gave Dubnov great joy. For the first time his many years of work became the object of detailed and thorough analysis. He had always craved understanding and agreement. Whether he was writing his early articles on reforms, or expounding the principle of national autonomy, or trying to discern patterns in the flux of historical events, he invariably turned to the invisible reader with ardent words of persuasion. And when the reader, like the hero of a Gogol tale, at last cried a resounding "I hear you,"[124] Dubnov felt more keenly than ever before that his life and work had been worthwhile.

Perhaps never before had the Berlin autumn seemed so fine and luxuriant as in the sunlit days when he wandered along leaf-strewn paths in the park, telling himself that the years of anxiety, searching, and ardor had not passed without trace. When he looked back at such moments he was conscious that a life spent in toil and deprivation had been a whole, a purposeful life, and, in its own way, a happy life. But the toiler conscious of the righteousness of his life's path was not vouchsafed the peaceful joy of the plowman reaping the harvest. The volcano of history was smoking ominously. Nineteen thirty was a year of crisis. Germany began to sink into the abyss of reaction.

Ten years earlier, Dubnov had decided to flee revolutionary chaos to preserve the peace necessary for work. Now he was overtaken by a time of troubles, a ferocious counterrevolution fed by the resentment of the upper echelons of society greedy for revenge, and the despair of the impoverished lower classes. A staunch democrat, he was filled with apprehension as the unstable structure of the Weimar Republic began to crack under the relentless pressure of destructive elements. The foul breath of zoological hatred spread over the country from the pages of a vulgar pamphlet distributed in tens of thousands of copies and from the columns of a bloodthirsty newspaper provocatively called *Angriff* (Attack). The main object of this hatred was world Jewry.

On the eve of Yom Kippur in the autumn of 1931 Dubnov wrote to Tcherikower: "I have returned to my own work, but the mood is that of the Day of Judgment. I feel a black storm cloud moving toward the world."

He worked on his memoirs, finished a short popular textbook of Jewish history, and wrote newspaper articles. The articles were printed in Yiddish dailies in Latvia and Lithuania, and, beginning in September 1932, chapters of his memoirs began to appear regularly in the New York *Zukunft*. A voluminous correspondence kept alive his connection with various countries. In the summer of 1932 Dubnov received news from distant, exotic Rio de Janeiro that the local Jewish young people had founded a library bearing his name. He was deeply moved, and in his reply expressed the wish that Brazil become one of the centers of Jewish culture in South America.

Attempts to shield his work from the storms of contemporary life were futile. More and more often a radio, carrying a hoarse voice, spitting rage, would rend the quiet of his study. Simon, Ida, and their grandson Alexander, who had come from Warsaw to study at Berlin University, listened gloomily to the howls of frenzy. The presence of the youth, who had brought joy and vitality into their home, became a constant source of anxiety. Ida Dubnov was particularly worried when her grandson pinned the three arrows,[125] a badge which aroused the hatred of the Hitler Youth, to his lapel before he left the house. The Hitler Youth were organizing attacks on their ideological opponents more frequently now; the toughs who used to distribute anti-Semitic pamphlets at the crossroads were quick to change their brown shirts for storm trooper uniforms. They were assuming the role of rulers of the country.

Dubnov searched feverishly for analogies in the past. The periods of mass psychosis and fanatical hatred directed at the disfranchised Jews sprang to mind. But the melancholy formula "there is nothing new under the sun" gave no comfort: a sixth sense suggested that the misfortune looming ahead could not be subsumed under any of the categories created by history.

The question that was now asked repeatedly in conversations with friends was—what next? The people who had settled in Berlin and planned to spend their lives there began to talk of fleeing Germany. Dubnov decided not to move for the time being. He was alarmed by the prospect of new wanderings, of transporting his library and archive, and a prolonged inter-ruption in his work. The thought of leaving depressed his wife still more. She had grown accustomed to the quiet, cozy nest; she liked their Berlin friends and feared that she lacked the physical and spiritual stamina to adapt to new circumstances. She sensed sadly that she was growing weaker every day. New, agonizing pains afflicted her joints, the first symptoms of the terrible disease which neither she, nor those about her, suspected.

These two, who had been fated to weather several historical storms, entered 1933 with anxiety and a gnawing feeling of helplessness. Their forebodings did not deceive them. Soon a majority of the German people gave the fate of Germany into the hands of Hitler.

30

In a New Nest

A new era in the history of Central Europe opened with a tragic paradox. The dictatorship achieved its victory over democracy with the aid of demo-cratic methods. After the March elections the flight from Germany began. The first to leave the country were the birds of passage, the recent emigrés. Many of them sought refuge in Austria, Czechoslovakia, and Palestine, but the main stream of emigration flowed into Paris. Sadly Dubnov saw off friends who were leaving. He was conscious that his days in Berlin were also numbered, but he vacillated in choosing his haven. Elias and Rebecca Tcherikower called him insistently to Paris, where the Jewish com-munity was thriving, but Dubnov was not attracted by the noisy, bustling world center. His thoughts turned to Switzerland; a half-forgotten image of Zurich awash in green floated into his memory. Long ago, as he had admired the splendor of the mountains and the azure blue of the lakes, the guest from the East had thought enviously of those fortunate men who could engage in scholarly study in that idyllic setting. Now, however, in these troubled, critical times the idyll seemed less attractive. The prospect of being separated from his children and from Jewish life disturbed him.

Work on his memoirs distracted him from gloomy thoughts. The galley proofs of the *History* arrived regularly from Palestine, where it was being printed. "May shines in all her beauty," Dubnov writes to Tcherikower, "but the air is laden with sorrow, the sorrow of parting. . . . My friends in Palestine are ready to excommunicate me for not moving there. Ten years ago I would have gone, now it is too late to break up my life." A short note from Ida Dubnov breathes resignation: "It's hard to think that we will have to leave our retreat. . . ."

Sometime later Dubnov informed his friends that his plans had crystallized:

> We are going to Riga, not to Zurich. . . . There is a great deal to be said for Riga: . . . the place is not so alien, it is closer to the children in the Soviet Union and Warsaw. We lead a sad life here, outwardly quiet but full of inner worry. This time of transition, this mood of emigration is hard on us. My friends in Palestine are astonished by my lack of desire to settle there. They do not understand that to change climate, language, the whole structure of life at our age would sap the rest of our strength, which may yet be needed. . . . I will scribble (just that, I won't write systematically) my memoirs. I have already reached 1908. . . . I will write more. Otherwise one could go mad from the daily newspapers and the horrible atmospheric pressures.

These letters, written in Russian (his correspondence with the Tcherikowers was usually conducted in Yiddish), are distinguished by a caution uncharacteristic of the writer called for by the ubiquitous censorship.

Luminous, cool summer days came, drenched in the honeyed perfume of flowering limes. Once more, as back in the early twenties, Dubnov took his solitary farewell walks along quiet streets and paths. He had experienced and pondered much in this setting. Many intimate conversations had taken place on the little bench in the park near the colorful flower bed. Now all that was history. All around dinned an alien, evil, hostile city inundated with brown-shirted troops.

The Dubnovs left Berlin in August. The suburb of Riga, awash in green, where they found a temporary refuge, reminded them of the retreat they had left, and Simon decided to settle there permanently. He liked the apartment in a white two-story house because of its similarity to his Berlin lodgings. Proximity to nature made up for a certain lack of comfort and luxury; the study windows stared directly into the green wall of the forest.

Once again his native North—stern yet gentle, with its mosses and heathers and the light morning frost, and the damp, bracing Baltic wind—breathed upon him.

The people who surrounded the guests with care and attention seemed familiar too. Dubnov met more than a few kindred spirits among them. Local Jewish life bore the stamp of provinciality, but integrity, initiative, and national commitment were quite evident. The preacher of autonomism had the opportunity to see at first hand the fruitfulness of autonomy guaranteed by law. Within a short time the efforts of the dedicated communal leaders had created in a small country a network of schools of various kinds, a permanent Jewish theater, and an independent press. Now, however, these accomplishments were in jeopardy. Chauvinism and anti-Semitism were gathering strength in Latvia under the influence of the infection from the West. Dubnov had fled Nazism but now feared for the fate of the country which had given him shelter. He shared his misgivings with his wife, but she was a gravely ill woman, and her grasp on reality was slipping. The beauties of the northern landscape did not gladden her, nor did the stories of visitors stir her. She sank more and more hopelessly into the quagmire of disease. After the Dubnovs settled into their new home, she almost ceased to move at all, and spent whole days in a deep armchair, her waxen fingers listlessly turning the pages of a book lying on her knees.

Having put his archive and library in order, Dubnov returned to his manuscripts and proofs after a long interval. At the end of September he writes to the Tcherikowers:

> I have already begun my customary work, but I do not complain of the frequent visitors from town. . . . Say what you like—they are our kind of people, spinning out the thread of our Russian-Jewish tradition. At every step I feel that living connection to my former reader, which now, in an atmosphere of memories, is very dear to me. . . . I have resumed work on the memoirs, but other work (editing translations, etc.) often distracts me.

His connection to the world and to the people dear to him was sustained by personal and business correspondence now more intense than ever before. Dubnov systematically read the proofs of his books coming out abroad. A major French publishing house was bringing out the *Recent History*, and the first volumes of the *World History* were in press in Palestine. Dubnov himself undertook a new edition of his textbook, which came out in Berlin in 1932, and added a concluding chapter to the original text. "I am working a great deal," he informed Tcherikower, to whom he was in the habit of entrusting all the details of his literary activities. "My brain is teeming with ideas for political articles, . . . I would have lapsed . . . into melancholia had it not been for my beloved work and that poetry of thought in solitude which has saved my spirit in the most difficult times of my life. I even look with philosophical calm at the current worldwide madness and only wonder if our generation will live to see the end of this epidemic. . . ."

A severe, snowy winter cut Lesnii Park off from the town. The forest sank deep into snowdrifts. Dubnov worked on his memoirs. Blizzard-swept winters of the past rose in his memory, and the new winter merged with them. Quiet reigned in the isolated house, broken only by the wind howling in the chimney. Dubnov would lay his manuscript aside and tiptoe into the bedroom. Each time his heart contracted in pain, as incurable resignation stared from the ill woman's sunken eyes. Her body had become almost weightless, losing the will to live: it seemed that the weariness Ida Dubnov had bravely overcome, decade upon decade, lay on her feeble shoulders now in all its weight. The family doctor came to the conclusion that it was pointless to hide the truth. He said aloud what those about her had long guessed—an operation was out of question, the patient's condition was hopeless, her days were numbered. It was decided to move her to a hospital.

Weeks of slow agony dragged on in the white hospital room. The ill woman was drugged with pain-killing narcotics and often lost consciousness. Only one wish lived in her dying brain—to see her children once more. Only her older daughter was able to come. Her son, Yakov, and her daughter Olga lived in Russia and could not obtain permission to leave. Ida Dubnov spent the last week of her life in a half-sleep. Sometimes the features of her face, taut with suffering, would suddenly soften; her parched lips moved in semi-consciousness and whispered something. It was impossible to make out the words, but it was clear that the ill woman was talking to her children. Death came to her as she slept, transfiguring her. The deep wrinkles furrowing her brow and cheeks were smoothed away, and the quiet, chaste quality which was the essence of her nature appeared on her still face. She lay in a small side room of the synagogue; stern, waxen, and pale with her finely etched profile astonishingly like the photograph taken of her when she was a girl.

Ida was buried at midday on 23 January, a sunlit, frosty day. Strangers gathered at the cemetery; she had had almost no friends in this town where she had come to die. The rabbi made a restrained speech, the prayer for the dead echoed solemnly, and the small, light coffin was lowered into the cold, alien earth.

Simon returned from the cemetery and took to his bed. His body could not stand the strain of the last few days. From time to time the doorbell rang tentatively, breaking the silence in the deserted rooms. Kind neighbors looked in; visitors came from town to shake his hand and express their sympathy. Daniel Charney, who had recently come from Germany, was a particularly frequent guest. In a quiet voice he related the political and literary news; sometimes he simply sat quietly by the sick man's bed for a long while. Father and daughter spent long hours alone now, talking in muted voices, recalling the past—people, cities, favorite verses. Their closeness had probably never been so complete as on those winter days at the edge of the forest. Shortly before his daughter's departure, Simon drew an envelope inscribed "for the family only" from a large cardboard folder. He read her extracts from his diary of a personal nature, and a chapter of his autobiography not intended for publication.

The next day his daughter did not find her father in his usual place, an armchair near the small table piled with newspapers. He was sitting at his desk. Before him lay a manuscript, peppered with corrections and notes in the margins. He was deep in thought, quietly humming his favorite Hasidic tune, his gaze as concentrated and as steady as ever. He had returned to work.

Each morning the snow-covered mailman drew a sheaf of letters from his bag. They came from all corners of the world, from old and new friends and acquaintances who had heard the news of Ida Dubnov's death. Simon was touched by the sincere grief of the few people who had been able to get close to the reticent, reserved woman and who valued her integrity, her silent fortitude, and her shy, inner warmth. Now their sorrow was mixed with fear for her companion of many years, left alone in his declining years in a foreign land.

Dubnov did not hide from his permanent correspondents that coping with loneliness would be far from easy. "I work still more diligently than before," he writes in March 1934, "therein lies my only salvation." He often gave himself up to memories of Berlin in the letters of this period.

In the spring of 1934 the first volume of the memoirs was finished and handed over to the printer. An edition of the book was being prepared in Palestine at the same time. Dubnov awaited the appearance of his autobiography with unusual emotion. This book brought to the surface long-concealed impulses of his youth. It occupied a special place on the long list of his works. There had been a time when the autodidact, shaken by his encounter with world literature, dreamed of artistic creation. Those dreams had not been realized. A novel he had written in a burst of enthusiasm proved unsuccessful, and his timid attempts at versifying remained forever in rough draft in his notebooks. But his youthful longing had not died away. Time and again a lyrical burst of emotion broke into his political prose, lending a special rhythm to a phrase, while many a passage in his historical narrative betrayed his attraction to the novel. Out of concern with the consistency of his scholarly style, Dubnov excised all alien elements in the final version. Only in intimate fragments of his autobiography did he give free rein to his secret impulses, and then the long-suppressed images poured forth in a mighty flood.

The first chapters of *The Book of My Life* were written at the beginning of the twenties, when the author was trying to find shelter from the storms of the present in the past. That need reasserted itself with new vigor almost fifteen years later, in the days when he was finishing the first volume. Immersion in the past also helped overcome the loneliness and depression engendered by the political situation. Poor, backward Latvia was in the throes of a grave political crisis. Neither its political independence nor its democratic structure had deep roots. The triumph of Nazism in neighboring Germany predetermined its fate. When, in May 1934, the ambitious peasant's son, the representative of the conservative rural elements, revoked the democratic constitution, the country did not even stir. The home-grown *kulak* fascism of little Latvia possessed neither the dynamism nor the bloodthirsty rhetoric of National Socialism. Local anti-Semitism was rooted in economic competition and was not, at least in the beginning, marked by pogroms. But the slogan "Latvia for the Latvians" was clear enough. The dictatorship aimed its heaviest blows at the progressive Jewish community.

Dubnov viewed the new triumph of reaction with profound dismay. His visitors complained bitterly of the harassment to which the Jewish national schools were being subjected. The independent press was seeing its last days. At the beginning of the summer the authorities closed the paper *Frimorgn*, where Dubnov occasionally published articles. His circle of acquaintances dwindled; Daniel Charney was one of the first to leave. One day the abrupt ring of the telephone interrupted a conversation the two friends were having in the sunlit study. Charney was called home. His unexpected guests proved to be agents of the secret police, who produced an order for him to leave Latvia immediately. Several days later Dubnov wrote to him in exile in Paris: "So we were not even able to say goodbye, . . . I feel completely orphaned in the paradise of Lesnii Park. May is in full bloom. I wander alone through the woods and give myself to reflection. It is fortunate that the Russian proofs take up so much time." In the next letter, dated 9 June, he returns to his habitual theme: "The only medicine for melancholia is constant work," he admits, "I take mammoth doses of this medicine myself. I have to read three galley proofs of the book, each consisting of twenty-six sheets."

Dubnov's distant friends anxiously followed events in the Baltic region. They were conscious that the new nest was built on a shifting foundation. The question of emigration again emerged as an important topic in his correspondence. The Tcherikowers were pressing their former plan. His daughter and son-in-law tried to persuade Dubnov to move to Poland and settle in a small summer resort outside Warsaw. The members of YIVO (Yiddish Scientific Institute) declared that the historian's place was in the oldest center of Jewish culture. He hesitated; he was weary of wanderings. "I travel more willingly in time than in space," he admitted in his letters.

The first volume of *The Book of My Life* came out in June. The dedication on the title page read: "To the memory of Ida, my life's companion for half a century." The author felt that the true memorial to his friend of so many years was not a gray tombstone in a deserted cemetery but the book in which she is always present, although her name is mentioned on few pages.

In July Dubnov went away to rest at the resort of Druskeniki, near the Polish-Lithuanian border, where his daughter's family was spending the summer. The luminous days flowed by, filled with the fragrance of warm pine needles. It was pleasant to look out on the green meadow from the steep slope overlooking the rushing Niemen and listen to the lilt of a shepherd's pipe winding through the sunset like a slow-running brook. The family atmosphere also gladdened the recluse. The grandsons whose childhood had passed beneath his gaze were his favorites, and firm friendship bound him to his son-in-law, Henryk Erlich. Despite some differing views they had much in common—demanding idealism, commitment to principle, calm courage. In their discussions they rarely overstepped the boundary beyond which personal rancor sets in.

The return journey from Druskeniki lay through Vilna. Dubnov strode down the narrow sidewalks of the quaint tangle of familiar streets, overcome by emotion: fate had brought him once more to that ancient city whose fascination neither poverty nor the petty bustle of the marketplace could destroy. An intense inner life could be felt here as in former years, but its substance had changed. Vigorous cultural activities had taken the place of abstract discussions about national culture. The week Dubnov spent in the "Jerusalem of Lithuania" whirled by. Visits to schools alternated with meetings at the Yiddish Scientific Institute, and there was no end to meetings and conversations in the intervening hours. He looked at the new people—the teachers, journalists, YIVO research fellows, socially minded physicians—with great interest. One feature distinguished them all—an organic link with the masses of the people. The arguments with the assimilationists, into which the author of the "Letters" had put so much passion, had almost ceased. The word *zhargon* had become a tiresome anachronism; the clear, melodious Vilna Yiddish rang out everywhere. It was the language of home and school, of scholarly gatherings and children's games.

On his return to Riga Dubnov tried to sum up his impressions. As he writes to Jacob Leshchinsky,

> I remain pleased with my journey to Poland. I saw at close range the world with which I parted twenty-eight years ago. . . . No dearth of hardship and worry, but so much commitment, readiness for struggle, even self-sacrifice (in the school movement for example!). In Vilna I visited schools of various orientations and saw that what they are doing there is no less than saving children, living in conditions of the most abject poverty, from ruin, and helping them to become human beings. YIVO, too, is a small island of culture in a sea of beggary.

Direct contact with the collective of dedicated scholars made the writer feel his connection with them still more strongly. The future of YIVO became one of his constant concerns. He dreamed of this Jewish academy becoming the main center of Jewish culture in the Diaspora. In letters to friends Dubnov laid plans for conducting a number of research seminars. He declared his readiness to go to Vilna each year for two months to lead a historical circle. Yet to move to Poland completely was a decision he was not prepared to make. He was alarmed by the atmosphere of acrimonious party contention. "It would disturb the entire plan for the last years of my life," he writes on 26 September, "which must be devoted to taking stock." The seclusion of his forest retreat seemed more suitable for completing his life's task.

It was not easy for Dubnov to live as a true recluse; people and social activities exerted a strong pull. The graveyard silence of Latvia, particularly striking in contrast with the bustling life of Vilna, weighed heavily on him. Over the last few months the last remnants of democracy in the country had been destroyed, and the opposition had gone underground or emigrated. The Jewish cultural organizations were in disarray. Only the conservative Agudah[126] enjoyed the government's protection. Dubnov complained bitterly of the absence of freedom of speech and urged his friends abroad to protest in print the crimes of the new regime.

As he strode along forest paths carpeted with crackling leaves, he tried to comfort himself with the thought that dictators are not eternal. Nomadic caravans of birds etched dark triangles against the northern sky, and he was overcome by a bitter feeling of his homelessness as he followed their flight. He was desperately straining to discern what the morrow would bring to those dear to him, to his people, to the world. Germany was in the grip of racist madness; a black shadow lay over the Baltic lands. Deep in thought, he would return home along a broad forest walk which his neighbors had named "Dubnov Avenue." A thick, almost palpable stillness had invaded his spacious rooms. At his desk he took out of a folder his diaries and the thin, yellowed pages of letters—the materials for the second volume of his memoirs. The distant years, the meetings, the arguments, the passions came to life. The whirlwind of events had shattered many illusions, but the gray-haired man with the glittering black eyes never faltered; he believed firmly in the final victory of humanity. Stubbornly he also refused to surrender, on the personal front, in the hard-fought duel with his two enemies, old age and loneliness. He had a powerful ally—History.

31

Victory over Loneliness

In one of the letters written in the mid-thirties Dubnov describes his current state of mind thus: "It is dreary here—all around is dead, everything sleeps. I feel this dreariness when I have to mingle with dead people, but in solitude I am never alone—the whole world is with me!"

In Berlin, to the great consternation of his friends, he had always refused invitations to the movies. "What do I need spectacle for," he would say, "if the film of Jewish history passes before me, every day, on a giant screen?" His working cell was populated with living images; his connection to the past was never broken. He feared only one thing—that hostile, outside forces would destroy this connection. While working on the second volume of memoirs he writes to the Tcherikowers: "I have no confidence that I will be able to work calmly in this new situation even here, at the edge of the woods. After all, you know that I follow closely all that is going on around me, and the worm of politics often gnaws at my soul." Ideas born of the bitter experiences of recent years clamored to be put down on paper. In an interval between two chapters of the memoirs Dubnov wrote a short article on the tragedy of contemporary Jewry for the bulletin of the Jewish World Congress. The article was in the nature of an appeal, and the author suggested to friends in Paris that it be translated into French and English and be widely distributed. Hitler's press turned their attention to it. The *Völkischer Beobachter* quoted the words "the house of Israel is in flames," and added gloatingly, "This is just what we wanted!"

Two events dealt the writer hard blows: in the summer of 1934 came the report of Bialik's death in Tel Aviv, and six months later of the demise of Dr. Cemach Szabad[127] in Vilna. The former brought Dubnov a wave of memories of the noontide of his life, of walks on the seashore, and of his circle of friends in Odessa. Snatches of poetry, which used to serve as the background to his work, floated into his brain. Often, as he paced about his study and pondered the next chapter, he would chant aloud lines from "The Cricket" or his favorite lines: "There was a fresh wind blowing, far distances opened wide—high skies grew deeper, clearer—and spring looked down from mountains into vales." Lately his correspondence with Bialik, the director of the Dvir publishing house, had tended toward business matters, but the lyric poet's youthful face lived on in his memory.

Dubnov experienced Szabad's death as the loss of a comrade-in-arms fallen at his post. Only a few months earlier they had spent long hours in the YIVO building, a comfortable two-story house on a quiet, tree-shaded street. Szabad had chaired the meeting at which Dubnov had read his paper on the aims of the Scientific Institute. It was difficult to imagine Vilna without Szabad, a tireless, ardent idealist and social activist.

In November 1934 the first chapter of a long-planned series, "Where Are We Going?" (*Vuhin geyen mir?*), appeared in the London journal *Dos fraye vort*. It was entitled "Will the Twentieth Century Be the Reverse of the Nineteenth Century?" Dubnov stated bitterly that the new century was out to destroy everything that had been won by the progressive elements of mankind over the last 125 years. In the nineteenth century even the reactionary governments which had crushed revolutions had been reluctant to eliminate civil liberties entirely. The twentieth century had brought a number of countries authoritarian regimes that extinguished even the demand for freedom. Nazism, which openly announced that the "German Revolution" was called upon to destroy the legacy of the French Revolution, was the most complete form of this dictatorship. At the present time a significant part of Europe was living under the flag of antidemocratism and antihumanism. The most sensitive barometer of mankind's ethical culture—the history of the Jewish people—testified to the fact that the standard of morality was lower in the twentieth century than in the Age of the Inquisition. The author asked in alarm: "What are these if not signs of psychical and ethical decline, of savagery spawned by the terrible world carnage? Is this a temporary phenomenon or the beginning of a new era, threatening us with a new Middle Ages? Where are we going?"

Several months later the article was reprinted in the New York *Zukunft*, and the author added two more chapters from the same cycle, "Bestiality and Humanism" and "The Ethical Criterion." He asserts:

The tragedy of contemporary life consists in the fact that we are witnessing a *crisis in social ethics*. Racism, which reduces man to the level of an animal (blood and breed), has dealt the heaviest blow to human morality. Racism is a degenerate form of nationalism typical of the twentieth century. Many oppressed peoples who fought for independence in the last century have in our time become themselves the persecutors of national minorities. The decline of pacifism is also a symptom of the ethical crisis. Italian Fascism and Nazism have created a cult of military power, while Soviet propaganda does not call for swords to be beaten into plowshares, but for turning weapons against the class enemy. National Socialism has abandoned all morality in theory and in practice, whereas Lenin's followers are convinced that good can be created by amoral methods. But man is an ethical rather than a political animal. Amoralism threatens to return mankind to the times of barbarity. This must be resisted; we must create a whole network of Societies of Ethical Culture.

The direct heirs to the biblical Prophets, who proclaimed the ideas of humanism and pacifism twenty-five centuries ago, must take the initiative by right of historical priority. Organized humanism must oppose organized bestiality.

Lines throbbing with outrage and apprehension were written in an idyllic winter setting. "My Lesnii Park is already arrayed in a snow-white robe, and it is unspeakably beautiful," Dubnov writes to Charney. "There is peace and stillness within my glass house; only rarely do guests come all the way here to look at a man who lives like a recluse among pine trees and slumbering homes." At the time Dubnov was finishing the second volume of his memoirs, and he was already looking forward to the appearance of fresh proofs. He loved to feel the uninterrupted flow of work and the welding of the links in the chain of his grand design. Illness usually overtook him in his brief periods of rest, forced or voluntary. "Without work I am always ill," he complained to his friends at such times. The instinct for self-preservation told him that the best way to preserve his physical and spiritual health was a combination of work and long walks.

In the spring of 1935 Dubnov happily accepted a proposal to lecture on Rambam, in connection with the great scholar's eight-hundredth anniversary, at a Jewish club organized by a group of intelligentsia. He wanted to express the ideas which had accumulated in the months of silence. The lecture was of a historical nature but its conclusions were highly topical. He sketched a fascinating image of the Jewish encyclopedist who had lived in a climate fed by the streams of three cultures: Jewish, Christian, and Moslem. The renowned codifier, who had systematized religious writing, had diligently studied the exact sciences and considered himself an Aristotelian. A thread can be traced running from Rambam to Spinoza, Mendelssohn, and the rationalists of the nineteenth century. Dubnov suggested that it was fitting to remember a progressive thinker of the Middle Ages at a time when "a new and dark Middle Ages threatens the European world. Now, when racist theory dominates a large European country, classifying men like cattle, according to breed, and declaring the most ancient civilized people the lowest race, it is appropriate to remember that eight hundred years ago there lived among these people a man who distinguished people . . . only by spiritual criteria." Dubnov wound up his lecture with these words:

We ourselves have sufficient protection from bestiality and antihumanism, this plague which has come upon mankind. We, the descendants of the Prophets . . . who created the ideals of humanism and justice three thousand years ago, the descendants of such thinkers as Rambam, must remember that throughout history we have survived as a spiritual nation thanks to our spiritual strength. And if the new devotees of Wotan, the apostles of brute force, want to destroy us, we must remind them that we have withstood the more sophisticated cults of Zeus and Apollo and the iron fist of ancient Rome!

The entire spring passed in work on the proofs of the second volume of *The Book of My Life*. After it came off the press Dubnov plunged into reading an abridged version of the *World History*, put together by Aaron Steinberg. With a feeling of satisfaction he declared that the translator of the ten-volume work had succeeded in abridging it and retaining its style without sacrificing anything essential. In August, Dubnov went to Vilna for a conference held in connection with the tenth anniversary of the founding of the Yiddish Scientific Institute.

In Vilna he plunged into the exhilarating atmosphere of a great cultural festival. The well-attended conference was a genuine celebration of Jewry's scholarly, literary, and social resources. It took place under singular circumstances. The ominous shadow of Nazism loomed large on the European horizon, but along with the growth of concern for the cultural values threatened by barbarism grew the determination to defend them to the utmost. Dubnov's speech at the opening of the conference reverberated with this determination. Right away, as though sensing that he spoke for the fifteen hundred people in the audience, he posed the question: was it not strange that, at a time when mortal danger threatened the Jews in one of the major European countries, at a time when a vile pestilence was poisoning the atmosphere of Europe, a scholarly conference had been organized? Was it possible to create cultural values during a moral earthquake? It was not only possible, it was necessary, he declared with conviction. Just as a physical earthquake could not break the laws of nature, so a moral crisis could not break the laws of history. It was necessary to cultivate genuine scholarship with special persistence at a time when scholarship was being falsified on a dictator's orders. The Jewish people were accustomed to creating their culture in the face of external obstacles. Now they were doing so along two channels. It was no accident that two scholarly festivals had coincided—the tenth anniversary of YIVO and the tenth anniversary of Hebrew University in Jerusalem. Cooperation between the two academies was the order of the day. Cultural and linguistic dualism was not a new phenomenon in Jewish history. It went back to the existence of the state of Judea as a Roman protectorate, when the cultural vitality of the academic centers of Babylon and Alexandria equaled that of Jerusalem. The Babylonian Talmud was valued by successive generations no less than the Jerusalem Talmud, and Aramaic was a literary medium equal to Hebrew. At the present time our academies complemented each other: the Palestine university was concentrating on studying the past, the institute in Vilna on contemporary problems and the training of cadres of scholars and teachers.

At the first plenary session of the conference Dubnov read a paper called

"The Contemporary State of Jewish Historiography." In his concise survey he showed how not only the form but also the content of scholarly research had changed over time. In the first, the theological stage, which had lasted for centuries, scholarly work was confined to scholastic commentary and excluded criticism. The content of the second, the spiritual stage, was the study of Judaism as the basis of the historical process; it was conducted in the spirit of a moderate traditionalism. In the third, the sociological stage, the life of the people in all its aspects—political, economic, cultural, and ethnographic—became the object of study; here a critical approach to the methods hallowed by tradition was used for the first time. The era of Graetz (1860–1890), which succeeded the era of Zunz (1820–1860), marked the transition to the sociological method, but at the very center of his *World History of the Jews* its creator placed the process of the development of religious writing and could not bring himself to repudiate the dogmatic treatment of the biblical period. Bible criticism called that treatment into question. The results of its researches, combined with the discoveries of prominent orientalists, made the murkiest, most legendary period of Jewish history the property of historical science. The scholarly achievements of the West coincided chronologically (the end of the nineteenth and the beginning of the twentieth century) with the flowering of the sociological method in Eastern Europe. It reinterpreted Judaism as the product and not the source of the people's life, Jewish history as part of the history of mankind. Recently one could observe a tendency among young historians to turn the sociological method into a socioeconomic one. For some (Schiper, Caro) this tendency was a reaction against the traditional disdain for economics; for others it stemmed from a Marxist conception of history. The speaker termed the method of historical materialism lopsided, but remarked that recently published monographs by young Marxist historians (Ringelblum, Friedman) had made substantive contributions to Jewish historiography.

In conclusion Dubnov returned to a subject he had touched on in his opening address—a comparison of the methods of work at the Vilna institute and the Jerusalem university. Comparing the tables of contents of issues of scholarly journals appearing simultaneously in Vilna and Jerusalem, he called attention to a striking difference in subject matter and pointed out that the publications of the two academies complemented one another, thus creating a single whole. The paper ended with these words:

> The historian's essential creative act is the resurrection of the dead. His task is not . . . to invent puppets dancing to the tunes of specific ideologies, but to recreate, on the basis of the materials, the past as it actually was. Ideology must be the outcome of historical research, not theories to which historiographical constructs are artificially fitted. . . . The ancient sages said, "The history of the world is the judgment of the world. . . ." Thus the history of world Jewry will serve as the tribunal for all the insults and persecutions

to which this nation has been subjected. We hope to see among the officers of this court the best and the most humane representatives of all the peoples of the world.

The plenary meetings were followed by section meetings. The activity of the historical section, which Dubnov had long chaired, was of particular interest to him. The papers read there confirmed his impression that Jewish historiography had made giant strides in the last few years. Dubnov was in excellent spirits. He enjoyed spending the hours of work and leisure with men close to him in spirit, the Berlin friends who were attending the conference as well as local figures—Zelig Kalmanovich,[128] Max Weinreich,[129] and Zalmen Rejzin.[130] At the end of the conference Dubnov went with his daughter and grandson to a summer place near Vilna. The conversations with old and new friends were transplanted to mossy glades and the green banks of the Vilija. Marc Chagall and his wife, who were staying nearby, became regular participants in the forest gatherings. Dubnov belonged to a generation which had shown little interest in the visual arts and recognized only crude, didactic realism in painting. Chagall's visionary art was alien to him, but he valued the artist's genuine folk roots.

Lately the Riga recluse had begun to favor the plan to move to Poland; his Vilna friends pressed this plan warmly. But an incident which occurred shortly before his departure caused new hesitations. On their way back from a walk one day Dubnov and his companions boarded a river steamer. A group of Poznan students on a pilgrimage to ancient Catholic shrines happened to be on deck. The arrival of Jews enraged the pilgrims. The bigoted bullies began to demand the removal of the heathen, and some of them started toward young Erlich, threatening to throw him overboard. The steamer rapidly made for the bank, and the frightened captain asked the Jewish passengers to take themselves off. Dubnov tried to keep calm during these outrageous proceedings but it cost him great effort. The incident, a vivid illustration of the newspaper reports on the growth of anti-Semitism in Poland, remained in his mind for a long time. It was difficult to forget the hate-filled eyes and the pogrom-like shouting.

Dubnov left the Jerusalem of Lithuania full of conflicting impressions.

32

Work Continues

I measure my life by the scale of my
work.
                    –Letter to a friend

The luminous days of autumn had arrived when Dubnov returned to the
forest glades gilded by a pale sun. His sense of well-being did not leave
him. In one of the letters of this period he observes: "I am persuaded
that I am built of durable, unaging material." Not even the newspaper
reports, which he devoured every day in immense quantities, could disturb his spiritual equilibrium; he attributed this to the beneficial influence
of nature and a strictly regulated life. He writes to Aaron Steinberg,

> My health is good, the wags say that I "grow younger every day." In any
> event, I do not feel old age in intellectual work, I often find it easier to write
> now than in former years. . . . *The Book of My Life* was a great moral success,
> . . . I received a cordial letter from Miliukov;[131] he said that much of my book
> could have gone into his *Book of Life* if only he had been able to write it.

Even Dubnov's seventy-fifth birthday brought no sense of old age; but
a secret, grim foreboding unexpectedly intruded in a letter to Steinberg
written soon after the anniversary:

> My life is now measured in quarters of a century. . . . It is a great blessing
> for a historian to live three "spans," in three generations, for he can penetrate
> the mystery of the changing eras more deeply. But it is also a curse if the
> change is for the worse, for then there is a danger that the thread of life will
> snap during a dark phase. We are living in a terrible time, and only a dual
> faith in life, the faith of a Jew and of a chronicler, gives me the strength to
> bear it all.

The 1935 anniversary was celebrated more modestly than the one five
years before. During those years the atmosphere in Europe had taken
a sharp turn for the worse. Nevertheless, Dubnov received numerous letters and telegrams of congratulation. "For a week now," he writes to
Charney, "I have been basking in the warm waters of my anniversary
—telegrams, letters, and articles. Not in the same quantity, it is true, as

five years ago in Berlin. This time, instead of a large banquet, they arranged a colloquium with forty participants."

The branches of the YIVO historical division in various cities had organized a number of lectures devoted to the aged scholar's career. The division set to work collecting materials for a Festschrift, which was to include original historical studies and unpublished archival documents. Work on the book required great effort, and the massive volume *Historishe shriftn* did not come out until 1937, under the editorship of Elias Tcherikower. A youthful face—albeit framed with gray—lit by a smile lurking in the corners of the eyes and mouth looks out of the portrait at the beginning of the book. A brief introduction described the recipient of the Festschrift as the creator of a new era in historiography and a tireless promoter of the study of history. Dubnov's younger colleagues maintained that "historicism" was for him a complete and efficacious world view; he thought of himself as a "missionary of history." As if continuing this line of thought, Samuel Abba Horodetzky,[132] who researched the genealogy of the Dubnov family, pointed out that his sense of mission had deep roots in the past. He saw the historian as the direct heir of a dynasty of talmudists and cabalists. From MaHaRal of Prague[133] to Bentsion Dubnov they were all renowned for their righteous lives as well as for their learning. Rabbi Joseph Yoske of Dubno,[134] a mystic and a visionary, a man of an ascetic bent who prayed daily for the insulted and the injured in Israel and other nations, was especially popular with the common people. The renowned cabalist, who found himself in constant communion with the world beyond, deemed it his duty to concern himself with earthly matters as well; he led the struggle against the *kahal* leaders who oppressed the poor. The researcher expressed his belief that the rebellious mood which seized the self-taught *maskil* in his youth was also deeply rooted in family tradition. Horodetzky drew the following conclusion:

Dubnov is the last bearer of the spirit which governed his family for centuries. However great the difference between him and his forefathers, there is no doubt that he received from them a rich heritage. His strong ties to the past, his attachment to the Jewish people, and his love of men were bequeathed to him by his distant great-great-grandfather Joseph Yoske of Dubno."

Among the original documents published in the Festschrift, documents from the scholar's own rich archive occupied a central place, for he had presented the archive he had taken out of Russia to YIVO. Of particular interest in another set of materials was a 1921 letter from a group of Petersburg Jewish communal leaders congratulating Dubnov on his sixtieth birthday and now published for the first time. Written in Yiddish, a rare occurrence among the Petersburg intelligentsia, it stated that the historian embodied the spirit of the generation which had entered the social arena in an era of pogroms. That generation, standing at a difficult crossroads in history, took their bearings from the idea of preserving the nation. The authors of the letter declared their intention of publishing a Festschrift and invited Jewish writers, regardless of orientation, to participate, claiming that Dubnov's work was a national treasure.*

At the end of 1935 Dubnov wrote an article on a subject which had long been on his mind—the necessity of convening an international Jewish congress to establish permanent representation in the League of Nations. Organized defense of Jewish rights in the international arena was one of the basic points of the program created by this theorist of Diaspora nationalism. The demand followed from the ideology of autonomism, indeed from his entire world view. Despite a number of bitter disappointments Dubnov still adhered to an optimistic liberalism, even in the antiliberal twentieth century. He believed doggedly in the inviolability of international treaties and the force of moral sanctions. At the very time reality was plainly demonstrating the powerlessness of the small states in the arena of the League of Nations, he saw in its representation of the weakest, stateless people a powerful bulwark in the struggle against anti-Semitism. His fervor infected very few people. The intellectual climate in which the ideology of Dubnovism evolved was foreign to assimilated American Jews, and the majority of Zionists were skeptical of the possibility of defending Jewish interests in the Diaspora. Dubnov writes bitterly to Tcherikower: "I do not see the kind of enthusiasm for the idea of the Congress, which, in a healthy people, could touch off a powerful movement." He felt that convening a Jewish parliament was particularly important at that juncture. In 1935, when the Nuremburg Laws were promulgated in Germany, the writer called them the "Declaration of the Disfranchisement of Man." The situation of the Jews had markedly deteriorated in many other European countries as well. The need to provide an "address for the Jewish people" became more imperative than ever.

The same idea was put forward in an appeal Dubnov wrote at Tcherikower's suggestion several months later. It averred that such phenomena as the paroxysm of vicious, zoological anti-Semitism in Germany, the economic boycott and outbreaks of pogroms in Poland, persecution in Rumania, and the virtual abrogation of equal rights in the small fascist Baltic states urgently required international intervention. A Jewish congress should be convened without delay, and it should be representative of the entire Jewish people. Taking to task the social organizations which refused to take part in the congress, Dubnov complained bitterly of the fragmentation of national energies and factional intolerance. To those who were indifferent he addressed an impassioned plea: "The thought that you are creating a worldwide organization for a worldwide people, an instrument for the defense of the most defenseless nation in the world, should

---

*Their intention was never realized.

inspire you. Every man who stands aside risks finding himself in complete isolation, outside the bounds of the living national organism."

As Dubnov worked on the third volume of the memoirs devoted to the recent past, he felt mired in the present, yet the only thing that could restore his spiritual equilibrium was a large-scale historical work. Such a project did materialize: a major Russian publisher expressed readiness to publish the ten-volume *History* in the original. The writer's spirits soared. A new project meant long months of uninterrupted work. It gave him the chance to revise the text of the *History* again and, above all, to add chapters documenting the events of the stormy last twenty-five years. There is a feeling of great animation in the letters of 1936. Dubnov quips that over the last few years he has grown accustomed to considering himself a historian on leave, and now he is happily returning to active duty. On 11 May he informs Aaron Steinberg:

> I have settled down to a large piece of work which gives me . . . great spiritual satisfaction. . . . For many years I have been tormented by the thought that I would not live to see my work in the language in which it was written. . : . A volume is to come out every three months; consequently I have made a compact with God for another thirty months, two and a half years. . . . Revisions and proofs once again. The third volume is indefinitely postponed. . . . I can endure the painful blows of the present relatively easily in my forest solitude, but at times they become unbearable. I save myself by my journey through the centuries. After all, decades of my life have been spent in this ark above the floodwaters—old habits die hard!

The letters to Tcherikower have the same cheerful tone, the same firm resolve: one must live, come what may, flying in the face of fate if need be, to bring the work to completion, and the angel of death would never dare approach a man fulfilling his life's vow. All the letters of this period contain an account of the progress of his work. The days were completely full again, as they were in St. Petersburg and Berlin: "I measure my life by the scale of my work: the volumes of the *History* appear one after the other, stacks of manuscripts and proofs pile up. . . . There is no time for anything else. The moment I tear myself away from work the distress of the world and the distress of Jewry in this accursed time crash down on me."

Proofs also came from France, where Dubnov's textbook was being printed, and from Palestine, where *The Book of My Life* was coming out in a Hebrew translation. Dubnov was obliged to give up a journey to Switzerland because of pressing work. "Our Geneva Congress is very much in my thoughts," he writes to Charney, "unfortunately I cannot attend it because I am once again in thrall to the muse of history. . . . Here I am like a fish in water, and I am reluctant to come out onto dry land. . . ."

Despite work on the *History* Dubnov found time to comment on various developments in literary and social life. His article "A Romantic of the

Revolution," written with great élan, was published in an issue of *Zukunft* devoted to the fortieth literary anniversary of Abraham Liessin.[135] The poetry of the Jewish poet-rebel reminded Dubnov of the poems of his beloved Victor Hugo, and he saw their main appeal in blending social and national commitment. Several months later he wrote a lengthy review article for the same journal devoted to a critique of a large historical work by Salo Baron, a professor at Columbia University. Dubnov valued Liessin highly, not only as a poet but also as an editor. The news that *Zukunft* might be forced to close disturbed him very much, and in print he vigorously urged the necessity of establishing a special fund to support the journal's continued existence.

The solitary study with wide windows looking into a green tangle of branches spun threads to all the centers of Jewish cultural and communal life. YIVO, the Congress, and the *Jewish Encyclopedia* were constant objects of Dubnov's concern. He closely followed Jewish periodicals all over the globe and made a special effort to find time for reading. Chaim Zhitlowsky's memoirs, in which Dubnov found much in common with *The Book of My Life*, made a strong impression on him. He writes to Zhitlowsky in March 1936:

> The milieu, your Vitebsk circle, the entire era which you depict so vividly, is very dear to me. . . . I myself went through the same process of development as you did several years earlier . . . with the difference that the problems of the individual stirred me more than did social problems, the world's woes more than our people's woes (the latter subsequently laid the former to rest).

He urged Zhitlowsky to keep writing his autobiography: "I think that a memoir is best, because it is the most intimate work of every reflective writer, provided it is written with the depth and veracity of a confession."

In the winter of 1937 Dubnov fell seriously ill; a severe cold was complicated by a gall bladder infection. His friends were at their wit's end. One consultation followed another. The condition of his heart alarmed the doctors. Dubnov, however, felt no fear. "I alone," he writes, "retained my composure among nervous and anxious people. No, I will not die until I have completed the remainder of my whole life's work." That the doctors would not permit him to read urgently needed proofs bothered him more than anything else. "My head has been in perfect working order throughout," he asserted, "even when I lie in bed. My work is more necessary to me than I am to it." Returning to his habitual way of life helped him to convalesce.

Correspondence occupied a large place in Dubnov's life and not solely as a matter of necessity, for he loved writing letters and was skilled in that art. Epistolary style suited him. He wrote slowly, thoughtfully, choosing his phrases with care. At times his gift for conciseness, for precise, succinct formulation, inspired by French models, is even more apparent in his letters than in his articles. Current events were the main subject of letters to his friends. No wonder that one day a polemic which began as correspondence should have ended in print. Its subject was the role of the Bund in the life of the Jewish community. The organizers of the celebration of the Bund's fortieth birthday, held in the autumn of 1937, were distressed by the fact that Dubnov was not moved to comment on the anniversary of an event which was a turning point in the life of Russian Jewry. Henryk Erlich said this frankly in a letter to his father-in-law. Dubnov decided that an exchange on the burning questions of contemporary life should not be confined to private correspondence. In June 1938 an article entitled "On the Isolation of the Bund and on the Zionist National Movement (A Letter to a Bundist Friend)" appeared in *Zukunft*. The "friend" was not named lest the argument look like a "family" matter. It proved impossible to avoid this, however. Erlich chose to eschew anonymity and signed his lengthy reply, which appeared in the same journal, with his full name. Dubnov argues in the article:

> The Bund's greatest sin is its tendency toward isolation. Its hostility toward the conservative Agudah is entirely understandable; however, the Bund categorically rejects the possibility of cooperation with the progressive, even the socialist, elements of the Jewish community if they are tinged by Zionism. Meanwhile, over the last forty years Zionism has become a national movement, and the rebirth of the Palestine center is one of the wonders of the world. The indisputable failings of Zionism—its lofty disdain for the Diaspora and its conviction of the superiority of Palestine Jewry to all other parts of the people—should not prevent some joint actions. We have seen "popular fronts," coalitions of all the progressive forces in a society, emerge in several European countries. Jewry also needs such a "popular front" to fight growing anti-Semitism and worldwide reaction. . . . If a double miracle comes to pass —the Bund repudiating its mistaken ideas and my living to see its fiftieth anniversary—then I will salute it wholeheartedly.

Dubnov was hard at work on the two concluding chapters of the *History*. "I have reworked the epilogue," he writes to Aaron Steinberg, "and I have brought it up to our own day—literally, for I cannot keep silent about the Austrian disaster, the Rumanian villainy, the Polish permanent pogrom. . . . You can imagine what it was like for me to write about all this without abandoning the 'calm' tone appropriate to a historian. . . ."

Some of Dubnov's works were being made available to larger audiences in abridged versions accessible to the average reader. The three-volume edition of the *World History* was appearing in German in Czechoslovakia; *The Book of My Life* came out in a single, slim, elegant volume in Berlin; and an abridged text of *Letters on Old and New Jewry* was published in Palestine. Despite the depressing political situation, Dubnov had the feeling of Galileo—"But it *does* move"—despite the repressive political situation. He lived as before, according to plan. In December 1937 he writes to Tcherikower: "All winter and part of the spring here I will work harder than I ever did these last years. And this is excellent. Work . . . helps me . . . drive away the demon of last year's illness." In fact, the editing of his large work did not always cure physical ailments, but it invariably drove off the "demon of despair." Dubnov tried to instill his own zest in his faraway friends. In a letter to the Tcherikowers we find such lines as: "They tell me . . . that all our brethren are dispirited. How can anyone give in to despair in our times? It is precisely in such terrible days that one shouldn't lose courage. . . ."

Soon, in a time of dreadful trials, courage would prove to be the only possession which human savagery could not take away from the writer.

33

The Twilight of Europe

The year 1938 was born in an atmosphere of anxiety: Europe was drawn inexorably into the orbit of catastrophe. Steel birds of prey flew over its southwestern tip, where the prologue to a worldwide bloodbath was enacted. The moral combat of Republican Spain against the forces of fascism was doomed to failure by the political "neutrality" of the great powers. And from the Olympian heights of "nonintervention" the democratic governments looked on as a small, unarmed people, whose destruction was essential to the nightmare program of Nazism, was crushed.

Unusually pessimistic notes can be heard in Dubnov's letters written in this period. On 3 January 1938 he writes to a Paris friend, the writer Nina Gurfinkel: "It has become very difficult to breathe in present-day Europe, which tramples all the ideals of the Declaration of Rights[136] into the mud. . . . The twentieth century *vs.* the nineteenth century—that is the meaning of the revolution from the right. . . . Hence the impotence of all our World Congresses and even the League of Nations. It is difficult to fight the savagery of entire nations."

Dubnov was preparing new volumes of the *History* for publication. Despite the entreaties of his friends he stubbornly refused to take a rest. "Can there be any talk of prolonged rest in such a time, gasping for breath as it races on, when the poisonous gases of politics are suffocating us?"

he writes to the Tcherikowers in September 1938. This was the time of the Munich capitulation to Hitler. Impotent anger stuck in Dubnov's throat; he groped for the words that would arouse the world's conscience. He had long insisted on the necessity of publishing a Jewish political journal in Paris or London, and he was pleased when his friends informed him the plan was close to realization. "I wish your enterprise, the forthcoming *Die fraye tribune*, well," he writes to Tcherikower. "I will probably send you an article about what is going on in the world now. We must wait and see what the nightmarish events of the last few days will bring. If Europe is sentenced to Nazi-Fascist hegemony it will be necessary to draw up a new battle plan." Several days later he writes:

> I am going to send a short piece to *Die fraye tribune*. I am taking advantage of a brief pause in my work in order to state concisely ideas which have preoccupied me lately. More than once in the course of fifty-seven years I have had to write articles of this kind in days of catastrophe. . . . And now it falls to my lot to react to a catastrophe more terrible than all those which have gone before. . . . I think my statement will also be heard as a memento to our World Congress, which ought to be reorganized and activated. I have now moved on to work on ancient history. That is the refuge where one can hide from this present time of troubles. . . . After all, if one couldn't find a firm footing in *all* eras, ours could drive one mad.

Events moved so rapidly that a month later Dubnov thought that the article, written in October 1938, was out-dated, and he decided to add an afterword. The wave of anti-Semitic terror had swelled to incredible heights in Germany (the expulsion of thousands of Jews to the Polish-German border zone, pogroms in Berlin and other cities, mass internments in concentration camps, indemnities). Dubnov writes to Elias and Rebecca Tcherikower, with whom he shared his moods and thoughts more and more often: "For the first time in all the centuries of modern history we are witnessing a government pogrom, but, on the other hand, for the first time there has been world protest. . . ."

In those dark days Dubnov was consumed by politics. He was disturbed by the news that the initiators of the Paris journal proposed the subtitle "an organ of Jewish thought" (*farn yidishn gedank*) as though emphasizing that it was apolitical. "In our day," he writes, "Jewish thought without politics was an impossibility. Incidentally, in working now on the chapters about ancient Prophetism, I too feel compelled to touch on questions of international politics."

Public misery did not dull his sensitivity to personal loss. The death of Abraham Liessin, whom he had valued as a poet, a journalist, and a man of stature, was a heavy blow. The survival of *Zukunft*, to which the deceased devoted so much effort, also concerned Dubnov deeply.

A letter to the Tcherikowers on 20 November 1938 ends with the words, "Amid sufferings and horror a new world will be born. Our grandchildren will, perhaps, live to see a calmer time; we were destined to witness the birth pangs."

His Paris friends urged him to send his contribution, but Dubnov hesitated. Rumors had reached him that the journal's *leitmotif* would be confessions by repentant representatives of the freethinking intelligentsia taken unaware by the events of recent years. These rumors worried him. To Tcherikower he writes:

> I repeat, it is better for me not to write for the *Tribune* until the first issue has appeared. This new breast-beating mood is quiet unknown to me although I follow the Jewish press closely. . . . I want to know what men a little younger than I are thinking. After all, back in the eighties I witnessed a period ringing with the repentant howl "Let's come home!" It should have a different resonance in our time. After the journal comes out I intend to speak my mind about this new virus in the *Tribune*. Now my attention is focused on two subjects: ancient history and the problems of contemporary life—more precisely, the problems of rousing world conscience (in connection with Roosevelt's campaign).

The tentacles of Nazism were reaching inexorably out toward new victims. In February Republican Spain fell. In March cohorts of storm troopers marched in a victory parade past the ancient buildings of silent, funereal Prague. The aggressor's new triumph spelled slavery for millions of Slavs and death for hundreds of thousands of Jews. Europe maintained a gloomy silence. Only isolated voices of protest testified that the will to resist was not completely paralyzed. During these dreadful days Dubnov worked feverishly on the article "The Awakening of World Conscience and the Role of Jewry (On the 150th Anniversary of the French Revolution)," which appeared in the April 1939 issue of the Paris journal *Russkie Zapiski*,[137] edited by P. Miliukov. The article showed that the true nature of Nazism had long been revealed as zoological anti-Semitism. It was entirely natural that a state which was cruelly persecuting a national minority should use cutthroat methods in dealing with its neighbors as well. It was time to realize that the Jewish question was an international question. The progressive circles of Jewry had long understood this and, back in 1919, created the Committee of Jewish Delegates to fight for the rights of Jewish minorities in the countries of Europe, as well as legal guarantees for the sanctuary in Palestine. Now that the League of Nations had collapsed the Jewish people had no means of recourse. Their only support lay with the progressive forces of mankind. It faced three urgent tasks: (1) the struggle for equal rights in individual countries in alliance with the democratic and socialist parties, (2) the struggle on an international scale through the medium of the World Jewish Congress and the American Jewish Congress, (3) the international organization of emigration. Dubnov noted bitterly the weakness of the Evian Emigration Committee[138] and the Arabophile orientation of British policy. He declared that other peoples would have to move over and make room for wandering Ahaspher.[139] A great shift in the major centers was beginning to take place before our very eyes. It was possible that only a third of the population of the Diaspora would remain in Europe, that America would become numerically the strongest center, and that a small Jewish state would arise in Palestine. The article concluded with an anxious question: Would Europe be able to destroy the present stronghold of reaction as the French destroyed the Bastille one hundred and fifty years before?

Dubnov thought the initiative taken by Roosevelt, who considered it essential to create a League to Resist European Aggression, a sign of the awakening of world conscience. This initiative ought, so the writer thought, to rouse to action even the Jewish Congress. He also outlined his plan in a short memorandum. A letter attached to this document, dated 1 May 1939, pointed out that the decisions made at the bureau's last session still remained on paper despite the fact that the condition of Jewry had significantly deteriorated over the last few months. The memorandum bore the title "The International League for the Defense of the Jewish People," and the text was published in the Jewish-American press. Dubnov wrote,

> President Roosevelt's appeal and the founding of the League to Resist European Aggression prompts one to ask: What fate awaits the Jewish people, persecuted by the aggressive governments of Germany and Italy, and subjected to restrictions in other countries? The Jewish people are a people without a state, therefore it cannot enforce its demands as a full-fledged member of the League he proposes. . . . But isn't systematic internal aggression directed against a defenseless nation no less criminal than the forced annexation of foreign territory by methods of external aggression?

Dubnov rehearsed the long litany of crimes committed by Nazism and observed that they had spawned chaotic, desperate waves of emigration. The victims of the terror wandered the seven seas, knocking in vain at doors in various countries that were slammed in their faces. The British administration drove them away from the ports of Palestine. For thousands of refugees the choice lay between a watery grave and countries of permanent pogrom. Only a body devoted to defending the rights of Jews could solve the tragic problem.

The Paris journal, which Dubnov had been waiting for impatiently, came out under the revealing title "At the Crossroads" (*Oyfn sheydveg*). The first issue confirmed his fears. On 4 May 1939 he writes to Tcherikower, one of the editors of the journal:

> I do not think this is the time for a reexamination of ideology. . . . The time for a reevaluation of values will come when the present turmoil has been laid to rest. But now, when the knife is at our throats, when millions of people do not know what the morrow will bring, it is inappropriate to concern oneself with breast-beating and worries about one's own soul. The only thing to do

during a fire is to carry water to pour on the flames and fight alongside the firemen—and that is all. I am going to say this in an article which might appear in the second issue; the title will be something like "What Should One Do in Haman's Times?" Here's the central idea: if they are rallying against us . . . to wipe us off the face of the earth, it is essential to concentrate all our energy on the struggle with these worldwide cutthroats. Sixteen million Jews is no mean force; it could easily spoil our enemy's game. If you wish, publish the article with a polemical editorial note . . ., but I cannot be silent. . . . Poland's reply to Hitler is due tomorrow. We do not know if it will be a step toward world war, but one thing is indisputable—everything except the struggle against the world aggressor must now be put aside. It is very sad that the World Jewish Congress is silent once again. . . . Have we reached such a pass that we no longer react to danger? . . . My health has been failing a little lately (symptoms of *angina pectoris*, it seems), but it does not prevent me from working. . . . I go out, I stroll through the woods, on the whole I feel quite all right. I do not think at all about the necessity of saving myself from the storms. The panic which prevails around me has not infected me, and anyway—where could I run to? One must hope that the small Baltic countries remain neutral.

The correspondence about the journal *Oyfn sheydveg* continued. In a letter of 12 June Dubnov encourages a plan of publishing in one and the same issue "Letters to the Editor" and an editorial response:

It will be, to use a modish term, a "symposium." I hope the war will be "peaceful," and that we—God willing—will not grow angry with each other. The success of *Oyfn sheydveg* gives me great pleasure. . . . We are at a crossroads in world politics now. . . . In a few days you will be celebrating the anniversary of the French Revolution in Paris. It is precisely in our time that this day should become an occasion of world significance, but the world is demoralized and sunk in apathy. . . . I live, as you see, in two worlds, in the past and in the present.

Work on the last volume of ancient history connected Dubnov to the past, while journalism paid its due to the contemporary world. Almost concurrently with his letter to the editor of *Oyfn sheydveg*, he wrote an article for *Evreiskii Mir*, a Russian periodical published in Paris which, both in spirit and in its list of contributors, continued the old, prerevolutionary tradition of Russian-Jewish journalism. In this article, entitled "The Jewish Intelligentsia, A Historical Survey," he returned to the subject of many of his previous articles and speeches—the defense of the multilingual principle in Jewish writing. Historical examples provided the heart of the main argument. The author polemicized with the Yiddishists and the Hebraists, pointing out that Jewish literature written in a non-Jewish language had a two-thousand-year-old lineage. The Greek Bible, the Septuagint, appeared in the first century B.C.E. In the following centuries one part of the Diaspora wrote in Greek and the other in Aramaic. The first major works in Jewish historiography appeared in German, and over the last one hundred and fifty years Russian-Jewish writing—scholarly, political, and artistic—had exercised an enormous influence on the formation of national self-awareness. At present, young men and women who neither spoke Yiddish nor read Hebrew expressed their Jewishness through the medium of the state language; this phenomenon was particularly characteristic of America.

The article drew attention to yet another aspect of the language question. As cultural centers migrated from country to country they left behind a heritage of universal values embodied in several world languages:

> Judaism is a national world view with a universal potential. . . . Within it lies the latent energy of spiritual expansion. From ancient times until the present the Jewish intelligentsia, who have come in contact with the surrounding world, have felt the need to share with it their cultural achievements. . . . We do not lock ourselves up in a national ghetto, we hold to a system of open doors. . . . As long as there is a multilingual Diaspora there will be a multilingual literature.

The author welcomed the growth of literature in Yiddish and Hebrew, and he reminded the reader that such representatives of Jewish thought as Maimonides, Mendelssohn, Graetz, and Herman Cohen had used the languages of the surrounding peoples. For them forced linguistic assimilation did not imply inner assimilation. Dubnov argued his case with particular passion. In vindicating the principle of multilingualism in the eyes of an imaginary reader he was defending the sixty years of his own literary career.

The polemic with the editorial board of *Oyfn sheydveg* was still more heated. In a tragic era heavy with the menace of catastrophe Dubnov seemed to have recaptured the militant ardor of the years when he had fought tradition in the name of freedom of thought. The article began with a historical note: by 1937 two thousand years had passed since a group of Jewish captives of war disembarked at a Roman port and began the European Diaspora: Dubnov claimed that "The knowledge that the descendants of the old German barbarians were trying to force us to move the centers of Jewry to America and Asia prevented us from celebrating that anniversary in a worthy manner." The Hitleriad has eclipsed all other historical disasters—the pogroms of the Crusaders, the expulsion from Spain, the Haimadak and Petliuran slaughters. "What can we do now?" The answer was simple. Fight the predator and save the victim. "We found ourselves now not at a spiritual crossroads, but on the field of battle. In such a situation it was wrong to surrender to defeatism. Jews everywhere must become the leaven of anti-aggression, rouse world conscience, insist on such measures as boycotts and sanctions, and, in the event of war, recruit volunteers from among us for anti-Hitler armies." The work in store would demand all their strength and more. It was incompatible with a sense of hopelessness and resignation, breast-beating, and mysticism. The time would come when it would be necessary "to save the lost souls of the young generation; meanwhile it is necessary to save human life. First the Jews and then the soul of Jewry."

The "breast-beating intelligentsia's" disdain of civil emancipation deeply offended the writer. "Yes, emancipation brought assimilation," he declared, "but it also brought liberation and a sense of human dignity, it roused the free man in the Jew." It was necessary to advocate not the rejection but the widening of the scope of emancipation. Flee Europe? But the deliverance of Europe from Nazism would also be the salvation of European Jewry. Now, when the anniversary of the French Revolution was being celebrated, was the time to declare for all to hear that this was the Jews' celebration too.

> We will live or die with mankind, with its progress or its regression. The call "Return to the ghetto!" is not new. . . . If it means a return to Jewish culture, to Judaism in the modern meaning of the word, then it coincides with the program of the national movement; but . . . the progressive elements of our people will never return to the medieval ghetto. . . . For a man who thinks freely, for himself, there can be no return to synagogue or church.

The article drew numerous responses, hostile as well as supportive. The polemical fervor, reminiscent of Dubnov's early political articles, seemed to have contributed to his feeling alive, indeed, rejuvenated. Summer that year was uncommonly fine. The sultry days were fragrant with the sharp smell of pine. The solitary suburban house came to life with the arrival of the Warsaw family. There were frequent visitors and many walks and picnics with poetry readings and choral singing. The host never lagged behind his young guests. He sang along with them "If tomorrow war comes, if tomorrow we're on the march,"[140] omitting the verse he disliked. Of the songs brought by his grandsons he especially loved the anthem of the young Jewish workers, "Here We Come" (*Mir kumen on*), and he sang with particular feeling "We are coming with a hungry gleam in the eye and longing for happiness in our hearts. . . ." The artless couplet could have been written about his own youth of poverty and dreams.

At the end of the summer father and daughter remained alone together. Their hearts were heavy. The newspaper reports filled them with dread —the talks in Moscow with the French and English representatives dragged on. Dubnov would declare with assurance, "Never mind, they'll reach an agreement soon." To quell their uneasiness they took books and went off into the woods in the company of a young woman, a neighbor who had regularly walked over in the winter to read aloud to Simon (after a recent attack of eye disease, his sight had begun to fail). He would be drawn into heated political arguments with his two companions and, to tease them, roundly abused Mayakovsky,[141] but the war crept more and more insistently into their conversations, driving out other subjects. A telegram from Warsaw required his daughter's return home; her visa expired in the middle of August. The silence that invaded the spacious rooms after she had gone was heavy with a foreboding of catastrophe.

Two weeks later propellers droned ominously in a scorching, cloudless sky over the towns of Poland. The country, stunned by the onslaught of the blitzkrieg, barely offered resistance. Terrible news struck Lesnii Park: the towns of Poland were in flames, Warsaw was on the brink of surrender, the populace was fleeing in panic, the army was retreating. While Dubnov suffered agonies not knowing the fate of his children, his friends, and the YIVO Institute in Vilna, his family was trudging through woods and along back roads, following the crowds of refugees and retreating troops toward the eastern border.

Dubnov wrote to the Tcherikowers on 9 October:

> What we feared has finally happened. At least we were psychologically prepared. Although we live in a neutral country, we too have had our share of anxiety. At first we were afraid that these small countries would be torn apart between the giants, but lately we have been reassured—the inviolability of the Baltic countries has been guaranteed. Therefore I have decided to decline my American friends' proposal to cross the ocean. This would destroy my spiritual equilibrium, which in times such as these is especially essential. . . . What particularly troubles me now is the fate of my children in Warsaw. . . . Being cut off from all my friends in Western Europe and America, and the absence of foreign newspapers also depress me.
>
> All my habitual interests have been set aside now. I work only for the salvation of my soul and not for publication. The edition of the cycle on ancient history is almost ready, more for the archive than anything else. I will then probably occupy myself with determining my literary bequests, also with a view to the future. . . . All the plans for publishing my books in different countries have been brought to a halt.

Several days later he informs Aaron Steinberg, "I feel well and bear up manfully under the dreadful events of our time. . . . Of course my plans for work are a shambles but I have not ceased writing—for myself. The only ray of light in the darkness is Lithuanian Vilna, where, perhaps, all of us are fated to meet again one day."

The notion of launching a political weekly in English, informing American public opinion about events in Europe, recurs repeatedly in the correspondence of that time. Dubnov writes to Steinberg on 18 November,

> If this plan can be implemented, you can count on my regular contributions. I have recently been brooding over a plan for some articles under the general title *Inter Arma II* similar to the series of articles I published in Petersburg in 1914–1915 during the World War. They will contain a mixture of history and topical commentary with a prognosis for the future. . . . Amid all . . .

the common and personal trials I nevertheless retain my spiritual equilibrium. . . . In a few days the last volume of the *World History* in its original Russian will come off the press and I will be able to say with a light heart: *"Nunc dimittis servum tuum in pace!"*[142] But . . . it is dreadful to be without intense intellectual work, so I am busy examining the third part of *The Book of My Life*, which has long lain in manuscript. . . . I am tormented by the thought that the three-volume edition of our history has perished in Moravska Ostrava during the Nazi pogrom.[143]

The yellowed cardboard sign with the inscription *Scripta manent* hung over Dubnov's desk as in former years. Once again, as in the days of the Revolution, the occupant of the study felt he was on an island amid the raging elements; once again he felt the need for the reminder that books were more enduring than men. . . . Newly printed volumes stood on a low rotating shelf. The Russian edition of his *magnum opus* was finished, and, over the last two years in Vilna, YIVO had printed the eight volumes of the *History* in a Yiddish translation.

The first news of his family's fate came in November. His daughter Sophie and his grandsons had reached Vilna after many hardships, and his son-in-law had been arrested by the Soviet authorities in Brest-Litovsk. Dubnov decided to join them in Vilna—now officially united with Lithuania—at the first opportunity, to help the wanderers settle down in their new surroundings. He also thought he might be able to obtain information through diplomatic channels about the fate of his son-in-law by relying on his formal Lithuanian citizenship. However, he had to postpone the journey until the third volume of his memoirs came off the press.

As he pondered the future on lonely winter evenings—winter that year happened to be exceptionally harsh, and the people living at the center of Riga almost never came to Lesnii Park—Dubnov laid plans for moving to Lithuania. As he writes to Elias and Rebecca Tcherikower on 18 December 1939,

> Lately I find myself in the grip of the emigration fever. I am not speaking of America, although my friends there have obtained a visa which has been waiting for me at the American consulate for over a month. I have decided to move to Lithuania in the spring, to Vilna or Kovno. Family considerations aside, . . . I am impelled to take this step by the oppressive social atmosphere in Latvia (a few remnants of democracy have been preserved in Lithuania) and by the hope that in Vilna I could be of help in restoring the Institute.

Vilna had long been dear to Dubnov, but the new tense atmosphere there troubled him. A pogrom organized after the withdrawal of the Red Army[144] revealed the intensity of ethnic prejudice. The prospect of war worried Dubnov very little in those days. He believed in the stability of the small Baltic nations, guaranteed by a treaty concerning military bases. "I think," he wrote to his friends in Paris, "that it is not yet time to think about moving YIVO to America. We should not give our European centers up for lost at the very moment when all that is best in mankind is fighting for a new Europe." To Charney's contention that it would be possible to work in more favorable conditions on the other side of the ocean, he replied: "Of course life is more peaceful in America, but we have no right to abandon the old nest." Gradually Lithuania began to assume the character of the promised land in Dubnov's imagination, a land where the fulfilment of his secret wishes awaited—a family circle, association with kindred spirits, permanent work at YIVO. A rainbow-colored mirage shimmered before the eternal wanderer at the end of his earthly journey. Carried away by his new plans, he invited friends menaced by Hitler in Western Europe to join him. In the letter to Charney cited above he expresses the hope of meeting him soon in Vilna. The Tcherikowers, he said, would in all probability be moving there soon as well.

Dubnov answered an invitation from the Jewish National Workers' Alliance in America with the following letter:

I was deeply moved by your friendly proposal to come to America, a proposal you have already acted upon; the visa you obtained with such great effort has long been waiting at the American consulate. Please believe that I find it very difficult to turn down the American plan, which would save me from all the misfortunes and turmoil in Europe, but I cannot act otherwise, and not only from considerations of health—at my age and under present conditions such a journey would be arduous—but also for reasons of larger import. Vilna's incorporation into Lithuania has raised the possibility of my moving to Vilna, where I could help restore the Scientific Institute, which has suffered badly from the war. . . . I propose to do this in the coming spring, when life in Vilna will have returned to normal.

Should the situation change, and should it turn out that staying in the Baltic region would be dangerous, then I would take advantage of the American visa. I intend to apply at the embassy for an extension. Let us hope, however, that the situation will improve and we live to see a free Europe. . . .

The dream of a liberated Europe and of redress for European Jewry savaged by Nazism guided all of Dubnov's plans. He informs Tcherikower of his literary affairs, adding:

Actually, all this is a sleeping pill to calm the nerves in time of war. I am strongly drawn to journalism. . . . My thoughts on the current situation give me no peace. . . . We must found a periodical in Paris or London to air opinions on the role of Jewry in a world war. . . . This is my plan: first we must . . . collect materials for a "Black Book" documenting the destruction of our Polish center, and second, begin putting out a weekly devoted to the question of Jewry in wartime and in the future "new Europe." Both the book and the paper must be in English, keeping in mind the outside world as well as the millions of English-speaking American Jews. . . . I have sent a letter to the editors of *The Times.* It says that it is essential to include on the list of war aims (Poland, Czechoslovakia, etc.) the restoration of the Jewish centers which have been destroyed and on which Hitler has declared the most merciless war. . . . However, I would also like to publish it in a Jewish journal, and not just this, but an entire cycle of articles in a similar vein. . . .

At the beginning of the winter of 1940 the first chapter of the series *Inter Arma*, entitled "Thoughts of a Jewish Historian on Aims of War and Peace," was written for the next issue of *Oyfn sheydveg*. The article is permeated with deep anguish, and it is couched almost entirely in a rhetorical tone uncharacteristic of the author. His direct appeal to the leaders of the anti-Hitler coalition intensifies the emotionalism. The *leitmotif* here is the idea that the Jewish people were experiencing their unexampled tragedy in total isolation, and that their physical sufferings were compounded by their moral sufferings caused by the indifference of the Allies.

The article began by comparing the two world wars. The first had been purposeless slaughter; only the authors of the peace program had tried to give it meaning. The purpose of the present war was clear. The democracies fighting the war where conscious that Nazism was a threat to mankind and must be crushed by military might. The declaration of the Allies promised to liberate Europe from Nazi barbarism, but they did not say a single word about the fate of the people against whom Hitler had been waging war for seven whole years. It would seem that the people fighting for a "new Europe" ought to be reaching out to the first victims of Nazism, but no one, with the exception of Roosevelt, had made any gesture of sympathy. Unfortunately not even the British Labour Party had done this, with their spokesman Dalton[145] claiming that the Jewish question would be automatically resolved by liberating the occupied countries. And this was precisely the moment when the *word* should become *deed*. Addressing the influential circles of the democratic coalition, Dubnov exclaimed bitterly,

> You want to evade the Jewish question by silence, but after the war it will quickly rise before you in all its magnitude. Representatives of Jewry will go to the forthcoming peace conference from all the ends of the earth, and they will seek from the "new Europe" justice for the people who have suffered more than any other from Hitler's campaign of terror.

Dubnov predicted that the delegates would demand international implementation of the principles of equal rights as well as unconditional emigration to America and Palestine. "The Jewish people," he says in conclusion, "will awaken after a war in which their sons too are shedding their blood, and they will make definite demands of the world, dictated by justice and humanitarianism."

According to the original plan the cycle *Inter Arma* was to have consisted of ten chapters. It was intended mainly for the non-Jewish reader. The author suggested to his translator, D. Movshovich, that he sent the article to the editors of the *Daily Chronicle*. Dubnov decided to set to work on additional chapters after the publication of the third volume of his memoirs. He was immersed in proofreading when an unexpected visitor from the West showed up at his blizzard-swept house. The young Jewish journalist brought with him a whiff of the hell of war-torn Europe. He tried to persuade Dubnov to leave strategically indefensible Riga for nearby Stockholm, the capital of a peaceful, prosperous country firmly committed to a tradition of neutrality. Dubnov rejected the proposal unequivocally. He explained to his visitor that he had once left Russia for the sake of completing his main work. That work was now finished, but his advanced years did not dispose him to travel. But, most important of all, in difficult times a Jewish writer should remain with his brethren and share their fate.

The beginning of spring brought new fears. The pincers of war had gripped Europe and were now beginning to tighten in the North. The stories of refugees from Poland about the nightmare of German occupation spawned horror and helpless confusion. Dubnov paced about his study for hours on end, trying to subdue his agitation; his solitary footsteps echoed in the silence of the empty rooms. The problems connected with publishing *The Book of My Life* tore him away from his bitter reflections. The first part of the new volume contained his recollections of the Berlin period (1922–1933), until his move to Latvia. To the chapters written earlier, he added a short elegiac epilogue in which he bade farewell in spirit to the native land he had left so long ago. The second part contained extracts from his diaries—his reflections on political, literary, and social matters.

In April Dubnov left for Kovno. There, in the home of his faithful friend Anna Beilenson, he realized once again how essential social intercourse was in times of hardship and crisis. Her hospitable home became a noisy club. There was no end to conversations, discussions, and consultations. Dubnov's paper on the fate of Jewry in wartime served as the focus of a colloquium organized by local journalists. An account of the speech published in a local paper had to be severely cut, as Lithuanian censorship did not permit criticism of Nazism. White splotches dotted even his short article "The Twentieth Century and the Middle Ages" in the Kovno paper *Yidishe shtime*, in which Dubnov showed that the first four decades of the twentieth century had brought more misery to the Jewish people than had the very darkest ages of the past. The article nonetheless concluded with an expression of confidence that humanity would triumph over barbarism.

Meetings with his family, colleagues, and disciples awaited Dubnov in Vilna. Despite its proximity to Poland, groaning beneath the German lash, the old city had not succumbed to resignation; the community life was extraordinarily active. The war emigrés—writers, pedagogues, cultural figures—added a special dimension to it. The YIVO Institute was teeming with people; its windows were flung open wide into the cool spring air of the young garden. The exhibits in a show organized on the twenty-fifth

anniversary of Y. L. Peretz's death were displayed in the sunlit rooms.
This literary wake lasted for several days and ended with a collective radio
broadcast in Yiddish, to which the visitor from Riga also contributed. The
broadcast was a major event in the life of Lithuanian Jews; it was the
first time the state-sponsored radio broadcast in their language.

Frequent meetings with Zelig Kalmanovich and other members of the
Institute strengthened Dubnov's conviction that his real place was among
the dedicated Vilna scholars, who were made, as he was, of resilient, fire-
proof material. With these thoughts he went back to his forest retreat,
having decided to prepare gradually for moving to Vilna. Gentle, sunlit
days washed over the Baltic lands, but distant shocks shattered the quiet
there. The German avalanche swept relentlessly down on the West, carrying off the frontier posts in its path. Dubnov especially feared for France,
a country he had long loved—the country of the Encyclopedists, the Revolution, and the Declaration of Human Rights. As he followed the advance
of enemy troops toward Paris, he prayed silently for a miracle, for another
Marne, for another patriotic uprising, as in the time of the Convention.
The capitulation of the French capital shocked him. The twilight of Europe
was pitch black.

Several days later the Red Army troops massed on the border marched
into the Baltic countries. Unexpectedly, in the fantastic circumstances of
war, Dubnov once more encountered Russia, a country to which he had
forever bade farewell in the afterword to *The Book of My Life*. The atmosphere of this encounter did not recall the stormy days after the October
Revolution. In Latvia the revolution was accomplished without bloodshed,
and representatives of the nonparty progressive intelligentsia were included in the first Provisional Government. In a letter to his daughter,
Dubnov described the new government as democratic and expressed satisfaction at the fall of Ulmanis's dictatorship, which had drawn the country
into the Nazi orbit.

Taking stock of one's life, as well as laying plans on the assumption that
the military situation had stabilized, turned out to be premature. Dubnov
had to abandon the idea of moving to Lithuania. The borders between
the separate Baltic republics, which were incorporated into the Soviet
Union in July, were sealed. Standing now on the threshold of eighty, Dubnov felt bitterly the impotence of a single human will before the elemental
forces of history. Now, chained fast to the little republic he had been about
to leave only yesterday, he strained in agony to guess what this new twist
of fate had in store for him and for that country.

At the end of the summer a prominent Jewish communist, whom Dubnov had chanced to meet in the prewar years, visited him. The visit was
of a semi-official nature. His guest declared that the change of regime
should not alarm Dubnov. The government, headed by a man of learning,
valued culture and its representatives. The visitor assured Dubnov that

his peace would be protected. Despite wartime difficulties his spacious home would not be requisitioned for compulsory "densification."[146]

Outward circumstances did in fact remain the same, but Dubnov's whole way of life changed drastically. The tireless worker found himself unemployed. The war had brought all translations of his books to a halt. The collapse of the plan for an English edition of the *History* was a particularly heavy blow. In Latvia itself the fact that his recently reissued textbook was declared incompatible with the spirit of a people's school showed which way the winds of change were blowing.

Dubnov felt his isolation particularly keenly on his eightieth birthday. A border guarded with bayonets separated him from his family. There was no news from his friends who had fled Paris and were wandering through southern France, waiting for a visa. America was totally silent, and communications had become difficult with Palestine, where his Odessa colleagues had sought refuge from the worldwide conflagration, and where his modest savings, his main source of income, were located. It was difficult to breathe in this suddenly constricted world.

When the news came in the autumn that his daugher Sophie and his grandsons were going to America, the sense of being cut off became still more oppressive. In his sorrow Dubnov turned his gaze to the East. Renewed correspondence revealed that his brother Vladimir was living out his last years in wretched circumstances in Moscow. Dubnov was taken by a new plan. Perhaps, he thought, it was fated that the brothers, who had been inseparable in youth, would spend their last years together. Vladimir answered his ardent summons vaguely, reluctant to reveal the bitter truth: stricken by paralysis, he was slowly wasting away and only the care of his nephew Yakov maintained the guttering flame of life.

The winter of 1940–41 was harsh and swept with blizzards. Dubnov was freezing in his spacious study; he remembered Petersburg winters of long ago. His daughter and grandsons had gone, and he followed their convoluted route, trembling for his six-week-old great-granddaughter Miriam, whom he called in a letter the "youngest of the transatlantic voyagers."

A hard, drastically changing life, rife with contradictions, clamored all about him, but it did not penetrate the recluse's retreat. The new reality was organically alien to him. It lacked the essential ingredients of his existence—constant communication with like-minded people scattered across the world and active participation in the cultural and social life of world Jewry. Each reply from afar, each new issue of a Jewish journal became an event in the monotonous rhythm of days. A letter from Dr. Meisel, the former librarian in Berlin's Jewish Community Center, who had moved to Jerusalem, stirred a host of memories. Bitterness overflowed Dubnov's soul and poured out in the lines of his reply, dated 5 March 1941:

Like any item of news from distant countries it was a great event in the life of a man incarcerated in the prison of war-torn Europe, though within the confines of a neutral country. The situation of our brethren in Palestine has somewhat improved now, thanks to British victories in Africa (may there be more like them!). There is hope that the plague of world slaughter will not reach you or desecrate the sacred places of our homeland. Palestine's special status in the eyes of God has been beneficial to me, too. Letters and printed materials from there reach me, albeit infrequently, while I have received not a single word from America since the end of the summer of 1940. . . . Our life now is full of miracles. By a miracle we remain among the living in a world where the angels of death (in the language of modern science they are called deadly bombs) and all kinds of other spirits of destruction swarm, even beyond the limits of the battlefield. But we are cut off from the source of our cultural life. After a long search I have finally been able to find a small Jewish calendar for 1941, the sole example of our "literature" for the past year. Foreign newspapers are unobtainable here. We know a little of what is going on in the world, but that little is made up according to a local prescription. And you, the possessors of riches, choose to lament the crisis of literature in your country!

Twenty years ago . . . at an uneasy time, I was in my native land and hoped to leave for Berlin in a year. Now I can go nowhere. All paths are closed. Berlin has turned into Sodom, and all our Jewish centers have been destroyed by the Sodomites. America and Palestine look to me from the different ends of the globe, and I turn my gaze toward them. But I know they are unattainable, and that I am fated to remain in this "great and gloomy wilderness." My "Talmud" has reached the end in these last years—the last volume of the Russian edition of the ten-volume *History* [Riga 1936–1939] has come out. And the "supplement to the Torah" is finished; the last volume of *The Book of My Life* (the Berlin period) came out in 1940, but unfortunately, due to various circumstances, I am in no position to send this book to you and other friends. I now write nothing for publication; instead I read world literature and make notes whenever my strength permits.

My friends worry about my fate, but I have only one concern. I am guarding the archival materials in my possession, fearing that they may be threatened with destruction. This valuable collection was originally intended for two academies, one in the Jerusalem of Lithuania and the other in ancient Jerusalem. Given present circumstances I would like to transfer one part to the National Library in Jerusalem and the other to YIVO in America, which has become a new center of Jewry. I intend to spell out this plan in my will, but the local powers-that-be may put obstacles in its path, and this worries me a great deal. My reply to your proposal to transfer some of the documents to the Bezazel archive should now be clear to you. When the flame engulfs the cedars, what's the use of worrying about blades of grass? A national archive should be the only place to preserve the thousands of letters on social and literary subjects I have accumulated over sixty years, as well as the hundreds of historical documents. An agonizing question sears my brain: Can I succeed in implementing this plan after the war, and will I live to see that day?

My family is now scattered all over the globe. My daughter and grandsons, refugees from Warsaw, were in Lithuania and recently left for America via

Russia and Japan. The other children have long since been living in the Soviet Union and could not obtain permission to travel to the Baltic lands to visit me. . . . Write to me of your life in Jerusalem, of the university which has suffered lately. . . . Any information at all about what is going on in our country will be received with the most heartfelt gratitude by the solitary inhabitant of the Baltic.

In May Dubnov received strange news from the distant exotic town of Kobe. At the end of a telegram containing belated congratulations on his eightieth birthday was scrawled the signature, "the Jewish community in Kobe. Your daughter Sophia." Some time later the mystery was revealed: representatives of the Jewish community in the Japanese port of Kobe, where a large group of emigrés was stranded for several months, had celebrated his eightieth birthday.

The last letter to his older daughter, written 12 June 1941, was suffused with sadness and resignation. Dubnov informed her that his days slipped by quietly and monotonously. In his declining years he had turned from a writer into a reader and returned to authors beloved in his youth in whom he found new delight. He was rereading *War and Peace* with relish. He had sufficient leisure for reading: the immense archive had long been set in order. All the materials were arranged and catalogued. Every day the mail brought the Moscow newspapers. The reports of what was happening in the West inspired fear for the civilized peoples who had fallen into the maw of the beast. His main connection to the outside world was Palestine, from where letters and journals arrived from time to time.

Ten days after those lines were written the German army crossed the border of the Soviet Union. On 29 June the first bombs were dropped on Riga. On 1 July German troops marched into the capital of Latvia.

Epilogue

At the beginning of July all Jews were moved out of the suburb where Dubnov lived. Friends helped him hide but Gestapo agents tracked him down and arrested him. An inhabitant of Riga who survived the destruction of the local Jewry and described it in detail, tells the story:

They were interested in his works written in Riga and demanded that he hand them over. The manuscripts had been hidden, and Dubnov declared that they had been left in Kaiserwald,[147] which he had left long ago. He was released, but arrested again shortly afterward. At the insistence of Schlitter, a Viennese Jew and a member of the Judenrat, Dubnov was again freed. He came out of prison completely broken and moved to the ghetto. Schlitter was arrested and shot on orders of the Gestapo.

In the ghetto the professor was given a small room in an old people's home on Liudza Street. But even there he did not remain idle. With a pencil, which, he said, had done duty for thirty-seven years, he was writing a chronicle, to be called *Ghetto*. During the short time he spent within the ghetto walls he was able to create a small center of Jewish intellectual life there. During the first "action" [30 November 1941] he was moved to another shelter for old people, and later, at the time of the second "action" [8 December 1941], to 56 Liudza Street. The families of the men serving in the Jewish police had taken shelter in that house. . . . The Latvian butcher Danskop, who came to inspect the house, asked the old professor whether he belonged to the family of any of the policemen. When he received a negative reply, he ordered him to join the columns marching by. Pandemonium broke out in the house, and one of the policemen [a German Jew, awarded the Iron Cross, name unknown] ran to catch up with the column, hoping to save Dubnov, but it was too late. The historian had made his last journey. He was killed in Rambuli outside Riga, where almost all the Jews of Riga died.*

Another witness** to the destruction of the Riga ghetto gives the following account:

When the Germans occupied Riga, they threw Dubnov out of his house and seized his entire immense library. They took the old writer to the Gestapo for interrogation. They let him go several days later. Dubnov was reluctant to speak of the interrogation, he only said that it was the first time in his life he had had dealings with such monsters. He moved into a shelter for old people in the temporary ghetto. On 25 October that ghetto was liquidated. . . . Then came the fateful 30 November. S. S. men and Gestapo butchers shot half the population of the ghetto that terrible night. . . . Those still alive spent the next week in a stupor. . . . Professor Dubnov was ill. He had fallen ill the night they drove the inhabitants of the ghetto out of their houses into the street. He was saved then by being moved to a part of the ghetto which the murderers had, for "technical reasons," decided not to "evacuate" at that time. Dubnov felt the end was near. . . . Then came the terrifying night of 7–8 December 1941. The same thing as the previous week was repeated, but in a more "organized" way. They loaded the sick and the feeble into dark blue buses. There wasn't enough room for everyone, and they shot many old people and pregnant women then and there, on the spot. When they drove Dubnov out into the street he had a high temperature—38.5 [degrees centigrade]. He hadn't the strength to climb the steps of the bus quickly. A drunken Latvian militiaman ran up and shot him point blank in the back of the head.

---

*Max Kaufman, *Die Vernichtung der Juden Lettlands* (Munich 1947).
**Gilel Melamed, *Zukunft* 1946, Vol. 4.

Dubnov fell dead. The next day they buried him in a mass grave in the old Jewish cemetery in the Riga ghetto.

Later a rumor began to pass from mouth to mouth that, as Dubnov walked to his death, he had repeated: "People, do not forget. Speak of this, people; record it all." Of those who could have heard those words hardly one is alive today. Only the legend lives, no less truthful than the life itself.

From the Author

The book proffered for the reader's attention is the fruit of more than two years' work. The basis for the first part (1860–1922) are the two volumes of my father's lengthy autobiography. Despite all efforts, the third volume could not be found; evidently the edition which appeared in Riga in 1940 was entirely destroyed by the German authorities. The events of the last period (1922–1941) had to be reconstructed from various unpublished as well as published materials and the correspondence at my disposal. I have endeavored to fill the many gaps with the material of my own recollections. They are a substantive part of the biography because the link between father and daughter was never broken, despite ideological disagreements and lengthy periods of separation.

The attentive reader may be struck by an imbalance in the structure of the book: the first part is more concise than the second. This violation of proportion is not accidental. I deemed it necessary to present facts published for the first time at greater length, realizing that, until the appearance of new, more-extensive researches, my work would be the sole source of information about my father's activities in the last years of his life.

I received invaluable assistance from people sympathetic to an undertaking associated with the name of Simon Dubnov. I wish to express my deep gratitude to all those who supplied me with materials and placed my father's correspondence at my disposal—Rebecca Tcherikower, Aaron Steinberg, Jacob Leshchinsky, Mark Wischnitzer, Daniel Charney, Nina Gurfinkel, and the staff of the Archive and Library of the YIVO Institute.

The publication of the book presented considerable difficulties. They were overcome thanks to the initiative and the indefatigable organizational work of L. O. Chekver, the activities of the members of the Dubnov Committee of the Union of Russian Jews, and the assistance rendered by L. and I. Rauzen and B. Shatzkin. To all of these people the author expresses her sincere gratitude.

January 1950
New York

Life with Grandfather

by Victor Erlich

The image which emerges from Mother's compact and affectionate biography and from Jonathan Frankel's illuminating introduction is that of a formidable and dedicated scholar, a seminal thinker, an impassioned spokesman, and a richly textured human being. I hasten to add another item to this impressive list: Simon Dubnov was also a thoroughly satisfying grandfather—caring, involved, richly instructive, and enjoyably zestful.

I feel fortunate to have known him as well as I did—a privilege which I owe in large measure to the close and abiding relationship between my parents and the Dubnovs. Only during the first three years of my life —a period of which my memories are less than vivid—did we all live in the same city, indeed, in the same house. Yet with so much goodwill on both sides there was ample motivation in two subsequent decades to overcome the distance that separated Warsaw from Berlin or Riga and to contrive occasions for family reunions, whether shared summer vacations on the German seashore or in the Polish countryside, or visits to my grandparents' home. Thus, throughout my childhood and adolescence, Grandfather was a vital and a significant presence. He affected my intellectual development in many ways, and across a wide spectrum. To indicate the scope of his influence, let me mention two widely disparate instances: It was Grandfather who was largely responsible for my falling under the spell of one of his favorite poets, Victor Hugo, whose verse and prose I would swallow in inordinate doses, and for my resulting fascination with the drama and the moral dilemmas of the French Revolution. And it was Simon Dubnov who managed to take enough time out of his exacting schedule to teach me the Hebrew alphabet.

Perhaps I should add that in making use of these cultural acquisitions, I must have been guided by a desire, conscious or otherwise, to merge Grandfather's teachings with the models provided by my parents. When at the age of twelve I embarked on a large-scale historical novel about the French Revolution, the main protagonist of which was an enlightened peasant with strong Menshevik leanings—a project which I wisely abandoned at the ripe age of fourteen—I was clearly seeking to combine Grandfather's vocation with my poet mother's commitment to imaginative literature. By the same token, I would for years, before my exposure to the classics of Yiddish literature, exercise my basic Jewish literacy primarily by reading the organ of the Jewish Labor Bund, *Naye folkstsaytung*, which Father edited.

In my fond recollections of Life with Grandfather, the period 1925–26 has pride of place. With Father embarked on a coast-to-coast speaking tour of the U.S. on behalf of the Jewish Labor movement in Poland, Mother eagerly accepted an invitation to do some research in the Bund archives in Berlin in order to spend a full academic year with her parents and to reimmerse herself in the congenial milieu of the Russian-Jewish intelligentsia, which, since leaving Petrograd in 1918, she had never ceased to miss. To my older brother, Alex, and me, aged respectively thirteen and eleven, this extended visit offered a golden opportunity to get to know Simon and Ida Dubnov and to become initiated in their way of life.

The Dubnov apartment, located in a quiet suburb of the teeming metropolis, seemed at times a rare instance of controlled bustle. Somehow, Grandfather's exacting writing schedule was made to absorb a stream of visitors —close associates and Jewish community leaders, self-assured pundits and timid apprentice historians. (One of the latter, I recall, was nearly turned away by Grandmother, who mistook him for an obnoxious Berlin peddler. Muttering her habitual "We don't need this," she was about to slam the door in the visitor's face, when Dubnov emerged from his study in time to recognize and rescue the hapless young scholar.) Yet above all, this was a household dominated by steady work. I have never since met anyone more methodical, more productive, more fully committed to writing than Dubnov. On visitor-free days the rigorous routine would be interrupted by two daily "constitutionals." Actually, "interrupted" is scarcely the right word; the walks were an integral part of the working schedule, clearly indispensable to the demanding pace Dubnov was determined to maintain. A man of modest, if not austere, habits where food, clothing, and quality of housing were concerned, he would allow himself only one, absolutely essential, luxury—a pleasant residential location, within walking distance of a park or woods.

I would often accompany him on these walks and got to learn their immutable pattern by heart. While we strolled down the quiet tree-lined streets of Schmargendorf or Grünewald, Grandfather would engage me in a conversation or, more typically, hold forth on a topic of mutual interest. Yet as soon as we would enter the path, he would stop talking, even if it meant interrupting himself in the middle of the sentence, raise his forefinger, and say with feeling: "Vitia, breathe." For some fifteen or twenty minutes we would breathe together in silence, as leaves rustled under our feet. If the story had not run its course or the point had not been made, the narrative or discursive flow would be resumed on our way back.

It was clear to me that Grandfather's insistence on "breathing" was not simply a matter of expanding one's lungs by inhaling maximal doses of healthful air. The silence which followed the injunction suggested near-religious reverence. Arguably, it was at such moments of wordless communion with nature that Dubnov came as close to a religious stance as he ever did.

It is a well-known fact that Grandfather was in the main a secular thinker. To be sure, as both Mother and Professor Frankel have demonstrated, the Dubnov I knew was no longer an *apikoyres*, a militant challenger of the rabbinical establishment. The premier historian of Jewry was bound to acquire a rich appreciation of Judaism's contribution to Jewish survival. But he was not an observant Jew, though he would attend the synagogue on the High Holidays—partly in deference to tradition, partly out of fondness for *Kol Nidre*. Predictably, his favorite Jewish holiday was Passover. He found its symbolism particularly congenial and enjoyed celebrating it in the company of friends. As it happens, one of the more vivid memories of our Berlin year involved a seder to which the Dubnovs were invited, with Mother, Alex, and me tagging along. The host, Dr. Isaac Steinberg, was a colorful and distinctive figure among the Russian-Jewish emigrés in Berlin. During the Revolution of 1917, he was one of the leaders of the ultra-radical group, the "Left-Wing S. R.," which seceded from the Socialist Revolutionary Party and joined Lenin's first government only to walk out on it in 1918 in protest against the Brest-Litovsk peace treaty with Germany. What made Dr. Steinberg a unique if not a bizarre phenomenon is that he managed throughout to be a rigorously observant Jew. (It is rumored that during his brief tenure as Commissar of Justice he refused to work on the Sabbath, much to Lenin's dismay.)

A spellbinding orator in at least three languages (Russian, Yiddish, and German), Dr. Steinberg seemed to me more a rhetorician than a thinker. In any case, his outlook was so different from Dubnov's that I have often wondered, in retrospect, what brought the two men together. I assume that the initial link was provided by Isaac's younger brother, Aaron Steinberg, an intellectual historian of depth and subtlety. Aaron became a much-valued friend and collaborator of Dubnov's as a splendid German translator of his monumental *World History of the Jewish People* and author of its masterful three-volume abridged version. Yet I also suspect that Grandfather was both bemused and fascinated by the coexistence of revolutionary maximalism with orthodox Judaism in Aaron Steinberg's ideological makeup.

Quite predictably, the seder at the Steinbergs' turned out to be a relentlessly ritualistic affair, in fact, the most protracted and "orthodox" seder I ever attended. The festivities were preceded by an awkward moment. As we were about to sit down at the table, our host produced skullcaps for all the males present. My brother, who at thirteen was a committed socialist and a principled secular thinker, balked at the *yarmulke*. The ensuing tension was relieved by Dubnov's quiet diplomacy. He took Alex aside and said something like, "Believe me, I would just as soon dispense with the skullcap myself, but since we are at Isaac's house, we should respect his feelings." My brother grudgingly relented. There was something beguiling about the spectacle of the architect of Jewish secular nationalism pleading with his teen-aged socialist grandson to show consideration for the religious beliefs of the first Soviet Commissar of Justice.

One of the fringe benefits of our year with the Dubnovs was the chance it gave my brother and me to see Grandfather "in the round," to glean facets of his personality to which only few intimates were privy. Among these was a lively and, at times, unexpectedly zany sense of humor. Once, as we were having our evening tea, Grandmother, who was usually somewhat reticent, was in a reminiscent mood. She began to relate an incident reaching back to the youth of my maternal uncle, Jacob, who at the time of her story was professor of mathematics at the University of Moscow. "When Yasha was in Kishinev," she began, only to be briskly interrupted by her husband. "He was never in Kishinev," announced Grandfather. "You must have confused Yasha with Pushkin." This far-fetched notion produced a great deal of merriment around the table. Grandmother, whose story was so whimsically undercut, was naturally reluctant to join in the laughter. She responded with a characteristic verbal shrug: "Oh, Semyon" —roughly a cross between "Here you go again" and "Boys will be boys." Ida Dubnov was too sober a person to side openly with Semyon's *jeux d'esprit* but too good-humored really to mind them.

There were nothing staid about Grandfather; even at his most didactic he was never pedantic or ponderous. Age failed to dim his vitality, to diminish his zest, even if it inevitably affected some of his responses. He could be sturdily and unabashedly old-fashioned. His attitude toward modern technology, including such eminently useful inventions as the telephone, was decidedly wary. I recall a scene when Mother got up from the dinner table and proceeded in the general direction of the telephone. Dubnov asked, somewhat apprehensively: "Where are you going, Sonia?" "I have to call Mr. X," answered Mother; whereupon Grandfather remonstrated, "Is it necessary? He'll call you." Being a reasonable man, he reluctantly conceded Mother's point that since it was she who needed some information from Mr. X it was proper for her to show initiative. But back in 1926 he clearly tended to view the telephone as a last resort. A positive obverse of this stance was his awe-inspiring promptness in answering letters. (Clearly, correspondence was for him a much more natural activity than a telephone conversation.) When congratulated on this admirable quality, he expressed genuine surprise. "What else? Postponing for days, let alone weeks, an answer to a letter is as rude as not responding immediately when one is greeted in the street."

Another area in which Dubnov showed himself unmistakably a nineteenth-century man was his literary taste. His abiding love of poetry forged early on a powerful bond between him and his favorite daughter, who learned to appreciate verse at her father's knee, only to become in the second decade of the century an accomplished poet, the author of limpid, controlled lyrics. Though Grandfather's intellectual outlook was shaped by positivism, he was keenly reponsive to the romantic and the lyrical. He was steeped in classical Russian poetry, finely attuned to the luminous genius of Alexander Pushkin, the romantic turmoil of Mikhail Lermontov, the civic muse of Nikolai Nekrasov, the haunting musicality of Afanasy Fet, the meditative eloquence of Fedor Tiutchev. He knew by heart many poems of Heinrich Heine and Victor Hugo. But his literary sensibility stopped at the century's edge. He found the quasi-mysticism of the Russian Symbolists too murky, their eroticism too enervating and "decadent." Needless to say, Grandfather had even less use for the verbal experimentation of the Russian Futurists, the more so since their most resonant spokesman, Vladimir Mayakovsky, became an ardent Bolshevik. It seems that at some point Mother and Dubnov agreed to disagree on "Modernism," but there were moments when he could not quite contain himself.

I recall one such moment in the Dubnovs' Berlin apartment. Grandfather picked up a volume of Mayakovsky's verse, which must have belonged to Mother, and opened it to the poem "Versailles," where the rhythmic flow was, in a true Futurist manner, broken into short lines consisting of a single word or word cluster. The first verse of the poem, in a literal translation, reads like this:

> On this
> Highway
> Hastening to the palace
> Innumerable Louises
> Shook
> In the silks
> Of gilded carriages
> Their heavy flesh

Dubnov viewed the text with undisguised dismay and proceeded to recite the poem, deliberately exaggerating the abrupt, staccato quality of the verse by pausing after each mini-line. Having gone on in this fashion to his total dissatisfaction, he turned to Mother: "Do you call this poetry? This is hiccoughs!"

The subsequent decade offered precious little room for humor or facetiousness. The sky over Europe grew darker every day, most notably over Germany. There was a shorter, cheerless visit with the Dubnovs in the summer of 1932. The city in which they had sought, and for a while had found, a relatively peaceful haven was now inundated by the "brown battalions" of the Nazi thugs. With a heavy heart the Dubnovs began to brace themselves for another move. Shortly after they had begun to settle into their new residence in Riga, Grandfather sustained a painful loss. His faithful companion of over fifty-five years, the quietly brave and undemonstratively caring woman who had stood by him through years of penury, often straining her resourcefulness to enable him to pursue his calling, died after a protracted illness. Dubnov's growing concern over Europe's future and over the deadly menace to European Jewry was compounded and, for a time, overshadowed by an acute sense of personal bereavement, of loneliness.

In 1935, Mother and I journeyed to Vilna to meet Grandfather and to join him at the Second Congress of YIVO, held on the tenth anniversary of the Institute's founding (Dubnov was one of its founders and honorary chairmen). Mother has spoken aptly of an "atmosphere of a major cultural festival." Yet it was an unmistakably Eastern European Jewish festival—intense, tumultuous, occasionally abrasive, teeming with ideas and projects, with methodological and ideological controversies. I vaguely recall a spirited debate about the relationship between politics and scholarship, in the course of which a forceful spokesman of the Bundist faction, S. Mendelson, took issue with the stance of the YIVO leadership. I remember having been impressed both by Mendelson's challenge and by Max Weinreich's counterattack, though as a budding Bundist I must have been leaning toward Mendelson's position. Yet as far as I was concerned, this was no more than an interesting sideshow. The main reason I came to Vilna was to hang around Grandfather and to see him in action. What I saw was consistently impressive. Dubnov clearly was one of the commanding figures at the Congress. His impassioned speech at the opening session, delivered in crisp, clear Yiddish, visibly stirred the large and attentive audience. His paper on "The Current State of Jewish Historiography" was one of the high points of the proceedings. During the same week, he delivered a moving eulogy of his old friend, a beloved Jewish community leader, Cemach Szabad, speaking at his grave in Vilna's Jewish cemetery.

The outpouring of affection and admiration for the doyen of Jewish historians must have been deeply gratifying. So was the palpable evidence of the vitality of the many fields of Jewish scholarship he helped pioneer. But the hectic pace of these events was draining. It seemed a good idea to adjourn for a few days to a quiet summer place near Vilna. In the small Jewish rooming house in which we landed we were soon joined by Marc and Bella Chagall, who had come to the Congress in conjunction with an exhibit of Chagall's Bible drawings. We saw a great deal of them during our brief stay at the rooming house. The Chagalls chose to take their meals with us and often accompanied us on our walks in the woods.

Our breakfast routine was especially memorable. Each morning the pert waitress would confront us with a thoroughly ethnic choice—chopped liver or herring. I recall that whenever Chagall's turn came to answer the standard question, he would turn to his wife, his large blue eyes pleading inability to tackle so mundane a matter, and say, "Bella, what do I feel like today?" It was noteworthy that Bella had no difficulty answering this query.

I must have been tickled to share the table with an internationally known painter. But I was fully aware that, while he seemed to enjoy Mother's company and expressed at some point a painterly interest in one of my profiles, which he rather fancifully labeled Ethiopian (I've been looking for it ever since), the real magnet in our trio was provided by Grandfather. It stands to reason that a Jewish artist as mindful of his roots as Marc Chagall would thrill to the opportunity to commune with the most distinguished Jewish historian of our time. But this, I assume, was only part, even if a major part, of the story. What may well have captivated Chagall was a rare blend of intense seriousness, with what I do not hesitate to describe as youthfulness—the blend that was Simon Dubnov at seventy-five.

It is this latter quality that dominates my recollection of what turned out to be our last meeting. The time was late spring, 1940; the place once again was Vilna. But in the meantime both the ancient city and our personal fortunes had undergone drastic change. We were no longer visitors to "the Jerusalem of Lithuania," but refugees, forced to flee there by the Nazi invasion and the fourth partition of Poland. Our family, which had expanded to include my wife and my sister-in-law, had been brutally truncated. In early October, Father was arrested by the NKVD in Brest-Litovsk. Our attempts to find out in which Soviet prison he was being held had proven futile. Vilna, which in September of 1939 was occupied by the Red Army, had been temporarily ceded to still-independent Lithuania, pending the creeping Sovietization of the entire country, which was to begin in the summer of 1940.

It was during this interlude, laden with uncertainty and anxiety, that Grandfather came down from Riga to see his friends and colleagues and to visit us. He fully shared our intense worry about Father and viewed Hitler's westward advance with increasing dismay. Yet characteristically he refused to surrender to gloom, let alone despair. He was full of plans for further activities—as vigorous, involved, and energetic as ever. What stands out most vividly in my memory is the brisk way he ran up the four flights of stairs leading to our Vilna apartment on the day of his departure. I remember thinking at the time that this near-octogenarian was, in spirit, one of the youngest men I would ever know, that he still had years of active and creative life in him.

The rest is history, which in 1941 meant nightmare. About a year after his return to Riga the great historian was struck by a Nazi murderer's bullet—a fate he could have easily avoided had he not chosen to remain with his people and bear witness to their ordeal. But the legend, as Mother has said, lives on. So does memory.

As I think back to our last glimpses of Grandfather, I am reminded of the closing lines of a late Pasternak poem, "Fame," a poem which, I am sure, he would have found congenial:

You must not for a single instant
Betray your nature or pretend,
But be alive, this alone matters,
Alive and living to the end.

GLOSSARY

Aggadah. (lit. narrative). The nonlegalistic portions of the Talmud—legends, parables, maxims, etc.

beys-medresh. A room or house for study and prayer; a small synagogue.

droshe. A sermon or formal textual exegesis offered by a Jewish scholar.

El male rahamim. (God full of mercy). Traditional Jewish prayer chanted on the occasion of burial and in memory of the dead.

Gemara. Compendium of commentaries on and supplements to the Mishnah, codified by rabbinical academies in Babylon and Jerusalem during the second through sixth centuries of the Common Era. The Mishnah and Gemara together constitute the Talmud; the term "Gemara" is also used to refer to the Mishnah and these commentaries.

Halachah. Rabbinic law; the legalistic portion of the Talmud, as opposed to *Aggadah*.

Haskalah. The Jewish Enlightenment movement, which first emerged in Berlin at the end of the eighteenth century; in Eastern Europe the *Haskalah* flourished in the nineteenth century.

High Holidays. The ten days from Rosh Hashanah, the Jewish New Year, to Yom Kippur, the Day of Atonement.

House of Hillel and House of Shammai. Two opposing schools of rabbinical interpretation of the Oral Law (Talmud). Their debates over interpretation of Jewish law during the last generations of the Second Temple period (first century B.C.E. through second century C.E.) are a prominent feature of talmudic dialectic.

Judenrat. Jewish self-government imposed by Nazi authorities in the ghettos they established for Jews in Central and Eastern Europe during World War II.

kahal. Jewish community; the leadership of a Jewish community.

kheyder (plural, *khadorim*). A school where Jewish children begin their traditional education, learning the letters of the Jewish alphabet as well as how to read the Bible and liturgy.

kitl. The white linen ceremonial robe worn by pious Jewish men on solemn occasions.

kulak. A well-to-do farmer in Russia who profited from the labor of poorer peasants.

ma'ariv. The evening service, recited daily after sunset.

mame-loshn (lit. mother tongue). An affectionate term for the Yiddish language.

maskil (plural, *maskilim*). An adherent of the Jewish Enlightenment movement (*Haskalah*), advocating the abandonment of much of Jewish traditional practice and the assimilation of modern Western mores.

melamed (plural, *melamdim*). A teacher of young children in the *kheyder*.

Midrash. The homiletical interpretation of Scripture; the literature of that interpretation among the early rabbis, which contains legends and tales as a supplement to the biblical narrative.

minhah. The afternoon daily prayer, recited some time between noon and sunset.

Mishnah. The code of Oral Law compiled by Rabbi Judah Ha-Nasi (ca. 135–217 C.E.) on the basis of previous collections and codified around the year 200 C.E., forming part of the Talmud.

misnaged (plural, *misnagdim*; adjective *misnagdic*). An opponent of Hasidism within Jewish orthodoxy.

narodnik (plural, *narodniki*). A Russian populist; one involved in a late nineteenth-century intellectual movement to celebrate the traditional culture of Russian peasantry.

nign (plural, *nigunim*). A melody, tune, or song without words. Creating and singing *nigunim* are an important feature of Hasidic spirituality.

Pale of Settlement. The eastern half of pre-partition Poland annexed by Russia during the late eighteenth and early nineteenth centuries. With this annexation, the Russian Empire acquired a large Jewish population. During the reign of Catherine II Jews were forbidden to settle anywhere in Russia east of this annexed territory.

Palestinophile. A proto-Zionist, one advocating Jewish settlement in Palestine in the years before the organized political and cultural Zionist movements were established.

pinkes (plural, *pinkeysim*). The book of records kept by a Jewish community.

responsa. The literature of medieval and later rabbinic correspondence regarding the interpretation of traditional Jewish law.

talmud-torah. School where Jewish children received their elementary, traditional Jewish education. Pedagogically similar to a *kheyder*, the *talmud-torah* was a public institution, whereas the *khadorim* were privately supported.

tefillin. Small boxes (phylacteries) containing biblical texts (Exodus 13:1–10, 13: 11–16, and Deuteronomy 6:4–9; 11:13–21) written on parchment, which are strapped to the arm and forehead with leather bands during weekday morning prayers by observant adult males.

tolstovka. A long belted man's shirt, a garment associated with Leo Tolstoy.

tsadik (plural, *tsadikim*). An especially pious, righteous, or spiritually pure man. A Hasidic leader, or *rebbe*, is often referred to as a *tsadik*.

tsadikism. Term used by Dubnov to describe Hasidic practice that focuses heavily on the role of the *tsadik* as the charismatic leader of a community.

yikhes. Family lineage and the prestige of one's ancestry.

zemstvo. Elective district council in pre-Revolutionary Russia.

zhargon. A term referring to the Yiddish language. Its use does not necessarily imply a pejorative meaning, although this was frequently the case.

EDITOR'S NOTES

1. Mendelssohn's Bible commentaries, known as the *Biur*, constitute one of the first major documents of the Jewish Enlightenment. Compiled between 1780 and 1783 by a group of scholars under Moses Mendelssohn's direction, the Hebrew-language commentaries accompanied Mendelssohn's German translation of the Bible printed in the Hebrew alphabet. Though the *Biur* relies primarily on traditional sources, it did introduce its readers to some modern theological concepts.

2. Abraham Mapu (1808–1867), generally credited as the creator of the modern Hebrew novel, was a principal exponent of the *Haskalah* in Eastern Europe. His first and most successful novel, *Ahavat Ziyyon* [Love of Zion, 1853], was followed by *Ayit Zaru'a* [The hypocrite], published in five parts from 1857 to 1861, which deals with the struggle of *maskilim* against the hypocrisy of the ultra-Orthodox.

3. Micah Joseph Lebensohn (1828–1852), one of the foremost Hebrew poets of the *Haskalah*, was the son of Abraham Dov Lebensohn, a leading intellectual and poet of his generation. The younger Lebensohn was known for his lyrical, romantic verses, many of which deal with biblical themes, as well as his translations of European classics.

4. *Ha-Karmel*, a Hebrew-language *Haskalah* periodical published in Vilna, which appeared weekly from 1860 to 1870, then monthly from 1871 to 1880.

5. Ludwig Börne (1786–1837), German political journalist and satirist.

6. *Hatte'ot Ne'urim* [The sins of youth], published in Vienna in 1876, is the autobiography of Moses Leib Lilienblum (1843–1910). A Hebrew writer, critic, and political journalist, Lilienblum was a major figure of the *Haskalah* in Eastern Europe and a leader of Hibbat Zion.

7. Dmitry Ivanovich Pisarev (1840–1868), radical social thinker and leading Russian nihilist, who wrote for several radical journals, including *Notes of the Fatherland* and *Russian World*.

8. Mikhail Iurevich Lermontov (1814–1842) was one of Russia's leading romantic poets. The quotation is from his narrative poem *Mtsyzi*.

9. Aleksei Vasilevich Koltsov (1809–1842) was known as the "Russian Robert Burns" for his verses on nature and peasant life.

10. Nikolai Alekseevich Nekrasov (1821–1877) was a major Russian poet whose verse combined a satirical bent with social compassion. Nekrasov was the owner and editor of the radical journal *Sovremennik* and later served as editor for *Annals of the Fatherland*.

11. Shimon Shmuel Frug (1860–1916) began writing in Russian and was the first poet to treat Jewish themes in Russian verse. He subsequently switched to writing in Yiddish. His Yiddish poems, often nationalist, Zionist, or socialist in sentiment, were frequently set to music and became very popular.

12. Sholem Aleichem (pseudonym of Sholem Rabinovitch, 1859–1916) was born in the Ukraine. He is regarded as one of the three "classical" Yiddish writers of the modern period. Sholem Aleichem was a leading advocate for the cultivation of Yiddish as a literary language. He edited and contributed to *Di yidishe folks-bibliotek* (1888, 1889), seminal collections of modern Yiddish poetry and prose. Sholem Aleichem achieved unparalleled popularity through the publication of numerous stories, monologues, plays, novels, and essays both in Eastern Europe and in America, where he lived from 1906 to 1907 and again from 1914 until his death in New York City in May 1916.

13. Mordecai Spector (1858–1925), Ukrainian-born Yiddish novelist and editor. Spector published his first novel in installments in the *Di yidishe folksblat*, and he later became its assistant editor. Spector's writing is said to have influenced Sholem

Aleichem to focus on provincial East European Jewish life in his fiction. Spector edited *Der hoyzfraynd*, a series of anthologies; and with Y. L. Peretz and Dovid Pinski, he issued the series *Yontev-bletlekh*. Both publications were landmarks in the development of late nineteenth-century Yiddish literature.

14. Theodor Mommsen (1817–1903), German classical scholar and historian, a vigorous opponent of anti-Semitism. A member of the Prussian and German parliaments as well as a leading scholar at the University of Berlin, Mommsen was also a major figure in the Verein zur Abwehr des Antisemitismus, established in 1890.

15. From the poem "Euthanasia."

16. A. L. Volynskii (pseudonym of Akim L. Flekser, 1863–1926), Russian literary critic and art historian. Volynskii wrote on Jewish topics for various Russian-language Jewish periodicals, and in 1884 he co-edited the anthology *Palestina*. In addition to writing on Jewish and non-Jewish literary figures, Volynskii authored several books on religious philosophy. After 1917 he abandoned literary criticism and became head of the Choreographic Institute in Leningrad, where he wrote about ballet.

17. The possessor of a "wolf's passport" in tsarist Russia was one denied permission to reside in the city of one's choice.

18. *Monish*, a satirical narrative poem by the Yiddish and Hebrew author Yitskhok Leyb Peretz (1852–1915), was first published in the watershed anthology of Yiddish literature *Di yidishe folksbibliotek* of 1888, edited by Sholem Rabinovitch (Sholem Aleichem). This poem, the first major Yiddish work by one of the three "classical" Yiddish writers, is considered a landmark in the development of modern Yiddish poetry.

19. *Ha-Zefira* [The dawn], Hebrew-language weekly published in Warsaw intermittently from 1862 to 1931. Originally *Ha-Zefira* was primarily devoted to articles about science and technology, although it also featured some coverage of Jewish scholarship and current events. In the 1880s the paper's contents became more diverse in subject matter and provided an opportunity for a new generation of Hebrew writers to publish.

20. Jacob Dineson (1856–1919), a pioneer of the Yiddish sentimental novel. Dineson was also active in modernizing elementary Jewish education through the creation of secular schools.

21. Ernest Renan (1823–1892), French philosopher and orientalist. Renan abandoned his university training for the priesthood in order to pursue independent scholarship on various religious topics. His writings include *Vie de Jésus*, a well-known secular biography of Jesus, as well as studies of biblical and medieval Jewry.

22. *Shulhan Arukh*, a concise guide to rabbinic law compiled by Joseph Caro and first published in Venice in 1565. It has served as the standard reference for observant Jewish practice to this day.

23. Mordecai Ben-Ammi (Rabinowicz) (1854–1932), Russian-language author and journalist. Ben-Ammi studied at the University of Odessa and spent most of his career in that city. He published articles on contemporary Jewish life in *Voskhod* and wrote a number of popular stories describing contemporary Russian Jewish life. Ben-Ammi was also active in the beginnings of the Zionist movement and settled in Palestine in 1923.

24. Yehoshua Hana Rawnitzki (1854–1944), Hebrew journalist and publisher, wrote for Hebrew and Yiddish periodicals. He was the first patron and the lifelong associate of the Hebrew poet Hayyim Nahman Bialik. In 1901, in Odessa, together with Bialik and S. Ben-Zion, Rawnitzki founded the Moriah publishing house, which published seminal textbooks in Hebrew as well as important anthologies

of modern Hebrew literature. In Palestine Rawnitzki, Bialik, and S. Levin established the Dvir publishing house.

25. *Di klyatshe* [The nag, 1873], a novel about a talking horse, with major digressive discussions of the ills of East European Jewish society, was written by Sholem Yankev Abramovich, known to his readers as Mendele Mokher Sforim (Mendele the Bookseller). Abramovich, a major figure of the East European *Haskalah*, is generally regarded as the father of the modern Yiddish and Hebrew novel. In the early part of his career he was also devoted to the promotion of modern secular education for the Jews of Eastern Europe and helped develop both Yiddish and Hebrew as modern literary and scholarly languages.

26. Berlin salons. During the late eighteenth and early nineteenth centuries the homes of such wealthy Jewish women as Henrietta Herz, Rachel Varnhagen, and Dorothea Schlegel provided meeting places for intellectual, "enlightened" Jews and non-Jews in Berlin's social elite. See notes 69–71.

27. Fedor Ivanovich Tiutchev (1803–1873), a major Russian lyrical poet, author of metaphysical, nature, and love poetry. Tiutchev was a university student and then entered the diplomatic service. In his later years he was known as a reactionary conservative and a Pan-Slavist.

28. Bund, known in full as Algemeyner Yidisher Arbeter Bund in Lite, Poyln un Rusland [General Jewish workers' union in Lithuania, Poland and Russia], a Jewish socialist party established in 1897 in Vilna. The Bund was the first workers' mass movement organized in Russia. It continued to play a vital role in Jewish politics of Eastern Europe until World War II, promoting Jewish cultural autonomy and socialist internationalism.

29. The Basle program, the original official program of the Zionist Organization. The Basle program was named after the site of the first Zionist Congress of 1897, where the program was formulated and adopted. The four-point program outlined the movement's goals of establishing a Jewish state in Palestine, organizing world Jewry, and promoting Jewish national consciousness.

30. Theodore Herzl (1860–1904) was a founder of "political" Zionism, which called for creating a Jewish state in Palestine, as opposed to the "spiritual" Zionism of Ahad Ha-am, who advocated the concept of a Jewish cultural center in Palestine which would "radiate" into the Diaspora. Herzl's *Der Judenstaat* was published in 1896, shortly after its author became involved in Zionist activities, and he convened the first Zionist Congress in Basle in 1897.

31. Afanasy Afanasevich Fet (1820–1892), the leading Russian lyrical poet of the nineteenth century, was also renowned for his translations of Shakespeare, Horace, Goethe, and others.

32. Dreyfus affair, the treason trials of French military officer Alfred Dreyfus (1859–1935), beginning with a closed trial in 1894. The charges brought against Dreyfus were based on forged evidence and appeared to have been motivated by anti-Jewish sentiments. At his first trial, Dreyfus was found guilty, sentenced to life imprisonment, and exiled to French Guiana to serve his sentence. The case became a subject of heated debate in French politics. Controversy over the trial raged in the press, climaxing with Emil Zola's article "J'accuse!" of 1898, forcing a second trial in 1899, at which Dreyfus was reconvicted, though his sentence was reduced. After a third examination of the evidence, he was finally acquitted without trial in 1906. The Dreyfus affair loomed large as a symbol of European anti-Semitism throughout the Continent for years afterward.

33. Jan Hus, religious leader after whom the Hussites, adherents of a Christian reform movement of fifteenth-century Bohemia, were named. Hus was burned at the stake in 1415 for his heresies against the Catholic church.

34. Tomás de Torquemada (?1420–1498), the first head of the Spanish Inquisition, was appointed Grand Inquisitor in 1483.

35. Gabriel Riesser (1806–1863), champion of Jewish emancipation in Germany. Riesser studied law at the universities of Kiel and Heidelberg but was denied the right to teach or practice as a notary because of his faith. His pamphlet *Über die Stellung der Bekenner des Mosaischen Glauben in Deutschland* (1831) marked a turning point in the Jewish struggle for civic rights in Germany. Opposed to the trend of Jewish intellectuals who were baptized so as to advance socially or professionally, Riesser argued for tolerance of Jews to believe and worship as they pleased. During the year following the 1848 revolution, he served in the Frankfurt Vorparlament and the National Assembly. He continued to play an active role in German politics and became a strong advocate of a united Germany.

36. Moritz Lazarus (1824–1903), a German-Jewish philosopher, received his doctorate from the University of Berlin and taught philosophy there and at the city's Royal Military Academy. He also studied psychology and established a branch of research known as *Völkerpsychologie* (national psychology). Lazarus was a member of several Jewish civic organizations and a founder of the Lehranstalt für die Wissenschaft des Judenthums, where he served as president of its board of curators. A prominent Jewish apologist, he devoted much energy to combatting anti-Semitism and promoting German nationalism.

37. Max Nordau (Simon Maximilian Suedfeld, 1849–1923), a writer, philosopher, orator, and physician, was co-founder of the World Zionist Organization. Nordau was the author of several controversial social tracts, among them *Die Conventionellen Leugen der Kulturmenschheit* (1883) and *Entartung* (1892). He befriended Theodore Herzl in Paris in 1892 and supported his Zionist activities. Nordau drafted the "Basle program" at the first Zionist Congress of 1897, and served as either vice president or president of the first ten congresses.

38. *Budushchnost'* [Future], a Russian-Jewish scholarly journal published weekly in St. Petersburg from 1899 to 1904, issued weekly with an annual literary almanac. Edited by Samuel Gruzenberg, the journal was an independent academic publication in the *maskilic* tradition.

39. Maxim Vinaver (1862–1926), lawyer, Russian politician, and Jewish communal leader. Vinaver studied law at the University of Warsaw and had a prestigious practice in St. Petersburg, where his legal analyses influenced court practices, though being Jewish prevented him from holding the title of judge until 1904. Following the Revolution of 1905, Vinaver was a founder and leader of the Constitutional Democratic Party (Kadets) and was elected to the first Duma of 1906. He was also active in the Society for the Promotion of Culture among the Jews of Russia and headed the Historical-Ethnographic Commission in St. Petersburg. He was elected to the Constituent Assembly following the 1917 Revolution, but soon left the Soviet Union for France, where he continued to work on behalf of Russian and Jewish emigrants.

40. Karl Renner (1870–1950), Austrian statesman. A moderate Social Democrat, Renner became the first chancellor of the new Austrian republic following World War I. His politics became more right-wing during the interwar period; in 1938 he advocated the Anschluss uniting Austria with Germany. Renner also played a major role in reestablishing Austrian home rule after World War II. Some of his writings appear under the pen name Rudolf Springer.

41. Hayyim Nahman Bialik (1873–1934) is considered the greatest modern Hebrew-language poet. He also wrote essays and short stories, and worked as an editor and translator. Bialik was born in Zhitomir but was largely based in Odessa from 1891 to 1921, when he left the Soviet Union for Berlin and then Palestine.

42. Herman Cohen (1842–1918), German philosopher, studied at the universities of Breslau, Berlin, and Halle. Cohen taught philosophy at the University of Marburg and later at the Hochschule für die Wissenschaft des Judentums in Berlin. His interpretation of Kant came to be known as the Marburg School of Neo-Kantianism. Also a proponent of humanistic socialism, Cohen regarded a nation's treatment of its working class as an index of its level of morality. While at Marburg, Cohen was called upon to respond to the issue of the Jewish question. He became more involved in the particulars of Jewish philosophy and of Jewish education during his years in Berlin.

43. Vladimir Jabotinsky (1880–1940), Zionist leader, soldier, orator, writer, and poet. Jabotinsky was renowned for his oratory at Zionist congresses and was the foremost Zionist lecturer and journalist in Russia from the early 1900s through the beginning of World War I. During the war Jabotinsky founded the Jewish Legion. He was head of Betar, a Zionist youth movement, and a founder of the Zionist Revisionist movement in 1925. Jabotinsky advocated the mass emigration of European Jewry to Palestine and the establishment of a Jewish army to fight with the Allies against Hitler at the beginning of World War II.

44. Bialik wrote two poems on the Kishinev pogrom of 1903: *Al ha-shehita* [On the slaughter] in 1903, and *Be-Ir ha-Haregah* [In the city of slaughter] in 1904.

45. In 1768 the Jewish community of the Ukrainian town of Uman was annihilated by Haidamak bands (see also note 94).

46. *Numerus clausus* [closed number], quotas restricting Jewish enrollment in universities. The first such laws were instituted in tsarist Russia by the Ministry of Education in 1887. They were abolished briefly during the 1905 Revolution and then reinstated until the Revolution of 1917 (though in some regions of southern Russia they were temporarily reinstated in 1919).

47. Viacheslav Konstantinovich von Plehve (1846–1904), Russian statesman, leader of reactionary circles under Alexander III and Nicholas II. Plehve was appointed Director of Police in the Ministry of Interior in 1881 and became Deputy Minister of the Interior in 1884 and Minister in 1902. He was known for his anti-Jewish and reactionary policies. Russian Jews and liberals accused him of responsibility for the pogroms in Kishinev in 1903. Plehve was assassinated by E. S. Sazonov, a Socialist Revolutionary, on July 15, 1904.

48. Sevastopol Campaign refers to Russia's war with England and France of 1854–1856, known in the West as the Crimean War. It preceded the "Great Reforms" of Alexander II by several years, the most notable change being the emancipation of the serfs in 1862.

49. Günzburg, a distinguished Russian family of bankers and philanthropists in the late nineteenth and early twentieth centuries. Baron Horace (Naphtali Herz) Günzburg (1833–1909), the best known, was one of the few Jews in the Russian Empire to be decorated by the tsar and to hold office (as a state councillor and an alderman). His home in St. Petersburg served as a meeting place for authors, artists, scholars, and other intellectuals. His son Baron David Günzberg (1857–1910), a scholar in Judaic and Oriental Studies, established a Jewish academy in St. Petersburg in 1908. It was known as the Courses in Oriental Studies, and Dubnov lectured there.

50. Leon (Leonty) Bramson (1869–1941), author and Jewish communal and political activist. Born in Kovno, Bramson studied law at the University of Moscow. He practiced in St. Petersburg, where he was active in the Society for the Promotion of Culture among the Jews, and director of the central committee of the Jewish Colonization Association from 1899 to 1906. Bramson wrote for *Voskhod* on the subjects of emigration, colonization, and Jewish education. He also directed a statistical study of the economic situation of Russian Jewry. A founder of the Jewish

Democratic Group, Bramson was elected to the first Duma in 1906 as a deputy for the province of Kovno. There he joined the labor faction (Trudoviki).

51. Mark Borisovich Ratner (1871–1917), Russian lawyer and socialist, wrote articles for *Russkoye Bogatstvo* on social and political issues. As a civil prosecutor in pogrom trials in the 1900s, he became more involved in Jewish issues. He was a leader of the Jewish Socialist Workers' Party (Sejmists) and a candidate for the second Duma. Ratner initiated the campaign for a Jewish section of the Socialist International.

52. Black Hundreds, armed gangs recruited by monarchist, right-wing societies, such as the Union of Russian People and the Double-Headed Eagle, to carry out pogroms against Jews and radicals in the early 1900s, beginning with the pogrom in Kishinev during Passover of 1903.

53. Stirnerian anarchism, the individualist school of anarchism articulated by Max Stirner (pseudonym of Kaspar Schmidt, 1805–1856) in *Der Einzige und sein Eigenthum* (1845).

54. Yehuda Novakovsky (1879–1933), a political activist and economist, was first involved with the Socialist Zionists, and later joined the Sejmists during the first decade of the twentieth century. He helped prepare evidence for the defense of Mendel Beilis (see note 73). Following the 1917 Revolution, Novakovsky served in the early Soviet government as a diplomat in Prague, Berlin, and London. From 1929 he lectured on economics in the Jewish section of the National University in Moscow. Novakovsky served as contributor or editor on a number of political journals and wrote in Yiddish on social and economic topics.

55. Sejmists, also known as the Jewish Socialist Workers' Party, the J.S. (Jewish Socialists), and SERP (its abbreviated name in Russian), a political party that advocated both national and socialist ideas, established in Kiev in April 1906. The Sejmists saw themselves as part of the international socialist movement but, because of the special conditions of European Jewry, demanded assurance of special legal status for Jews as a national group, embodied in an extraterritorial national personal autonomy. The Sejmists drew their ideological inspiration from Zhitlowsky and were also influenced by Dubnov and the Austrian Social Democrats. They conceived of a Jewish national Sejm (parliament) that would oversee individual Jewish communities. Sejmist publications included *Folksshtime* and *Shtimme* in Yiddish and *Serp* [Sickle] in Russian. After 1917, the Sejmists united with the Zionist Socialists to form the United Jewish Socialist Workers' Party.

56. Sh. An-sky (Solomon Zainwil Rapaport, 1863–1920), author and folklorist. As a young man, An-sky was involved in the *narodnik* movement, living with Russian peasants and practicing traditional trades. Later he became active in the Socialist-Revolutionary Party. An-sky headed the Jewish ethnographic expedition funded by Baron Horace Günzburg, which documented Jewish folkways in small towns throughout Volhynia and Podolia during the years 1911–1914. In 1919 An-sky founded the Jewish Ethnographic Society in Warsaw. He wrote stories and poems which drew on folklore motifs, and his most famous literary work is the play *The Dybbuk*.

57. Piotr Frantsevich Lesgaft (1837–1909), progressive Russian educator and physician. The author of texts on anatomy, Lesgaft also instituted progressive programs in Russian physical education. He organized the Free University in St. Petersburg in 1905, which offered classes to laborers and women. Lesgaft's activism incurred the ire of the tsarist regime.

58. *Codex Hammurabi*, a collection of Babylonian laws compiled during the reign of Hammurabi (1792–1750 B.C.E.). The stela on which the code was recorded was discovered in Susa in 1901 by the French orientalist Jean-Vincent Scheil.

59. Joseph Gedaliah Klausner (1874–1958), literary critic, historian, and Zionist activist. In 1902 Klausner succeeded Ahad Ha-Am as editor of the Hebrew journal *Ha-Shilo'ah*, a post he held for twenty-eight years. An ardent Hebraist, Klausner was active in the Va'ad ha-Lashon [Academy of Hebrew language] after settling in Palestine in 1919. He was appointed professor of Hebrew Literature at the newly established Hebrew University in 1925.

60. Chaim Zhitlowsky (1865–1943), Yiddishist, social philosopher, and writer. Zhitlowsky was the chief theoretician of Diaspora nationalism and Yiddishism. He helped found the Russian Socialist-Revolutionary Party in 1893 and was active in the Bund from 1897 until 1903, when he shifted toward Territorialism. Zhitlowsky was elected to the second Duma and chaired the Czernowitz Yiddish Conference of 1908. After 1908 he lived in the United States.

61. Czernowitz Yiddish Conference, the first international, interparty conference on the role of the Yiddish language in Jewish life, held from 30 August through 4 September 1908, in the town of Czernowitz. The seventy participants included many prominent Yiddish writers, among them Jacob Gordon, Dovid Pinski, Y. L. Peretz, Abraham Reisen, Sholem Asch, H. D. Nomberg, and Mordecai Spector. The conference dealt with issues such as the promotion of modern Yiddish literature, theater, education, and press, as well as the standardization of Yiddish spelling and grammar. After some debate, the participants proclaimed Yiddish "a Jewish national language."

62. Petr Arkadevich Stolypin (1862–1911), Russian statesman. From 1906, Stolypin served as Minister of Interior and Chairman of Council of Ministers. A liberal conservative, he supported cultural, social, and economic reforms while harshly suppressing revolutionary activity. He was assassinated in 1911.

63. Meir Balaban (1877–1942), historian of Jewish communal life in Poland, considered the founder of the historiography of Polish Jewry. Balaban taught in the rabbinical seminary Tahkemoni of Warsaw as well as at the University of Warsaw. He was one of the founders of the Institute for Jewish Studies in Warsaw (1927) and served as its director for several years. Balaban wrote major studies on the Jewish communities of Lvov, Cracow, and Lublin. He coedited a volume of the *Istoriia evreiskogo naroda v Rossii* and contributed over 150 articles to the *Evreiskaia Entsiklopediia*.

64. Moses Schorr (1874–1941), a Polish rabbi and scholar, was professor of Semitic languages and ancient oriental history at the universities of Lemberg and Warsaw. He was also a preacher at the liberal Tlomacka Street Synagogue in Warsaw and was a member of that city's rabbinical council. Schorr was a founder of the Institute for Jewish Studies, established in Warsaw in 1928, where he lectured on the Bible and on Hebrew. He was also a member of the Polish Academy of Sciences and a member of the Polish Senate from 1935 to 1938.

65. Ignacy (Yitskhok) Schiper (1884–1943), historian and public worker. Active from his youth in Zionist organizations, Schiper served in the Polish Sejm from 1922 to 1927. He lectured at the Institute for Jewish Sciences in Warsaw on the history of Jewish economy. The focus of his historical writings was the economics and popular culture of Polish Jewry.

66. Julius Isidorovich Hessen (1871–1940?), historian of Russian Jewry, focused on Russian Jewry's quest for emancipation. He translated Pinsker's *Autoemanzipation* into Russian and prepared documentation for the Duma on Russian Jewish life and Russian laws regarding Jews. In addition to publishing several volumes of his own historical studies of Russian Jewish life, Hessen played a key role in researching and publishing the *Evreiskaya Entsiklopediia*. His *Istoriia evreev v Rossii* (1914) and *Istoriia evreiskogo naroda v Rossii* (1916–1927) remain standard works on Russian Jewish history from its beginnings to the late nineteenth century.

After the 1917 Revolution, Hessen worked with other historians on histories of the labor movement and on anti-Semitism in Russia.

67. Mark Wischnitzer (1882–1955), historian, sociologist, and community leader. He edited the European Jewish history section of *Evreiskaia Entsiklopediia* and lectured on oriental affairs and Jewish scholarship at the Institute founded by Baron Günzberg in St. Petersburg. He was an organizer and editor of *Istoriia evreiskogo naroda* in the years 1914–1916 and edited a section of the *Encyclopaedia Judaica* in Berlin in the 1920s. Together with his wife, Rachel, Wischnitzer published the Jewish art journals *Rimon* and *Milgroym* in Berlin in the 1920s. He also worked on behalf of European Jewry as secretary of the Hilfverein der Deutschen Juden and the American Jewish Joint Distribution Committee during the interwar years. After World War II he worked for the Council of Jewish Organizations and Welfare Funds in the United States.

68. Maria Gavrilovna Savina (1854–1915), Russian actress, renowned for her performances in dramatic works by Gogol, Turgenev, Chekhov, Tolstoy, Ostrovsky, and others.

69. Henriette Herz (1764–1847), a society leader in Berlin, was renowned for her intelligence and beauty. Her salon was frequented by Moses Mendelssohn and Solomon Maimon, among many other intellectuals. Herz was involved with other wealthy "enlightened" Berlin Jews in the Tugenbund, a youth group dedicated to furthering ethical values. She was baptized in 1817.

70. Dorothea von Schlegel (née Mendelssohn) (1763–1839), eldest daughter of Moses Mendelssohn. Like Henriette Herz, she ran a salon for intellectuals and artists in her Berlin home. She was married to banker Simon Veit, but later divorced him. She lived with the philosopher and Romantic writer Friedrich von Schlegel (1772–1829), whom she eventually married after both converted to Catholicism. Their home in Vienna was also a social and intellectual center in the early 1800s.

71. Wilhelm von Humboldt (1767–1835), a German philologist and statesman, championed Jewish civic rights at the Congress of Vienna and was instrumental in getting Jews admitted to the University of Berlin. His brother, Alexander (1769–1839), a geographer and naturalist, was also a dedicated philo-Semite.

72. "The Green Noise of Spring" is a poem by Nekrasov.

73. Beilis affair. Menahem Mendel Beilis, a Russian Jew, was charged in July 1911 of the ritual murder of a twelve-year-old non-Jewish boy near Kiev in March of that year. Despite police evidence to the contrary, the Russian court yielded to pressure from anti-Semitic groups and arrested Beilis. He remained in prison for more than two years. The case prompted an international outcry against the baseless charge of blood libel. At his trial in 1913, Beilis was pronounced not guilty and set free.

74. Vladimir Galaktionovich Korolenko (1853–1921), Russian writer, prominent among turn-of-the-century Russian liberal intelligentsia. Korolenko was active in many humanitarian causes and was an outspoken opponent of Russian anti-Semitism. In his fiction and journalism he denounced the Kishinev pogroms and the Beilis blood-libel case.

75. Semyon Afanasyevich Vengerov (1855–1920), literary historian and critic, who wrote extensively on Russian and other European literatures. Vengerov taught at the university in St. Petersburg and was appointed Minister of Education in 1899.

76. Abraham Merezhin (1880–193?), educator, journalist, author, and community activist. Merezhin was a champion of Yiddishism, beginning with his activities as a teacher in the modern Jewish school movement in Odessa. He was an initiator of modern Yiddish children's literature, helping to establish the press Farlag Blimelekh. Merezhin became active in the Bund in Odessa after the 1917

Revolution. Later, as a member of the Communist Party, he was associated with its Jewish section (Evsektsiia) in Moscow and was active in organizing Jewish laborers and agricultural colonists. He was arrested and executed in the 1930s along with other Evsektsiia leaders.

77. Abraham Menahem Mendel Usishkin (1863–1941) began his Zionist activities as a member of Hovevei Zion in the 1880s. In 1897 he was elected Hebrew secretary of the first Zionist Congress, and in 1898 he was elected to the Zionist General Council, on which he served for the rest of his life. Usishkin was instrumental in promoting Jewish settlement of Palestine as central to the Zionist agenda; as head of the Jewish National Fund from 1923 until 1941 he led the drive to purchase land in Palestine. Usishkin also helped found Hebrew University in Jerusalem and served on its Board of Trustees and Executive Committee.

78. "Let my soul die with the Philistines" are Samson's last words as he topples the Philistine temple (Judges 16:30).

79. Helots, inhabitants of the island of Helos enslaved by the Spartans, dating from the Dorian invasion of Peleponnesus. Considered property of the state, Helots were assigned as laborers for individual Spartan citizens and were also forced to fight in battle on the Spartans' behalf.

80. Albert (Abraham Elijah) Harkavy (1835–1919), Russian orientalist and scholar of Jewish history and literature. Harkavy published articles on the natural and physical sciences as well as ·on the issues of contemporary education and literature in the *Haskalah* journals *Ha-Karmel* and *Ha-Meliz*. He worked in the department of Jewish literature and oriental manuscripts of the Imperial Library in St. Petersburg, serving as department head from 1877 until his death. Harkavy wrote historical works on Jewish language, the Khazars, and the Kharijites. He also published annotated editions of a number of important Jewish manuscripts from the Imperial Library.

81. Maxim Gorky (pseudonym of Aleksey Maximovich Peshkov, 1868–1936), Russian author and the major pre-Revolutionary writer sympathetic to Bolshevism. Gorky was also prominent among Russian intellectuals who spoke out against anti-Semitism. Sympathetic portraits of Jews appear in his fiction and essays, and in 1916 he co-edited an anthology, *Shchit* [The shield], which featured statements by leading Russian authors and intellectuals decrying the persecution of Jews.

82. Leonid Nikolaevich Andreev (1871–1919), Russian prose writer and dramatist. A friend of Gorky's, Andreev contributed to the anthology *Shchit*.

83. Fedor Sologub (pseudonym of Fedor Kuz'mich Teternikov, 1863–1927), Russian poet, novelist, and playwright. Sologub was one of the major figures in Russian Symbolism. An opponent of the Bolshevik Revolution of 1917, he was condemned as a "decadent" writer by the official Soviet critics.

84. General Lavr Georgevich Kornilov (1870–1918), Russian military leader. As commander-in-chief of all Russian forces in August 1917, Kornilov believed that the provincial government was incapable of dealing with any threat from the Bolsheviks, and mistakenly believing that Alexander Kerensky was in agreement, he organized his troops to march on Petrograd but was arrested on Kerensky's orders. This action strengthened the Bolsheviks, and after the fall of Kerensky, Kornilov escaped to join the anti-Bolshevik forces of Anton Denikin on the Don, where he was killed in action.

85. The cruiser *Aurora* firing on the Winter Palace was the central event of the October Revolution of 1917, the Bolshevik assault on the seat of the Provisional Government.

86. "In hutted, stolid Russia" is a quotation from "The Twelve" (1918), a major poem of the Revolution by the leading Russian Symbolist poet and dramatist Aleksandr Aleksandrovich Blok (1880–1921).

87. "We will fan the world fire to the grief of all bourzhooys," ibid.

88. Aleksei Maksimovich Kaledin (1861–1918), Cossack leader and commander of a Russian cavalry division from 1914 to 1917. Kaledin returned to the Don region, where he was elected the Cossacks' hetman and organized an anti-Bolshevik campaign. After repeated defeats, he committed suicide.

89. Grigorii Eseevich Zinoviev (1883–1936), the leading Bolshevik advocate of world revolution, was the principal architect of the Communist International and its first chairman. He joined Lenin in exile between the revolutions of 1905 and 1917. Zinoviev became Lenin's closest collaborator and accompanied him on his return to Russia following the revolt of February 1917. After the October Revolution, Zinoviev was Chairman of the Petrograd Soviet. He served in the Politburo from 1919 to 1936, during which time he was also chair of the executive committee of the Communist International. Following Lenin's death he helped drive Trotsky into political isolation but later sided with him against Stalin. Zinoviev was tried for treason and executed in 1936.

90. *"Noli tangere circulos meos,"* literally, "Don't touch my circles"; apparently intended to mean "My work endures."

91. Admiral Alexander Vasilevich Kolchak (1873?–1920), naval commander during the Russo-Japanese War and World War I. Kolchak was the leader of anti-Bolshevik troops in Siberia from 1918 to 1920. There he briefly led a provisional government; he was later captured and executed.

92. Anton Ivanovich Denikin (1872–1947), a Russian general during World War I, supported Kornilov against Kerensky. Following the Bolshevik seizure of power, Denikin led the White Army in the occupation of the Ukraine and the southern Caucasus. In 1920 he abandoned the struggle against the Red Army. He died in exile in France.

93. Nicholas Nikolaevich Iudenich (1862–1933), a general in the Russo-Japanese War and World War I. In 1919 Iudenich led a White Army based in the Baltic against Petrograd, but was defeated. He died in exile.

94. Haidamak, the name given in the eighteenth century to armed bands of Ukrainian serfs and other impoverished outcast elements of Ukrainian society who fled Polish landowners and lived in the steppes beyond the Dnieper. Their uprisings against Polish nobility, reminiscent of the Cossack raids of the sixteenth century, involved violence against Jews living in the Ukraine, who were regarded as allies of Polish landowners as well as economic competitors. The Haidamak movement was eventually suppressed by Russian and Polish armies but has remained a part of Ukrainian lore and literature.

95. Anatolii Vasilevich Lunacharskii (1875–1933), Bolshevik leader and author, joined the Bolsheviks at the turn of the century, working for the party journal *Vperiod*. Between the revolutions of 1905 and 1917 he led an experimental workers' school in exile together with Maxim Gorky and Alexander Bogdanov. In 1917 Lunacharskii was appointed People's Commissar for Education. During the 1920s he introduced many educational innovations.

96. Michael Kulisher (1847–1919), grandson of *Haskalah* adherent Moses Kulisher, was a historian, ethnographer, and communal worker. He was a member of the Society for the Promotion of Culture among the Jews, a founder of the Jewish Society for History and Ethnography, and one of the founders of the Jewish Democratic Group in 1906.

97. Joseph Kulisher (1878–1934), son of Michael Kulisher, was a noted historian of European economics. He wrote on Jewish economic life in the Middle Ages and in eighteenth-century Prussia.

98. Israel (Sergei) Zinberg (1873–1939), historian of Jewish literature. Although he pursued scholarship as an avocation (he was by profession a chemical engineer),

Zinberg wrote major studies on Yiddish and Hebrew literature. He was editor and chief contributor to the Jewish literature department of the *Evreiskaia Entsiklopediia* (1907–1914). Zinberg's major work, *Geshikhte fun der literatur bay yidn*, is an eight-volume study of Jewish literature from the Spanish period through the end of the Russian *Haskalah* (1929–1937, last volume published posthumously in 1965). Zinberg was arrested in 1938 and deported to Siberia, where he died.

99. Aaron Steinberg (1891–1975), author, intellectual historian, and translator, wrote an important book on Dostoyevsky. Aaron Steinberg was the younger brother of Isaac Nahman Steinberg (see note 112). He left the Soviet Union in 1922 for Berlin and then for London. He translated Dubnov's ten-volume *World History of the Jewish People* and also compiled an abridged, three-volume edition entitled *Weltgeschichte des jüdischen Volkes*. In addition to his scholarly activities, Aaron Steinberg worked in the West for the World Jewish Congress and UNESCO.

100. *Shekel ha-geulah*, literally "coin of redemption" in Hebrew. Refers to an annual contribution by Diaspora Jews to a Zionist organization toward the purchase of land and the promotion of Jewish settlement in Palestine.

101. "Volunteers" (Russian: *Dobrovoltsy*), a frequent designation of those who fought in the ranks of the White Army.

102. Michael Nikolaevich Pokrovskii (1868–1932), Russian historian, appointed to the People's Commissariat for Education and Director of Central Archives in 1918.

103. Cheka, the All-Russian Extraordinary Commission for Fighting Counter-Revolution and Sabotage, was established on 7 December 1917 and was replaced by the GPU in 1922.

104. Following the 1917 Revolution, four letters of the traditional Russian alphabet were dropped and other orthographic reforms were introduced.

105. Joseph Opatoshu (1886–1954), Yiddish novelist and short-story writer. Born near the Polish town of Mlawe, Opatoshu emigrated to the United States in 1907. From 1910 he regularly contributed stories, essays, and novels in serial form to Jewish periodicals and anthologies. *In poylishe velder* [In Polish woods] (1921), the first novel of a trilogy, which deals with the decline of the Hasidic dynasty of Kotsk in the early 1800s, is his best-known work.

106. Heinrich Graetz (1817–1891), Jewish historian and Bible scholar. His multi-volume *Geschichte der Juden von den ältste Zeiten bis zur Gegenwart*, published from 1853 to 1870, is regarded as the first comprehensive attempt to write a history of the Jewish people from a Jewish perspective.

107. Isaac Marcus Jost (1793–1860), German educator and historian. His *Geschichte der Israeliten seit der Zeit der Maccabaeen bis auf unsere Tage*, in ten volumes, published from 1820 to 1847, was an important pioneering effort in modern Jewish scholarship in the early days of the *Haskalah*.

108. Martin Philippson (1846–1916), historian and communal leader. As head of the Lehranstalt für die Wissenschaft des Judentums, he was commisioned to write his three-volume *Neueste Geschichte der jüdischen Volkes*, published from 1907 to 1911.

109. Grani was founded by a group of Russian emigrés living in Germany in the 1920s. In addition to publishing Dubnov's history, it issued books on art, children's literature, Russian literature, Russian translations of works in other languages, and, in 1922 and 1923, two volumes of a literary almanac entitled *Grani*.

110. Elias Tcherikower (1881–1943), Jewish historian who contributed to the *Evreiskaia Entsiklopediia* and wrote a history of the Society for the Promotion of Culture among the Jews of Russia in 1914. Tcherikower went to the Ukraine after the 1917 Revolution and helped document anti-Semitic pogroms of the post-Revolutionary period. His *Antisemitizm un pogromen in Ukraine 1917–1918* featured an introduction written by Dubnov. One of the founders of YIVO, Tcherikower established its history

section and edited three volumes of its *Historishe shriftn* (1929–1939). For YIVO he also wrote or edited histories of Jewish life in France and the Ukraine as well as a history of the Jewish labor movement in the United States. His wife, Rebecca (1884–1963), assisted him in some of his political and scholarly activities.

111. Jacob Leshchinsky (1876–1966), a pioneer in the social, economic, and demographic study of Jewish life, was active in Zionist movements as a young man and helped found the Zionist Socialist Party. Leshchinsky began publishing his studies of European Jewry in 1903. During the February 1917 Revolution he helped found the United Jewish Socialist Party. Leshchinsky left the Soviet Union in 1921 for Berlin, where he was a correspondent for the *Forward* and where he helped establish the Institute for Research into Contemporary Jewry and Judaism. During the 1920s he directed YIVO's economics and statistics division. Leshchinsky left Europe for the United States in 1938 and moved to Israel in 1959.

112. Isaac Nahman Steinberg (1888–1957), author and jurist. In 1917 Steinberg was one of the leaders of the left-wing Socialist Revolutionaries (SR's) and was Commissar of Justice in Lenin's short-lived coalition government. Exiled in 1923, he lived in Berlin, London, and New York. Steinberg wrote and spoke extensively on socialism, revolution, and Territorialism. This last cause led him to pursue establishing a Jewish colony in Australia and, later, in Surinam. His brother Aaron was a professor of philosophy (see note 99).

113. Daniel Charney (1888–1959), Yiddish poet and journalist, co-edited *Yidishe emigratsie* with Elias Tcherikower. Charney wrote for American and European Yiddish dailies about the conditions of the Jewish populations of Lithuania, Latvia, and Poland during the interwar years. He lived and wrote in New York after 1941.

114. The Council of the Four Lands was the central institution of Jewish self-government in Poland and Lithuania from the mid-1500s until 1764. The Council (*Vaad*), which supervised local Jewish communities (known as *kahals*), was the most extensive form of autonomy ever achieved by European Jewry. Composed of rabbis representing the constituent communities, the Councils were convened during large fairs. Their responsibilities included the collection of taxes, rabbinical adjudications, political relations with co-territorial non-Jewish governments and communities, and such internal communal affairs as education and charities.

115. Martin Buber (1878–1965), philosopher and theologian. Buber studied philosophy at several German universities. At the age of twenty-six he was drawn to the study of Hasidism, largely out of an aesthetic interest. This resulted in his free renderings of Hasidic lore into German (*Die Geschichtes des Rabbi Nachman*, 1906, and *Die Legende des Baalschem*, 1908). His major philosophical work, *Ich und Du*, was published in 1923. He taught Jewish religion and ethics at the University of Frankfurt until 1933. In 1938 Buber emigrated to Palestine, where he was appointed professor of social philosophy at Hebrew University. In the 1940s he wrote two theological studies on Hasidism.

116. Vilna Gaon (Elijah ben Solomon Zalman, 1720–1797), the spiritual and intellectual leader of Lithuanian Jewry and the *misnagdim*. Descended from a renowned scholarly family, Elijah was a child prodigy. In addition to his excellence in talmudic and cabalistic studies, he was self-educated in mathematics, geography, and astronomy. He also advocated the study of Hebrew grammar and supported the translation of works of natural science into Hebrew, although he opposed the *Haskalah*. Elijah devoted virtually his entire adult life to study. His scholarship was preserved and widely disseminated by his students. Under Elijah's leadership, Vilna became the center of traditional rabbinical scholarship and the opponents of Hasidism. More than seventy works are attributed to Elijah but none were published during his lifetime.

117. Vladimir Medem (pseudonym M. Vinitski, 1879–1923), a prominent leader

and theoretician in the Jewish Labor Bund. Medem was active in radical politics as a student in Minsk before joining the Bund, writing for its various periodicals during the first decade of the twentieth century. A major architect of Bundist ideology, Medem elaborated its doctrine of promoting an autonomous Jewish national culture simultaneously with pursuing universal socialist goals. He was also a leading advocate for Yiddish educational and cultural programs as part of the Bund's agenda. He emigrated to the United States in 1921, where he worked as a journalist.

118. Rambam (Moses ben Maimon, 1135–1204), rabbinic authority, philosopher, physician, and a leading intellectual figure of medieval Jewry. Born in Cordova, he and his family traveled to Fez and later to Cairo in pursuit of religious freedom and economic opportunity. Rambam wrote talmudic commentaries as well as medical texts in Arabic (having served as court physician to an Egyptian sultan). His major philosophical work is *More Nevukhim* [Guide to the perplexed]. Written from 1176 to 1191, it attempts to reconcile traditional Jewish beliefs with Aristotelean philosophy. The Arabic text has been translated into Hebrew, Latin, and most European languages.

119. Yiddish Scientific Institute, original English translation of *Yidisher visnshaftlekher institut*—YIVO, the name of a center, established in Vilna in 1925, for the scholarly study of East European Jewish life. The international headquarters of the Institute were relocated in New York City in 1940, where it is now known in English as the YIVO Institute for Jewish Research.

120. Shalom Schwarzbard (1886–1938), soldier and Yiddish poet. Schwarzbard was active in the 1905 Revolution and helped organize Jewish self-defense during pogroms. After serving in the French Foreign Legion during World War I, he returned to Russia to join the Red Guard, where he fought against Petliura's Cossacks. Schwarzbard assassinated Petliura in Paris in May 1926. His autobiography, *Inem loyf fun yorn*, appeared in 1934.

121. Semyon Vasilyevich Petliura (1879–1926), Ukrainian patriot and leader of the struggle for Ukrainian independence. Petliura was both chairman of the Ukrainian provisional government and chief commander of its army. In 1920 he fought against both the Red Army and the anti-Soviet forces of Denikin. Petliura died while leading the Ukrainian government in exile in Paris.

122. Nikolai Aleksandrovich Berdiaev (1874–1948), religious philosopher and Christian existentialist. Once a Marxist, Berdiaev became involved in the turn-of-the-century religious revival and joined the Russian Orthodox Church. He was a professor of philosophy at Moscow University for a brief time. Berdiaev was forced to leave the Soviet Union in 1922. In 1924 he founded a religious philosophical academy in Paris.

123. Piotr Lavrovich Lavrov (1823–1900), Russian socialist thinker, mathematician, and populist leader. In his *Historical Letters* (1868–1869), Lavrov set forth his philosophy of history. This work, which was widely influential in both academic and popular circles, stressed the significance of the individual in history.

124. "I hear you" is quoted from "Taras Bulba" (1836), a story by Russian writer and dramatist Nikolai Vasilevich Gogol (1809–1852).

125. Three arrows was the emblem of the German Social Democratic movement.

126. Agudat Israel (also called "Agudah"), an international Jewish organization established in 1912, committed to promoting traditional adherence to rabbinic law and the application of its principles to organizing Jewish community life.

127. Dr. Cemach Szabad (1864–1935), physician and community activist. Szabad was a leading figure in the Vilna Jewish community as a cultural and political organizer. A native of Vilna, he studied medicine at Moscow University and then returned to his native town, where he practiced medicine and eventually became director of a hospital. He was active in the vocational training work of ORT and

YEKOPO and helped found Vilna's branch of OZE, a public health organization. Szabad wrote in Yiddish on medical research and public health. He also helped organize the TSYSHO secular Yiddish school system and the YIVO Institute.

128. Zelig Kalmanovich (1881–1944), Yiddish writer, philologist, and translator, who joined the staff of YIVO in 1929. He served as editor of *YIVO-bleter*, the Institute's scholarly journal, and wrote on Yiddish dialects and syntax. His translations into Yiddish include Dubnov's *History of the Jews* (1910–1911). His diary of the Vilna ghetto during World War II was published by YIVO in 1951.

129. Max Weinreich (1894–1969), Yiddish linguist, historian, and educator. Active as a youth in Yiddish cultural organizations in his native Latvia, Weinreich wrote his doctoral dissertation on Yiddish philology at the University of Marburg. He subsequently played a leading role in establishing modern Yiddish linguistic scholarship. A co-founder of YIVO, he directed the Institute's linguistic studies and its research training division. Weinreich relocated YIVO's central headquarters in New York City in 1940, following the Soviet occupation of Vilna, and served as the Institute's director there until his death. In addition to his masterwork, the four-volume *Geshikhte fun der yidisher literatur* (1970), Weinreich edited numerous YIVO publications, translated Homer and Freud into Yiddish, and wrote a number of scholarly studies on Jewish history, language, and psychology.

130. Zalmen Rejzin (1887–1941), Yiddish literary historian, philologist, journalist, and translator. With his older brother, the poet Abraham Reisin, he wrote Yiddish educational materials and children's literature. In 1920 he published his *Gramatik fun der yidisher literatur*, which helped establish standards for modern Yiddish. He compiled a biographical and bibliographical listing of Yiddish writers in his *Leksikon fun der yidisher literatur un prese*, issued in a single volume in 1914 and later in an expanded four-volume edition (*Leksikon fun der yidisher literatur, prese un filologi*) in Vilna in 1926–1929. A founder of YIVO, Rejzin was active in its philological and literary divisions.

131. P. Miliukov (1859–1943), a historian, was a leading figure of Russian liberalism and the head of the Constitutional Democratic party from 1905 until 1918. He served in the third and fourth Dumas and was Minister of Foreign Affairs in the Provisional Government in 1917.

132. Samuel Abba Horodetzky (1881–1957), scholar and historian of Jewish mysticism and Hasidism. His genealogy of Simon Dubnov appeared in YIVO's *Historishe shriftn II* (1938) and was issued in English translation in *YIVO Annual for Jewish Social Science* VI (1951):9–18.

133. MaHaRal of Prague (Judah Loew ben Bezalel, 1525?–1609), rabbi, talmudist, moralist, and mathematician. The MaHaRal was renowned for his scholarship, piety, and asceticism. He was also a pedagogical innovator and prolific author of rabbinic commentaries, sermons, and responsa. According to legend, the MaHaRal is associated with the creation of the Golem of Prague.

134. Rabbi Joseph Yoske of Dubno (1659–1702), scholar, moralist, and cabalist. He was born in Lublin and became rabbi of Dubno in 1698. Renowned for his piety, he wrote a morality book, *Yesod Yosef*, which was first printed in Shklov in 1785.

135. Abraham Liessin (pseudonym of Abraham Walt, 1872–1938), Yiddish poet and editor. Liessin was active in the founding of the Jewish Labor Bund. He emigrated to the United States in 1897, where he wrote for the *Forward*. From 1913 until his death he was editor of *Zukunft*, in which he regularly published editorials as well as his poetry. His collected works, *Lider un poemen*, were issued in three volumes in 1938.

136. Declaration of Rights (*Declaration du droits humains*, of 4 August 1789), one of the key documents to emerge from the French Revolution.

137. *Russkie Zapiski* (*Annales russes*), Russian-language sociopolitical and literary journal published in Paris from 1937 until September 1939. The journal appeared irregularly at first, then monthly from May 1938, when its editor was P. N. Miliukov. Others closely involved with the journal include H. D. Avksentev, I. I. Bunakov, M. V. Vishniak, and V. V. Rudnev.

138. Evian Emigration Committee. Thirty-one countries met at Evian-les-Bains in July 1938 to discuss the problem of European refugees. Known as the Evian Conference, it led to the establishment of the Inter-Governmental Committee to organize emigration and resettlement in cooperation with the League of Nations and the International Labor Organization. The Committee attempted to negotiate with Germany to establish orderly emigration procedures and to open refugee quotas in the United States, Australia, and Europe, but it met with limited success. It continued to function through World War II and afterward worked with UNRWA to repatriate displaced persons; eventually the Committee merged with the International Refugee Organization of the United Nations.

139. Ahaspher, the legendary figure of the Wandering Jew. According to Christian literature and lore, he is condemned by Jesus to wander the earth until the Second Coming for having mocked or struck Jesus on the way to his death.

140. The opening lines of a popular Red Army song, sung in the Soviet Union on the eve of World War II.

141. Vladimir Vladimirovich Mayakovsky (1894–1930), Russian poet and playwright, and the leading representative of the Russian Futurist school. In 1917 Mayakovsky became a totally engagé poet of the Revolution. He committed suicide in 1930.

142. *"Nunc dimittis servum tuum in pace"* (Now let your servant depart in peace) Luke 2:29.

143. Moravska Ostrava. A pogrom occurred in this Moravian town shortly after the Nazi invasion of Czechoslovakia.

144. Soviet forces entered Vilna on 19 September 1939, but soon withdrew. Vilna was ceded to Lithuania on 31 October, at which time a Lithuanian pogrom against the Jews of Vilna erupted.

145. Hugh Dalton (1887–1962), socialist economist and authority on international trade. Dalton was a Labour Party Minister of Parliament for many years and served in Churchill's war cabinet as Minister of Economic Warfare.

146. "Densification" (Russian: *uplotnenie*), the early Soviet practice of assigning two or more families to live in one apartment.

147. Kaiserwald, a concentration camp established by the Nazis near Riga in the summer of 1943. Kaiserwald was used to house surviving inmates of the liquidated ghettos of Riga, Daugavpils, Liepaja, and, later, Vilna. Following Soviet victories in the summer of 1944, surviving inmates of Kaiserwald were deported by the Nazis to Stutthof, a camp near Danzig.

BIBLIOGRAPHY

Bibliographies of Dubnov's Writings

Dubnov, S. M. *Kniga zhizni* [The book of my life], vol. III, pp. 163–89. Riga, 1940; New York: Izdanie Soiuza Russkikh Evreev, 1957. The fullest bibliography of Dubnov's works, covering the period 1881–1933.

Duker, Abraham G. *"Evreiskaia Starina.* A Bibliography. . . ." *Hebrew Union College Annual*, vols. VII–IX. Covers the years 1909–1930 of the publication that Dubnov edited for many years.

Meisl, Josef. "Simon Dubnows Abhandlungen und Schriften," in *Festschrift zu Simon Dubnows siebzigsten Geburtstag*, Ismar Elbogen, Josef Meisl, and Mark Wischnitzer, eds., pp. 266–95. Berlin: Jüdischer Verlag, 1930. A chronological bibliography covering the years 1880–1930.

————. "Sifre Shimeon Dubnov umaamarav beivrit," in *Sefer Shimeon Dubnov*, Simon Rawidowicz, ed., pp. 236–39. Jerusalem and London: Ararat Publishing Society, 1954. Covers Dubnov's Hebrew publications for the years 1892–1950.

Dubnov's Major Works

Ob izuchenii istorii russkikh evreev [On the study of Russian Jewish history]. St. Petersburg, 1881 (in *Voskhod* anthology and as a separate brochure).

Bek i Brann. Evreiskaia istoria [Bäck and Brann: Jewish history], revised and expanded by S. M. Dubnov, 2 vols. Odessa, 1896–1897.

Uchebnik evreiskoi istorii [Jewish history for students], 3 vols. Odessa, 1898–1901. Rev. ed. Vilna and St. Petersburg, 1906–1907. Yiddish translation, New York, 1915–1917.

Vseobshchaia istoriia evreev [Universal Jewish history], 3 vols. Odessa, 1901–1905. Rev. ed. vol. I, St. Petersburg, 1910. Yiddish translation, Vilna, 1910.

Emantsipatsiia evreev [Emancipation of the Jews], *1789–1791*. Vilna, 1906.

Pis'ma o starom i novom evreistve [Letters on old and new Jewry], 1897–1907. St. Petersburg, 1907. Hebrew translation, Tel-Aviv, 1937. Yiddish translation, Mexico City, 1959.

Oblastnoi Pinkes . . . (Community record book of the Jews of Lite). Hebrew text with Russian translation by Y. Tuvim with introduction and annotations by Dubnov. St. Petersburg, 1909–1918 (supplement to *Evreiskaia Starina*; also published separately in 2 vols.).

Noveishaia istoriia evreiskago naroda [Most recent history of the Jewish people], *1789–1881*. St. Petersburg, 1914. 2nd ed. Petrograd, 1919. 3rd ed., Berlin, 1923. German translation, Berlin, 1920, 1923. Hebrew translation, Berlin, 1923–1924. Yiddish translation: vol. I, Berlin, 1923; vol. II, Warsaw, 1926; vol. III, Warsaw, 1928.

Chego khotiat evrei [What Jews want]. St. Petersburg, 1917.

Istoriia evreiskago soldata [History of a Jewish soldier]. St. Petersburg, 1918. French translation, Paris, 1929.

Evrei v tsarstvovanie Nikolaia II [Jews under the reign of Tsar Nicholas II], *1894–1914*. Petrograd, 1922.

Evrei v Rossii i zapadnoi Evrope v epokhu antisemitskoi reaktsii [Jews in Russia and Western Europe in the age of anti-Semitic reaction], *1881–1914*. Moscow and Petrograd, 1923.

Vsemirnaia istoriia evreiskogo naroda [World history of the Jewish people], 2 vols.

Berlin, 1924–1925. German translation, Berlin, 1925–1929. Yiddish translation, Vilna, 1933.

Fun zhargon tsu yidish [From *zhargon* to Yiddish]. Vilna, 1929.

Toldot Ha-Hasidut [History of Hasidism]. Tel-Aviv, 1930–1931. German translation, Berlin, 1931. Yiddish translation, Vilna, 1930–1933; Buenos Aires, 1957–1958.

Yidishe geshikhte dertseylt far kinder [Jewish history for children]. Berlin, 1932; Riga, 1934–1939.

Kniga zhizni [The book of my life], 3 vols. Vols. I–II, Riga, 1934–1935. Vol. III, Riga, 1940; New York, 1957. German translation, vols. I–II, Berlin, 1937. Hebrew translation, vol. I, Tel Aviv, 1937.

Istoriia evreev v Evrope [The history of the Jews in Europe], 4 vols. Riga, 1936–1937.

Istoriia evreiskogo naroda na Vostoke [History of the Jewish people in the Orient], 3 vols. Riga, 1939.

Dubnov's Works in English

In *Jewish Encyclopedia* (New York, 1903–1904): "Council of Four Lands," vol. IV, pp. 304–308; "Jacob Frank," vol. V, pp. 475–78; "Hasidism," vol. VI, pp. 251–58.

Jewish History: An Essay in the Philosophy of History. Philadelphia: Jewish Publication Society, 1903. Translated from the German by Henrietta Szold (originally written in Russian).

"The Leading Motives of Modern Jewish History," *Jewish Review*, London, May 1911. Translated from the Russian.

History of the Jews in Russia and Poland, 3 vols. Philadelphia: Jewish Publication Society, 1916–1920. Translated from the Russian by I. Friedlaender. Reprint, New York: KTAV Publishing House, 1975.

"A Sociological Conception of Jewish History," *Menorah Journal*, New York, 1928, no. 3, pp. 257–67.

"World Jewry since 1914," in *Herzl's Memorial Book*, pp. 282–96. New York: New Palestine, 1928.

In *Encyclopedia of Social Sciences*. New York: Columbia University, 1931–1932. Articles on "Diaspora," "Graetz," "Josephus Flavius," "Jewish Autonomy."

An Outline of Jewish History, 3 vols. New York: M. Maisel, 1925. Translation of "Jewish History for Students" (Russian).

A Short History of the Jewish People. London, 1936. Translation of "Jewish History for Children" (Yiddish).

Nationalism and History: Essays on Old and New Judaism. Philadelphia: Jewish Publication Society, 1958. Edited with an introduction by Koppel S. Pinson.

History of the Jews, 5 vols. South Brunswick, N.J.: T. Yoseloff, 1967–1973. Translated by Moshe Spiegel from "the fourth definitive revised edition" of *Istoriia Evreiskogo Naroda na Vostoke*, vols. 1–10.

Works in English about Dubnov

Davis, Moshe. "Jewry East and West: The Correspondence of Israel Friedlaender and Simon Dubnow," *YIVO Annual for Jewish Social Science*, vol. IX (1954), pp. 9–62.

Fraenkel, Josef. *Dubnow, Herzl and Ahad Ha-am: Political and Cultural Zionism*. London: Ararat Publishing Society, 1963.

Friedlaender, Israel. *Dubnow's Theory of Jewish Nationalism*. New York: The Maccabaean Publishing Company, 1905.

Kochan, Lionel. "Graetz and Dubnow: Two Jewish Historians in an Alien World," in *Essays in Honour of E. H. Carr*, C. Abramsky, ed., pp. 352–66. Hamden, Connecticut: Archon Books, 1974.

———. "The Apotheosis of History: Dubnow," in *The Jew and His History*, pp. 88–98. New York: Schocken Books, 1977.

Seltzer, Robert M. "Simon Dubnow: A Critical Biography of His Early Years." Ph.D. diss., Columbia University, 1970.

———. "Coming Home: The Personal Basis of Simon Dubnow's Ideology," *AJS Review*, vol. 1 (1976), pp. 283–301.

———. "From Graetz to Dubnov: The Impact of the East European Milieu on the Writing of Jewish History," in *The Legacy of Jewish Migration*, David Berger, ed. New York: Social Science Monographs, Brooklyn College Press, distributed by Columbia University Press, 1983.

———. "Ahad Haam and Dubnow: Friends and Adversaries," in *At the Crossroads: Essays on Ahad Haam*, Jacques Kornberg, ed., pp. 60–73. Albany: State University of New York Press, 1983.

Simon Dubnov: The Life and World of a Jewish Historian. New York: YIVO, 1961. Exhibition catalog, issued simultaneously in Yiddish.

Steinberg, Aaron, ed. *Simon Dubnow: The Man and His Work: A Memorial Volume on the Occasion of the Centenary of his Birth* (1860–1960). Paris: World Jewish Congress, 1963. Essays on Dubnov's life and historiography in English, French, German, Hebrew, Italian, and Yiddish.

Index

Abramovich, Sholem Yankev (Mendele), 96, 104, 149, 152, 160: and Bialik, 119; death of, 176; neutrality of, 113; and the Odessa literary circle, 92–93; and Yiddish, 196–97; *Di Klyatshe*, 98, 261n25

Abuya, Elisha ben, 27

"Affirmation of the Diaspora, The" (Dubnov), 150

"After the Thirty-Year War" (Dubnov), 158

Akher, Elisha, 70, 71, 99, 183

Akiba, Rabbi, 70, 99

Aleichem, Sholem (Rabinovitch), 96, 259n12, 260n18: death of, 162, 168; and *Di yidishe folksblat*, 71; in Kiev, 90; and Yiddish, 87, 195, 196; *Dos meserl*, 84

Alexander II, 263n48

Alexander III, 80

Algemeyner Yidisher Arbeter Bund. *See* Bund

All-Russian Cheka, 185, 269n103

All-Russian Jewish National Assembly, 134

America (United States), 84, 244: cultural centers in, 158; and the Diaspora, 233; and the Immigration Act, 24; Jewish communities in, 20; Jewish emigration to, 5, 18, 71, 123, 240; Jewish representatives in, 31n90

American Jewish Congress, 232

Anarchism, 172: Stirnerian, 135, 264n53

Andreev, Leonid Nikolaevich, 167, 267n82

An-sky, Sh. (Solomon Zainwil Rapaport), 137, 151, 264n56: death of, 182

Asch, Sholem, 265n61

Assimilation, Jewish, 81, 109: of German Jews, 158; and the intelligentsia, 70, 135; and Jewish historiography, 194; vs. nationalism, 6, 7, 112

Autonomism, 134, 138–39: cultural-national, 117, 118, 176, 200; in the Diaspora, 17, 150; Jewish national, 1, 130, 194, 203; in Riga, 212; vs. spiritual Zionism, 104, 161

"Autonomism, the Basis of a National Program" (Dubnov), 117

Avrom-Yoel, Rabbi, 47

"Awakening of World Conscience and the Role of Jewry, The" (Dubnov), 232

Baal-Shem-Tov, Israel (the Besht), 84, 86, 198: and Jesus, 113. *See also* Hasidism

Babylonian exile, 194

Bäck, Dr. Samuel, 106

Balaban, Meir, 151, 265n63

Balfour Declaration, 175–76, 203

Baron, Salo Wittmayer, 2, 17, 228

Basle program, 108, 261n29, 262n37

Beilenson, Anna, 241

Beilis, Menahem Mendel, 264n54, 266n73

Beilis affair, 158, 266n73

Ben-Ammi, Mordecai (Rabinowicz), 95, 104, 260n23: his manifesto to the Jews of Russia, 18

Ben-Zakai, Yohanan, 8

Ben-Zion, S., 260n24

Berdiaev, Nicholai Aleksandrovich, 206, 271n122

Besht. *See* Baal-Shem-Tov, Israel

"Bestiality and Humanism" (Dubnov), 219

Beyer, Fritz, 205

Bialik, Hayyim Nahman, 262n41: death of, 218; and Hebrew, 159, 161; and the Kishinev pogrom, 122; his manifesto to the Jews of Russia, 18; and the Moriah Publishing House, 152, 260n24; and the Odessa literary circle, 119, 160; and Palestine, 184

Bible criticism, 222

Black Hundreds, 131, 132–33, 264n52

Blok, Aleksandr Aleksandrovich, 169, 267n86

Blood libel, 158, 160, 266n73, 266n74

Bney Moyshe, 94

Bogdanov, Alexander, 268n95

Book of My Life, The, 45, 56, 62, 248: on autonomism, 118; on Bentsion, 78, 89–90, 99–100; on the Book of Ecclesiastes, 44; on the French Revolution, 88; on historicism, 91, 111; on the intelligentsia, 71–72; on the move from Odessa, 124; on the Odessa literary circle, 96; origins of, 131; publication of, 215; on Tolstoy, 86; writing of, 214–15

Börne, Ludwig, 82, 259n5: on freedom, 72; influence of, 50, 51, 159

Bramson, Leon, 263n50: and the Historical-Ethnographical Commission, 16; and the Trudovik group, 130

Brann, Marcus, 106

Bruno, Giordano, 70

Brutzkus, Julius, 16

Buber, Martin, 197, 270n115

Buckle, Henry Thomas: and cosmopolitanism, 113, 134; influence of, 12; and rationalism, 54; *History of Civilization*, 53

Budushchnost' (journal), 262n38: "Changing Trends in Russian-Jewish Journalism," 112–13

Bund (Algemeyner Yidisher Arbeter Bund), 207, 261n28: and the Jewish community, 229; and the Odessa literary circle, 105; in Vilna, 126; and YIVO, 254

Byron, George Gordon, Lord, 77, 81

Cabala, 16, 81

Caro, Joseph, 94, 260n22
Censor, 80: and Dubnov's textbook, 116; and Graetz's *History of the Jews*, 101
Chagall, Bella, 254
Chagall, Marc, 223, 254, 255
"Changing Trends in Russian-Jewish Journalism" (Dubnov), 113
Charney, Daniel, 191, 270n113: and America, 239; and the death of Ida Dubnov, 213; in exile, 215; letters to, 220, 224, 227
Chernyshevsky, Nikolai Gavrilovich, 3, 10
Cherviakov, 202
Christianity, 113–14, 171: converts to, 159–60; and the Essenic movement, 127, 198
Cicero, 97
Civil emancipation, Jewish, 76
Class struggle, 172, 175
Cohen, Herman, 120, 235, 263n42
Collective individualism, 109. *See also* Individualism
Commission for the Amelioration of Scholars' Living Conditions, 181
Committee of Nationalization, 116, 119–20: and the Jewish Independent Workers' Party, 121
Comte, Auguste, 57, 58, 63, 72, 78: *Philosophy of Positivism*, 183
Condorcet, Marquis de, 11, 72, 81
Consciousness, historical, 16, 97
Constituent Assembly, 172–76
Constitutional Democratic Party, 130, 134
"Contemporary State of Jewish Historiography, The" (Dubnov), 222
Cosmopolitanism, 4, 81: and Buckle, 53; and nationalism, 80, 134, 207
Courses in Oriental Studies, 11, 146, 153: and historicism, 166; police infiltration of, 157; and Tolstoy, 155; and Zionism, 150
"critically thinking individual," 74
Criticism, historical, 29n41
Criticus (Simon M. Dubnov), 74, 84, 86, 195
"cultural nation," 202
Czernowitz Conference, 147, 200, 265n61

Da Costa, Uriel, 70, 71, 99
Dalton, Hugh, 240, 273n145
"Deeds of My Youth, The" (Dubnov), 50
Dembovetskii (Governor), 89
Den' (newspaper): "The Sources of the Ritual Lie," 160
Denikin, Anton Ivanovich, 179, 181, 267n84, 268n92
Depping: *History of the Jews in the Middle Ages*, 53
Diaspora: and America, 233; and historical consciousness, 100; history of, 194; and nationalism, 17, 130, 137, 193, 207; and Yiddish, 150; and Zionism, 122, 149–50
Diderot, Denis, 72

Dineson, Jacob, 86, 260n20: and Yiddish, 196
Dinur, Benzion, 7
"Divided and a United National Party, A" (Dubnov), 117
Dizengoff, Meir, 119: manifesto to the Jews of Russia, 18
Dobroliubov, Nikolai Aleksandrovich, 10
Dreyfus affair, 112, 261n32
Dubno, Yosef, 40
Dubnov, Bentsion (Rabbi), 43, 50, 78, 82, 153–54, 225: amnesty of, 89–90; death of, 99–100; and hasidic mysticism, 40; and the yeshiva, 48, 49
Dubnov, Ber, 127
Dubnov, Ida (née Freidlin), 60–61, 72, 83, 182, 252: in Berlin, 191, 209–10; cancer of, 156–57, 212; death of, 213–16, 253–54; marriage of, 73, 77; in Odessa, 102–103; and the Odessa literary circle, 95; and the 1917 Revolution, 175; in St. Petersburg, 142, 193; as wife, 3, 75–76, 183; youth of, 54, 55, 57–58
Dubnov, Isaac, 42, 46
Dubnov, Meyer-Yakov, 41, 50, 78: death of, 85
Dubnov, Olga, 125, 142, 185: birth of, 82; and death of Ida Dubnov, 213; youth of, 110
Dubnov, Risa, 41, 42
Dubnov, Sheyne, 41–42, 43, 48, 49, 50, 85, 107: death of, 117
Dubnov, Simon M.: arrest by the Gestapo, 245; birth of, 40; campaign against reaction, 89; death of, 246–47; emigration from Russia, 187; eye disease of, 79–80, 83, 86; on history, 103; and Ida Freidlin, 54, 57–58, 72, 73, 75, 77; at the *kheyder*, 3, 43–47; at Kovno, 185; at the Linka retreat, 144–47, 153–54, 156–57; literary influences of, 9, 50–51; love of nature, 3, 108, 250–51; manifesto to the Jews of Russia, 18; as "missionary of history," 99, 225; moves to Berlin, 189; moves to Odessa, 21, 90; moves to Riga, 211; moves to St. Petersburg, 59–60, 83, 89, 90, 140; moves to Vilna, 123–24; self-education, 9, 63, 76–79; in Switzerland, 108; his textbook, 110, 116; at the yeshiva, 48–49; and the Zurich Conference, 201–202
Dubnov, Sophie, 107, 160, 216, 245, 250: as biographer, 2, 248; birth of, 79; and death of Ida Dubnov, 213, 214; education of, 87; escape to Vilna, 238; marriage of, 29n37; moves to America, 243; and poetry, 110, 253; in St. Petersburg, 142; at the university, 125; and World War II, 236–37
Dubnov, Volf (Vladimir), 42, 47, 82, 88, 243: education of, 50, 51; and the Freidlin sisters, 54; and Odessa, 105–106; and Palestine, 72, 80; and St. Petersburg, 59–60

Dubnov, Yakov (Yasha), 110, 142, 213, 243: birth of, 86; exile of, 155; illness of, 102, 168

Duma: of 1906, 136–39; the second, 142, 144

Ecclesiastes, 44

Education, national: 115–16, 118, 120, 153

Elbogen, Ismar, 192, 205

Emancipation of the Jews During the Great French Revolution 1789–1791, The (Dubnov), 138

Emanuil, Roza, 144

Emigration, Jewish, 135: to America, 5, 18, 71, 123, 240

Encyclopedists, 81

Erlich, Alexander, 1, 209, 250

Erlich, Henryk, 216: arrest of, 238, 255; and the Bund, 29n37, 229

Erlich, Miriam, 243

Erlich-Dubnov, Sophie. *See* Dubnov, Sophie

Essenic movement: and Christianity, 127, 198

"Eternal and the Ephemeral Ideals of Jewry, The" (Dubnov), 93

"Ethical Criterion, The" (Dubnov), 219

Evian Emigration Committee, 232, 273n138

Evolutionism, 8, 9, 19

Evreiskaia Nedelia (journal): "The Story of a Jewish Soldier," 168, 171

Evreiskaia Starina (*Jewish Antiquity*, journal), 158, 165, 177: founding of, 16, 149; and the Historical-Ethnographic Society, 150–51

Evreiskii Mir (*Jewish World*, journal), 149, 150, 151: "The Affirmation of the Diaspora," 150

Externus (Simon M. Dubnov), 74, 76

Festschrift zu Simon Dubnows siebzigsten Geburtstag, 205–206

Fet, Afanasy Afansevich, 107, 253, 261n31: and Sophie Dubnov, 110, 142

First Zionist Congress (Basle), 105

Flavius, Joseph, 44

Flekser, Akim. *See* Volynskii, A. L.

Folk (journal), 201

Folksblat (journal), 201

Folkspartey (United National Group), 6, 149, 157, 172: and the Diaspora, 142–43; and emigration, 20

Forverts (*Jewish Daily Forward*, newspaper), 190

Frank, Jacob, 84

Frankism, 15, 74, 106

Fraye vort (journal): "Will the Twentieth Century Be the Reverse of the Nineteenth Century?" 219

Fraynd (newspaper), 143

Freidlin, Chaim, 54, 57

Freidlin, Fanny, 54, 57–58, 82

Freidlin, Ida. *See* Dubnov, Ida

Freidlin, Mera (Miriam), 54, 57, 77–78

Frevil-Abramovich, Manefa, 156

Friedlaender, Dr. Israel, 2, 123

Frimorgn (journal), 201

Frug, Shimon Shmuel, 70, 82, 96, 140, 160, 259n11: death of, 168; and *Evreiskii Mir,* 149; and Yiddish, 87, 196; and *Di yidishe folksblat,* 71

Galileo, 70

Gaon of Vilna, 198, 270n116

Gemara, 44

Germany: Nazism in, 215; Weimar, 190, 209. *See also* Nazism

Gestapo. *See* Nazism

Ginzberg, Osher. *See* Ha-Am, Ahad

Goethe, Johann Wolfgang von, 77, 164–65

Gordon, Jacob, 265n61

Gordon, Judah Leib, 71, 195

Gorky, Maxim (Aleksey Maximovich Peshkov), 182, 267n81, 268n95: and the Commission for the Amelioration of Scholars' Living Conditions, 181; and the League to Combat Anti-Semitism, 167; and "The Story of a Jewish Soldier," 168

Graetz, Heinrich, 2, 27, 189, 269n106: and the Diaspora, 193; influence of, 12, 74, 99–100; and Jewish mysticism, 15; and the language question, 154, 235; and martyrdom, 14; *History of the Jews,* 60, 100, 101, 222

Grani, 190, 269n109

"Great French Revolution and the Jews, The" (Dubnov), 88

Gressman, Hugo, 205

Gruzenberg, Samuel, 262n38

Günzburg, Baron David, 11, 263n49

Günzburg, Baron Horace, 129, 146, 263n49, 264n56, 266n67

Gurfinkel, Nina, 230

Ha-Am, Ahad (Osher Ginzberg), 7, 93–95, 106, 161: and the Committee of Nationalization, 116; death of, 199, 201; on the Diaspora, 150; and "Dubnovism," 109; and the First World War, 167–68; and Hebrew, 195; illness of, 182; and Jewish education, 118; and Jewish history, 207; and the language question, 200–201; in London, 146; manifesto to the Jews of Russia, 18; and Neo-Palestinism, 103; in Odessa, 21; and the pogroms, 123; in Polesia, 115; and spiritual Zionism, 130, 261n30; and the Union Congress, 136–37; and the Vilna Bund, 126; and the Wissotsky Tea Company, 11; "The Negation of the Diaspora," 150; "Slavery in Freedom," 94

Ha-Aretz (journal), 201

Haidamak, 179, 268n94

Ha-Karmel (journal), 49, 259n4
Ha-Olam (journal), 201
Harkavy, Albert, 166, 267n80
Ha-Shilo'ah (journal), 109, 119: "The Negation and Affirmation of the Diaspora in Ahad Ha-Am's Thought," 161
Hasidism, 15, 48, 85–86, 111: and Ahad Ha-Am, 94; and Christianity, 113–14; history of, 195, 197–98; and nationalism, 84
Haskalah, 47, 48, 49–50, 71: and Hasidism, 197, 198
Ha-Tekufah (journal), 201
Ha-Zefirah (journal), 51, 86
Hebrew, 74, 99–100, 159, 235: and national education, 153; as national language, 147; in Palestine, 20; vs. Yiddish, 13, 71, 196
Hegel, Georg W. F., 7, 82
Heine, Heinrich, 50, 81, 159, 253
Herz, Henrietta, 261n26, 266n69
Herzl, Theodore, 122, 262n37: and Zionism, 20, 109, 261n30
Hessen, Julius Isidorovich, 151, 265n66
"Historic Moment, A" (Dubnov), 18, 123
"Historical Report" (Dubnov), 103
Historical-Ethnographic Commission (later Historical-Ethnographic Society), 16, 98, 113, 130, 148, 153, 166, 185: and the Beilis affair, 158; and *Evreiskaia Starina*, 151; and Peretz, 156; and Zionism, 150
Historicism, 91, 100, 166
Historicus (Simon M. Dubnov), 149
"Historiographer of Jewry, The" (Dubnov), 99
Historiography, Jewish, 206, 207
Historishe shriftn (monograph), 225
History, Jewish, 83–84, 222–23: and Judaism, 6; and nationalism, 8, 194; pattern of, 17, 26
History of Hasidism, The (Dubnov), 15, 25, 85–86, 100, 195, 197
"History of the Hasidic Schism" (Dubnov), 88, 98
Hitler, Adolf, 210, 218, 231, 234
Hitler Youth, 209
Horodetzky, Samuel Abba, 225, 272n132
House of Shammai, 44
Hugo, Victor, 77, 121, 174, 228, 249, 253: on history, 83–84
Humanism: and nationalism, 75, 108, 117–18, 125, 148
"Humanization and Nationalization" (Dubnov), 149
Humboldt, Wilhelm von, 266n71
Hus, Jan, 112, 261n33

Idealism, 26, 73: vs. history, 12, 14, 18
Idelson, Abraham, 149
Immortality, collective, 91
Individualism, 126, 134: Christian, 154; Jewish, 55; of Mill, 135

Inner Life of the Jews in Poland and Lithuania in the Sixteenth Century, The (Dubnov), 114
Inquisition, Age of, 70, 219
Institute for Jewish Studies, 265n64
"Intelligentsia in Disarray, The" (Dubnov), 121
"Introduction to the History of Hasidism, An" (Dubnov), 86
Itliberg, Switzerland, 108
Iudenich, Nicholas Nikolaevich, 179, 180, 181, 268n93

Jabotinsky, Vladimir, 122, 203, 263n43
Jacobinism, 135
Javitz, B., 104
"Jerusalem of Lithuania." *See* Vilna
Jesus of Nazareth, 113
Jewish congress, 226–27
Jewish Democratic Group, 142
Jewish Encyclopedia, 145–47
Jewish Independent Workers' Party, 121
Jewish Lexicon, 201
Jewish Literary Society (St. Petersburg), 147–48
Jewish National Council, 177
Jewish National Workers' Alliance in America, 239
Jewish People's University, 179, 180
Jewish Scientific Society (Berlin), 192
Jewish Socialist Workers' Party, 264n55
Jewish Teachers' Institute, 51
Jews: Allies' indifference to, 240; of the Diaspora, 122; duality of, 118; emancipation of, 235–36; and the First World War, 164–65, 176; in the nineteenth century, 117; and revolutions, 129, 202. *See also* History, Jewish; Judaism
Jews in Russian and Western Europe in the Age of Anti-Semitic Reaction, The (Dubnov), 190
Jost, Isaac Marcus, 189, 269n107
Judaism: "historical consciousness" of, 100; and Jesus, 114; and the language question, 235; legalism of, 61; reform in, 5–6; ritualism of, 75

Kabala, 16, 81
Kagan, Marcus, 60, 110, 115, 178
Kaledin, Aleksei Maksimovich, 175, 268n88
Kalmanovich, Zelig, 223, 242, 272n128
Karo, Joseph. *See* Caro, Joseph
Kerensky, Alexander, 267n84, 268n92
Kheyder, 39, 43–44, 79: reform of, 118
Khmelnitskii, Bogdan, 14, 15, 73
Khronika Voskhoda (journal), 87, 89
Klausner, Joseph Gedaliah, 146, 161, 265n59
Koigen, David, 192
Kolchak, Admiral Alexander Vasilevich, 179, 181, 268n91

Koltsov, Aleksei Vasilevich, 57, 259n9
Kornilov, General Lavr Georgevich, 172, 267n84, 268n92
Korolenko, Vladimir Galaktionovich, 158, 266n74
Kovno (Lithuania), 185, 187–88
Kovno University, 185
Kule, Rabbi, 43
Kulisher, Joseph, 179, 268n97
Kulisher, Michael I., 24, 25, 179, 268n96
Kulisher, Moses, 268n96

Land and Freedom, 55
Landau, Adolph, 11, 75, 76, 80, 140
Language: in the *Kheyder*, 118; the question of, 13, 147, 161, 195, 200, 234–35
"Last Word of Condemned Jewry, The" (Dubnov), 76
Latvia: Soviet absorption of, 242–43
Lavrov, Piotr Lavrovich, 207, 271n123
Lazarus, Moritz, 112, 262n36
League of Nations, 23, 202, 226
League to Combat Anti-Semitism, 167
League to Resist European Aggression, 233
Lebensohn, Abraham Dov, 259n3
Lebensohn, Micah Joseph, 49, 107, 259n3
Lenin, 178, 182, 219, 268n89
Leontiev, K., 80
Lermontov, Mikhail Iurevich, 51, 56, 110, 142, 253, 259n8
Lesgaft, Piotr Frantsevich, 139, 140, 264n57
Leshchinsky, Jacob, 191, 207, 216, 270n111
Leshchinsky, Liya, 191
"Lessons from the Terrible Days" (Dubnov), 18
Letopis' (journal), 168
"Letter from Mstislavl," 60
Letters on Old and New Jewry (Dubnov), 25, 108–109, 111, 207: German edition of, 123; and Jewish self-government, 17; and spiritual nationalism, 1, 94, 104, 138; "Autonomism, the Basis of a National Program," 117; "A Divided and a United National Party," 117; "The Intelligentsia in Disarray," 121; "Spiritual Nationalism and Zionism," 109
Levin, Shmariia, 127, 138
Levinsohn, Isaac Baer, 29n41
Liberalism, 9, 26
Liessin, Abraham, 228, 231, 272n135
Lilienblum, Moses Leib, 52, 71, 94
Literarishe bleter (journal), 201
"Literature of the Time of Troubles, The" (Dubnov), 103
Lunacharskii, Anatolii Vasilevich, 179, 268n95
Luzzato, Moses, 84

MaHaRal of Prague, 225, 272n133

Mahler, Raphael, 22, 207
Maimon, Solomon, 266n69
Maimonides, 9, 154, 235
Mamontov, 180
Mapu, Abraham, 47, 259n2
Margulies, M., 121
Marxism, 7, 9, 19, 23, 135, 141: and Jewish historiography, 222
Maskilim. See Haskalah
Materialism, historical, 126, 222
Mayakovsky, Vladimir, 237, 253, 273n141
Medem, Vladimir, 200, 270n117
Meisel, Dr., 243
Meisl, Josef, 205, 206
Mendele. *See* Abramovich, Sholem Yankev
Mendelson, S., 254
Mendelssohn, Moses, 53, 220, 266n69: commentaries by, 45, 259n1; and the language question, 154, 235; and "Prophetism," 9
Merezhin, Abraham, 161, 266n76
Meshcherskii (Prince), 89
Miliukov, P., 224, 232, 272n131
Mill, John Stuart, 58, 77, 78: individualism of, 135; and self-education, 63, 87; *On Liberty*, 10, 57, 72, 183
Minor, Rabbi, 87
Mirskii, Prince Sviatopolk, 128
Mishnah, 44
Modern History of the Jews (Dubnov), 21–22
Modernism, 253
Mommsen, Theodor, 81, 260n14
Montesquieu, 72
Moral of Terrible Days, The (Dubnov), 133, 135, 137
Movshovich, D., 240
Mstislavskii, S. (Simon M. Dubnov), 73, 74
"My Philosophy" (Dubnov), 55
Mysticism: Hasidic, 40; Jewish, 15, 81

National Socialism, 215, 219
Nationalism, 75: vs. assimilation, 7, 115; as collective individualism, 109; and cosmopolitanism, 80, 134; cultural-historical, 104–105; in the Diaspora, 1, 137; and humanism, 26, 108, 117–18, 125, 148; Jewish, 4, 91, 105, 154; and racism, 219; spiritual, 8, 94, 99, 112, 126, 138, 199–200; and trilingualism, 161
Nazism, 215, 219, 221, 230: as anti-Semitism, 232; and the Brown Shirts, 204; and emigration, 233; in Riga, 245–46
"Negation and Affirmation of the Diaspora in Ahad Ha-Am's Thought, The" (Dubnov), 161
Nekrasov, Nikolai Alekseevich, 70, 110, 142, 253, 259n10
Neo-Palestinism, 103
Nicholas II, 127, 128, 171: and the Duma, 131, 144

Nietzsche, Friedrich Wilhelm, 108
Niger, Sh., 207–208
"Nihilism or Anarchism?" (Dubnov), 150
Nineteenth century, 117, 219
Nomberg, H. D., 265n61
Nordau, Max, 112, 262n37
Novakovsky, Yehuda, 136, 264n54
Novyi Voskhod (journal), 167: "Rights and Du-
    ties," 166
Nuremburg Laws, 226

Odessa, 89: literary circle of, 91, 95, 119–20,
    122–23
"On the Study of Jewish History" (Dubnov),
    97, 98, 103, 113, 148
"On the Supremacy of National Politics in
    the Life of an Oppressed Nationality"
    (Dubnov), 137
Opatoshu, Joseph, 188, 190, 193, 269n105
Oyfn sheydveg (journal), 233, 234: "Thoughts
    of a Jewish Historian on Aims of War and
    Peace," 240

Pale of Settlement, 59: and the First World
    War, 164; pogroms in, 122–23, 131; reac-
    tion against Jews in, 89; and the 1905 Revo-
    lution, 129
Palestine, 178, 180: and the Balfour Declara-
    tion, 203; cultural centers in, 158; emigra-
    tion to, 157, 240; as spiritual center, 150;
    and the Second World War, 240
Palestinophilia, 4, 71, 74, 75
Pardes, 99
Pascal, 100
"Path of Thorns, The" (Dubnov), 60
Peretz, Yitskhok Leyb, 149, 242, 265n61:
    Monish, 84, 155–56, 260n18
Peshkov, Aleksey Maximovich. See Gorky,
    Maxim
Petliura, Semyon Vasilyevich, 181, 201,
    271n121
Pharisees, 81, 114
Philippson, Martin, 189, 269n108
Pinsker, 74
Pinski, Dovid, 265n61
Pinson, Koppel S., 2, 29n32
Pipler, Itse (Rabbi), 44
Pisarev, Dmitry Ivanovich, 3, 10, 52, 56,
    259n7: and the "critically thinking" indi-
    vidual, 55
Plehve, Viacheslav Konstantinovich von,
    127, 263n47
Pogroms, 14, 62: in Alexandria, 127; in Bialy-
    stok, 139; by the Black Hundreds, 131 (see
    also Black Hundreds); of 1881, 70, 71; in
    Elizavetgrad, 4; of the German govern-
    ment, 231; at Gomel, 126–27; the Hai-
    damak, 198; in Kishinev, 18, 122–23,
    263n44, 263n47, 264n52, 266n74; and the

Russian civil war, 181; in Vilna, 132–33,
    238
Poincaré, Raymond, 162
Pokrovskii, Michael Nikolaevich, 184,
    269n102
Positivism, 52, 57, 58, 74
"De profundis" (Dubnov), 167
Pushkin, Alexander, 51, 110, 253: on Russia,
    187

Rabbinism, 6. See also Hasidism
Rabinovitch, Sholem. See Aleichem, Sholem
Rafes, Moyshe, 13
Rambam (Moses ben Maimon), 220, 271n118
Rapaport, Solomon Zainwil. See An-sky, Sh.
Rasputin, 169
Rationalism, 54, 126, 134
Ratner, Mark Borisovich, 130, 264n51
Rawnitzki, Yehoshua Hana, 95, 96, 99, 152,
    260n24: manifesto to the Jews of Russia, 18;
    and the use of Hebrew, 159
Razsvet, "The People's Yiddish Newspaper"
    (journal), 62, 143, 149: and nationalism,
    70; and Palestinophilia, 71, 72–73
Realism, 52
Recent History of the Jewish People, The (Dub-
    nov), 155, 160, 165, 189, 190, 193
Reflections on the Eternal People (Dubnov), 149
Reform: educational, 79; religious, 5, 74
Reinus, Maria, 205
Reisen, Abraham, 265n61, 272n130
Rejzin, Zalmen, 223, 272n130
Renan, Ernest, 4, 86, 260n21
Renner, Karl, 118, 139, 262n40
Revolution: French, 8, 88; of 1905, 129, 132,
    136; of 1917, 23, 169–73
Riesser, Gabriel, 112, 202, 262n35
Riga (Latvia), 187: fascism in, 215, 217; Nazi
    occupation of, 245, 246
"Rights and Duties" (Dubnov), 166
Rights, national, 1, 117. See also Nationalism
"Rise of Tsadikism, The" (Dubnov), 88
"Romantic of the Revolution, A" (Dubnov),
    227–28
Romi, Immanuil, 81
Roosevelt, Franklin, 233, 240
Rosenfeld, Yakov, 62
Rousseau, Jean Jacques, 72
Russian language, 154. See also Language, the
    question of
Russkii Evrei (journal), 60, 61, 62–63, 70
Russkie Zapiski (journal): The Awakening of
    World Conscience and the Role of Jewry,"
    232

S. D. D. (Simon M. Dubnov), 74
Sabbateanism, 15
St. Petersburg: Free University of, 139, 140–
    41; Literary Society of, 147–48

Savina, Maria Gavrilovna, 156, 266n68
Sazonov, E. S., 263n47
Schiller, Johann Christoph Friedrich von, 55, 73
Schiper, Ignacy, 151, 265n65
Schlegel, Dorothea von (née Mendelssohn), 261n26, 266n70
Schlegel, Friedrich von, 266n70
Schlitter, 246
Schlosser, Friedrich Christoph, 78
Schmidt, Kaspar. *See* Stirner, Max
Schorr, Moses, 151, 265n64
Schwarzbard, Shalom, 201, 271n120
Sejmists, 136, 264n55
Sev, L., 120
Sevastopol Campaign, 127, 263n48
Sforim, Mendele Mokher. *See* Abramovich, Sholem Yankev
Shelley, Percy Bysshe, 76, 77
Shneerson, Zalman, 100
Shulman, Kalmen, 46
Skepticism, 4, 81
Slutsky, Yehuda, 7
Smolenskin, Peretz, 5, 19
"Social and Spiritual Life of Jews in Poland in the Eighteenth Century, The" (Dubnov), 111
Society for the Promotion of Enlightenment among Jews of Russia (Odessa committee), 100, 115–16, 118
Sokolow, Nahum, 86
Sologub, Fedor, 167, 267n83
Solovev, Vladimir, 73
"Sources of the Ritual Lie, The" (Dubnov), 160
Spector, Mordecai, 71, 86, 259n13, 265n61: and Yiddish, 195, 196
Spencer, Herbert, 63, 78
Spinoza, Benedict, 15, 70, 74, 99, 220
Springer, Rudolf. *See* Renner, Karl
Steinberg, Aaron, 224, 227, 229, 237, 269n99: in Berlin, 191, 192; and Jewish historiography, 205–206; and the Jewish People's University, 179; as translator of the *World History*, 32n98, 221, 251
Steinberg, Isaac Nahman, 3, 191, 251, 269n99, 270n112
Stirner, Max, 264n53. *See also* Anarchism, Stirnerian
Stolypin, Petr Arkadevich, 147–48, 265n62
"Story of a Jewish Soldier, The" (Dubnov), 168, 171
"Struggle for the Rights of the Jewish People, Past and Present, The" (Dubnov), 202
Sue, Eugene, 47
Szabad, Dr. Cemach, 218, 219, 254, 271n127
Szold, Henrietta, 122

Talmud, 221: historical justification for, 100;

as taught in the *kheyder*, 44–45
Tcherikower, Elias, 188, 189, 190, 209, 212, 227, 269n110: and the appeal for a Jewish congress, 226; and *Die fraye tribune*, 231, 232; on Dubnov's thought, 206–207; and *Historishe shriftn*, 225; in Paris, 210
Tcherikower, Rebecca, 210, 212
Tchernowitz, Chaim, 119
Teternikov, Fedor Kuz'mich. *See* Sologub, Fedor
"Third Haidamak Massacre, The" (Dubnov), 190
"Thoughts of a Jewish Historian on Aims of War and Peace" (Dubnov), 240
Tiutchev, Fedor Ivanovich, 100, 110, 199, 253, 261n27
Tog (newspaper), 201: "The Struggle for the Rights of the Jewish People, Past and Present," 202
Tolstoy, Lev, 4, 77, 80, 86: anti-Semitism of, 87; death of, 155
Torquemada, Tomás de, 112, 262n34
Trudovik group, 130
"*Tsadik* in the St. Petersburg Fortress, A" (Dubnov), 100
Tsadikim, 85
Turgenev, Ivan Sergeevich, 51, 55, 58, 77, 156

Ulmanis, Karlis, 242
Union for the Attainment of Equal Rights for the Jewish People in Russia, 6, 131, 134, 135–37; dissolution of, 142, 143
United National Group, 157. *See also* Folkspartey
United States. *See* America
Usishkin, Abraham Menahem Mendel, 161, 162, 267n77
Utopians, 174

Varnhagen, Rachel, 261n26
Veit, Simon, 266n70
Vengerov, Semyon Afanasyevich, 159, 266n75
Versailles Treaty, 23
Vilna, 50–51: Bund in, 126, 254; pogrom in, 132–33; and the 1905 Revolution, 132
Vinaver, Maxim, 16, 142, 175, 262n39: and the Historical-Ethnographic Commission, 113, 130, 148
"Vision of the Sacred Language, A" (Dubnov), 47
Volin, Y., 121
Volynskii, A. L., 82, 260n16
Voskhod (journal), 11, 70, 71, 74, 80, 83, 112: "Autonomism, the Basis of a National Program," 117; and the censor, 98; closing of, 149; "A Divided and a United National Party," 117; "The Great French Revolu-

tion," 88; "A Historic Moment," 123; "Historical Report," 103; "The Historiographer of Jewry," 99; "History of the Hasidic Schism," 88; "The Intelligentsia in Disarray," 121; "An Introduction to the History of Hasidism," 86; "The Last Word of Condemned Jewry," 76; "Letters on Old and New Jewry," 120, 121; and *The Moral of Terrible Days*, 135, 137; "On the Study of History," 113; "On the Study of Jewish History," 98; "On the Supremacy of National Politics in the Life of an Oppressed Nationality," 137; "The Rise of *Tsadikism*," 88; "What Kind of Emancipation Do Jews Need?" 75; and *World History of the Jewish People*, 121

Walt, Abraham. *See* Liessin, Abraham
War: First World, 163–64, 167; Russian civil, 179; Russo-Japanese, 127; Second World, 240; Spanish civil, 230, 232. *See also* Revolution
Warsaw, 85: Nazi sack of, 237
Weil, Gotthold, 192
Weimar Republic, 190, 209
Weinreich, Max, 223, 254, 272n129
What Do the Jews Want? (Dubnov), 22
"What Is Jewish History?" (Dubnov), 100, 101, 121–22
"What Kind of Emancipation Do Jews Need?" (Dubnov), 75
"What Should We Do at the World Congress?" (Dubnov), 178
"Will the Twentieth Century Be the Reverse of the Nineteenth Century?" (Dubnov), 219
Wilson, Woodrow, 22
Wischnitzer, Mark, 151, 188, 192, 205, 266n67
Wischnitzer, Rachel, 192
Women's Free University, 125
World History of the Jewish People, 25, 121, 153, 188–89: and the biblical period, 114, 115; and Christianity, 126–27, 171; and Eastern Jewry, 167; German edition, 192–95; and the Middle Ages, 128; reception of, 205; and the 1917 Revolution, 175, 177; Russian edition, 227
World Jewish Congress, 232, 233, 234
World Peace Congress, 178

Yiddish (*zhargon*), 71, 87–88, 130, 143, 235: and Jewish autonomy, 150; as Jewish national language, 13, 147, 265n61; and national education, 153; significance of, 195–97; and the Yiddish Scientific Institute, 203–204
Yiddish Scientific Institute (YIVO), 16, 201, 208, 221, 269n110, 271n119: and Lithuania, 237, 239, 241; Second Congress of, 254; and Cemach Szabad, 219; and Yiddish, 196, 203
Yidishe Folkspartey. *See* Folkspartey
Di Yidishe velt (journal): "After the Thirty-Year War," 158
YIVO. *See* Yiddish Scientific Institute
Yoske, Rabbi Joseph, 225, 272n134

Zaichik, Robert, 108
Zasulich, Vera, 55
Zealots, 81, 114
Zederbaum, Alexander, 196
Zelig, Rabbi, 45
Zemstvo, 128
Zevi, Sabbatai, 15, 74, 84
Zhargon. *See* Yiddish
Zhitlowsky, Chaim, 1, 146, 203, 228, 265n60
Zinberg, Israel, 179, 268n98
Zinoviev, Grigorii Eseevich, 177, 268n89
Zionism, 9, 17, 105, 180: and the Balfour Declaration, 176, 203; and the Basle program, 108; and the Diaspora, 122, 149–50; vs. "Dubnovism," 109; and the Jewish question, 20; political, 112, 127, 261n30; spiritual, 104, 130, 161, 200
Zionist party, 105
Zola, Emile, 103, 261n32
Zukunft (journal), 228
Zunz, 193, 222

SOPHIE DUBNOV-ERLICH, a poet, critic, and journalist, was born in 1885 in Mstislavl, Russia, the oldest child of Simon and Ida Dubnov. She attended the Bestuzhev Higher Courses for Women in St. Petersburg, studied at the Sorbonne in Paris, and, after the Russian Revolution of 1905, enrolled in the history and philology faculty at the University of St. Petersburg. Her first collection of poems, *Osenniaia svirel'* (The Autumn Reed Pipe) was published by the Symbolist journal *Apollo* in 1910. During this period Sophie Dubnov became active in socialist politics, and in 1911 she married Henryk Erlich, a leading figure in the Jewish Labor Bund.

Fleeing to Poland in 1918, the Erlichs and their two sons, Alexander and Victor, spent the interwar years in Warsaw, where Dubnov-Erlich became a prominent drama critic and journalist in the Yiddish-language Bundist press. In December 1941 Henryk Erlich was arrested and executed by the NKVD, several days before Simon Dubnov was shot by the Nazis in the Riga ghetto. Dubnov-Erlich, her sons, and their wives made their way to the United States in 1942. Settling in New York, she continued her involvement in both Jewish and world affairs and remained a productive writer until the age of ninety-five. This biography of her father, written in Russian, was published in 1950; Yiddish and Hebrew translations appeared soon afterward. Dubnov-Erlich died in New York City in 1986 at age 101.